Fundamentals and Methods
of Machine and Deep Learning

Scrivener Publishing
100 Cummings Center, Suite 541J
Beverly, MA 01915-6106

Publishers at Scrivener
Martin Scrivener (martin@scrivenerpublishing.com)
Phillip Carmical (pcarmical@scrivenerpublishing.com)

Fundamentals and Methods of Machine and Deep Learning

Algorithms, Tools and Applications

Edited by

Pradeep Singh

Department of Computer Science Engineering,
National Institute of Technology,
Raipur, India

WILEY

This edition first published 2022 by John Wiley & Sons, Inc., 111 River Street, Hoboken, NJ 07030, USA and Scrivener Publishing LLC, 100 Cummings Center, Suite 541J, Beverly, MA 01915, USA
© 2022 Scrivener Publishing LLC
For more information about Scrivener publications please visit www.scrivenerpublishing.com.

Wiley Global Headquarters
111 River Street, Hoboken, NJ 07030, USA

For details of our global editorial offices, customer services, and more information about Wiley products visit us at www.wiley.com.

Library of Congress Cataloging-in-Publication Data

ISBN 978-1-119-82125-0

Cover image: Pixabay.Com
Cover design by Russell Richardson

Contents

Preface

Over the past two decades, the field of machine learning and its subfield deep learning have played a main role in software applications development. Also, in recent research studies, they are regarded as one of the disruptive technologies that will transform our future life, business and the global economy. The recent explosion of digital data in a wide variety of domains, including science, engineering, internet of things, biomedical, healthcare and many business sectors, has declared the era of big data, which cannot be analyzed by classical statistics but by the more modern, robust machine learning and deep learning techniques. Since machine learning learns from data rather than by programming hard-coded decision rules, an attempt is being made to use machine learning to make computers that are able to solve problems like human experts in the field.

The goal of this book is to present a practical approach by explaining the concepts of machine learning and deep learning algorithms with applications. Supervised machine learning algorithms, ensemble machine learning algorithms, feature selection, deep learning techniques, and their applications are discussed. Also included in the eighteen chapters is unique information which provides a clear understanding of concepts by using algorithms and case studies illustrated with applications of machine learning and deep learning in different domains, including disease prediction, software defect prediction, online television analysis, medical image processing, etc. Each of the chapters briefly described below provides both a chosen approach and its implementation.

Chapter 1 assists in learning supervised machine learning algorithms and their applications.

Chapter 2 discusses the detection of zonotic diseases using ensemble machine learning algorithms.

Chapter 3 provides machine learning model evaluation techniques.

Chapter 4 analyzes MSEIR and LSTM models for the prediction of COVID-19 using RMSLE.

Chapter 5 discusses the significance of feature selection techniques in machine learning.

Chapter 6 provides insight into the development of disease prediction systems using machine learning and deep learning.

Chapter 7 discusses the detection of diabetic retinopathy using ensemble learning techniques.

Chapter 8 presents a case study for medical analysis of heart disease using machine learning and deep learning.

Chapter 9 discusses a novel convolutional neural network model to predict software defects.

Chapter 10 familiarizes the reader with the process of predictive analysis on online television videos using machine learning algorithms.

Chapter 11 discusses a combinational deep learning approach to visually evoked EEG-based image classification.

Chapter 12 gives a comparative analysis of machine learning algorithms with balancing techniques for credit card fraud detection.

Chapter 13 describes crack detection in civil structures using deep learning.

Chapter 14 discusses measuring urban sprawl using machine learning.

Chapter 15 is all about the applications of deep learning algorithms in medical image processing.

Chapter 16 assists in understanding the simulation of self-driving cars based on deep learning.

Chapter 17 discusses assistive technologies for visual hearing and speech impairments using machine learning and deep learning solutions.

Chapter 18 provides insight into the role of deep learning in remote sensing.

Finally, I would like to express my heartfelt thanks to all authors, reviewers, and the team at Scrivener Publishing for their kind co-operation extended during the various stages of processing this book.

Pradeep Singh
November 2021

Supervised Machine Learning: Algorithms and Applications

Shruthi H. Shetty*, Sumiksha Shetty†, Chandra Singh‡ and Ashwath Rao§

Department of ECE, Sahyadri College of Engineering & Management, Adyar, India

Abstract

The fundamental goal of machine learning (ML) is to inculcate computers to use data or former practice to resolve a specified problem. Artificial intelligence has given us incredible web search, self-driving vehicles, practical speech affirmation, and a massively better cognizance of human genetic data. An exact range of effective programs of ML already exist, which comprises classifiers to swot e-mail messages to study that allows distinguishing between unsolicited mail and non-spam messages. ML can be implemented as class analysis over supervised, unsupervised, and reinforcement learning. Supervised ML (SML) is the subordinate branch of ML and habitually counts on a domain skilled expert who "teaches" the learning scheme with required supervision. It also generates a task that maps inputs to chosen outputs. SML is genuinely normal in characterization issues since the aim is to get the computer, familiar with created descriptive framework. The data annotation is termed as a training set and the testing set as unannotated data. When annotations are discrete in the value, they are called class labels and continuous numerical annotations as continuous target values. The objective of SML is to form a compact prototype of the distribution of class labels in terms of predictor types. The resultant classifier is then used to designate class labels to the testing sets where the estimations of the predictor types are known, yet the values of the class labels are unidentified. Under certain assumptions, the larger the size of the training set, the better the expectations on the test set. This motivates the requirement for numerous area specialists or even different non-specialists giving names to preparing the framework. SML problems are grouped into classification and regression. In Classification the result

---

**Corresponding author*: shruthihshetty02@gmail.com
†*Corresponding author*: sumikshashetty7@gmail.com
‡*Corresponding author*: chandrasingh146@gmail.com
§*Corresponding author*: ashu1280@gmail.com

Pradeep Singh (ed.) Fundamentals and Methods of Machine and Deep Learning: Algorithms, Tools and Applications, (1–16) © 2022 Scrivener Publishing LLC

has discrete value and the aim is to predict the discrete values fitting to a specific class. Regression is acquired from the Labeled Datasets and continuous-valued result are predicted for the latest data which is given to the algorithm. When choosing an SML algorithm, the heterogeneity, precision, excess, and linearity of the information ought to be examined before selecting an algorithm. SML is used in a various range of applications such as speech and object recognition, bioinformatics, and spam detection. Recently, advances in SML are being witnessed in solid-state material science for calculating material properties and predicting their structure. This review covers various algorithms and real-world applications of SML. The key advantage of SML is that, once an algorithm swots with data, it can do its task automatically.

Keywords: Supervised machine learning, solid state material science, artificial intelligence, deep learning, linear regression, logistic regression, SVM, decision tree

1.1   History

The historical background of machine learning (ML), in the same way as other artificial intelligence (AI) concepts, started with apparently encouraging works during the 1950s and 1960s, trailed by a significant stretch of accumulation of information known as the "winter of AI" [9]. As of now, there has been an explosive concern essentially in the field related to deep learning. The start of the primary decade of the 21st century ended up being a defining moment throughout the entire existence of ML, and this is clarified by the three simultaneous patterns, which together gave an observable synergetic impact. The first pattern is big data and the second one is the reduction in the expense of equal processing and memory, and the third pattern is acquiring and building up the possibility of perceptron using deep learning algorithms. The investigation of ML has developed from the actions of a modest bunch of engineers investigating whether a machine could figure out how to solve the problem and impersonate the human mind, and a field of insights that generally overlooked computational reviews, to a wide control that has delivered basic measurable computational hypotheses of learning measures.

1.2   Introduction

ML is one of the quickest developing fields in software engineering. A lot of studies have been carried out to make machines smart; learning is one of the human characters which are made as necessary aspects of the machine too. For example, we are standing at a crowded railway station waiting for a friend. As we wait, hundreds of people pass by. Each one looks different, but when our friend arrives we have no problem picking her out of the crowd. Recognizing people's faces is something we humans do effortlessly, but how would we program a computer to recognize a person? We could try to make a set of rules. For example, our friend has long black hair and brown eyes, but that could describe billions of people. What is it about her that you recognize? Is it the shape of her nose? But can we put it into words? The truth is that we can recognize people without ever really knowing how we do it. We cannot describe every detail of how we recognize someone. We just know how to do it. The trouble is that to program a computer, we need to break the task down into its little details. That makes it very difficult or even impossible to program a computer to recognize faces. Face recognition is an example of a task that people find very easy, but that is very hard for computers. These tasks are often called artificial intelligence or AI. ML is the subset of AI [1]. Earlier data was stored and handled by the companies. For example, each time we purchase a product, visit an official page, or when we walk around, we generate data. Every one of us is not just a generator yet also a buyer of information. The necessities are needed to be assumed also interests are to be anticipated. Think about a supermarket that is marketing thousands of products to millions of consumers either at stores or through the web store. What the market needs is to have the option to predict which client is probably going to purchase which item, to augment deals and benefits. Essentially every client needs to find the best suitable product. We do not know precisely which individuals are probably going to purchase which item. Client conduct changes as expected and by geological area. However, we realize that it is not arbitrary. Individuals do not go to store and purchase things irregular, they purchase frozen yogurt in summer and warm clothes in winter. Therefore, there are definite outlines in the data.

An application of AI strategies to an enormous information base is termed data mining [4, 17]. Data mining is an enormous volume of information handled to develop a basic model with significant use, for instance, having high perspective accuracy. To be insightful, a framework that is in a changing climate ought to be able to learn. If the framework can learn and receive such change, then the framework designer need not anticipate and give answers for every conceivable circumstance. An exact range of effective programs of ML already exists, which comprises classifiers to swot e-mail messages to study that allows us to distinguish between unsolicited mail and non-spam messages. For an immense size of data, the manual foreseeing gives an unpredictable task to individuals. To overthrow this issue, the machine is trained to foresee the future, with the assistance of training and test datasets. For the machine to be trained, different types of ML algorithms are accessible. The computer program is supposed to study from the experience E regarding few classes of task T from performance P extent. The estimated performance of a task improves with experience [8].

ML can be implemented as class analysis over supervised, unsupervised, and reinforcement learning (RL). These algorithms are structured into a taxonomy constructed on the estimated outcome.

Unsupervised learning (UL) is a kind of AI that searches for previously undetected samples in an informational set without prior marks and with the least human management. Cluster analysis and making data samples digestible are the two main methods of UL. SML works under defined instructions, whereas UL works for the unknown condition of the results. The UL algorithm is used in investigating the structure of the data and to identify different patterns, extract the information, and execute the task [12, 15].

R) can be an idea of a hit and a preliminary strategy of knowledge. For each activity performed, the machine is given a reward point or a penalty point. On the off chance that the alternative is right, the machine picks up the prize point or gets a penalty point if there should be an occurrence of an off-base reaction. The RL algorithm is the communication between the atmosphere and the learning specialist [14]. The learning specialist depends on exploitation and exploration. The point at which the learning specialist follows up on experimentation is called exploration, and exploitation is the point at which it plays out an activity-dependent on the information picked up from the surrounding

Supervised learning (SML) algorithms function on unidentified dependent data which is anticipated from a given arrangement of identified predictors [20, 21].

1.3   Supervised Learning

SML is genuinely normal in characterization issues since the aim is to get the computer to get familiar with a created descriptive framework. In SML, the data annotation is termed as a training set, whereas the testing set is unannotated data. When annotations are discrete in the value they are called class labels while the continuous numerical annotations are so-called continuous target values. SML problems are grouped into classification and regression. Classification is the type of SML where the result has discrete value and the aim is to predict the discrete values fitting to a specific class. Regression is the type of SML that is acquired from the labeled datasets and continuous-valued result are predicted for the latest data which is given to the algorithm [8].

In SML, every model is a pair comprising of an input object and the desired output value. SML requires pre-labeled information. For masked occurrences, an ideal situation will take into consideration to accurately calculate and decide the class labels. This requires the taking in algorithms, to sum up from the training data to unobserved states in a "sensible" way. SML algorithm investigates the training data set and produces a derived capacity, which is utilized for planning new models. By this process, the informational set should have inputs and known outputs. SML can be classified into two types: regression and classification [12]. Regression is the sort of SML that studies the labeled datasets and anticipates a persistent output for the new information set to the algorithm. In this method, the required result is in the form of a number. Taking an example, a regression model that decides the cost of a pre-owned vehicle, ought to have numerous instances of used vehicles recently sold. It should essentially know the data sources and the subsequent output to assemble a model. In classification, the algorithm needs to plan the new information that is found in any of the two classes that are present in the dataset. The classes should be planned to one or 0 which is considered as "Yes" or "No", "snows" or "does not snow", etc. The result will be both of the classes and not a number as it was in regression. For instance, the classifier decides if an individual has an illness, the algorithm should consist of sources of input and it must be able to predict the outcome.

Some of the known SML algorithms are linear regression, logistic regression, decision tree, support vector machine (SVM), etc. [3].

1.4 Linear Regression (LR)

LR is the simplest method of regression; it is a linear approach to model the link between a scalar response and one or more descriptive variables. Few examples of the LR algorithm are predicting the stock price, exam scores, etc. In other words, it is a statistical regression process used for predictive evaluation, mainly used to solve the regression problem in ML. Assume a model with a linear relationship among the input (x) and the single output value (y). Precisely that y can be estimated through a linear combination of input (x). The input with a single value is referred to as simple LR and input with multiple values is often referred to as multiple LR. For example, consider a linear equation which consolidates a set of (x) input variable

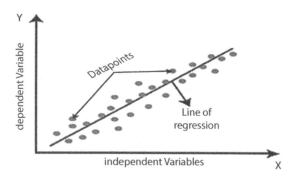

Figure 1.1 Linear regression [3].

resulting in a predicted outcome (y) for the given set of input. Hence, both the input (x) and the output value are numeric. The line equation allows one scaling factor to every input value which is called a coefficient. Another extra coefficient is added, which is often known as the intercept. To learn the LR model is to estimate the coefficient values used in the illustration of available data. Various techniques are to train the data; the most common technique used is ordinary least squares (OLS) [6]. Figure 1.1 characterizes the conspiracy between data points and LR line.

1.4.1 Learning Model

1] Simple linear regression: Single input is used to esti-mate the coefficients. This involves statistical calculations such as mean, standard deviations (SD), correlations, and covariance.

2] OLS: This technique is used when there is more than one input, to calculate the coefficients. This OLS method looks for minimizing the summation of the squared residuals. That is, for a given regression line through the input, the distance is calculated from every data point concerning the regres-sion line then square it, and all together sum the squared errors. Assuming the data as a matrix, this approach uses linear algebra to calculate the coefficient values. Sufficient memory and data should be available to fit the data and to complete matrix operation [6].

3] Gradient descent: For more than one input value, the pro-cess of optimizing the coefficient values can be achieved by iteratively minimizing the errors on training data. This procedure is termed gradient descent and works for random values for every coefficient. For every couple of input data and output, the summation of the squared errors is estimated. The coefficient values are updated in the path of diminishing the error. This procedure is repetitive up to a minimum sum-squared error is attained or no added progress is possible [6].

4] Regularization: This method looks for minimizing the sum-squared error on the training data (using OLS) and also to decrease the complexity in the model. These approaches are said to be operative when the input values are collinear and OLS overfits the training dataset [6].

1.4.2 Predictions With Linear Regression

Predicting values are more like solving an equation for the specified input. Consider an example where weight (y) is predicted from height (x). The LR equation is represented as [6]

$$y = B_0 + B_1 * x \tag{1.1}$$

or

$$weight = B_0 + B_1 * height \tag{1.2}$$

These equations can be conspired as a line in 2-dimension as shown in Figure 1.2.

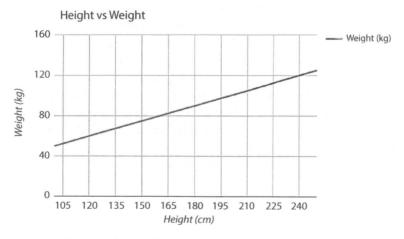

Figure 1.2 Height vs. weight graph [6].

Let B_0 be the bias coefficient and B_1 be the height column coefficient. To find the coefficients, the above learning techniques are used. Later, different height values are used to calculate the weight. For example, let $B_0 = 0.2$ and $B_1 = 0.4$, for an individual of height of 185 cm, the weight is calculated as follows [6]:

$$weight = 0.2 + 0.4 * 185 \qquad (1.3)$$

$$weight = 74.2 \qquad (1.4)$$

1.5   Logistic Regression

Logistic regression is well-known ML algorithms, which is under the SML technique. It is utilized for anticipating the dependent factor by making use of a given set independent factor, it is used for the classification problems, and it is dependent on the idea of probability. Logistic regression calculates the yield of a dependent variable. Thus, the outcome is a discrete value. It may be either yes or no, zero or one, and valid or invalid [3, 7]. However, instead of giving the definite value as 0 and 1, it provides the probabilistic values which lie in the range of 0 and 1. For instance, consider that you are being given a wide scope of riddles/tests trying to comprehend which concept you are acceptable at. The result of this investigation would be considered a geometry-based issue that is 70% prone to unravel. Next is the history quiz, the chance of finding a solution is just 30%. Consider an event of detecting the spam email. LR is utilized for this event; there is a constraint of setting a limit depending on which classification is possible. Stating if the class is spam, predicted consistently is 0.4 and the limit is 0.5, the information is categorized as not a spam mail, which can prompt the outcome progressively. Logistic regression is classified as binary, multinomial, and ordinal binary can have only two possible values either yes or no or true or false where multinomial can have three or more possible values and Ordinal it manages target factors with classifications. For instance, a grade can be arranged as "very poor", "poor", "great", and "excellent".

Logistic regression is well defined as [16].

$$\sigma(t) = \frac{e^t}{e^t + 1} = \frac{1}{1 + e^{-t}} \qquad (1.5)$$

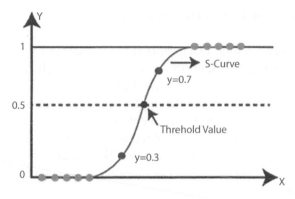

Figure 1.3 Logistic regression [3].

Figure 1.3 shows the function curve between the values 0 and 1.

1.6 Support Vector Machine (SVM)

SVMs are an influential yet adaptable type of SML which are utilized both for classification and regression. They are mainly utilized for classification problems. They use a Kernel capacity which is an essential idea for the greater part of the learning process. These algorithms make a hyperplane that is utilized to group the different classes. The hyperplane is produced iteratively, by the SVM with the target to minimize the error. The objective of SVM is to split the datasets into different classes to locate a maximum marginal hyperplane (MMH). MMH can be located using the following steps [10].

- SVM creates hyperplanes iteratively that separates the classes in a most ideal manner.
- Then, it picks the hyperplane that splits the classes accurately.

For example, let us consider two tags that are blue and black with data features p and q. The classifier is specified with a pair of coordinates (p, q) which outputs either blue or black. SVM considers the data points which yield the hyperplane that separates the labels. This line is termed as a decision boundary. Whatever tumbles aside of the line, will arrange as blue, and anything that tumbles to the next as black.

The major terms in SVM are as follows:

- Support Vectors: Datapoints that are nearby to the hyperplane are called support vectors. With the help of the data points, the separating line can be defined.
- Hyperplane: Concerning Figure 1.4, it is a decision plane that is parted among a set of entities having several classes.
- Margin: It might be categorized as the gap between two lines on data points of various classes. The distance between the line and support vector, the margin can be calculated as the perpendicular distance.

There are two types of SVMs:

- Simple SVM: Normally used in linear regression and classification issues.
- Kernel SVM: Has more elasticity for non-linear data as more features can be added to fit a hyperplane as an alternative to a 2D space.

SVMs are utilized in ML since they can discover complex connections between the information without the need to do a lot of changes. It is an incredible choice when you are working with more modest datasets that have tens to a huge number of highlights. They normally discover more precise outcomes when contrasted with different calculations in light of their capacity to deal with little, complex datasets.

Figure 1.4 shows the hyper-plane that categorizes two classes.

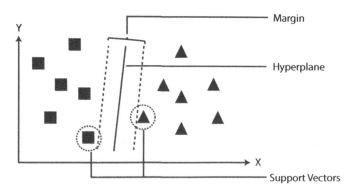

Figure 1.4 SVM [11].

1.7   Decision Tree

Decision tree groups are dependent on the element values. They utilize the strategy for Information Gain and discover which element in the dataset, give the best of data, making it a root node, etc., till they can arrange each case of the dataset. Each branch in the decision tree speaks to an element of the dataset [4, 5]. They are one of the most generally utilized calculations for classification. An analysis of the decision tree, the decision tree is utilized to visually and signify the decision and the process of decision making. As the term suggests it utilizes a tree-like representation of choices. Tree models are the objective variable that can take a discrete arrangement of values termed as classification trees; in this tree model, leaves signify the class labels, and combinations of features of class labels are signified by the branches.

Consider an example of listing the students eligible for the placement drive. Now, the scenario is whether the student can attend the drive or not? There are "n" different deciding factors, which has to be investigated for appropriate decision. The decision factors are whether the student has qualified the grade, what is the cut-off, whether the candidate has cleared the test, and so on. Thus, the decision tree model has the following constituents. Figure 1.5 depicts the decision tree model [2]:

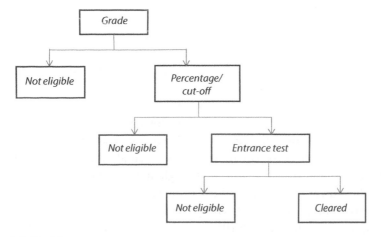

Figure 1.5 Decision tree.

- Root Node: The root node in this example is the "grade".
- Internal Node: The intermediate nodes with an incoming edge and more than 2 outgoing edge.
- Leaf Node: The node without an out-going edge; also known as a terminal node.

For the currently developed decision tree in this example, initially, the test condition from the root hub is tested and consigns the control to one of the active edges; thus, the condition is again tried and a hub is allocated. The tree is supposed to be ended when all the test conditions lead to a leaf hub. The leaf hub consists of class-labels, which vote against or in favor of the choice.

1.8   Machine Learning Applications in Daily Life

Some of the main areas where we use ML algorithms are in traffic alert systems in Google maps, social media sites like Facebook, in transportation and commuting services like Uber, Product recommendation systems, virtual personal assistant systems, self-driving cars, Google translators, online video streaming services, fraud detection, etc [13].

1.8.1   Traffic Alerts (Maps)

Nowadays, when we decide to go out and in need of assistance for directions and traffic situations on the road we have decided to travel, we usually take the help of Google maps. If in case you decided to travel to a city and decide to take the highway, and the Google traffic alert system suggested that "Even though there is heavy traffic, you are on the fastest route to your destination", how does the system know all these things? In short, it is a combined data of people actively using the service, the previous data of the route collected over the years, and also involves some own tricks which are acquired by the company to efficiently calculate the traffic. Most of the people who are currently using the Google maps service is indirectly providing their location, speed, and the routes they are going to take in which they are traveling, which helps Google collect data about the traffic, which will help the Google map algorithm predict the traffic and recommend the best routes for future users.

1.8.2   Social Media (Facebook)

Social media applications like Facebook use ML to detect and recognize faces that are used for automatic friend tagging suggestions. The algorithm compares the detected faces with the database of pictures it already has and gives users suggestions. Facebook's DeepFace algorithm which uses deep learning runs behind the Facebook application to recognize faces and identify the person in the picture. It also provides alternative tags to images already uploaded on Facebook.

1.8.3   Transportation and Commuting (Uber)

Transportation and commuting apps like Uber use ML to provide good services to their clients. It provides a personalized application that is unique to you, for example, it automatically detects your location and gives options either to go home or office or any other frequent places which will be purely based on your search history and patterns. The application uses a ML algorithm on top of historic data on trips to make accurate ETA predictions. There was an increase of 26% in the accuracy of delivery and pickup after implementing ML on their application.

1.8.4   Products Recommendations

This tells you how powerful is the ML recommendation systems are these days. Take for example, you liked an item on Amazon, but add it to your wish list because you cannot afford the item at the current price. Surprisingly, the day after, when you are watching videos on YouTube or some other application you encounter an ad for the item which you have wish-listed before. Even when you switch to another app, say, Facebook, you will still see the same ad on that website. This happens because Google tracks your search history and recommend ads depending on the activities you do. About 35% of Amazon's wealth is generated by using product recommendation systems like these [18].

1.8.5   Virtual Personal Assistants

Here, virtual assistant finds some useful information when the user asks some questions via text or voice. There are many applications of ML which are being in these kinds of applications. Applications involve speech verification and identification systems, speech-text conversions, NLP, and text-to-speech conversion. The only thing you have to do is ask a simple question like, "What is my schedule for tomorrow?" or maybe "Show my upcoming booking", then assistants search for information related to questions to collect information. Recently, chatbots use a personal assistant, which is being used in many food ordering company applications, online coaching or training sites, and also many in many transport applications [19].

1.8.6   Self-Driving Cars

This may be one of the most breath taking the implementation of ML in the modern world. Tesla uses deep learning and other algorithms to build a self-driving car. As the computation required for this is very high, we need matching hardware to run these algorithms, NVIDIA provides the necessary hardware to run these computationally expensive models.

1.8.7   Google Translate

Before when you remember the times when you go to a new place where the language used there is completely new to you and you find it difficult to communicate with the locals or find places you wanted to go, this was mainly because you could not understand what is written on the local spots. But nowadays, Google's GNMT is a neural machine algorithm that has a dictionary of thousands of millions of words of many different languages, uses natural language processing to very efficiently and accurately translate any sentences or words. Even the tone of every sentence matters, it uses techniques like NER.

1.8.8   Online Video Streaming (Netflix)

More than a 100 million users use Netflix, and there is no doubt that it is the most-streamed web service in the whole world. Netflix application use ML algorithms which collect a massive amount of data about the users, when the user pauses, rewinds, or fast forwards. It also takes data depending on the day you watch the content, the date and time, and mainly the rating pattern and search pattern. The application collects these data from each of their users they have and use their recommendation systems and a lot of algorithms related to ML approaches.

1.8.9   Fraud Detection

Currently, online credit card fraud detection is 32 billion dollars market in 2020. That is approximately higher than the profit made by many MNC companies combined. Nowadays, the number of payment channels like a credit card, debit card, numerous wallets, UPI, and much more has increased the number of criminals. ML approaches fraud detection as a classification problem.

1.9   Conclusion

In the anticipating years, ML will embrace a significant reason in the divulgence of data from the abundance of information that is at present open in a different zone of utilization. The supervised learning strategies are developing constantly by the information researchers, which contain an enormous arrangement of algorithms. This zone has the consideration of numerous engineers and has picked up generous advancement in the most recent decade. The learning strategies accomplish magnificent execution that would have been hard to get in the earlier many years. Given the reckless development, there is a lot of room for the engineers to work effectively and to develop the SML strategies.

References

1. Iqbal, M. and Yan, Z., Supervised Machine Learning Approaches: A Survey. *Int. J. Soft Comput.*, 5, 946–952, 2015, 10.21917/ijsc.2015.0133.
2. Nasteski, V., An overview of the supervised machine learning methods. *Horizons. B.*, 4, 51–62, 2017, 10.20544/HORIZONS.B.04.1.17.P05.
3. Sharma, R., Sharma, K., Khanna, A., Study of Supervised Learning and Unsupervised Learning. *Int. J. Res. Appl. Sci. Eng. Technol. (IJRASET)*, 8, VI, June 2020.
4. Kotsiantis, S.B., Supervised Machine Learning: A Review of Classification Techniques, in: *Proceedings of the 2007 conference on Emerging Artificial Intelligence Applications in Computer Engineering: Real Word AI Systems with Applications in eHealth*, HCI, Information Retrieval and Pervasive Technologies, The Netherlands, 2007.
5. Osisanwo, F.Y., Akinsola, J.E.T., Awodele, O., Hinmikaiye, J.O., Olakanmi, O., Akinjobi, J., Supervised Machine Learning Algorithms: Classification and Comparison. *Int. J. Comput. Trends Technol. (IJCTT)*, 48, 3, 128–138, June 2017.
6. Brownlee, J., Linear Regression for Machine Learning – Machine Learning Mastery, [online] Machine Learning Mastery https://machinelearningmastery.com/linear-regression-for-machine-learning/.

7. Brownlee, J., Logistic Regression for Machine Learning – Machine Learning Mastery, [online] Machine Learning Mastery Available at: https://machine-learningmastery.com/logistic-regression-for-machine-learning/.
8. Mitchell, T., *Machine Learning*, 432pp., McGraw Hill, Carnegie Mellon University, 2015.
9. https://www.javatpoint.com/machine-learning
10. https://www.tutorialspoint.com/machine_learning_with_python/classification_algorithms_support_vector_machine.htm
11. https://www.edureka.co/blog/supervised-learning/
12. https://machinelearningmastery.com/supervised-and-unsupervised-machine-learning algorithms/
13. Fabris, F., Magalhães, J.P., Freitas, A.A., A review of supervised machine learning applied to ageing research. *Biogerontology*, 18, 2, 171–188, 2017.
14. Ayodele, T., Types of Machine Learning Algorithms, InTech Open, 2010, https://www.intechopen.com/chapters/10694
15. Musumeci, F. *et al.*, An Overview on Application of Machine Learning Techniques in Optical Networks. *IEEE Commun. Surv. Tutorials*, 21, 2, 1383–1408, Secondquarter 2019.
16. https://en.wikipedia.org/wiki/Logistic_regression
17. https://www.edureka.co/blog/decision-trees/
18. Mohri, M., Rostamizadeh, A., Talwalker, A., *Foundations of machine learning*, MIT Press, Cambridge, MA, 2012.
19. Cioffi, R., Travaglioni, M., Piscitelli, G., Petrillo, A., De Felice, F., Artificial Intelligence and Machine Learning Applications in Smart Production: Progress, Trends, and Directions. *Sustainability*, 12, 492, 2020.
20. Behera, R. and Das, K., A Survey on Machine Learning: Concept, Algorithms and Applications. *Int. J. Innov. Res. Comput. Commun. Eng.*, 5, 2, 1301–1309, 2017.
21. Domingos, P., A few useful things to know about machine learning. *Commun. ACM*, 55, 10, 14–20, 2012.

2

Zonotic Diseases Detection Using Ensemble Machine Learning Algorithms

Bhargavi K.

Department of Computer Science and Engineering, Siddaganga Institute of Technology, Tumakuru, India

Abstract

Zonotic diseases are a kind of infectious disease which spreads from animals to humans; the disease usually spreads from infectious agents like virus, prion and bacteria. The identification and controlling the spread of zonotic disease is challenging due to several issues which includes no proper symptoms, signs of zoonoses are very similar, improper vaccination of animals, and poor knowledge among people about animal health. Ensemble machine learning uses multiple machine learning algorithms, to arrive at better performance, compared to individual/stand-alone machine learning algorithms. Some of the potential ensemble learning algorithms like Bayes optimal classifier, bootstrap aggregating (bagging), boosting, Bayesian model averaging, Bayesian model combination, bucket of models, and stacking are helpful in identifying zonotic diseases. Hence, in this chapter, the application of potential ensemble machine learning algorithms in identifying zonotic diseases is discussed with their architecture, advantages, and applications. The efficiency achieved by the considered ensemble machine learning techniques is compared toward the performance metrics, i.e., throughput, execution time, response time, error rate, and learning rate. From the analysis, it is observed that the efficiency achieved by Bayesian model combination, stacking, and Bayesian model combination are high in identifying of the zonotic diseases.

Keywords: Zonotic disease, ensemble machine learning, Bayes optimal classifier, bagging, boosting, Bayesian model averaging, Bayesian model combination, stacking

Email: bhargavi.tumkur@gmail.com

Pradeep Singh (ed.) Fundamentals and Methods of Machine and Deep Learning: Algorithms, Tools and Applications, (17–32) © 2022 Scrivener Publishing LLC

2.1   Introduction

Zonotic diseases are a kind of infectious disease which spreads from animals to human beings; the disease usually spreads from infectious agents like virus, prion, virus, and bacteria. The human being who gets affected first will, in turn, spread that disease to other human beings likewise the chain of disease builds. The zonotic disease gets transferred in two different mode of transmission, one is direct transmission in which disease get transferred from animal to human being, and the other is intermediate transmission in which the disease get transferred via intermediate species that carry the disease pathogen. The emergence of zonotic diseases usually happens in large regional, global, political, economic, national, and social forces levels. There are eight most common zonotic diseases which spread from animal to humans on a wider geographical area which include zonotic influenza, salmonellosis, West Nile virus, plague, corona viruses, rabies, brucellosis, and lyme disease. Early identification of such infectious disease is very much necessary which can be done using ensemble machine learning techniques [1, 2].

The identification and controlling of spread of zonotic disease is challenging due to several issues which includes no proper symptoms, signs of zoonoses are very much similar, improper vaccination of animals, poor knowledge among the peoples about animal health, costly to control the world wide spread of the disease, not likely to change the habits of people, prioritization of symptoms of disease is difficult, lack of proper clothing, sudden raise in morbidity of the humans, consumption of spoiled or contaminated food, inability to control the spread of zonotic microorganisms, reemerging of zonotic diseases at regular time intervals, difficult to form coordinated remedial policies, violation of international law to control the disease, transaction cost to arrive at disease control agreements is high, surveillance of disease at national and international level is difficult, unable to trace the initial symptoms of influenza virus, wide spread nature of severe acute respiratory syndromes, inability to provide sufficient resources, climate change also influences on the spread of the disease, difficult to prioritize the zonotic diseases, increasing trend in the spread of disease from animals to humans, and continuous and close contact between the humans and animals [3, 4].

Ensemble machine learning uses multiple machine learning algorithms, to arrive at better performance, compared to individual/stand-alone machine learning algorithms [5, 6]. Some of the potential ensemble learning algorithms like Bayes optimal classifier, bootstrap aggregating (bagging), boosting, Bayesian model averaging (BMA), Bayesian model combination, bucket of models, stacking, and remote sensing. Some of the advantages offered by ensemble machine learning compared to traditional machine learning are as follows: better accuracy is achieved in prediction, scalability if the solution is high as it can handle multiple nodes very well, combines multiple hypothesis to maximize the quality of the output, provides sustainable solution by operating in an incremental manner, efficiently uses the previous knowledge to produce diverse model-based solutions, avoids overfitting problem through sufficient training, models generated are good as they mimics the human like behavior, complex disease spreading traces can be analyzed using combined machine learning models, misclassification of samples is less due to enough training models, not sensitive toward outliers, cross-validation of output data samples increases performance, stability of the chosen hypothesis is high, measurable performance in initial data collection is high, will not converge to local optimal solutions, exhibits non-hierarchical and overlapping behaviors, several open source tools are available for practical implementation of the models, and so on [7–9].

The main goal of applying ensemble machine learning algorithms in identifying the zonotic diseases are as follows: decreases the level of bagging and bias and improves the zonotic disease detection accuracy with minimum iteration of training, automatic identification of diseases, use of base learners make it suitable to medical domain, easy to identify the spread of disease at early stage itself, identifies the feature vector which yields maximum information gain, easy training of hyper parameters, treatment cost is minimum, adequate coverage happens to large set of medical problems, reoccurrence of the medical problems can be identified early, high correlation between machine learning models leads to efficient output, training and execution time is less, scalability of the ensemble models is high, offers aggregated benefits of several models, non-linear decision-making ability is high, provides sustainable solutions to chronic diseases, automatic tuning of internal parameters increases the convergence rate, reusing rate of the clinical trials gets reduced, early intervention prevents spread of disease, capable to record and store high-dimensional clinical dataset, recognition of neurological diseases is easy, misclassification of medical images with poor image quality is reduced, combines the aggregated power of multiple machine learning models, and so on [10, 11].

2.2 Bayes Optimal Classifier

Bayes optimal classifier is a popular machine learning model used for the purpose of prediction. This technique is based on Bayes theorem which is principled by Bayes theorem and closely related to maximum posteriori algorithm. The classifier operates by finding the hypothesis which has maximum probability of occurrence. The probable prediction is carried out by the classifier using probabilistic model which finds the most probable prediction using the training and testing data instances.

The basic conditional probability equation predicts one outcome given another outcome, consider A and B are two probable outcomes the probability of occurrence of event using the equation $P(A|B) = (P(B|A)^*P(A))/P(B)$. The probabilistic frameworks used for prediction purpose are broadly classified into two types one is maximum posteriori, and the other is maximum likelihood estimation. The important objective of these two types of probabilistic framework is that they locate most promising hypothesis in the given training data sample. Some of the zonotic diseases which can be identified and treated well using Bayes optimal classifier are Anthrax, Brucellosis, Q fever, scrub typhus, plague, tuberculosis, leptospirosis, rabies, hepatitis, nipah virus, avian influenza, and so on [12, 13]. A high-level representation of Bayes optimal classifier is shown in Figure 2.1. In the hyperplane of available datasets, the Bayes classifier performs the multiple category classification operation to draw soft boundary among the available datasets and make separate classifications. It is observed that, with maximum iteration of training and overtime, the accuracy of the Bayes optimal classifier keeps improving.

Some of the advantages of advantages of Bayes optimal classifier which makes it suitable for tracking and solving the zonotic diseases are as follows: ease of implementation, high accuracy is achieved over less training data, capable of handling both discrete and non-discrete data samples,

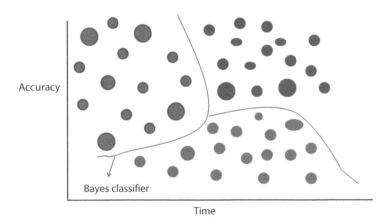

Figure 2.1 A high-level representation of Bayes optimal classifier.

scalable to any number of data samples, operates at very speed, suitable for real-time predictions, achieves better results compared to traditional classifiers, not much sensitive to outliers, ease generalization, achieves high computational accuracy, works well on linear/nonlinear separable data samples, interpretation of the results is easy, easily mines the complex relationship between input and output data samples, provides global optimal solutions, and so on [14].

2.3   Bootstrap Aggregating (Bagging)

Bootstrap aggregating is popularly referred as bagging is a machine learning–based ensemble technique which improves the accuracy of the algorithm and is used mostly for classification or aggregation purposes. The main purpose of bagging is that it avoids overfitting problem by properly generalizing the existing data samples. Consider any standard input dataset from which new training datasets are generated by sampling the data samples uniformly with replacement. By considering the replacements, some of the observations are repeated in the form of the unique data samples using regression or voting mechanisms. The bagging technique is composed of artificial neural networks and regression tree, which are used to improve the unstable procedures. For any given application, the selection between bagging and boosting depends on the availability of the data. The variance incurred is reduced by combining bootstrap and bagging [15, 16].

Bagging and boosting operations are considered as two most powerful tools in ensemble machine learning. The bagging operation is used concurrently with the decision tree which increases the stability of the model by reducing the variance and also improves the accuracy of the model by minimizing the error rate. The aggregation of set of predictions made by the ensemble models happens to produce best prediction as the output. While doing bootstrapping the prominent sample is taken out using the replacement mechanism in which the selection of new variables is dependent on the previous random selections. The practical application of this technique is dependent on the base learning algorithm which is chosen first and on top of which the bagging of pool of decision trees happen. Some of the zonotic diseases which can be identified and treated well using bootstrap aggregating are zonotic influenza, salmonellosis, West Nile virus, plague, rabies, Lyme disease, brucellosis, and so on [17]. A high-level representation of bootstrap is shown in Figure 2.2. It begins with the training dataset, which is distributed among the multiple bootstrap sampling units. Each of

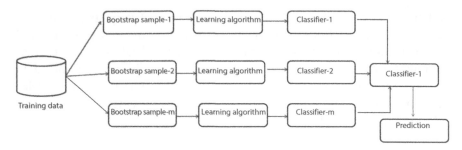

Figure 2.2 A high-level representation of Bootstrap aggregating.

the bootstrap sampling unit operates on the training subset of data upon which the learning algorithm performs the learning operation and generates the classification output. The aggregated sum of each of the classifier is generated as the output.

Some of the advantages offered by bootstrap in diagnosing the zonotic diseases are as follows: the aggregated power of several weak learners over runs the performance of strong learner, the variance incurred gets reduced as it efficiently handles overfitting problem, no loss of precision during interoperability, computationally not expensive due to proper management of resources, computation of over confidence bias becomes easier, equal weights are assigned to models which increases the performance, misclassification of samples is less, very much robust to the effect of the outliers and noise, the models can be easily paralyzed, achieves high accuracy through incremental development of the model, stabilizes the unstable methods, easier from implementation point of view, provision for unbiased estimate of test errors, easily overcomes the pitfalls of individuals machine learning models, and so on.

2.4 Bayesian Model Averaging (BMA)

It is one of the popularly referred ensemble machine learning model which applies Bayesian inference to solve the issues related to the selection of problem statement, performing the combined estimation, and produces the results using any of the straight model with less prediction accuracy. Several coherent models are available in BMA which are capable of handling the uncertainty available in the large datasets. The steps followed while implemented the MBA model is managing the summation, computation of integral values for MBA, using linear regression for predictions, and transformation purposes [18, 19].

Basically, BMA is an extended form of Bayesian inference which performs mathematical modeling of uncertainty using prior distribution by obtaining the posterior probability using Bayes theorem. For implementing the BMA, first prior distribution of each of the models in the ensemble network needs to be specified then evidence needs to be found for each of the model. Suppose the existing models are represented by M_l, where the value of l varies from 1 to k which basically represent the set of probability distributions. The probability distribution computes likelihood function $L(Y|\theta_l, M_l)$, where θ_l stands for parameter which are model specific dependent parameter. According to the Bayes theorem, the value for posterior probability is computed as follows [20]. A high-level representation of BMA is shown in Figure 2.3. Bayesian model representation begins with the data set which is distributed among multiple data subsets. Each subset of data is fed as input to the learner then average operation is performed

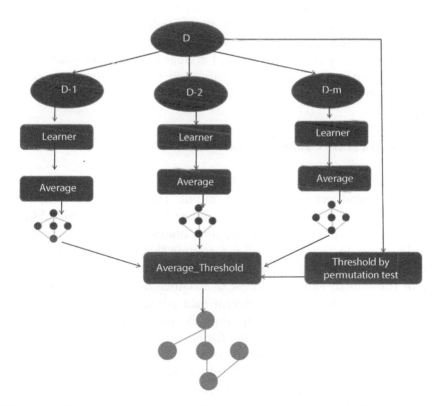

Figure 2.3 A high-level representation of Bayesian model averaging (BMA).

finally compared with the average threshold and tested using permutation threshold to generate the Bayesian model as output.

$$\pi(\theta_l | \theta_l, M_l) = \frac{L(Y | \theta_l, M_l) * \pi(\theta_l | \theta_l, M_l)}{\int L(Y | \theta_l, M_l) * \pi(\theta_l | \theta_l, M_l) d\theta_l}$$

Some of the advantages offered by BMA in diagnosing the zonotic diseases are as follows: capable of performing multi-variable selection, generates overconfident inferences, the number of selected features are less, easily scalable to any number of classes, posterior probability efficiency is high, deployment of the model is easier, correct estimation of uncertainty, suitable to handle complex applications, proper accounting of the model, combines estimation and predictions, flexible with prior distribution, uses mean candidate placement model, performs multi-linear operation, suitable of handling the heterogeneous resources, provides transparent interpretation of the large amount of data, error reduction happens exponentially, the variance incurred in prediction is less, flexibility achieved in parameter inference is less, prediction about model prediction is less, high-speed compilation happens, generated high valued output, combines efficiency achieved by several learner and average models, very much robust against the effect caused by misspecification of input attributes, model specification is highly dynamic, and so on.

2.5   Bayesian Classifier Combination (BCC)

Bayesian classifier combination (BCC) considers k different types of classifiers and produces the combined output. The motivation behind the innovation of this classifier is will capture the exhaustive possibilities about all forms of data, and ease of computation of marginal likelihood relationships. This classifier will not assume that the existing classifiers are true rather it is assumed to be probabilistic which mimics the behavior of the human experts. The BCC classifier uses different confusion matrices employed over the different data points for classification purpose. If the data points are hard, then the BCC uses their own confusion matrix; else, the posterior confusion matrix will be made use. The classifier identifies the relationship between the output of the model and the unknown data labels. The probabilistic models are not required; they share information about sending or receiving the information about the training data [21, 22].

The BCC model the parameters which includes $\pi_j^k = \{\pi_{j,1}^k, \pi_{j,2}^k, \pi_{j,3}^k, \ldots \pi_{j,J}^k\}$, hyperparameters $\alpha_j^k = \{\alpha_{j,1}^k, \alpha_{j,2}^k, \alpha_{j,3}^k, \ldots \alpha_{j,J}^k\}$. Based on the values of the prior posterior probability distribution of random variables with observed label classes, the independence posterior density id computed as follows:

$$P(P, \pi, t, \alpha | C) = \prod_{i=1}^{i=I} \left\{ pt_i \prod_{k=1}^{k=K} \pi_{c_i, t_i}, \right\} P(P|V) * P(\pi|\alpha) * P(\alpha|\lambda)$$

The inferences drawn are based on the unknown random variables, i.e., P, π, t, V, and α which are collected using Gibbs and rejection sampling methodology. A high-level representation of BCC is shown in Figure 2.4. First parameters of BCC model, hyperparameters, and posterior probabilities are summed to generate final prediction as output.

Some of the advantages offered by BCC in diagnosing the zonotic diseases are as follows: performs probabilistic prediction, isolates the outliers which causes noise, efficient handling of missing values, robust handling of irrelevant attributes, side effects caused by dependency relationships can be prevented, easier in terms of implementation, ease modeling of dependency relationships among the random variables, learns collectively from labeled and unlabeled input data samples, ease feature selection, lazy learning, training time is less, eliminates unstable estimation, high knowledge is attained in terms of systems variable dependencies, high accuracy achieved in interpretation of the results, confusion matrix–based processing of data, low level of computational complexity, easily operates with less computational resources, requires less amount of training data, capable

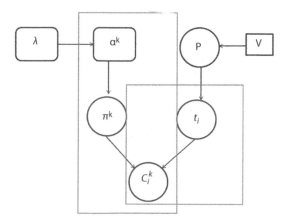

Figure 2.4 A high-level representation of Bayesian classifier combination (BCC).

enough to handle the uncertainty in the data parameters, can learn from both labeled and unlabeled data samples, precise selection of the attributes which yields maximum information gain, eliminates the redundant values, lower number of tunning parameters, less memory requirement, highly flexible classification of data, and so on [23].

2.6 Bucket of Models

The bucket of models is one of the popular ensemble machine learning techniques used to choose the best algorithm for solving any computational intensive problems. The performance achieved by bucket of models is good compared to average of all ensemble machine learning models. One of the common strategies used to select the best model for prediction is through cross-validation. During cross-validation, all examples available in the training will be used to train the model and the best model which fits the problem will be chosen. One of the popular generalization approaches for cross-validation selection is gating. In order to implement the gating, the perceptron model will be used which assigns weight to the prediction product by each model available in the bucket. When the large number of models in the bucket is applied over a larger set of problems, the model for which the training time is more can be discarded. Landmark-based learning is a kind of bucket-based model which trains only fast algorithms present in the bucket and based on the prediction generated by fast algorithms will be used to determine the accuracy of slow algorithms in the bucket [24]. A high-level representation of bucket of models is shown in Figure 2.5. The data store

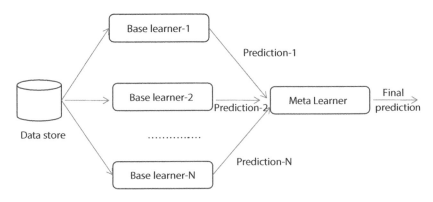

Figure 2.5 A high-level representation of bucket of models.

maintains the repository of information, which is fed as input to each of the base learners. Each of the base learners generates their own prediction as output which is fed as input to the metalearner. Finally, the metalearner does summation of each of the predictions to generate final prediction as output.

One of the best suitable approaches for cross-validation among multiple models in ensemble learning is bake off contest, the pseudo-code of which is given below.

Pseudo-code: Bucket of models

For each of the ensemble model present in the bucket do
      Repeat constant number of times
            Divide the training set into parts, i.e., training set and test set randomly
            Train the ensemble model with training set
            Test the ensemble model with test set
Choose the ensemble model that yields maximum average score value

Some of the advantages offered by bucket of models in diagnosing the zonotic diseases are as follows: high quality prediction, provides unified view of the data, negotiation of local patterns, less sensitive to outliers, stability of the model is high, slower model gets benefited from faster models, parallelized automation of tasks, learning rate is good on large data samples, payload functionality will be hidden from end users, robustness of the model is high, error generation rate is less, able to handle the random fluctuations in the input data samples, length of the bucket is kept medium, easier extraction of features from large data samples, prediction happens by extracting the data from deep web, linear weighted average model is used, tendency of forming suboptimal solutions is blocked, and so on [25, 26].

2.7   Stacking

Stacking is also referred as super learning or stacked regression which trains the meta-learners by combining the results generated by multiple base learners. Stacking is one form of ensemble learning technique which is used to combine the predictions generated by multiple machine learning models. The stacking mechanism is used to solve regression or classification problems. The typical architecture of stacking involves two to three models which are often called as level-0 model and level-1 model. The level-0 model fit on the training data and the predictions generated by it gets compiled. The level-1 model learns how to combine the predictions generated by the predictions obtained from several other models. The simplest approach followed to prepare the training data is k-fold cross-validations of level-0 models. The implementation of stacking is easier and training and maintenance of the data is also easier. The super learner algorithm works in three steps first is to setup the ensemble, train the ensemble which is setup, and after sufficient training test for the new test data samples [27, 28].

The generalization approach in stacking splits the existing data into two parts one is training dataset and another is testing dataset. The base model is divided into K-NN base models, the base model will be fitted into K−1 parts which leads to the prediction of the Kth part. The base model will further fit into the whole training dataset to compute the performance over the testing samples. The process gets repeated on the other base models which include support vector machine, decision tree, and neural network to make predictions over the test models [29]. A high-level representation of stacking is shown in Figure 2.6. Multiple models are considered in parallel, and training data is fed as input to each of the model. Every model generated the predictions and summation of each of the predictions is fed as input to generalizer. Finally, generalizer generates final predictions based on the summation of the predictions generated by each of the model.

Some of the advantages offered by stacking in diagnosing the zonotic diseases are as follows: easily parallelized, easily solves regression problems, simple linear stack approach, lot more efficient, early detection of local patterns, lower execution time, produces high quality output,

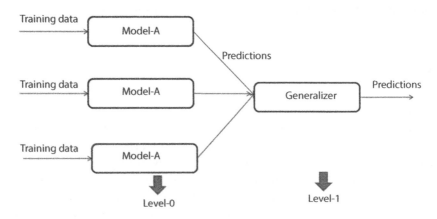

Figure 2.6 A high-level representation of stacking.

chances of misclassification is less, increased predictive accuracy, effect of outliers is zero, less memory usage, less computational complexity, capable of handling big data streams, works in an incremental manner, classification of new data samples is easy, used to solve multiple classification problems, approach is better than classical ensemble method, suitable to solve computation intensive applications, generalization of sentiment behind analysis is easy, able to solve nonlinear problems, robust toward large search space, training period is less, capable of handling noisy training data, collaborative filtering helps in removal of noisy elements from training data, suitable to solve multi-classification problems, less number of hyperparameters are involved in training, evolves naturally from new test samples, very less data is required for training, and so on.

2.8   Efficiency Analysis

The efficiency achieved by the considered ensemble machine learning techniques, i.e., Bayes optimal classifier, bagging, boosting, BMA, bucket of models, and tacking, is compared toward the performance metrics, i.e., accuracy, throughput, execution time, response time, error rate, and learning rate [30]. From the analysis, it is observed that the efficiency achieved by Bayesian model combination, stacking, and Bayesian model combination

Technique	Accuracy	Throughput	Execution time	Response time	Error rate	Learning rate
Bayes optimal classifier	Low	Low	High	Medium	Medium	Low
Bagging	Low	Medium	Medium	High	Low	Low
Boosting	Low	Medium	High	High	High	Low
Bayesian model averaging	High	High	Medium	Medium	Low	Low
Bayesian model combination	High	High	Low	Low	Low	High
Bucket of models	Low	Low	High	Medium	Medium	Low
Stacking	High	High	Low	Low	low	Medium

are high compared to other ensemble models considered for identification of zonotic diseases.

2.9   Conclusion

This chapter provides introduction to zonotic diseases, symptoms, challenges, and causes. Ensemble machine learning uses multiple machine learning algorithms to identify the zonotic diseases in early stage itself. Detailed analysis of some of the potential ensemble machine learning algorithms, i.e., Bayes optimal classifier, bootstrap aggregating (bagging), boosting, BMA, Bayesian model combination, bucket of models, and stacking are discussed with respective architecture, advantages, and application areas. From the analysis, it is observed that the efficiency achieved by Bayesian model combination, stacking, and Bayesian model combination are high compared to other ensemble models considered for identification of zonotic diseases.

References

1. Allen, T., Murray, K.A., Zambrana-Torrelio, C., Morse, S.S., Rondinini, C., Di Marco, M., Daszak, P., Global hotspots and correlates of emerging zoonotic diseases. *Nat. Commun.*, 8, 1, 1–10, 2017.
2. Han, B.A., Schmidt, J.P., Bowden, S.E., Drake, J.M., Rodent reservoirs of future zoonotic diseases. *Proc. Natl. Acad. Sci.*, 112, 22, 7039–7044, 2015.
3. Salata, C., Calistri, A., Parolin, C., Palu, G., Coronaviruses: a paradigm of new emerging zoonotic diseases. *Pathog. Dis.*, 77, 9, ftaa006, 2019.
4. Mills, J.N., Gage, K.L., Khan, A.S., Potential influence of climate change on vector-borne and zoonotic diseases: a review and proposed research plan. *Environ. Health Perspect.*, 118, 11, 1507–1514, 2010.
5. Ardabili, S., Mosavi, A., Várkonyi-Kóczy, A.R., Advances in machine learning modeling reviewing hybrid and ensemble methods, in: *International Conference on Global Research and Education*, 2019, September, Springer, Cham, pp. 215–227.
6. Gao, X., Shan, C., Hu, C., Niu, Z., Liu, Z., An adaptive ensemble machine learning model for intrusion detection. *IEEE Access*, 7, 82512–82521, 2019.
7. Yacchirema, D., de Puga, J.S., Palau, C., Esteve, M., Fall detection system for elderly people using IoT and ensemble machine learning algorithm. *Pers. Ubiquitous Comput.*, 23, 5–6, 801–817, 2019.
8. Zewdie, G.K., Lary, D.J., Levetin, E., Garuma, G.F., Applying deep neural networks and ensemble machine learning methods to forecast airborne ambrosia pollen. *Int. J. Environ. Res. Public Health*, 16, 11, 1992, 2019.

9. Dang, Y., *A Comparative Study of Bagging and Boosting of Supervised and Unsupervised Classifiers For Outliers Detection* (Doctoral dissertation), Wright State University, Dayton, Ohio, United States, 2017.

10. Wiens, J. and Shenoy, E.S., Machine learning for healthcare: on the verge of a major shift in healthcare epidemiology. *Clin. Infect. Dis., 66*, 1, 149–153, 2018.

11. Bollig, N., Clarke, L., Elsmo, E., Craven, M., Machine learning for syndromic surveillance using veterinary necropsy reports. *PLoS One, 15*, 2, e0228105, 2020.

12. Shen, X., Zhang, J., Zhang, X., Meng, J., Ke, C., Sea ice classification using Cryosat-2 altimeter data by optimal classifier–feature assembly. *IEEE Geosci. Remote Sens. Lett., 14*, 11, 1948–1952, 2017.

13. Dalton, L.A. and Dougherty, E.R., Optimal classifiers with minimum expected error within a Bayesian framework—Part II: properties and performance analysis. *Pattern Recognit., 46*, 5, 1288–1300, 2013.

14. Boughorbel, S., Jarray, F., El-Anbari, M., Optimal classifier for imbalanced data using Matthews Correlation Coefficient metric. *PLoS One, 12*, 6, e0177678, 2017.

15. Hassan, A.R., Siuly, S., Zhang, Y., Epileptic seizure detection in EEG signals using tunable-Q factor wavelet transform and bootstrap aggregating. *Comput. Methods Programs Biomed., 137*, 247–259, 2016.

16. Hassan, A.R. and Bhuiyan, M.I.H., Computer-aided sleep staging using complete ensemble empirical mode decomposition with adaptive noise and bootstrap aggregating. *Biomed. Signal Process. Control, 24*, 1–10, 2016.

17. Pino-Mejías, R., Jiménez-Gamero, M.D., Cubiles-de-la-Vega, M.D., Pascual-Acosta, A., Reduced bootstrap aggregating of learning algorithms. *Pattern Recognit. Lett., 29*, 3, 265–271, 2008.

18. Hinne, M., Gronau, Q.F., van den Bergh, D., Wagenmakers, E.J., A conceptual introduction to Bayesian model averaging. *Adv. Methods Pract. Psychol. Sci., 3*, 2, 200–215, 2020.

19. Ji, L., Zhi, X., Zhu, S., Fraedrich, K., Probabilistic precipitation forecasting over East Asia using Bayesian model averaging. *Weather Forecasting, 34*, 2, 377–392, 2019.

20. Liu, Z. and Merwade, V., Separation and prioritization of uncertainty sources in a raster based flood inundation model using hierarchical Bayesian model averaging. *J. Hydrol., 578*, 124100, 2019.

21. Isupova, O., Li, Y., Kuzin, D., Roberts, S.J., Willis, K., Reece, S., Computer Science, Mathematics, BCCNet: Bayesian classifier combination neural network. *arXiv preprint arXiv:1811.12258*, 8, 1–5, 2018.

22. Yang, J., Wang, J., Tay, W.P., Using social network information in community-based Bayesian truth discovery. *IEEE Trans. Signal Inf. Process. Networks, 5*, 3, 525–537, 2019.

23. Yang, J., Wang, J., Tay, W.P., IEEE Transactions on Signal and Information Processing over Networks, Using Social Network Information in Bayesian Truth Discovery. *arXiv preprint arXiv:1806.02954*, 5, 525–537, 2018.
24. Dadhich, S., Sandin, F., Bodin, U., Andersson, U., Martinsson, T., Field test of neural-network based automatic bucket-filling algorithm for wheel-loaders. *Autom. Constr.*, 97, 1–12, 2019.
25. Leguizamón, S., Jahanbakhsh, E., Alimirzazadeh, S., Maertens, A., Avellan, F., Multiscale simulation of the hydroabrasive erosion of a Pelton bucket: Bridging scales to improve the accuracy. *Int. J. Turbomach. Propuls. Power*, 4, 2, 9, 2019.
26. Lora, J.M., Tokano, T., d'Ollone, J.V., Lebonnois, S., Lorenz, R.D., A model intercomparison of Titan's climate and low-latitude environment. *Icarus*, 333, 113–126, 2019.
27. Chen, J., Yin, J., Zang, L., Zhang, T., Zhao, M., Stacking machine learning model for estimating hourly PM2. 5 in China based on Himawari 8 aerosol optical depth data. *Sci. Total Environ.*, 697, 134021, 2019.
28. Dou, J., Yunus, A.P., Bui, D.T., Merghadi, A., Sahana, M., Zhu, Z., Pham, B.T., Improved landslide assessment using support vector machine with bagging, boosting, and stacking ensemble machine learning framework in a mountainous watershed, Japan. *Landslides*, 17, 3, 641–658, 2020.
29. Singh, S.K., Bejagam, K.K., An, Y., Deshmukh, S.A., Machine-learning based stacked ensemble model for accurate analysis of molecular dynamics simulations. *J. Phys. Chem. A*, 123, 24, 5190–5198, 2019.
30. https://archive.ics.uci.edu/ml/index.html

3

Model Evaluation

Ravi Shekhar Tiwari

University of New South Wales, Kensington, Sydney, Australia

Abstract

We are in a technology-driven era, where 70% of our activities are directly dependent on technology and the remaining 30% is indirectly dependent. During the recent time, there was a breakthrough in computing power and in the storage devices —which gave rise to technology such as cloud, Gpu, and Tpu—as a result of our storage and processing capacity increased exponentially. The exponential increase in storage and computing capabilities enables the researcher to deploy Artificial Intelligence (A.I.) in a real-world application.

A.I. in real-world application refers to the deployment of the trained Machine Learning (ML) and Deep Learning (DL) models, to minimize the human intervention in the process and make the machine self-reliant. As we all know, for every action, there is a positive and negative reaction. These breakthroughs in the technology lead to the creation of a variety of ML/DL models but the researchers were stupefied between the selection of models. They were bewildered which model they should select as to correctly mimic the human mind—the goal of A.I. As most of us are solely dependent on the accuracy metric to justify the performance of our model, but in some cases, the accuracy of the simple model and complex model are almost equivalent. To solve this perplexity, researchers came up with a variety of the metrics which are dependent on the dataset on which the ML/DL model was trained and on the applications of the ML/DL models. So, that individual can justify their model—with the accuracy metric and the metrics which are dependent on the dataset as well as the application of the respective model. In this chapter, we are going to discuss various metrics which will help us to evaluate and justify the model.

Keywords: Model evaluation, metrics, machine learning models, deep learning models, Artificial Intelligence

Email: tiwari11.rst@gmail.com

Pradeep Singh (ed.) Fundamentals and Methods of Machine and Deep Learning: Algorithms, Tools and Applications, (33–100) © 2022 Scrivener Publishing LLC

3.1   Introduction

We are expected to enter in the era of Machine General Intelligence, which allows machine to have intelligence to perform most of the human work technically but its foundation lies on the various techniques of the Machine Learning (ML) and one of the most important part of ML is evaluation of model. In recent days, we are aware of the scenario where more than one model exists for our goal or objective. Some of the models are complex—lacks explain ability where as some of them are simple and can be explained. Recent development in the Artificial Intelligence (A.I.) has given us the capacity to explain the prediction of the models using Shapley, LIME, and various ML explain ability tools, but still we are in dilemma when it comes to choose the best model for our objective.

"Swords cannot be replaced Needle"—although it has unlimited power when compared to needle. Similarly, it is better to choose simple model with respect to the complex model when there is minute difference in the accuracy because it will be computational economical when compared to complex model which uses far more resources. But in some use cases, we cannot rely totally on the accuracy—it is just the quantitative value of correct prediction from model with respect to the total number of samples. Accuracy can prove inefficient as well as incorrect quantitative value when it comes to imbalance dataset. Imbalance dataset is the term use to denote the dataset when sample from the classes is not equal; in this case, accuracy is not in a position to justify our model.

Model evaluation is one of the core topics in ML which help us to optimize the model by altering its parameter during training phase. Though accuracy is one of the pillars of model evaluation, it is reinforced with over supporting evaluation metric to justly the usefulness of the model. In this chapter, we are going to learn metrics some of them acts as a pillar for the ML models, and some of them acts as a supporting metrics. The chapter is basically categorized into four parts: regression, correlation, confusion metric, and natural language processing metric with pseudo code, which brings the clarity about the metrics, and their uses, as well as pros and cons, respectively.

3.2   Model Evaluation

Model evaluation is one of the most crucial processes after training and testing the model because we have restriction of computation as well as on the bandwidth of data which will serve as an input to these trained models;

hence, it is not feasible to deploy complex model whose accuracy is almost equivalent to simple model because most of the time accuracy metric is not enough to justify our model (in case of imbalance class) [1]. We need to justify our model productivity by comparing it with another trained model or base model, so we need different types of metrics such as R^2, adjusted R^2, and RMSE, to describe the trend of data concerning the regression line, error, as well as other statistical quantitative metrics [7].

Figure 3.1 is a brief representation of the process or the procedures which take place before the deployment of any ML/DL model.

Regression is defined as the statistical term which attempts to determine the relationship between the independent variable (IV) which will be denoted by X and dependent variable (DV) which will be denoted by Y [3]. In the regression model, we train the model on IV, i.e., X, and try to predict DV, i.e., Y, where the value of X and Y ranges from [−infinity, +infinity]. Classification refers to the process of categorizing or assigning the input data in one of the classes.

Let us first make some assumptions and understand some terminologies which will help to understand the coming evaluation metrics easily.

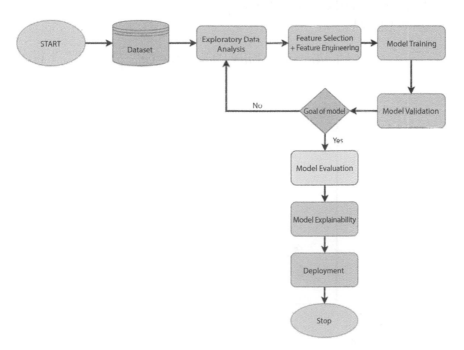

Figure 3.1 ML/DL model deployment process.

3.2.1   Assumptions

Suppose you build a regression model whose equation is $Y = mx + c + \varepsilon$, where m is the slope of line, c is the intercept, ε is the error, and x is the input variable [6]; in the case of linear regression, m and c refer to weight and bias, which are learned by the model oven e epochs on n samples. The predicted value from the model is O and the actual value is Y.

3.2.2   Residual

It is defined as the difference between actual value $Y_{(i)}$ and predicted value $O_{(i)}$. Refer to Figure 3.2 where dots represent the actual value Y and the value predicted value O by our model. Since our model is the regression model, I have shown it with line denoted by $Y = mx + c$, whose output will be a point on the line Y which is dependent on x. It is also known as residual [3].

$$Residuals(error) = Y_{(i)} - O_{(i)}, \tag{3.1}$$

If we substitute the value of $Y = mx_{(i)} + c + \varepsilon$ and $O = mx_{(i)} + c$ in Equation (3.1), we will get

$$Residual(error) = Emx_{(i)} + c + \varepsilon) - (mx_{(i)} + c) \tag{3.2}$$

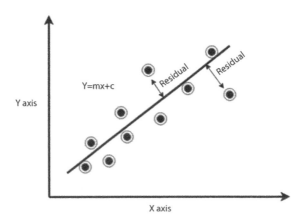

Figure 3.2 Residual.

3.2.3 Error Sum of Squares (*Sse*)

It quantifies how much the data points $Y_{\{i\}}$ is far from points on the regression line, i.e., $Y_{\{i\}} = mx_{\{i\}} + c + \varepsilon$, varies around the estimated regression line, i.e., and $O_{\{i\}} = mx_{\{i\}} + c$ [4].

$$Sse = \sum_{i}^{n} (Y_{\{i\}} - O_{\{i\}})^2 \qquad (3.3)$$

If we substitute the value of $Y = mx_{\{i\}} + c + \varepsilon$ and $O = mx_{\{i\}} + c$ in Equation (3.3), then we will get

$$Sse = \sum_{i}^{n} (mx_{\{i\}} + c + \varepsilon - (mx_{\{i\}} + c))^2 \qquad (3.4)$$

3.2.4 Regression Sum of Squares (*Ssr*)

It quantifies how much the predicted output "O" estimated from the line $O_{\{i\}} = mx_{\{i\}} + c$ is far from the "no relationship line", i.e., $\overline{y} = mx + c + \varepsilon$ [4].

$$Ssr = \sum_{i}^{n} \left(O_{\{i\}} - \overline{y}_{\{i\}}\right)^2 \qquad (3.5)$$

If we substitute the value of $\overline{y} = mx_{\{i\}} + c + \varepsilon$ and $O = mx_{\{i\}} + c$ in Equation (3.5), then we will get

$$Ssr = \sum_{i}^{n} (mx_{\{i\}} + c + \varepsilon - (mx_{\{i\}} + c))^2 \qquad (3.6)$$

3.2.5 Total Sum of Squares (*Ssto*)

It is defined as the sum of *Ssr* and *Sse*, which quantifies, by how much data point from regression line, i.e., $Y_{\{i\}} = mx_{\{i\}} + c + \varepsilon$ vary around their mean, i.e., $\overline{y}$ [4].

$$Ssto = Sse + Ssr \qquad (3.7)$$

If we substitute the value from *Sse* [Equation (3.3)] and *Ssr* [Equation (3.6)] in Equation (3.7), then we will get

$$Ssto = \sum_i^n (Y_{\{i\}} - O_{\{i\}})^2 + \sum_i^n (O_{\{i\}} - \overline{y}_{\{i\}})^2 \qquad (3.8)$$

By solving this equating using Equation (3.8), then we will get

$$Ssto = \sum_i^n (y_{\{i\}} - \overline{y})^2 \qquad (3.9)$$

3.3 Metric Used in Regression Model

As we say, the building is as strong as its foundation, we have built our foundation, and it is quite strong. So, we can start building floors one by one; hence, we will start with metrics which are extensively used in the regression model.

3.3.1 Mean Absolute Error (*Mae*)

Mae stands for Mean Absolute Error. Mae used to calculate overall mean variation between the prediction O from the estimated line $O = mx_{\{i\}} + c$ and actual value Y line $Y = mx_{\{i\}} + c + \varepsilon$ [6]. If we try to traverse from right to left, then we can split the terms into three individual terms: Error, Absolute, and Mean, respectively. These three words are related to each other in order of their split-up.

Error: It is also known as residuals (Figure 3.2), defined as the difference in the predicted value O and the actual value Y

$$Error = Y_{\{i\}} - O_{\{i\}} \qquad (3.10)$$

Absolute: The error or residual of the model can have positive as well as a negative value. If we consider the negative value along with the positive value, then there are chances that positive and negative residuals of the same magnitude can negate each other which can have an adverse effect while backpropagation. Suppose our model has residuals of 2, 4, 6, 7, and −2, and if we take the mean of the error then value with the same magnitude, but the opposite sign can cancel each other, hence it will have an adverse effect on the model. So, by considering only the strength or magnitude of the error by taking absolute value, i.e., modulus of error, it is highly affected by the outlier [7].

$$Absolute = |\, Error \,| \qquad\qquad (3.11)$$

If we substitute the value of Equation (3.10) in Equation (3.11), then we will get

$$Absolute = |\, Y_{\{i\}} - O_{\{i\}} \,| \qquad\qquad (3.12)$$

Mean: We repeat the above steps, i.e., Error and Absolute for n-samples, i.e., the number of samples of which model is trained or tested and calculate mean and select the model which has minimum Mean Absolute Error.

$$Mae = \frac{(\sum_{i}^{n}(Absolute))}{n} \qquad\qquad (3.13)$$

If we substitute the value of Equation (3.12) in Equation (3.13), then we will get

$$Mae = \frac{\left(\sum_{i}^{n}(|\, Y_{\{i\}} - O_{\{i\}} \,|)\right)}{n} \qquad\qquad (3.14)$$

The pseudo-code is given below for *Mse*:

For I in no._samples:
    Error = Y$_{\{i\}}$ – O$_{\{i\}}$
    Absolute = | Error |
    Total Error = Total Error + Absolute
Mae = Total Error / no._samples

3.3.2   Mean Square Error (*Mse*)

Mse stands for Mean Square Error. Mae used to calculate overall mean square of variation between the prediction *O* from the estimated line $O = mx_{\{i\}} + c$ and actual value *Y* estimated line $Y = mx_{\{i\}} + c + \varepsilon$ [8]. If we try to traverse from right to left, we can split the term into three individual terms Error, Square, and Mean, respectively. These three words are related to each other in order of their split-up.

Error: It is also known as residuals (Figure 3.2), defined as the difference in the predicted value O and the actual value Y.

$$Error = Y_{\{i\}} - O_{\{i\}} \tag{3.15}$$

Square: The error or residual of the model can have positive as well as a negative value. If we consider the negative value along with the positive value, then there are chances that positive and negative residuals of the same magnitude can negate each other which can have an adverse effect while backpropagation. Suppose our model has residuals of 2, 4, 6, 7, and −2, and if we take the mean of the error then value with the same magnitude, but the opposite sign can cancel each other, hence it will have an adverse effect on the model. So, we square the error to handle the above-mentioned issue, whereas in Mae, we use the modulus operator [8].

$$Square = Error^{\{2\}} \tag{3.16}$$

If we substitute the value of Equation (3.15) in Equation (3.16), then we will get

$$Square = (Y_{\{i\}} - O_{\{i\}})^{\{2\}} \tag{3.17}$$

Mean: We repeat the above steps, i.e., Error and Square for n-samples, i.e., the number of samples of which model is trained or tested and calculate mean and select the model which has minimum Mean Square Error.

$$Mse = \frac{(\sum_{i}^{n}(Square))}{n} \tag{3.18}$$

If we substitute the value of Equation (3.17) in Equation (3.18), then we will get

$$Mse = \frac{\left(\sum_{i}^{n}(Y_{\{i\}} - O_{\{i\}}^{\{2\}})\right)}{n} \tag{3.19}$$

The pseudo code is given below for Mse:
For I in no._samples:
    Error = $Y_{\{i\}} - O_{\{i\}}$

Square = (Error)$^{\{2\}}$
Total Error = *Total Error* + *Square*
Mse = *Total Error* / *no._samples*

3.3.3   Root Mean Square Error (*Rmse*)

Rmse stands for Root Mean Square Error. Rmse used to calculate the overall root of the mean square of the variation between the prediction O from the estimated line $O = mx_{\{i\}} + c$, and actual value Y line $Y = mx_{\{i\}} + c + \varepsilon$. It is derived from the mean square error and is highly affected by the presence of outliers [10]. In RMSE, root empowers to show a large number of deviations, and when compared to Mae, it gives high weights to error and hence punishes the large errors [12]. If we try to traverse from right to left, then we can split the term into four individual terms: Error, Square, Mean, and Root, respectively. These four words are related to each other in order of their split-up.

Error: It is also known as residuals (Figure 3.2), defined as the difference in the predicted value O and the actual value Y.

$$Error = Y_{\{i\}} - O_{\{i\}} \qquad (3.20)$$

Square: The error or residual of the model can have positive as well as a negative value. If we consider the negative value along with the positive value, then there are chances that positive and negative residuals of the same magnitude can negate each other which can have an adverse effect while backpropagation. Suppose our model has residuals of 2, 4, 6, 7, and −2, and if we take the mean of the error then value with the same magnitude, but the opposite sign can cancel each other, hence it will have an adverse effect on the model [10].

$$Square = Error^{\{2\}} \qquad (3.21)$$

If we substitute the value of Equation (3.20) in Equation (3.21), then we will get

$$Square = (Y_{\{i\}} - O_{\{i\}})^{\{2\}} \qquad (3.22)$$

Mean: We repeat the above steps, i.e., Error and Square for n-samples, i.e., number of samples of which model is trained or tested and calculate mean. It is highly affected by outliers [11].

$$Mse = \frac{(\sum_i^n (Square))}{n} \tag{3.23}$$

If we substitute the value of Equation (3.22) in Equation (3.23), then we will get

$$Mse = \frac{\left(\sum_i^n (Y_{\{i\}} - O_{\{i\}})^{\{2\}}\right)}{n} \tag{3.24}$$

Root: After calculating the mean of the square of the error, we raise it to power ½, i.e., we take second root of Mse, hence $Rmse = Mse^{\{\frac{1}{2}\}}$. Second root gives high weight to the error, and as a result, it punishes large errors. We select the model which has minimum Mean Square Error.

$$Rmse = Mse^{\{\frac{1}{2}\}} \tag{3.25}$$

If we substitute the value of Equation (3.24) in Equation (3.25), then we will get

$$Rmse = \left(\frac{\left(\sum_i^n (Y_{\{i\}} - O_{\{i\}})^{\{2\}}\right)}{n}\right)^{\{\frac{1}{2}\}} \tag{3.26}$$

The pseudo-code below for Rmse:

For I in no._samples:
    Error = $Y_{\{i\}} - O_{\{i\}}$
    Square = $(Error)^{\{2\}}$
    Total Error = Total Error + Square
Mse = Total Error / no._samples
$Rmse = (Mse)^{\{\frac{1}{2}\}}$

3.3.4   Root Mean Square Logarithm Error (*Rmsle*)

Rmsle stands for Mean Square Logarithm Error. Rmsle used to calculate the root of mean logarithm square of the variation between the prediction O from the estimated line $O = mx_{\{i\}} + c$, and actual value Y line $Y = mx_{\{i\}} + c + \varepsilon$.

It is derived from the root mean square error and used when we do not want to penalize the huge error [16]. If we try to traverse from right to left, then we can split the term into five individual terms: Error, Logarithm, Square, Mean, and Root, respectively. These five words are related to each other in order of their split-up.

Logarithm: In this, we take the logarithm of the target value $Y_{(i)}$ and the predicted value $O_{(i)}$ and then we calculate the error. We all add 1 to these values to avoid taking the log of 0 [11, 16].

$$Logarithm\ of\ target = \log(Y_{(i)} + 1) \tag{3.27}$$

$$Logarithm\ of\ prediction = \log(O_{(i)} + 1) \tag{3.28}$$

Error: It is also known as residuals (Figure 3.2), defined as the difference in the predicted value O and the actual value Y, but in Rmsle calculate error by taking the log of target and predicted value.

$$Error = Logarithm\ of\ target - Logarithm\ of\ prediction \tag{3.29}$$

If we substitute the value of Equation (3.27) and of Equation (3.28) in Equation (3.29), then we will get

$$Error = \log(Y_{(i)} + 1) - \log(O_{(i)} + 1)) \tag{3.30}$$

Square: The error or residual of the model can have positive as well as a negative value. If we consider the negative value along with the positive value, then there are chances that positive and negative residuals of the same magnitude can negate each other which can have an adverse effect while backpropagation. Suppose our model has residuals of 2, 4, 6, 7, and −2, and if we take the mean of the error then value with the same magnitude, but the opposite sign can cancel each other, hence it will have an adverse effect on the model.

$$Square = Error^{\{2\}} \tag{3.31}$$

If we substitute the value of Equation (3.30) in Equation (3.31), then we will get

$$Square = (\ (\log(Y_{(i)} + 1) - \log(O_{(i)} + 1))^{\{2\}} \tag{3.32}$$

Mean: We repeat the above steps, i.e., Error and Square for n-samples, i.e., number of samples of which model is trained or tested and calculate mean.

$$msle = \frac{(\sum_i^n (Square))}{n} \tag{3.33}$$

If we substitute the value of Equation (3.32) in Equation (3.33), then we will get msle (mean square log of error)

$$msle = \frac{\left(\sum_i^n \left(((\log(Y_{\{i\}}+1) - \log(O_{\{i\}}+1))^{\{2\}}) \right) \right)}{n} \tag{3.34}$$

Root: After calculating the mean of the square of the error, we raise it to power ½, i.e., we take second root of Msle, $Rmse = (Msle)^{\{\frac{1}{2}\}}$. Second root gives high weight to the error, and as a result, it punishes large errors. We select the model which has minimum Mean Square Error.

$$Rmsle = Msle^{\{\frac{1}{2}\}} \tag{3.35}$$

If we substitute the value of Equation (3.34) in Equation (3.35), then we will get

$$Rmsle = \left(\frac{\left(\sum_i^n \left(((\log(Y_{\{i\}}+1) - \log(O_{\{i\}}+1))^{\{2\}}) \right) \right)}{n} \right)^{\{\frac{1}{2}\}} \tag{3.36}$$

The pseudo-code is given below for Rmsle:

For I in no._samples:
    Logarithm of target = log $(Y_{\{i\}} + 1)$
    Logarithm of prediction = log $(O_{\{i\}} + 1)$
    Error = Logarithm of target – Logarithm of prediction
    Square = (Error$)^{\{2\}}$
    Total Error = Total Error + Square
Msle = Total Error / no._samples
$Rmsle = (Msle)^{\frac{1}{2}}$

If value O and Y values are small, then RMSE is equal to RMSLE, i.e., RMSE == RMSLE.

If any one of O and Y values are big, then RMSE is greater than RMSLE, i.e., RMSE > RMSLE.

If value O and Y values are big, then RMSE is very greater RMSLE, i.e., RMSE >> RMSLE.

3.3.5 R-Square (R^2)

R^2 is also known as the coefficient of determination and is used to determine the goodness of fit, i.e., how well the model fits the line or how data fit the regression model [31]. It determines the proportion of variance in the DV that can be explained by IV. It ranges between [0, 1], where the model whose R^2 value is close to 1 is considered a good model, but in some cases, this thumb rule also fails to validate [17]. It can be calculated by squaring the correlation between predicted and the actual value [30]. So, we need to consider the other factors also along with the R^2 [18]. In simple words, we can say how good is our model when compared to the model which just predicts the mean value of the target from the test set as predictions [12].

$$R^{\{2\}} = 1 - \left(\frac{Sse}{Ssto} \right) \tag{3.37}$$

where Sse is Error Sum of the square from Equation (3.38) and Ssto is Total Sum of the square from Equation (3.39), and replacing the values, respectively, then we get

$$Sse = \sum_i^n (Y_{\{i\}} - O_{\{i\}})^2 \tag{3.38}$$

$$Ssto = Sse + Ssr \tag{3.39}$$

$$Ssto = \sum_i^n (Y_{\{i\}} - \overline{Y})^2 \tag{3.40}$$

By solving expanding Equation (3.37) using Equations (3.38), (3.39), and (3.40), we will get

$$R^{\{2\}} = \left(\frac{Ssr}{Ssto}\right) \tag{3.41}$$

$$R^{\{2\}} = \left(\frac{\sum_i^n (O_{\{i\}} - \overline{y}_{\{i\}})^2}{\sum_i^n (Y_{\{i\}} - \overline{Y})^2}\right) \tag{3.42}$$

So, Equation (3.42) can also be defined as

$$R^{\{2\}} = \frac{MSE(model)}{MSE(baseline)} \tag{3.43}$$

In simple words, we can say how good is our model when compared to the model which just predicts the mean value of the target from the test set as predictions.

3.3.5.1   Problem With R-Square (R^2)

As I have mentioned above, R^2 determines the proportion of variance in the DV that can be explained by IV and in Equation (3.43) to maximize the R^2, we need to maximize MSE (model) or decrease MSE (baseline model) which predicts mean of the target variable. So, when we increase the IV and estimated equation change from $Y = mx_{\{i\}} + c + \varepsilon$ to $Y = mx_{\{i\}} + c + \varepsilon$. Now, if the IV is not significantly correlated, then MSE (Baseline model) should increase and MSE (model) should decrease as a result of Equation (3.43), R^2, the value should decrease but it was found that in reality the value of R^2 does not decrease it keeps increasing [12]. As a result, adjusted R^2 came to existence which is an improvised version of R^2.

3.3.6   Adjusted R-Square (R^2)

We have already discussed the problem related to R-square (R^2), which is biased, i.e., R^2 is biased—if we add new features or IV, then it does not penalize the model respective of the correlation of the IV. It always increases or remains the same, i.e., no penalization for uncorrelated IV [12]. To counter this problem, penalizing factor has been introduced in the Equation (3.41), which penalize R^2.

$$AdjustedR^{\{2\}} = 1 - (1 - R^{\{2\}})\left[\frac{n-1}{n-(k+1)}\right]$$ (3.44)

where k = number of features and n = number of samples in the training set.

Now, from Equation (3.44), if we add more features the denominator, i.e., $(n - (k + 1))$ should decrease, so the whole Equation (3.44) should increase. We have R^2 in the equation and if R^2 does not increases $(1 - R^{\{2\}})$ term will be close to 1. Overall, we are deducting larger value from 1, hence $AdjustedR^{\{2\}}$ will be close to 0. So, we can summarize that the added IV does not have a significant correlation with the DV hence does not add any value of the model.

Since, we have a basic idea of $AdjustedR^{\{2\}}$ from the above paragraph and we can proceed $|Y_{\{i\}} - O_{\{i\}}|$ forward with mathematical intuition. Our aim is to make the LHS of the Equation (3.44) close to 1. So, we need to minimize the term which can be split into two parts, i.e.,

$$(1 - R^{\{2\}})\left[\frac{n-1}{n-(k+1)}\right]$$ (3.44a)

For the Equation (3.44a), to be minimum, we need R^2 to be maximum, hence the bigger number will be subtracted from 1 which will result in a smaller term.

$$\left[\frac{n-1}{n-(k+1)}\right]$$ (3.44b)

For Equation (3.44b), by adding an independent term in the denominator, the value of the denominator will increase; hence, overall value of the equation will be minimum. Overall, if we analyze by considering both Equations (3.44a) and (3.44b), then we are mainly dependent on (3.44a) to be minimum (when R^2 is greater), i.e., by adding an IV R^2 increases, then the IV is adding value to the model; else, it does not add any value to the model.

3.3.7 Variance

Variance is defined as how far point/points of points from the mean of the data points are. It is used in decision trees as well as random forest and ensemble algorithms to decide the split of the node which has a continuous sample [12, 24]. It is inversely proportional to the homogeneity, i.e., more variance in the node less the homogeneity. It is highly affected by the outliers.

$$Variance = \frac{\sum_i^n (X - mean(X))^2}{n} \qquad (3.45)$$

where X= data point, mean(X) = mean of all data point, and n = number of samples.

3.3.8   AIC

AIC refers to Akaike's Information Criteria that is a method for scoring and selecting a model by considering *Sse*, number of parameter, and number of samples, developed by Hirotugu Akaik. AIC shows the relationship between Kullback-Leibler measurement and the likelihood estimation of the model [24]. It penalizes the complex model less, i.e., it emphasizes more on the training dataset by penalizing the model with an increase in the IV. AIC selects the complex model; the lower the value of AIC, better the model [24].

$$AIC = -2/N * LL + 2 * k/N, \qquad (3.46)$$

where N = number of parameters, LL = Log of Likelihood, and N = Number of samples

$$2 * \frac{k}{N} \geq 0 \qquad (3.46a)$$

$$-2/N * LL \qquad (3.46b)$$

Here, in Equation (3.46), LL refers to the Log of Likelihood of the model for regression models; we can take LL as Mse and Ssr, and for classification, we can take Binary Cross Entropy. If we analyze Equation (3.46a), the term $2 * k/N$ will be always positive since N and k are positive so this term will be greater than or equal to zero; also, in Equation (3.46b), the term $-2/N$

$*$ LL will be negative always; the whole equation is a dependent parameter of the model instead of the number of samples, i.e., bigger the value of k, minimum the value of AIC.

3.3.9 BIC

BIC is a variant of AIC known as Bayesian Information Criterion [32]. Unlike the BIC, it penalizes the model for its complexity and hence selects the simple model [24]. The complexity of the model increases, BIC increases hence the chance of the selection decreases [24, 32]. BIC selects the simple model; the lower the value of BIC, the better the mode.

$$BIC = -2 * LL + log(N) * k, \tag{3.47}$$

where N = number of parameters, LL = Log of Likelihood, and N = Number of samples

$$log(N) * k \tag{3.47a}$$

$$-2 * LL \tag{3.47b}$$

Here, in Equation (3.47), LL refers to the Log of Likelihood of the model for regression models; we can take LL as Mse and Ssr, and for classification, we can take Binary Cross Entropy. If we analyze Equation (3.47a), the term $log(N) * k$ will be always positive since N and k are positive so this term will be greater than or equal to zero; also, in Equation (3.47b), the term $-2 * LL$ will be negative always, and the whole equation is dependent on the number of samples of the training data of model, i.e., N increases, Equation (3.47b) increases, hence the value of Equation (3.47) decreases.

3.3.10 ACP, Press, and R^2-Predicted

ACP is defined as Amemiya's Prediction Criterion. The lower the value, the better the model.

$$APC = \left(\frac{n+p}{n(n-p)} \right) * Sse \tag{3.48}$$

where N = number of parameters, LL = Log of Likelihood, and N = Number of samples.

Press is a model approval technique used to evaluate a model's prescient capacity that can likewise be utilized to look at relapse models [54]. For an informational collection of size n, Press is determined by precluding every perception exclusively, and afterward, the rest of the n − 1 perception is utilized to ascertain a relapse condition which is utilized to foresee the estimation of the discarded reaction esteem (which, in review, we indicate by $O_{\{ii\}}$. We point that the ith Press remaining as the distinction $Y_{\{i\}} - O_{\{ii\}}$.

$$PRESS = \sum_i^n (Y_{\{i\}} - O_{\{ii\}})^2 \tag{3.49}$$

More modest the Press values, the better the model's predicting capacity [54]. Press can likewise be utilized to compute the anticipated R^2 (indicated by $R^2_{\{pred\}}$) which is commonly more instinctive to decipher than Press itself. It is characterized as follows:

$$R^2_{\{pred\}} = 1 - \left(\frac{Press}{Ssto} \right) \tag{3.50}$$

What is more, it is a useful method to estimate the prediction capacity of your model without choosing another example or parting the information into preparing and approval sets to evaluate the prediction of trained models. Together, Press and $R^2_{\{pred\}}$ can help forestall overfitting because both are determined utilizing predictions excluded from the model assessment [54]. Overfitting alludes to models that seem to give a solid match to the informational index within reach, however, neglect to give substantial expectations to novel predictions. You may see that and R^2 are comparative in structure [31, 54]. While they would not be equivalent to one another, it is conceivable to have R^2 very high comparative with $R^2_{\{pred\}}$, which suggests that the fitted model is overfitting the example information. Be that as it may, dissimilar to R^2, $R^2_{\{pred\}}$ goes from values under 0 to 1. $R^2_{\{pred\}} < 0$ happens when the fundamental PRESS gets expanded past the degree of the SSTO. In such a case, we can just shorten $R^2_{\{pred\}}$ at 0. At long last, if the PRESS value gives off an impression of being enormous because of a couple of exceptions, at that point, a minor departure from Press (utilizing the supreme incentive as a proportion of separation) may likewise be determined [54].

3.3.11   Solved Examples

As we have understood several metrics, it will be better if we do one example from the above metrics. Let us assume that the predicted value is $O =$ [2, 9, 4, 7, 8, 4, 1] and actual value, i.e., target value, is $Y =$ [2, 6, 3, 5, 7, 8, 3], and the number of samples is 7, i.e., $n(O) = n(Y) = 7$ and number of parameters be 3.

By solving according to the formula of the metric, we will get the value which is mentioned in Table 3.1, and by using the above-mentioned formulas, we will get

Ssr	$= 36$
Ssto	$= 56$
Mae	$= (0 + 3 + 1 + 2 + 1 + 4 + 2)/7 = 1.85$
Mse	$= (0 + 9 + 1 + 4 + 1 + 16 + 4)/7 = 5$
Rmse	$= (Mse)^{\frac{1}{2}} = 2.23$
Rmsle	$= (0 * 0 + 0.176 * 0.176 + 0.125 * 0.125 + 0.147*0.147 + 0.058$

$* 0.058 + -0.301 * -0.301 + - 0.477 * -0.477)/7 = 0.389704 /7 = 0.055672$

$R^{\{2\}}$	$= Ssr/Ssto = 36/56 = 0.642$
Adjusted R{2}	$= 0.284$
Variance (O)	$= 8$
Variance (Y)	$= 4.4081$
AIC	$= 6.74$ (*by taking ln* (Mse))
BIC	$= -0.68358$ (*by taking ln* (Mse))

Table 3.1 Calculation and derived value from the predicted and actual values.

Y	O	Y – O	|Y – O|	(Y – O)^2	Log(Y + 1)	Log(O + 1)	Log(Y + 1) – Log(0 + 1)
2	2	0	0	0	0.301	0.301	0
9	6	3	3	9	0.954	0.778	0.176
4	3	1	1	1	0.602	0.477	0.125
7	5	2	2	4	0.845	0.698	0.147
8	7	1	1	1	0.903	0.845	0.058
4	8	–4	4	16	0.602	0.903	–0.301
1	3	–2	2	4	0	0.477	–0.477

3.4 Confusion Metrics

Confusion metric is one of the most widely used metrics for classification [27]. From the confusion metric, several metrics can be derived which can be used to evaluate binary class classification models as well as multi-class classification such as TPR, accuracy, precision, and many others, which we are going to discuss. It applies to ML as well as DL models—the task is to predict labels of the input data into specific classes like dog or cat, bus, or car, which are encoded numerically [34].

Confusion metric is a metric of size m * m (m is no. of classes); if we traverse row-wise, i.e., left to right, then it represents Predicted Value, i.e., number of samples which were predicted correctly as well as predicted incorrectly [32, 34]. Similarly, if we traverse column-wise only, then it represents Actual Value, and the combination of the row and column gives the magnitude of the True Positive (TP), True Negative (TN), False Positive (FP), and False Negative (FN).

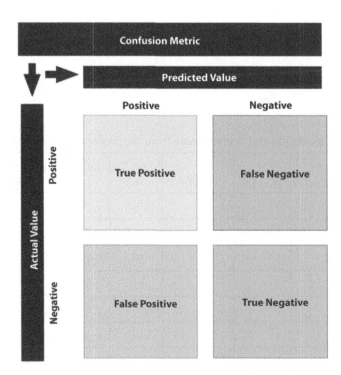

Figure 3.3 Confusion metric.

3.4.1 How to Interpret the Confusion Metric?

From Figure 3.3, we can split the confusion metric into four separate elements, i.e., TP, TN, FP, and FN [40]. As I have mentioned earlier and it is clear from Figure 3.3, the column represents Predicted Value, and the row represents the Actual Value. We all know that we read the elements of the metric by Row and then column. So, we will use True (T) and False (F) to denote the value column, i.e., actual value, and we will

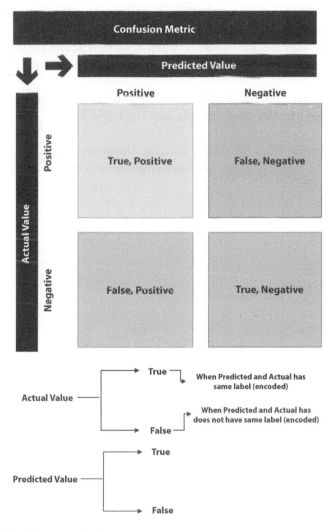

Figure 3.4 Confusion metric interpretation.

use Positive (P) and Negative (T) to denote the value row, i.e., predicted value.

If we analyze from the Figure 3.4, we will see if the model predicts the label as Negative and in actual the value is Negative so we will call it as TN, True—since predicted and the actual value is same, and Negative—because model predicted the label as negative. Similarly, if the model predicts the label as Positive, and in reality, the value is Negative, so we will call it as FP, False—since predicted and the actual value is not the same, and Positive—because the model predicted the label as Positive.

From the confusion metric, we can derive the following data, which can be used to derive other metrics which will support the accuracy metric [55, 57].

FN = Prediction from the model is negative and the actual value is positive, so the trained model prediction is incorrect and known as FN—Type 2 error [56].

FP = Prediction from the model is positive and the actual value is negative, so the trained model prediction is incorrect and known as FP—Type 1 error [56].

TN = Prediction from the model matches the actual value, i.e., the model predicted the negative value, and the actual value is also negatively known as TN [56].

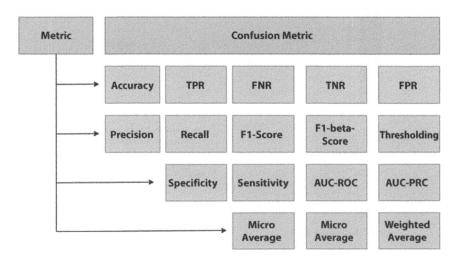

Figure 3.5 Metric derived from confusion metric.

TP = Prediction from the model matches the actual value, i.e., the model predicted the positive value, and the actual value is positively known as TP [56].

$$\text{Total Sample correctly Predicted by the model} = TP + TN \quad (3.51)$$

$$\text{Total number of samples} = TP + FP + FN + TN \quad (3.52)$$

Confusion metric elements can be used to derive other metrics because the model which we train is dependent on the use case. These use cases sometimes vary where we want to prioritize accuracy or TPs or FPs. So, we need to justify the accuracy with other supporting metrics because in some cases accuracy fails to justify our model [1, 6]. Figure 3.5 shows the list of the metrics derived from the confusion metric.

Here, we will discuss each of the metrics mentioned in Figure 3.5 in detail.

3.4.2 Accuracy

Accuracy is defined as the ratio of the total number of correctly predicted samples by the model to the total number of samples [55].

$$Accuracy = \frac{\text{Total Sample correctly Predicted by the model}}{\text{Total number of samples}} \quad (3.53)$$

If we substitute the value of Equations (3.54) and (3.55) in Equation (3.56), then we will get

$$\text{Total Sample correctly Predicted by the model} = TP + TN \quad (3.54)$$

$$\text{Total number of samples} = TP + FP + FN + TN \quad (3.55)$$

So,

$$Accuracy = \frac{TP + TN}{TP + FP + FN + TN} \quad (3.56)$$

$$Accuracy (\%) = \left(\frac{TP + TN}{TP + FP + FN + TN} \right) * 100 \quad (3.57)$$

3.4.2.1   *Why Do We Need the Other Metric Along With Accuracy?*

Suppose we have a dataset which has 90 dog images and 10 cat images, and a model is trained to predict dog, where a trained model predicted 80 correct samples and 20 incorrect samples.

So, in this case, if we calculate accuracy from Equation (3.52), then we will get the following:

From confusion metric, we can say,

$$Total\ Sample\ correctly\ Predicted\ by\ the\ model = 80$$

$$Total\ number\ of\ samples = 100$$

So,

$$Accuracy = \frac{80}{100} = 0.80$$

$$Accuracy(\%) = Accuracy * (100)$$

$$Accuracy(\%) = 0.80 * (100) = 80\ \%$$

Accuracy is quite good, so we can select the model!

No, because the dataset is imbalanced, and hence, we cannot depend totally on accuracy because 80% of the tie model is predicting—the image is not the cat. So, it is biased toward one class. So, we need supporting metrics to justify our model [6, 7].

3.4.3   True Positive Rate (TPR)

TPR is known as True Positive rate, which is the ratio of TP: $(TP + FN)$ or, in simple words, ratio of correctly predicted positive labels to the total actual positive labels [24, 31]. The value of TPR is directly proportional to the goodness of model, i.e., TPR increases, model becomes better and hence can be used as an alternative to the accuracy metric.

$$Correct\ predicted\ positive\ label = TP \tag{3.58}$$

$$Total\ actual\ positive\ labels = (TP + FN) \tag{3.59}$$

$$TPR = \frac{Correct\ predicted\ positive\ label}{Total\ actual\ positive\ labels} \tag{3.60}$$

If we substitute Equations (3.58) and (3.59) in Equation (3.60), then we will get

$$TPR = \frac{TP}{TP + FN} \qquad (3.61)$$

3.4.4   False Negative Rate (FNR)

FNR is known as False Negative rate, which is the ratio of FN: $(TP + FN)$ or, in simple words, ratio of incorrect predicted positive labels to the total actual positive labels [24, 31]. The value of FNR is inversely proportional to the goodness of model, i.e., FNR decreases, model becomes better and hence can be used as an alternative to the accuracy metric.

$$\text{Incorrectly predicted positive label} = FN \qquad (3.62)$$

$$\text{Total actual positive labels} = (TP + FN) \qquad (3.63)$$

$$FNR = \frac{\text{Incorrectly predicted positive label}}{\text{Total actual positive labels}} \qquad (3.64)$$

If we substitute Equations (3.62) and (3.63) in Equation (3.64), then we will get

$$FNR = \frac{FN}{TP + FN} \qquad (3.65)$$

3.4.5   True Negative Rate (TNR)

TNR is known as True Negative rate, which is ratio of TN: $(FP + TN)$ or, in simple words, ratio of correct predicted negative labels to the total actual negative labels [24, 31]. The value of TNR is directly proportional to the goodness of model, i.e., FPR increases, model becomes better and hence can be used as an alternative to the accuracy metric.

$$\text{Correct predicted negative label} = TN \qquad (3.66)$$

$$\text{Total actual negative labels} = (FP + TN) \qquad (3.67)$$

$$TNR = \frac{\text{Correct predicted negative label}}{\text{Total actual negative labels}} \qquad (3.68)$$

If we substitute Equations (3.66) and (3.67) in Equation (3.68), then we will get

$$TNR = \frac{TN}{FP + TN} \qquad (3.69)$$

3.4.6 False Positive Rate (FPR)

FPR is known as False Positive rate, which is ratio of FP: $(FP + TN)$ or, in simple words, ratio of incorrect predicted negative labels to the total actual negative labels [24, 31]. The value of FNR is indirectly proportional to the goodness of model, i.e., FPR decreases, model becomes better and hence can be used as an alternative to the accuracy metric.

$$\text{Incorrect predicted negative label} = FP \qquad (3.70)$$

$$\text{Total actual negative labels} = (FP + TN) \qquad (3.71)$$

$$FPR = \frac{\text{Incorrect predicted negative label}}{\text{Total actual negative labels}} \qquad (3.72)$$

If we substitute Equations (3.70) and (3.71) in Equation (3.72), then we will get

$$FPR = \frac{FP}{FP + TN} \qquad (3.73)$$

3.4.7 Precision

Precision tells us how many of the positive samples were predicted correctly to all positive predicted samples, i.e., TP: $(TP + FP)$. We cannot afford to have more FP because it will degrade our model [22, 28].

$$\text{Correct predicted positive label} = TP \qquad (3.74)$$

$$\text{Total positive predicted labels} = (TP + FP) \qquad (3.75)$$

$$Precision = \frac{\text{Correct predicted positive label}}{\text{Total positive predicted labels}} \qquad (3.76)$$

If we substitute Equations (3.74) and (3.75) in Equation (3.76), then we will get

$$Precision = \frac{TP}{TP + FP} \qquad (3.77)$$

Suppose classification model is trained to identify the patients who will be vulnerable to death by Covid-19 by considering various features like age, lungs condition, medical history, and various explicit as well as implicit factors, it categorizes patient in two classes, i.e., class 0—low chance of death and class 1—high chance of death. In this, we cannot allow the model to give us the high value of FP, i.e., Type 1 error—the person is at high risk and the model is predicting the person is at low risk. Hence, we try to minimize the FP and maximize TP. This metric is used extensively in healthcare applications [34].

3.4.8   Recall

Recall tells us how many of the samples were predicted correctly to all the actual positive samples, i.e., $TP : (TP + FN)$. We cannot afford to have more FN because it will degrade our model [22].

$$\text{Correct predicted positive label} = TP \qquad (3.78)$$

$$\text{Actual positive labels} = (TP + FN) \qquad (3.79)$$

$$Recall = \frac{\text{Correct predicted positive label}}{\text{Total positive labels}} \qquad (3.80)$$

$$Recall = \frac{TP}{TP + FN} \qquad (3.81)$$

Suppose the classification model is trained to identify the persons who are criminal and have a high chance of indulging in illegal activities. In this case, our priority will be to reduce FN, i.e., Type 1 error. If FN is high, then there is an increased chance that a person who can indulge in illegal activities can escape and the innocent person can be put behind bars; hence, it will increase the crime rate in our society. Hence, we try to minimize the FN and maximize TP [35].

3.4.9   Recall-Precision Trade-Off

Recall considers actual positive label, whereas precision considers total predicted positive labels as their denominator, respectively [24, 25, 34].

$$Precision = \frac{TP}{TP + FP} \tag{3.82}$$

$$Recall = \frac{TP}{TP + FN} \tag{3.83}$$

So, they are inverse of each other where if one increases another decreases and vice versa. Hence, we have to choose among these two metrics according to the application of the trained ML/DL model.

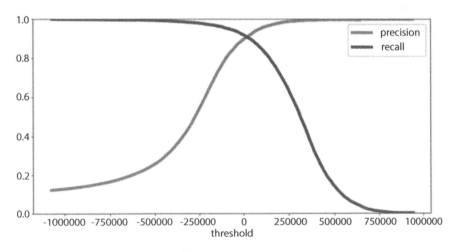

Figure 3.6 Precision-recall trade-off.

As shown in Figure 3.6, if we plot precision and recall, they intersect each other at a point where *Precision == Recall* [34]; this is known as precision-recall trade-off because if we move leftward or rightward from the intersection of these two lines, one value will decrease, and another will increase [24].

3.4.10 F1-Score

As we have discussed above that precision and recall are inversely related and, in some cases, where we are unable to decide between precision and recall, we proceed with F1-score which is the combination of precision and recall [43]. Precision is the harmonic mean of precision and recall has a maximum value when precision and recall are equal, i.e., they intersect each other. It is always used with other evaluation metrics because it lacks interpretation.

$$Precision = \frac{TP}{TP + FP} \quad (3.84)$$

$$Recall = \frac{TP}{TP + FN} \quad (3.85)$$

$$F1 - score = \frac{(Recall^{-1} + (Precision)^{-1}}{2} \quad (3.86)$$

By solving Equation (3.86), then we will get

$$F1 - score = 2 * \left(\frac{Precision * Recall}{Precision + Recall} \right) \quad (3.87)$$

3.4.11 F-Beta Sore

We have discussed earlier that F-score uses geometric mean instead of the arithmetic mean because Harmonic mean punishes penalize bigger value more when compared to the arithmetic mean [43].

Consider a case where Precision = 0 and Recall = 1, then

$$Arithmetic\ Mean = \frac{Precision + Recall}{2} \qquad (3.88)$$

By substituting the value of Precision and Recall in Equation (3.88), then we will get

$$Arithmetic\ Mean = \frac{1+0}{2}$$

$$Arithmetic\ Mean = 0.5$$

And if we take harmonic mean, i.e., F1-score, then we will get

$$F1-score = 2*\left(\frac{Precision * Recall}{Precision + Recall}\right) \qquad (3.89)$$

$$F1-score = 2*\left(\frac{0*1}{1+0}\right)$$

$$F1 - score = 0$$

If we analyze these two values, i.e., arithmetic mean and harmonic mean (F1-Score), and if we analyze the output of any random model that is equal to the arithmetic mean, hence F1-score (harmonic mean) penalizes the bigger value more as compared to the arithmetic mean.

F-beta score is the improvised version of the F1-score where the individual can give desired weight to the precision or recall [22, 43] according to the business case, or as per the requirement, the weight is known as beta which has ranged between [0, 1]. Formulae are given as follows:

$$F - score(controlling - precision) = (1 + (\beta)^2) * \left(\frac{Precision * Recall}{(\beta^2 * Precision + Recall)}\right)$$

$$(3.90)$$

$$F-score(controlling-Recall)=(1+(\beta)^2)*\left(\frac{Precision*Recall}{(Precision+\beta^2*Recall)}\right)$$

$$(3.91)$$

3.4.12 Thresholding

Thresholding is a technique which is applied to the probability of the pre-diction of the models (Table 3.2). Suppose you have used "SoftMax" as the activation layer in the output layer, which gives the probability of the different classes [7]. In thresholding, we can select a particular value so that if the predicted probability is higher to the particular value, i.e., threshold value, then we can classify into one class/label, and if the predicted prob-ability is lower than the particular value, then we can classify into another class/label [9]. This particular value is known as threshold and the process is called thresholding.

If we take, *threshold* = 0.45 then,
Predicted Class = 0, if predicted probability < threshold, i.e., 0.45 or
Predicted Class = 1, if predicted probability => threshold, i.e., 0.45

From Table 3.3, if we analyze, we can calculate confusion metric, and hence, we can further calculate TP, TN, FN, and FP. The threshold is deter-mined by considering the value of TP, TN, FN, and FP, as well as the busi-ness scenario.

Table 3.2 Predicted probability value from model and actual value.

S. no.	Actual class	Predicted probabilities
1	0	0.56
2	1	0.76
3	1	0.45
4	0	0.32
5	1	0.04

Table 3.3 Predicting class value using the threshold.

S. no.	Actual class	Predicted probabilities	Predicted class (Threshold = 0.45)
1	0	0.56	1
2	1	0.76	1
3	1	0.45	1
4	0	0.32	0
5	1	0.04	0

3.4.13   AUC-ROC

AUC is referred to as Area Under the Curve, i.e., the amount of area which is under the line (linear or nonlinear) [33]. ROC means Receiver Operating Characteristic; initially, it was used for differentiating noise from not noise, but in recent years, it is used very frequently in binary classification [3] Figure 3.7.

ROC gives the trade-off between TP and the FP where x-axis represents FPR and y-axis represents TPR. The total area of ROC is 1 unit because TPR and FPR value has range [0, 1] [33]. It can be analyzed that more the area under the curve better the model as it can differentiate between positive and negative class but AUC in ROC should be greater than 0.5 unit [3].

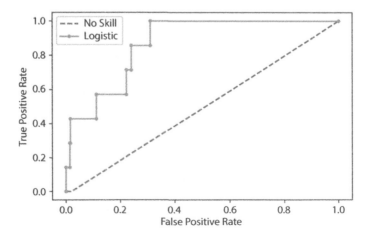

Figure 3.7 AUC-ROC curve.

If AUC of ROC = 1, then the binary classification model can perfectly classify the entire positive and negative class points correctly [29].
If AUC of ROC = 0, then the binary classifier is predicting all negative labels as positive labels, and vice versa [4].
If 0.5 < AUC of ROC < 1, then there is a high chance that the binary classification model can classify positive labels and negative labels. This is so because the classifier is able to differentiate between TPs and TNs than FNs and FPs [5].
If AUC of ROC = 0.5, then the classifier is not able to distinguish between positive and negative labels, i.e., the binary classification model is predicting random class for all the dataset [3].

In some book, the y-axis can be represented as Sensitivity which is known as TPR and the x-axis can be represented as Specificity which can be determined by 1 – FPR [3].
Steps to construct AUC-ROC:

1. Arrange the dataset on the basis on the predictions of probability in decreasing order.
2. Set the threshold as the ith row of the prediction (for first iteration, take first prediction; for second iteration, take second as the threshold).
3. Calculate the value of TPR and FPR.
4. Iterate through all the data points in the dataset and repeat steps 1, 2, and 3.
5. Plot the value of TPR (Sensitivity) and FPR (Specificity = 1 – FPR).
6. Select the model with maximum AUC.

The pseudo-code for the calculation of the AUC-ROC is as follows:
TPR = []
FPR = []
Sorted_predictions = sort(probability_prediction)
For I in Sorted_predictions:
    Threshold = I
    TPR.append(Calculate TPR)
    FPR.append(Calculate FPR)
Plot_AUC_ROC (TPR, FPR)

3.4.14   AUC-PRC

AUC is referred to as Area Under the Curve, i.e., the amount of area which is under the line (linear or nonlinear). PRC means Precision-Recall Curve; it is used very frequently in binary classification [33].

PRC gives the trade-off between precision and recall where the x-axis represents precision and y-axis represent recall. The total area of PRC is 1 unit because precision and recall value has range [0, 1] [33]. It can be clearly analyzed that more the area under the curve better the model as it can clearly differentiate between positive and negative class but AUC in PRC should be greater than 0.5 unit because of imbalance in the dataset as small change in prediction can show a drastic change in AUC-PRC curve [3] (Figure 3.8).

A binary classification model with correct predictions is depicted as a point at a coordinate of (1, 1). A skillful model is represented by a curve that bends toward a coordinate (1, 1) [5]. A random binary classification model will be a horizontal line on the plot with a precision that is proportional to the number of positive examples in the dataset. For a balanced dataset, this will be 0.5 [4]. The focus of the PRC on the minority class makes it an effective diagnostic for imbalanced binary classification models. Precision and recall make it possible to assess the performance of a classifier on the minority class [29]. PRCs are recommended for highly skewed domains where ROC curves may provide an excessively optimistic view of the performance [5].

Steps to construct AUC-PRC:

1. Arrange the dataset on the basis on the predictions of probability in decreasing order.
2. Set the threshold as the ith row of the prediction (for first, take 1 prediction; for second, take second as the threshold).

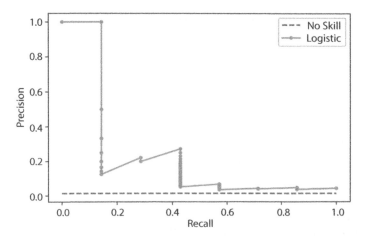

Figure 3.8 Precision-recall curve.

3. Calculate the value of precision and recall.
4. Iterate through all the data points in the dataset and repeat steps 1, 2, and 3.
5. Plot the value of precision and recall.
6. Select the model with maximum AUC.

The pseudo-code for the calculation of the AUC-ROC is as follows:

Precision = []
Recall = []
Sorted_predictions = *sort(probability_prediction)*
For I in Sorted_predictions:
    Threshold = *I*
    Precision.append(Calculate Precision)
    Recall.append(Calculate Recall)
Plot_AUC_PRC (Precision, Recall)

3.4.15   Derived Metric From Recall, Precision, and F1-Score

The micro average is the precision or recall of F1-score of classes.

$$Micro\ avg\ Precision = \frac{TP1 + TP2}{TP1 + TR2 + FP1 + FP2} \qquad (3.92)$$

The macro average is defined as the average of precision or recall of F1-score of classes (more than one class).

$$Macro\ average\ (Precision) = \frac{P1 + P2}{2} \qquad (3.93)$$

$$Macro\ average\ (Recall) = \frac{R1 + R2}{2} \qquad (3.94)$$

$$Macro\ average\ (F1\_Score) = \frac{F1\_class1 + F1\_class2}{2} \qquad (3.95)$$

The weighted average is the weight associated with precision or recall or F1-score of the classes where we control the precision or recall or F1-score of the classes by giving importance to one class and penalizing the other class [48]. It is the improvised version of the macro average.

Since we have discussed confusion metric and metric related to it, for better understanding, let us solve one example where dataset consists of 460 samples from two classes.

3.4.16 Solved Examples

From Figure 3.9, i.e., confusion metric, we can deduce the following metrics:

TP = 200
FN = 60
FP = 20
TN = 180

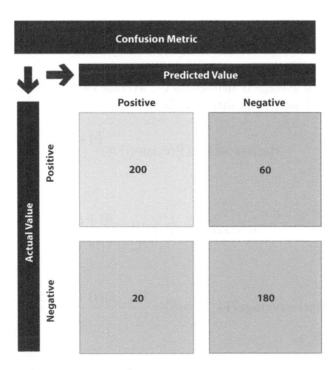

Figure 3.9 Confusion metric example.

So, here, we have all the information required for calculation of the metrics which are as follows:

$$Accuracy = \frac{TP + TN}{TP + FP + FN + TN} \tag{3.96}$$

$$Accuracy = \frac{200 + 180}{200 + 60 + 20 + 180} = 0.82$$

$$Accuracy(\%) = 0.82 * 100 = 82$$

$$TPR = \frac{TP}{TP + FN} \tag{3.97}$$

$$TPR = \frac{200}{200 + 60} = 0.76$$

$$FNR = \frac{FN}{TP + FN} \tag{3.98}$$

$$FNR = \frac{60}{200 + 60} = 0.23$$

$$TNR = \frac{TN}{FP + TN} \tag{3.99}$$

$$TNR = \frac{180}{20 + 180} = 0.90$$

$$FPR = \frac{FP}{FP + TN} \tag{3.100}$$

$$FPR = \frac{20}{20 + 180} = 0.10$$

$$Precision = \frac{TP}{TP + FP} \tag{3.101}$$

$$Precision = \frac{200}{200 + 20} = 0.09$$

$$Recall = \frac{TP}{TP + FN} \tag{3.102}$$

$$Recall = \frac{200}{200 + 60} = 0.76$$

$$F1 - score = 2 * \left(\frac{Precision * Recall}{Precision + Recall} \right) \tag{3.103}$$

$$F1 - score = 2 * \left(\frac{0.09 * 0.76}{0.09 + 0.76} \right) = 0.160941$$

3.5   Correlation

Correlation is defined as the relationship between two variable IV and DV; it ranges between [−1, 1], whereas −1 means highly negative correlation, i.e., increase in DV will tend to decrease in IV, or vice versa, 0 means no correlation, i.e., no relationship exists between IV and DV, and 1 means highly positive correlation, i.e., increase in DV will tend to increase in IV, or vice versa [16].

While in implementation, we use to set the threshold for both sides so that we can incorporate the IV which are highly correlated in terms of the absolute value of magnitude and then we process further to build the model [16]. Correlation estimation is done before building the model but, in some cases, where we have limitations like computing power and storage scarcity, we use correlation metric to justify our regression model by showing the relation between IV and DV. Below are the correlation metrics which are used widely to justify the model indirectly, i.e., justifies the model by justifying its predictors/features (X = IV and Y = DV, respectively) [15]:

3.5.1   Pearson Correlation

Pearson correlation is defined as the covariance of two variable normalized by the product of the standard deviation of the variables denoted by r.

It measures a linear association between two variables—parametric correlation [14]. It is also known as the product-moment correlation coefficient between two variables IV and DV which ranges from $[-1, 1]$ where $0 =$ no relation, $1 =$ positive relation, and $-1 =$ negative relation, respectively [14].

Assumptions:

1. IV and DV are normally distributed.
2. Both IV and DV are continuous and as linearly related.
3. No outliers are present in the IV and DV (it affects the mean).
4. IV and DV are homoscedasticity (homogeneity of variance).

Formulae:

$$r = \frac{Cov(X,Y)}{\sigma(X)*\sigma(Y)} \tag{3.104}$$

where

$$\sigma = standard\ deviation$$

$$Cov(X,\ Y) = Covariance$$

$$Cov(X,Y) = \frac{\sum_{i=1}^{n}(X_i - \bar{X})*\sum_{i=1}^{n}(Y_i - \bar{Y})}{N-1} \tag{3.105}$$

$$N = Number\ of\ Samples$$

$$(\overline{X}) = Mean\ of\ X,\ similarly\ for\ Y$$

Steps of Pearson correlation:

1. Find the covariance of X and Y.
2. Find the standard deviation of X and Y.
3. Multiply the covariance of X and Y and divide by multiplication of the standard deviation of X and Y.

3.5.2 Spearman Correlation

Spearman correlation is a non-parametric test which is used to measure the association between the two variables [19]. It is equal to the Pearson correlation, and it is calculated as same as the Pearson correlation, but instead of the value, we use the rank of the variable denoted by ρ [21]. It ranges from $[-1, 1]$ where 0 = no relation, 1 = positive relation, and -1 = negative relation, respectively.

Assumption:

1. IV and DV are linear and monotonous.
2. IV and DV are continuous and ordinal.
3. IV and DV are normally distributed.

Formulae:

$$\rho = \frac{Cov(rank(X), rank(Y))}{\sigma(rank(X)) * \sigma(rank(Y))} \quad (3.106)$$

where

$$\sigma = standard\ deviation$$

$$Cov(rank(X), rank(Y)) = Covariance\ of\ rank\ of\ X\ and\ Y$$

$$Cov(X, Y) = \frac{\sum_{i=1}^{n}(rank(X_i) - \bar{X}) * \sum_{i=1}^{n}(rank(Y_i) - \bar{Y})}{N - 1} \quad (3.107)$$

$$N = Number\ of\ Samples$$

$$(\overline{X}) = Mean\ of\ rank\ (X),\ similarly\ for\ Y$$

Or,

$$\rho = 1 - \frac{6 * \sum_{i=1}^{n}(d_i^2)}{N(N^2 - 1)} \quad (3.108)$$

where
$N = Number\ of\ Samples$
$d = Difference\ in\ rank\ of\ X\ and\ Y$

Steps of Spearman correlation:

1. Rank the variable X and Y.
2. Calculate the difference of the rank, i.e., d = R(x) – R(y).
3. Raise d to the power of 2 and perform summation.
4. Calculate N * (N – 1), where n is no of the variable.
5. Substitute the respective value in the below formulae.
6. (Optional) you can use the rank of the variable in Pearson's formula and calculate the Spearman correlation.

3.5.3   Kendall's Rank Correlation

It is a non-parametric measure of the relationship between the columns of the ranked data. It is preferred over Spearman correlation because of the low GES (gross error sensitivity) and the asymptotic variance [19, 23]. It ranges from [–1, 1] where 0 = no relation, 1 = positive relation, and –1 = negative relation, respectively.

Assumption:

1. IV and DV are linear and monotonous.
2. IV and DV are continuous and ordinal.
3. IV and DV are normally distributed.

Formulae:

$$\tau = \frac{(C-D)}{\left(\dfrac{N}{2}\right)} \tag{3.109}$$

where
N = *Number of Samples*
C = *Number of Concordant Pair*
D = *Number of Discordant Pair*

A quirk test can produce a negative coefficient, hence making the range between [–1, 1], but when we are using ranked data, the negative value does not mean much. Several version of tau correlations exists such as τ A, τ B, and τ C. τ A is used with a squared table (no. of row == no. of columns), and τ C for rectangular columns [24].

Briefly, concordant [23] means ranks are ordered in same order irrespective of the rank (X increases, Y also increases) and discordant [23] (X increases, Y also decreases) means ranks are ordered in opposite way irrespective of rank.

Steps of Kendall's rank correlation:
  Steps to find concordant:

1. Take any column X or Y.
2. For the first value in the selected count no. of values in the respective column starting from the next row which is greater than the selected value in row. Suppose you are calculating a concordant for ith row, so you will take values from (i+1)th row from the Interview column.

  Steps to find discordant:

1. Take any column X or Y.
2. For first value in the selected feature, i.e., Interviewer 2, count no of value in the respective column starting from next row which is smaller than the selected value in row. Suppose you are calculating a concordant for ith row, so you will take values from (i+1)th row from the interview column.

3.5.4   Distance Correlation

Distance correlation is used to test the relation between the IV and DV which are linear or nonlinear, in contrast with the Pearson which applies to only linear related data [51]. Statistical test of dependence can be performed with a permutation test. It ranges from [0, 1] where 0 = no relation, 1= positive relation, and −1 = negative relation, respectively.
  Steps of distance correlation:

1. Calculate the distance metric of X and Y.
2. Calculate doubly center for X and Y each element.
3. Multiply the doubly center of X and Y for each term take the summation and finally divide by N raised to 2.

  Formulae:

$$a_{j,k} = |X_j - X_k| \tag{3.110}$$

$$b_{j,k} = |Y_j - Y_k| \tag{3.111}$$

$$A_{j,k} = a_{j,k} - \overline{a}_j - \overline{a_k} - \overline{a} \tag{3.112}$$

$$B_{j,k} = b_{j,k} - \overline{b}_j - \overline{b_k} - \overline{b} \tag{3.113}$$

$$d\,Cov^2(X,Y) = \frac{1}{N^2} * \sum_{i=0}^{n} \sum_{j=0}^{n} (A_{j,k}, B_{j,k}) \tag{3.114}$$

Or, for two random variables,

$$dCor(X,Y) = \frac{dCov(X,Y)}{(dVar(X)*dVar(Y))^2} \tag{3.115}$$

where
N = No. of Samples.
j, k = i to N.
$a_{j,k}, b_{j,k}$ = Distance metric with each point to all other point.
$\overline{a}, \overline{b}$ = Grand Mean i.e. Mean of X and Y, respectively.
$\overline{a}_j, \overline{a_k}, \overline{b}_j, \overline{b_k}$ = j^{th} row mean, k^{th} column mean, respectively.
$d\,Cov^2(X, Y)$ = Distance covariance.

3.5.5   Biweight Mid-Correlation

This type of correlation is median base instead of the traditionally mean base, also known as bicorr, which measures similarity between samples [50]. It is less affected by outliers because it is independent of mean. It ranges from [0, 1] where 0 = no relation, 1 = positive relation, and −1 = negative relation, respectively.

Assumptions:

1. IV and DV are normally distributed.
2. Both IV and DV are continuous or ordinal.

Formulae:

$$u\_i = (X\_i - Med(X))/(9 * MAD\,(X)) \tag{3.116}$$

$$v_i = \frac{Y_i - Med(Y)}{9 * MAD(Y)} \tag{3.117}$$

$$W_i^x(1-u_i^2)*I*(1-|u_i|)$$ (3.118)

$$W_i^y(1-v_i^2)*I*(1-|v_i|)$$ (3.119)

$$I = 1 \ if, X > 0, \ else \ I = 0$$

$$\bar{X} = \frac{(X_i - Med(X)*W_i^x)}{\left(\left(\sum_{j=0}^{N}\left[(X_i - Med(X))*W_j^x\right]^2\right)^{\frac{1}{2}}\right)}$$ (3.120)

$$\bar{Y} = \frac{(Y_i - Med(Y)*W_i^y)}{\left(\left(\sum_{j=0}^{N}\left[(Y_i - Med(Y))*W_j^y\right]^2\right)^{\frac{1}{2}}\right)}$$ (3.121)

Finally,

$$Bicorr(X,Y) = \sum_{i=0}^{N}(\bar{X},\bar{Y})$$ (3.122)

where
N = No. of Samples.
$Med(X)$, $Med(Y)$ = Median of X and Y, respectively.
$MAD(A)$, = Mean Absolute Value, i.e., $|A_i - \bar{A}|$ where $\bar{A}$ is mean of A.

3.5.6 Gamma Correlation

It is the measurement of rank correlation equivalent to the Kendal rank correlation [49]. It is robust to outliers and denoted by gamma, i.e., γ. Its goal is to predict where new value will rank. It applies to data which are tied with their respective rank [50]. It ranges from [0, 1] where 0 = no relation, 1 = positive relation, and −1 = negative relation, respectively.
Formulae:

$$\gamma = \frac{N_C - N_D}{N_C - N_D}$$ (3.123)

where
   N_c = *Number of Concordant Pair.*
   N_d = *Number of Discordant Pair.*

3.5.7   Point Biserial Correlation

This type of correlation is used to calculate the relationship between the dichotomous (binary) variable and continuous variable works well then IV and DV are linearly dependent [53]. It is same as the Pearson correlation; the only difference is that it works with dichotomous and continuous variable and denoted by r_{pb} [53]. It ranges from [0, 1] where 0 = no relation, 1 = positive relation, and −1 = negative relation, respectively.
   Assumptions:

   1. IV and DV are normally distributed, i.e., mean − 0 and variance = 1 or bell-shaped curve.
   2. Anyone of them IV or DV should be continuous or ordinal and another should be dichotomous.

   Formulae:

$$r_{pb} = \frac{(M_1 - M_0)}{S_n} * (p*q)^{\frac{1}{2}}$$
(3.123)

Or,

$$r_{pb} = \frac{(M_1 - M_0)}{S_n} * \left(\left(\frac{n_o}{n} \right) * \left(\frac{n_1}{n} \right) \right)^{\frac{1}{2}}$$
(3.124)

where
   M_0 = *Mean of data with group 0.*
   M_1 = *Mean of data with group 1.*
   S_n = *Standard deviation of Continuous data.*
   p = *Proportion of cases in group 0* $\left(p = \frac{n_o}{n} \right)$.
   q = *Proportion of cases in group 1* $\left(q = \frac{n_o}{n} \right)$.
   n = *Total Number of observation.*
   n_0 = *Number of observation in group 0.*
   n_1 = *Number of observation in group 1.*

3.5.8   Biserial Correlation

Biserial correlation is almost the same as point biserial correlation, but one of the variables is dichotomous ordinal data and has an underlying continuity and denoted by r_b [53]. It ranges from [0, 1] where 0 = no relation, 1 = positive relation, and −1 = negative relation, respectively.

Assumptions:

1. IV and DV are normally distributed.
2. Anyone of them IV or DV should be ordinal which has underlying continuity, and another should be dichotomous.

Formulae:

$$r_b = \frac{[(Y_1 - Y_o) * ((p * q)/Y]}{\sigma_y} \qquad (3.125)$$

where
Y_o = *Mean Score of data point at X = 0.*
Y_1 = *Mean Score of data point at X = 1.*
p = *Proportion of data pairs for X = 1.*
q = *Proportion of data pairs for X = 0.*
σ_y = *Population standard deviation.*
Y = *Height of standard Normal Distribution.*

3.5.9   Partial Correlation

The partial correlation measures the strength of correlation between the variables by controlling one or more variables [51]. Like if the dataset has 5 IV, then we calculate correlation with 1 IV and DV and then we calculate the correlation between 2 IV and DV and so on. Therefore, some discrepancies are there when we compare t and p-value from other correlation methods [52].

3.6   Natural Language Processing (NLP)

Evaluation of the NLP model is a little tricky to evaluate because the output of these model is text/sentence/paragraph. So, we have to check the syntactical, semantic, and the context of the output of the model [41]; so, we use different types of techniques to evaluate these models, some of the metric based on word levels, sentence level, and so on. Let us have some basic intuition about NLP models. NLP deals with Natural Language—humans use to communicate with each other, i.e., it deals with the text data [49]. We all know that ML models take input as numerical value, i.e., numeric tensor, and give numeric output. So, we need to convert these text data into numerical format. For this, we have various pre-processing techniques such as Bog of Words, Word2vector, Doc2vector, Term Frequency (TF), Inverse Term Frequency (ITF), and Term Frequency-Inverse Term Frequency (TF-IDF) [41], or you can do manually by various techniques. For now, you do not need to get carried away just assume that text has been converted by some algorithm or method into numerical value and vice versa.

3.6.1   N-Gram

In ML, gram is referred as a word and N is an integer. So, N-gram refers to the count of words in a sentence [49]; if a sentence is made-up of 10 words, then it will be called as 10-gram. It is used to predict the probability of the next word in the sentence depending how the model is trained, i.e., om Bigram trigram and so on using the probability of occurrence of the word related to its previous word.

$N - Gram = N (Natural) + Gram (word)$

Reference Sentence: I am a human.

So,

1 – *Gram* (*UniGram*): *I, am, a, human.*

2 – *Gram* (*BiGram*): *I, am, am a, a human.*

3 – *Gram*: (*TriGram*) *I am a, am a human.*

Similarly, we can group the words in a sentence according to N-Gram. and we predict the next word in the sentence irrespective of the context.

3.6.2   BELU Score

BELU stands for the Bi-Lingual Evaluation Understudy—it was invented to evaluate the language translation from one language to another [41, 49].

Steps to calculate BELU are as follows:

Step 1: From the predicted word, assign the value 1 if the word matches with the training set else assign 0.

Step 2: Normalize the count so that it has range of [0–1], i.e., total count/ no. of words in reference sentence.

The below example shows how the BELU score of the predicted sentence is calculated by implementing the above-mentioned steps.

Original sentence: A red car is good.

Reference sentence 1: A red car is going.

BELU score: $(1 + 1 + 1 + 1 + 0)/5 = 4/5$

Reference sentence 2: A red car is going fast and looks good.

BELU score: $(1 + 1 + 1 + 1 + 1)/5 = 5/5 = 1$

Reference sentence 3: On the road the red car is good.

BELU score: $(1 + 1 + 1 + 1 + 1)/5 = 5/5 = 1$

As we can see from the above example, that Reference Sentence 2 and Reference Sentence 3 have BELU score of 1 respective but the meaning of them were completely different from the original sentence. Hence, BELU score did not consider the meaning of the sentence; it just took the present of the word in the respective sentence to calculate the BELU score; to counter this problem, BELU score with N-Gram was introduced which is discussed below.

3.6.2.1   BELU Score With N-Gram

BELU score with N-Gram is almost same as the BELU score but we use combination of the word, i.e., N-Gram to calculate the BELU score [41]. BELU score with N-Gram also limits the number of times the word has been used in the document or in sentence which helps us to avoid unnecessary repetition of words. Finally, we try to mitigate the loss if the detail in the predicted sentence by introducing brevity penalty, i.e., we try to keep the predicted output from the model to be greater than the reference sentence [41].

$$BELU\ Score\ with\ N - Gram = 1 - Gram * 2 - Gram * 3 - Gram \ldots$$
$$N - Gram * brevity\ penalty \tag{3.126}$$

where brevity penalty = 1, if length of output sentence predicted by the NLP model is greater than the length of the shortest sentence referenced, i.e., length of the shortest reference sentence in the training set.

$$brevity\ penalty = e\left(\frac{length\ of\ output\ sentence\ predicted\ by\ the\ NLP\ model}{length\ of\ the\ shortest\ sentence\ referenced}\right) - 1,$$
$$\tag{3.127}$$

for the else part.

BELU score is not able to consider the meaning, structure as well as it cannot handle morphological rich language [41].

3.6.3   Cosine Similarity

It is a metric which is used to define the similarity between two documents earlier commonly used approach which was used to match similar documents is based on counting the maximum number of common words between the documents [47]. But this approach has flaws, i.e., the size of the document increases, the number of common words tends to increase even if the two documents are unrelated. As a result, cosine came into existence which removed the flaws of the count the common word or the Euclidean distance [47].

Mathematically, cosine is the measurement of the angle between two vector projected in a multi-dimensional space. In this context with the NLP, the two vectors arrays of word counts are associated with the two documents. Cosine calculates the direction instead of the magnitude, whereas the Euclidean distance calculates magnitude [47, 49]. It is advantageous because even if the two similar documents are far apart by the Euclidean distance because of the size (like, the word "cricket" appeared 50 times in one document and 10 times in another), they could still have a smaller angle between them. The smaller the angle, the higher the similarity.

Formulae:

$$Cos\theta = \frac{(\vec{a})*(\vec{b})}{(|\vec{a}|)*(|\vec{b}|)} \qquad (3.128)$$

where

$$\vec{a}*\vec{b} = \sum_i^n a_i * b_i \qquad (3.129)$$

$$(|\vec{a}|)*(|\vec{b}|) = \sqrt{\sum_i^2 (a_i)^2} * \sqrt{\sum_i^2 (b_i)^2} \qquad (3.130)$$

Let us assume that we have three documents, and after tokenization, we found the below information from Table 3.4 and we have project its cosine similarity on 3D plane in Figure 3.10.

Table 3.4 Document information and cosine similarity.

Document name	Number of similar words	$Cos\theta$
Document 1 and Document 2	70	0.15
Document 2 and Document 3	57	0.23
Document 1 and Document 3	27	0.77

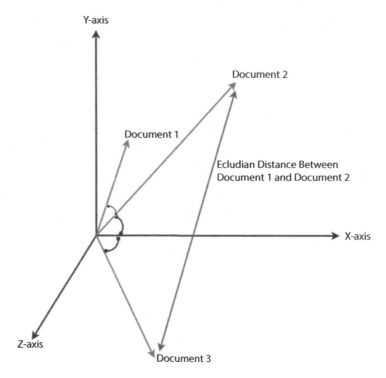

Figure 3.10 Cosine similarity projection.

From Table 3.4 and Figure 3.10, Document 1 and Document 2 as well as Document 2 and Document 3 have more similar word, i.e., 70 and 57 words, respectively; hence, the value of $Cos\theta$ will be less, i.e., 0.15 and 0.23, respectively; as a result, when we will project these documents in 3D plane, they will be close to each other and hence they will have more similarity. If we consider Document 1 and Document 3, we can see from the table that number of similar word is 27; as a result, Cos(theta) is close to 1, i.e., 0.77, and when we project these information in 3D plane, the orientation of the

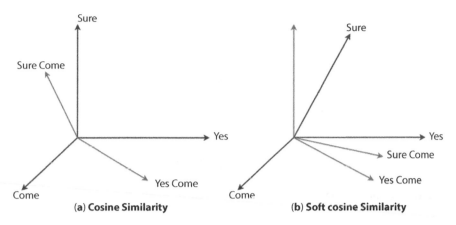

Figure 3.11 (a) Cosine similarity. (b) Soft cosine similarity.

Document 1 and Document 3 will be far from each other, as shown in Figure 3.10. So, we can conclude that smaller the value of $Cos\theta$, documents are similar. $Cos\theta$ lies between 0 and 1; hence, $Cos\theta$ close to 0 similarity increases and vice versa.

If you have another set of documents on a completely different topic, say "food", you want a similarity metric that gives higher scores for documents belonging to the same topic and lower scores when comparing docs from different topics. So, we need to consider the semantic meaning, i.e., words similar in meaning should be treated as similar [49]. For example, "President" vs. "Prime minister", "Food" vs. "Dish", "Hi" vs. "Hello" should be considered similar. For this, converting the words into respective word vectors and then computing the similarities can address this problem by soft cosine [25, 49]. Soft cosine is very useful when you have to compare the semantic similarity of the word. Figure 3.11.a represents the cosine similarity which is close to 1, i.e., they are not similar, but if we consider Figure 3.11.b which is close to 0, i.e., they are similar hence it considers semantic meaning of the words before calculating the similarity.

3.6.4   Jaccard Index

Jaccard index is defined as the Jaccard similarity coefficient, which is used to understand the similarity or diversity between two finite sample sets [44] and have range [0, 1]. If the data is missing in the sample set, then it is replaced by zero, mean or the missing data is produced by the k-nearest algorithm or expectation-maximization algorithm (EM algorithm) [20, 36].

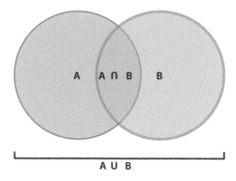

Figure 3.12 Intersection and union of two sets A and B.

Formulae:

By referring Figure 3.12 mathematically Jaccard Index can be defined as:

$$Jaccard\ Index, J(A,B) = \frac{(A \cap B)}{(A \cup B)} = \frac{(A \cap B)}{(|A| + |B| - |A \cap B|)} \qquad (3.131)$$

$$Jaccard\ Distance = (1 - J(A,\ B)) \qquad (3.132)$$

By substituting Equation (3.131) in Equation (3.132), then we will get

$$Jaccard\ Distance = 1 - \frac{(A \cap B)}{(|A| + |B| - |A \cap B|)} \qquad (3.133)$$

3.6.5   ROUGE

ROGUE stands for Recall-Oriented Understudy for Gisting Evaluation, which is collection of the metric for evaluation of the transcripts produced by the machine, i.e., generation of the text and the text generation by NLP model based on overlapping of N-grams [25].

The metrics which are available in ROGUE are as follows:

ROUGE-N: overlap of N-grams between the system and reference summaries.

ROUGE-1: refers to the overlap of *unigram (each word)* between the system and reference summaries.

ROUGE-2 refers to the overlap of *bigrams* between the system and reference summaries.

ROUGE-L: Longest Common Subsequence (LCS)–based statistics. Longest common subsequence problem takes into account sentence-level structure similarity naturally and identifies the longest co-occurring in sequence n-grams automatically.

ROUGE-W: Weighted LCS-based statistics that favors consecutive LCSes.

ROUGE-S: Skip-bigram–based co-occurrence statistics. Skip-bigram is any pair of words in their sentence order.

ROUGE-SU: Skip-bigram plus unigram-based co-occurrence statistics.

3.6.6   NIST

NIST stands for National Institute of Standard and Technology situated in the US. This metric is used to evaluate the quality of text produced by the ML/DL model [49]. NIST is based on BELU score, which calculates n-gram precision by giving equal weight to each one, whereas NIST calculates how much information is present in N-gram, i.e., when model produces correct n-gram and the n-gram is rare, then it will be give more weight. In simple words, we can say that more weight or credit is given to the n-gram which is correct and rare to produce as compared to the n-gram which is correct and easy to produce [49].

Example, if the trigram "task is completed" is correctly matched, then it will receive lower weight as compared to the correct matching of trigram "Goal is achieved", as this is less likely to occur.

3.6.7   SQUAD

SQUAD refers to the Stanford Question Answering Dataset [41]. It is the collection of the dataset which includes the Wikipedia article and questions related to it. The NLP model is trained on this dataset and tries to answer the questions [41]. SQUAD consists of 100,000+ question-answer pairs and 500+ articles from Wikipedia [49]. Though it is not defined as a metric it is used to judge the model usability and predictive power to analyze the text and answer questions which is very crucial in NLP applications like a chatbot, voice assistance, and chatbots.

The key features of SQUAD are as follows:

1. It is closed dataset, i.e., questions and answers are always a part of the dataset and in series like Name of the spacecraft was Apollo 11.
2. Most of the answers, i.e., almost 75% are less than or equal to 4.

3. Finding an answer can be simplified as finding the start index and the end index of the context that corresponds to the answers

3.6.8   MACRO

MACRO stands for Machine Reading Comprehension Dataset similar to SQUAD; MACRO also consists of 1,1010,916 anonymized questions collected from Bing's Query Log's with answers purely generated by humans [49]. It also contains human written 182,669 question answers—extracted from 3,563,535 documents.

NLP models are trained on this dataset and try to perform the following tasks:

1. Answer the question based on the passage. As mentioned above, the question can be an anonymous or original question. So, custom or generalized word2vec, doc2vector, or Gloves are required to train the model—Question Answering
2. Rank the retrieved passage given in the question—Passage Ranking.
3. Predict whether the question can be answered from the given set of passages, if yes, then extract and synthesize the predicted answer like a human.

3.7   Additional Metrics

There are few metrics which are used rarely, or they are derived from the other metric used unfrequently are listed below:

3.7.1   Mean Reciprocal Rank (MRR)

Mean Reciprocal Rank is a measure to evaluate systems that return a ranked list of answers to queries. This is the simplest metric of the three. It tries to measure "Where is the first relevant item?". It is closely linked to the binary relevance family of metrics. For a single query, the *reciprocal rank* where rank is the position of the highest-ranked answer. If no correct answer was returned in the query, then the reciprocal rank is 0 [58].

This method is simple to compute and is easy to interpret. This method puts a high focus on the first relevant element of the list. It is best suited for targeted searches such as users asking for the "best item for me". Good for known-item search such as navigational queries or looking for a fact. The MRR metric does not evaluate the rest of the list of recommended items. It focuses on a single item from the list. It gives a list with a single relevant item just as much weight as a list with many relevant items [58]. It is fine if that is the target of the evaluation. This might not be a good evaluation metric for users that want a list of related items to browse. The goal of the users might be to compare multiple related items.

Formulae:

$$MRR = \left(\frac{1}{|Q|}\right) * \sum_{i=0}^{Q}\left(\frac{1}{rank_i}\right) \quad (3.134)$$

3.7.2   Cohen Kappa

Kappa is similar to accuracy metric score, but it considers the accuracy that would have been happened through random prediction [54]. It can be also defined as how the model exceeded random prediction in terms of the accuracy metric.

$$Kappa = \frac{Observed\ Accuracy - Expected\ Accuracy}{1 - Expected\ Accuracy} \quad (3.135)$$

3.7.3   Gini Coefficient

As we have discussed AUC-ROC curve in confusing metric section (3.4.13), Gini coefficients is derived from AUC-ROC curve; it is an indicator which shows how well the model outperforms the random prediction [54]. It is also used to explain how the model exceeded random model prediction in terms of AUC-ROC curve.

$$Gini\ Coefficient = (2 * Auc - ROC\ Curve) - 1 \quad (3.136)$$

3.7.4   Scale-Dependent Errors

Scale-dependent errors, such as mean error (ME) mean percentage error (MPE), mean absolute error (MAE), and root mean squared error (RMSE), are based on a set scale, which for us is our time series, and cannot be used to make comparisons that are on a different scale [55]. For example, we would not take these error values from a time series model of the sheep population in Scotland and compare it to corn production forecasts in the United States.

Mean Error (Me) shows the average of the difference between actual and forecasted values.

Mean Percentage Error (Mpe) shows the average of the percent difference between actual and forecasted values. Both the ME and MPE will help indicate whether the forecasts are biased to be disproportionately positive or negative [55].

Root Mean Squared Error (Rmse) represents the sample standard deviation of the differences between predicted values and observed values [56]. These individual differences are called residuals when the calculations are performed over the data sample that was used for estimation and are called prediction errors when computed out-of-sample. This is a great measurement to use when comparing models as it shows how many deviations from the mean the forecasted values fall.

Mean Absolute Error (MAE) takes the sum of the absolute difference from actual to forecast and averages them [57]. It is less sensitive to the occasional very large error because it does not square the errors in the calculation.

3.7.5   Percentage Errors

Percentage errors, like *Mape*, are useful because they are scale-independent [49], so they can be used to compare forecasts between different data series, unlike scale-dependent errors. The disadvantage is that it cannot be used in the series and has zero values.

Mean Absolute Percentage Error (Mape) is also often useful for purposes of reporting [49], because it is expressed in generic percentage terms it will make sense even to someone who has no idea what constitutes a "big" error in terms of dollars spent or widgets sold.

3.7.6   Scale-Free Errors

Scale-free errors were introduced more recently to offer a scale-independent measure that does not have many of the problems of other errors like percentage errors.

Mean Absolute Scaled Error (MASE) is another relative measure of error that applies only to time series data. It is defined as the mean absolute error of the model divided by the mean absolute value of the first difference of the series [49]. Thus, it measures the relative reduction in error compared to a naive model. Ideally, its value will be significantly less than 1 but is relative to comparison across other models for the same series. Since this error measurement is relative and can be applied across models, it is accepted as one of the best metrics for error measurement.

3.8   Summary of Metric Derived from Confusion Metric

Suppose we have a confusion metric as shown above in Figure 3.13, and by taking this as an example, we can derive a few more metrics mentioned in Table 3.5.

		Truth	
Predicted	**1**		**0**
1	A		B
0	C		D

Figure 3.13 Confusion metric.

Table 3.5 Metric derived from confusion metric.

Metric	Formulae	Interpretation
Sensitivity	$\dfrac{A}{A+D}$	What percentage of all 1 was correctly predicted?
Specificity	$\dfrac{B}{B+D}$	What percentage of all 0 was correctly predicted?
Prevalence	$\dfrac{A+C}{A+B+C+D}$	Percentage of true 1's in the sample
Detection Rate	$\dfrac{A}{A+B+C+D}$	Correctly predicted 1 as a percentage of entire samples.
Detection Prevalence	$\dfrac{A+B}{A+B+C+D}$	What percentage of full sample was predicted as 1?
Balanced Accuracy	$\dfrac{Sensivity + Specificity}{2}$	A balance between correctly predicting 1 and 0.
Youden's Index	$Sensivity + Specificity - 1$	Similar to balance accuracy

3.9   Metric Usage

Table 3.6 Metric usage.

Metric	Formulae	Usage
Mean Absolute Error	$$Mae = \frac{\left(\sum_{i}^{n} \left(|Y_{\{i\}} - O_{\{i\}}|\right)\right)}{n}$$	Regression, Time Series
Mean Square Error	$$Mse = \frac{\left(\sum_{i}^{n} \left(Y_{\{i\}} - O_{\{i\}}\right)^{\{2\}}\right)}{n}$$	Regression, Time Series
Root Mean Square Error	$$Rmse = \left(\frac{\sum_{i}^{n} \left(Y_{\{i\}} - O_{\{i\}}\right)^{\{2\}}}{n}\right)^{\left[\frac{1}{2}\right]}$$	Regression, Time Series, Classification
Root Mean Square Logarithm Error	$$Rmsle = \left(\frac{\sum_{i}^{n} \left(\left(\log(Y_{\{i\}} + 1) - \log(O_{\{i\}} + 1)\right)^{\{2\}}\right)}{n}\right)^{\left[\frac{1}{2}\right]}$$	Regression, Time Series, Classification

(Continued)

Table 3.6 Metric usage. (*Continued*)

Metric	Formulae	Usage
R-square(R^2)	$$R^{(2)} = \left(\frac{\sum_i^n \left(O_{\{i\}} - \overline{y}_{\{i\}}\right)^2}{\sum_i^n (Y_{\{i\}} - \overline{Y})^2} \right)$$	Regression, Time Series
Adjusted R-square	$$AdjustedR^{(2)} = 1 - (1 - R^{(2)}) \left[\frac{n-1}{n - (k+1)} \right]$$	Regression, Time Series
Variance	$$Variance = \frac{\sum_i^n (X - mean(X))^2}{n}$$	Regression
AIC	$$AIC = -2/N * LL + 2 * k/N$$	Regression, Time Series, Classification
BIC	$$BIC = -2 * LL + log(N) * k$$	Regression, Time Series, Classification

(*Continued*)

Table 3.6 Metric usage. (*Continued*)

Metric	Formulae	Usage
ACP	$APC = \left(\dfrac{n+p}{n(n-p)} \right) * Sse$	Regression, Time Series
Press	$PRESS = \sum_{i}^{n} \left(Y_{\{i\}} - O_{\{ii\}} \right)^{2}$	Regression, Time Series
R^2-predicted	$R^{2}_{\{pred\}} = 1 - \left(\dfrac{Press}{Ssto} \right)$	Regression, Time Series
Accuracy	$Accuracy = \dfrac{TP + TN}{TP + FP + FN + TN}$	Regression, Classification
TPR	$TPR = \dfrac{TP}{TP + FN}$	Regression, Classification
FNR	$FNR = \dfrac{FN}{TP + FN}$	Regression, Classification
TNR	$TNR = \dfrac{TN}{FP + TN}$	Regression, Classification

(Continued)

Table 3.6 Metric usage. (*Continued*)

Metric	Formulae	Usage
FPR	$FPR = \dfrac{FP}{FP+TN}$	Regression, Classification
Precision	$Precision = \dfrac{TP}{TP+FP}$	Regression, Classification
Recall	$Recall = \dfrac{TP}{TP+FN}$	Regression, Classification
F1-Score	$F1 - score = 2*\left(\dfrac{Precision*Recall}{Precision+Recall}\right)$	Regression, Classification
Threshold		Classification, NLP
AUC-ROC	Graph	Binary Classification
AUC-PRC	Graph	Binary Classification
KS Statistic	$Max(Cumulative\% \ of \ 1 - Cumulative\% \ of \ 2)$	Classification
Concordance	Proportion of Concordance Pairs	Classification
Somers D	$(Concordance \ Pair - Discordant \ Pair)/Totals \ Pairs$	Classification

3.10   Pro and Cons of Metrics

Table 3.7 shows the pro and cons of Metrics.

Table 3.7 Metric pros and cons.

Metric	Pros	Cons
Mean Absolute Error	Avg. of absolute error	Not robust to outliers
Mean Square Error	Robust to outliers	Punishes error equally
Root Mean Square Error	Root enables it to show large number of deviation, punishes large error severely.	Affected by outliers
Root Mean Square Logarithm Error	Punishes large errors severely.	Affected by outliers, equivalent to Rmse
R-square (R^2)	Compare the trained model with base model	Does not take account of usefulness of the features
Adjusted R-square (R^2)	Take account of usefulness of the features	Dependent on R-square
Variance	Calculates Homogeneity of Nodes	Affected by outliers
AIC	Penalizes the model based on complexity	Dependent on Likelihood of the model
BIC	Penalizes the model based on complexity	Does not take account of the usefulness of the features
Accuracy	Calculates correctly predicted labels	Does not take account of the imbalance dataset

(Continued)

Table 3.7 Metric pros and cons. (*Continued*)

Metric	Pros	Cons
TPR	Proportional to goodness of model	Take account of the imbalance dataset
FNR	Indirectly proportional to goodness of model	Take account of the imbalance dataset
TNR	Proportional to goodness of model	Take account of the imbalance dataset
FPR	Indirectly proportional to goodness of model	Take account of the imbalance dataset
F1-Score	Takes account of Precision and Recall	Lacks interpretability
N-Gram	Split the word into N- integers	Does not consider the semantic nature of the sentence
Cosine	3D-vector representation of the word	Does not consider the semantic nature of the sentence
Soft-Cosine	3D-vector representation of the word, with semantic representation	Computational Expensive

3.11   Conclusion

Model evaluation is one of the trending as well as vast topics in ML because it involves indepth understanding of the models along with dataset and objective. As we can see in Table 3.6, there is no concrete rule which states that the particular metric should be used with this type of dataset and model. Thus, choice of metric is totally dependent on the model, dataset, and our use case. In this chapter, in model evaluation,

I have covered metrics which are widely used in Regression Classification, NLP, and Reinforcement Learning model theoretically but it is always suggested to have in-depth knowledge of the metric, which optimizes the model. We are just stepping into the era of Machine General Intelligence and knowing correct metrics always helps to optimize the model and validate the result of the problem statement easily.

References

1. Chawla, Nitesh & Japkowicz, Nathalie & Kołcz, Aleksander. (2004). Editorial: Special Issue on Learning from Imbalanced Data Sets. SIGKDD Explorations. 6. 1–6. 10.1145/1007730.1007733.
2. Tom Fawcett,An introduction to ROC analysis, Pattern Recognition Letters, 27, 8, 2006, pp. 861-874, ISSN 0167-8655, https://doi.org/10.1016/j.patrec.2005.10.010.
3. Davis, J. and Goadrich, M., The relationship between precision-recall and ROC curves, in: *Proc. of the 23rd International Conference on Machine Learning*, pp. 233–240, 2006.
4. Drummond, C. and Holte, R.C., Cost curves: An Improved method for visualizing classifier performance. *Mach. Learn.*, 65, 95–130, 2006.
5. Flach, P.A., The Geometry of ROC Space: understanding Machine Learning Metrics through ROC Isometrics, in: *Proc. of the 20th Int. Conference on Machine Learning (ICML 2003)*, T. Fawcett and N. Mishra (Eds.), pp. 194–201, AAAI Press, Washington, DC, USA, 2003.
6. Garcia, V., Mollineda, R.A., Sanchez, J.S., A bias correction function for classification performance assessment in two-class imbalanced problems. *Knowledge-Based Syst.*, 59, 66–74, 2014. *Int. J. Data Min. Knowl. Manage. Process (IJDKP)*, 5, 2, 10, March 2015.
7. Garcia, S. and Herrera, F., Evolutionary training set selection to optimize C4.5 in imbalance problems, in: *Proc. of 8th Int. Conference on Hybrid Intelligent Systems (HIS 2008)*, IEEE Computer Society, Washington, DC, USA, pp. 567–572, 2008.
8. Garcia-Pedrajas, N., Romero del Castillo, J.A., Ortiz-Boyer, D., A cooperative coevolutionary algorithm for instance selection for instance-based learning. *Mach. Learn.*, 78, 381–420, 2010.
9. Gu, Q., Zhu, L., Cai, Z., Evaluation Measures of the Classification Performance of Imbalanced Datasets, in: Z. Cai, et al., (Eds.), ISICA 2009, CCIS 51, pp. 461–471 Springer-Verlag, Berlin, Heidelberg, 2009.
10. Han, S., Yuan, B., Liu, W., Rare Class Mining: Progress and Prospect, in: *Proc. of Chinese Conference on Pattern Recognition (CCPR 2009)*, pp. 1–5, 2009.

11. Hand, D.J. and Till, R.J., A simple generalization of the area under the ROC curve to multiple class classification problems. *Mach. Learn.*, 45, 171–186, 2001.

12. Hossin, M., Sulaiman, M.N., Mustapha, A., Mustapha, N., A novel performance metric for building an optimized classifier. *J. Comput. Sci.*, 7, 4, 582–509, 2011.

13. Hossin, M., Sulaiman, M.N., Mustapha, A., Mustapha, N., Rahmat, R.W., OAERP: a Better Measure than Accuracy in Discriminating a Better Solution for Stochastic Classification Training. *J. Artif. Intell.*, 4, 3, 187–196, 2011.

14. Hossin, M., Sulaiman, M.N., Mustapha, A., Mustapha, N., Rahmat, R.W., A Hybrid Evaluation Metric for Optimizing Classifier, in: *Data Mining and Optimization (DMO), 2011 3rd Conference on*, pp. 165–170, 2011.

15. Huang, J. and Ling, C.X., Using AUC and accuracy in evaluating learning algorithms. *IEEE Trans. Knowl. Data Eng.*, 17, 299–310, 2005.

16. Huang, J. and Ling, C.X., Constructing new and better evaluation measures for machine learning, in: *Proc. of the 20th International Joint Conference on Artificial Intelligence (IJCAI 2007)*, R. Sangal, H. Mehta and R. K. Bagga (Eds.), Morgan Kaufmann Publishers Inc., San Francisco, CA, USA, pp. 859–864, 2007.

17. Japkowicz, N., Assessment metrics for imbalanced learning, in: Imbalanced Learning: Foundations, Algorithms, and Applications, pp. 187–210, Wiley IEEE Press, 2013.

18. Joshi, M.V., On evaluating performance of classifiers for rare classes, in: *Proceedings of the 2002 IEEE Int. Conference on Data Mining (ICDN 2002) ICDM'02*, IEEE Computer Society, Washington, D. C., USA, pp. 641–644, 2002.

19. Kohonen, T., *Self-Organizing Maps*, 3rd ed., Springer-Verlag, Berlin Heidelberg, 2001.

20. Kuncheva, L.I., and Bezdek, J.C., Nearest Prototype Classification: Clustering, Genetic Algorithms, or Random Search? *IEEE Trans. Syst. Man Cybern.-Part C: Appl. Rev.*, 28, 1, 160–164, 1998.

21. Lavesson, N. and Davidsson, P., Generic Methods for Multi-Criteria Evaluation, in: *Proc. of the Siam Int. Conference on Data Mining*, SIAM Press, Atlanta, Georgia, USA, pp. 541–546, 2008.

22. Lingras, P. and Butz, C.J., Precision and recall in rough support vector machines, in: *Proc. of the 2007 IEEE Int. Conference on Granular Computing (GRC 2007)*, IEEE Computer Society, Washington, DC, USA, pp. 654–654, 2007.

23. MacKay, D.J.C., *Information, Theory, Inference and Learning Algorithms*, Cambridge University Press, Cambridge, UK, 2003.

24. Mitchell, T.M., *Machine Learning*, MacGraw-Hill, USA, 1997.

25. Prati, R., Batista, G., Monard, M., A survery on graphical methods for classification predictive performance evaluation. *IEEE Trans. Knowl. Data Eng.*, 23, 1601–1618, 2011.

26. Provost, F., Domingos, P. Tree Induction for Probability-Based Ranking. Machine Learning 52, 199–215 (2003). https://doi.org/10.1023/A:10240 99825458

27. Rakotomamonyj, A., Optimizing area under ROC with SVMs, in: *1st Int. Workshop on ROC Analysis in Artificial Intelligence (ROCAI 2004)*, J. Hernandez-Orallo, C. Ferri, N. Lachiche and P. A. Flach (Eds.), Valencia, Spain, pp. 71–80, 2004.

28. Ranawana, R. and Palade, V., Optimized precision-A new measure for classifier performance evaluation, in: *Proc. of the IEEE World Congress on Evolutionary Computation (CEC 2006)*, pp. 2254–2261, 2006.

29. Rosset, S., Model selection via AUC, in: *Proc. of the 21st Int. Conference on Machine Learning (ICML 2004)*, C.E. Brodley (Ed.), p. 89, ACM, New York, NY, USA, 2004. *Int. J. Data Min. Knowl. Manage. Process (IJDKP)*, 5, 2, 11, March 2015.

30. Skalak, D.B., Prototype and feature selection by sampling and random mutation hill climbing algorithm, in: *Proc. of the 11th Int. Conference on Machine Learning (ICML 1994)*, W.W. Cohen and H. Hirsh (Eds.), pp. 293–301, Morgan Kaufmann, New Brunswick, NJ, USA, 1994.

31. Marina Sokolova, Guy Lapalme, A systematic analysis of performance measures for classification tasks, Information Processing & Management, 45, 4, 427–437, 2009, ISSN 0306-4573, https://doi.org/10.1016/j.ipm.2009.03.002.

32. Tan, P.N., Steinbach, M., Kumar, V., *Introduction to Data Mining*, Pearson Addison Wesley, Boston, USA, 2006.

33. Vuk, M. and Curk, T., ROC curve, lift chart and calibration plot. *Metodološki zvezki*, 3, 1, 89–108, 2006.

34. Hossin, Mohammad and M.N, Sulaiman. A Review on Evaluation Metrics for Data Classification Evaluations. International Journal of Data Mining & Knowledge Management Process. 5. 1–11, 2015.

35. Wilson, S.W., Mining oblique data with XCS, in: *Advances in Learning Classifier Systems: Third Int. Workshop (IWLCS 2000)*, P.L. Lanzi, W. Stolzmann, S.W. Wilson (Eds.), pp. 283–290, Springer-Verlag, Berlin, Heidelberg, 2001.

36. Zhang, H. and Sun, G., Optimal reference subset selection for nearest neighbor classification by tabu search. *Pattern Recognit.*, 35, 7, 1481–1490, 2002.

37. Senthilnathan, S., Relationships and Hypotheses in Social Science Research, https://ssrn.com/abstract=3032284 or http://dx.doi.org/10.2139/ssrn.3032284, New Zealand, 2017.

38. Smith, M.D., Handshoe, R., Handshoe, S., Kwan, O.L., Demaria, A.N., Comparative accuracy of two-dimensional echocardiography and Doppler pressure half-time methods in assessing severity of mitral stenosis in patients with and without prior commissurotomy. *Circulation*, 73, 1, Jan, 100–107, 1986.

39. Helen Victoria, A. and Maragatham, G., Automatic tuning of hyperparameters using Bayesian optimisation. *Evolving System*, 12, 217–223, 2021.

40. Ramasamy, Pitchai & Babu, Ch & Perumal, Supraja & Challa, Mahesh. Cerebrum Tumor Segmentation of High Resolution Magnetic Resonance Images Using 2D-Convolutional Network with Skull Stripping. *Neural Processing Letters,* 53, 1–14, 2021.

41. Papineni, K.; Roukos, S.; Ward, T.; Zhu, W. J. (2002). BLEU: a method for automatic evaluation of machine translation (PDF). ACL-2002: 40th Annual meeting of the Association for Computational Linguistics. pp. 311–318. CiteSeerX 10.1.1.19.9416.

42. Tan, P.N., Steinbach, M., Kumar, V., Introduction to Data Minning, Addison-Wisely,, Pearnson, 97–114, 2005.

43. Chicco, D. and Jurman, G., The advantages of the Matthews correlation coefficient (MCC) over F1 score and accuracy in binary classification evaluation. *BMC Genomics,* 21, 1, 6-1–6-13, January 2020.

44. Sven Kosub, A note on the triangle inequality for the Jaccard distance, Pattern Recognition Letters, 120, pp. 36–38, 2019, ISSN 0167-8655, https://doi.org/10.1016/j.patrec.2018.12.007.

45. Joseph Lee Rodgers and W. ALan Nicewander, Thirteen Ways to Look at the Correlation Coefficient, The American Statistian, https://doi.org/10.1080/00031305.1988.10475524

46. D. G. Beech, 1962. "The Advanced Theory of Statistics. Volume 2, Inference and Relationship," Journal of the Royal Statistical Society Series C, Royal Statistical Society, 11(1), pp. 67–68, March.

47. Sirodovo, G., Gelbukh, A., Gomerz-Adorono, Pinto, D., Soft Similarity and Soft Cosine Measure: Similarity of the Feature in Space Model, 2014. arXiv:1910.19129v2 [cs.IR] 31 Oct 2019.

48. Chicco, D. and Jurman, G., The Advantage of Mathew Correlation over F1 score and accuracy in Binary Classification. *BMC Genomics,* 2020.

49. Ming, T.K., Sammut, C., Webb, G., Encyclopedia of Machine Learning, Springer, 2017.

50. Damghani, M. and Babak, N.K., Measuring and Testing Independence by Correlation of Distances. *Ann. Statist.,* 2007.

51. Dr. Arati Shah ,International Journal of Social Impact,Volume 5, Issue.

52. F. E. Croxton, D. J. Cowden, S. Klein, Prentice-Hall, Inc., Englewood Cliffs, N. J, "Applied General Statistics, Third Edition. 1967." *Journal of the American Statistical Association,* 63(322), p. 738.

53. Linacre, J., The Expected Value of the Point Biserial Correlation, Rash Measurement Transaction, 2008.

54. Lehman, A., *Jmp for Basic Univariate and Multivariate Statistic: A step by Step Guide,* SAS Press, Cary, NC, 2005.

55. Supraja, P. and Jayashree, S., Optimised Neural Network for Spectrum Prediction Scheme in Cognitive Radio. *Wirel. Pers. Commun.,* Springer, 24, 2, pp. 357–364.

56. Supraja, P., Gayatri, V.M., Pitchai, R., Optimise Neural Network for Spectrum Prediction using Genetic Algorithm in Cognitive Radio Network. *Cluster Comput.*, Springer, 2017.

57. Shanthini, A., Vinodhini, Chandrasekaran, Supraja, P., A Taxonomy on Impact of Label Noise and Feature Noise using Machine Learning Techniques. *Soft Comput.*, Springer, 2019, Pub Date : 2019-04-08,

58. Zhao Song and Wen Sun Efficient Model-free Reinforcement Learning in Metric Spaces in Machine Learning (cs.LG); Machine Learning (stat.ML) arXiv:1905.00475 [cs.LG]

59. Cowers, D.M.W., Evaluation, Evaluation From Precisin, ecall F-Measur To ROC, Informdmedness, Markedness and Correlation, *Journal of Machine Learning Technologies*, 2, 1, pp. 37–63, 2011.

4

Analysis of M-SEIR and LSTM Models for the Prediction of COVID-19 Using RMSLE

Archith S., Yukta C., Archana H.R.* and Surendra H.H.

Department of Electronics and Communication Engineering, BMS College of Engineering, Bangalore, India

Abstract

During an epidemic period, it is important to perform the time forecasting analysis to track the growth of pandemic and plan accordingly to overcome the situation. The paper aims at performing the time forecasting of coronavirus disease 2019 (COVID-19) with respect to confirmed, recovered, and death cases of Karnataka, India. The modified mathematical epidemiological model used here are Susceptible - Exposed - Infectious - Recovered (SEIR) and recurrent neural network such as long short-term memory (LSTM) for analysis and comparison of the simulated output. To train, test, and optimize the model, the official data from Health and Family Welfare Department - Government of Karnataka is used. The evaluation of the model is conducted based on root mean square logarithmic error (RMSLE).

Keywords: COVID-19, modified SEIR, neural networks, LSTM, RMSLE

4.1 Introduction

Severe acute respiratory syndrome corona virus 2 (SARS-CoV-2), also known as COVID-19 virus, was first found in Hubei province of China in November 2019. Virus was spread to other parts of world to almost all the countries. In India, the first case was reported during January from the state of Kerala. Around 20 lakh individuals are infected by the COVID-19 virus in India and around 1.5 lakh individuals are infected

---

*Corresponding author: archanahr.ece@bmsce.ac.in

Pradeep Singh (ed.) Fundamentals and Methods of Machine and Deep Learning: Algorithms, Tools and Applications, (101–120) © 2022 Scrivener Publishing LLC

in Karnataka state alone [1]. The case trend in Karnataka is as shown in Figures 4.1 and 4.2. To contain the spread, government adopted nation-wide lockdown and many other policies such as large-scale quarantine, strict control of travel, social distancing norms, and monitoring the suspected cases. In this paper, integration of COVID-19 collected date using modified susceptible exposed infectious removed (SEIR) model known as SEIRPDQ is considered to derive the epidemic curve. Performance of the time forecasting using recurrent neural network (RNN) with LSTM (long short-term memory) is rained and evaluated to predict the epidemic.

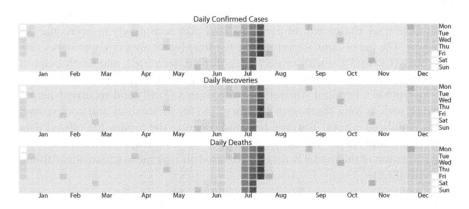

Figure 4.1 Cases in Karnataka, India.

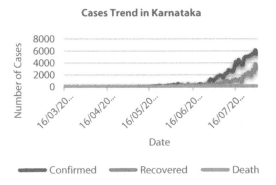

Figure 4.2 Cases trend in Karnataka, India.

4.2   Survey of Models

4.2.1   SEIR Model

SEIR model is a numerical model used to characterize the dynamics of epidemic outburst. This can be further used to predict the infection rate of growth based on metaheuristic method. Differential equations can be used to represent the variation of data based on infected, dead, recovered, quarantined, and protected using BFGS optimization algorithm [15].

4.2.2   Modified SEIR Model

The SEIR model which uses the time-series data is used to predict the contagion scenarios of the epidemic outbreak.

The interaction with six different parameters, namely, susceptible (S), exposed (E), infective (I), recovered (R), protected (P), quarantined (Q), and deaths (D) is shown in Figure 4.3.

SEIRPDQ model is described by a series of ordinary differential equations (4.1) [2]:

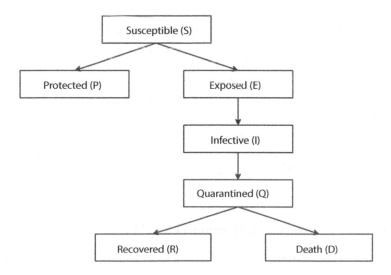

Figure 4.3 Modified SEIR.

$$\frac{dS}{dt} = -\frac{\beta IS}{N} - \alpha S$$

$$\frac{dP}{dt} = \alpha S$$

$$\frac{dE}{dt} = -\frac{\beta IS}{N} - \gamma E \tag{4.1}$$

$$\frac{dI}{dt} = \gamma E - \delta I$$

$$\frac{dQ}{dt} = \delta I - \theta Q - \tau Q$$

$$\frac{dR}{dt} = \theta Q$$

These equations depend on parameters β, α, γ, δ, θ, and τ [12].
β is infection rate.
α is the protection rate.
γ is the inverse of the average latent time
δ *is the inverse of the average time*
required to quarantine a person with symptoms.
θ is the recovery rate.
τ is the death rate.
Susceptible (S) is a group of individuals who are exposed to contagious people and possibility is high to get infected if they are in contact. If strict lockdown and social distancing regulations are followed, then the susceptible populations are protected (P). The infective population represents the infected people who have contacted with the contagious person. The quarantine (Q) group is that population who are quarantined in hospitals or home. They represent the actual cases detected that are able to pass the disease to susceptible people. Recovered (R) people get immunity so that they are not susceptible to the same illness anymore. Death indicates the deceased population [4, 5].

4.2.3   Long Short-Term Memory (LSTM)

To predict the growth of an epidemic, the information of the history of the events is required. It is difficult for a traditional neural network to predict the future based on the history. The class of neural network is known as RNN which will address the issue. These networks have a feedback path allowing the history of events to persist [6]. The RNNs has good performance in connecting the previous information to the present task. Traditional RNNs cannot connect the present task to the long running history of events due to an issue called vanishing the gradients. Here, the effect of past event will connect to the present gradient. This RNN connects the present task to its history with small number of events occurred [13].

To address the issue in the RNN, a class of RNN that works better than the traditional RNN in various fields such as natural language processing, stock market predictions, and sentiment prediction was considered. This model was used for the prediction of COVID-19 and the exact manifestation is still limited because availability of quality data. A LSTM model was designed to predict the cases in China by training the model over 2003 SARS data, and it was predicted that the cases will be hiked in February 2020 followed by gradual decrease [3]. By default, LSTMs are designed to learn the long-term dependencies. In general, all RNNs have chain like structure of repeating blocks/models of simple neural network [6]. The LSTM is able to learn term dependencies and remember the long-term values as per the requirement [7].

The basic structure of the LSTM is as shown in Figure 4.4. Each block/model has three main gates, namely, Forget gate (f), Update gate (i), and Output gate (o). The value of this gate ranges from 0 to 1. The gates decide the percentage of data to be remembered from the previous value which needs to be updated to the present value from the learned history.

As shown in Figure 4.4, the LSTM cell will have three inputs in which two inputs are from the previous cell which will contribute to remember

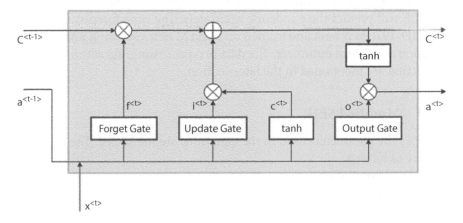

Figure 4.4 LSTM cell.

the history of events. These inputs are called as memory component $C^{<t>}$ and activation component $a^{<t>}$. The third input is the tth time stamp $x^{<t>}$ of the data set X. The LSTM cell validates the inputs and updates the remembering and forgetting capacities which, in turn, produces the memory and the activation component for the next timestamp. The LSTM cell is a standard cell activation function and all the linear combinations are predefined by Equation (4.2) [7].

$$f^{<t>} = \sigma(W_f[a^{<t-1>}, x^{<t>}] + b_f)$$

$$i^{<t>} = \sigma(W_u[a^{<t-1>}, x^{<t>}] + b_u)$$

$$o^{<t>} = \sigma(W_o[a^{<t-1>}, x^{<t>}] + b_o) \qquad (4.2)$$

$$c^{<t>} = tanh(W_c[a^{<t-1>}, x^{<t>}] + b_c)$$

$$C^{<t>} = f^{<t>} * C^{<t-1>} + i^{<t>} * c^{<t>}$$

$$a^{<t>} = o^{<t>} * tanh(c^{<t>})$$

4.3   Methodology

The algorithm used for prediction of epidemic using both modified SEIR and LSTM model is discussed. SEIR methodology describes the deduction of a differential equation with the considered parameters. The change in the values of the parameters affects the response of the S, E, I, R, P, and Q values. For the parameter optimization, the curve with low value of RMSLE will predict the pandemic accurately. The time forecasting of the COVID-19 data is built and trained on a LSTM network using RMSLE loss function and Adam optimizer. The data pre-processing, algorithm, and the prediction are mentioned in the later section.

4.3.1   Modified SEIR

STEP 1: The parameters used in the equations are initialized. The parameters are as follows:
   N: Total population
   I: Infected (1)
   R: Recovered (0)
   E: Exposed (0)

S: N-I-R-E-P-Q
Beta: infectious rate (B)
Gama: 1/average latent time (G)
Lambda: recovery rate (L)
Kappa: death rate (K)
Alpha: protection rate (A)
Sigma: quarantine factor (S)

STEP 2: SEIRDP function is defined which returns the differential equations as indicated in Equation (4.3)

$$\frac{dS}{dt} = -\frac{\beta IS}{N} - \alpha S$$

$$\frac{dP}{dt} = \alpha S$$

$$\frac{dE}{dt} = \frac{\beta IS}{N} - \gamma E \qquad (4.3)$$

$$\frac{dI}{dt} = \gamma E - \delta I$$

$$\frac{dQ}{dt} = \delta I - \theta Q - \tau Q$$

$$\frac{dR}{dt} = \theta Q$$

STEP 3: To solve the equations
Generally, to solve the linear differential equations, we can use Laplace transforms. Here, we use python SciPy. Integrate package using function **ODEINT**

Integrating equation using odient function:
Solution = odient(model, y0,t)

- Model is the SEIRDP function which contains all the model equation.
- Initializing the differential states and time points are defined.

Integration and returning SEIRPQ values.

STEP 4: The differential equations and solutions should be trained to our model in order to fit the data curve with the actual curve. In total, 80% of data is used to train the model and 20% data is used to test the model [9].

STEP 5: Defining the opt_seir function and err_seir function which returns integration and root mean squared value respectively which are used to optimize the parameters.

Opt_seir function is used to optimize the parameters below which was previously initialized. Optimization is done using a function called BFGS the optimized parameter values are obtained

> Beta: infectious rate (B)
> Gama: 1/average latent time (G)
> Lambda: recovery rate (L)
> Kappa: death rate (K)
> Alpha: protection rate (A)
> Sigma: quarantine factor (S)

STEP 6: Optimization is done using a function called Broyden Fletcher Goldfarb Shanno (BFGS); the optimized parameter values are obtained:
Solution = odient(model,y0,t)

- Model is the SEIRDP function which contains all the model equation.
- Optimized parameter values are uploaded here.
- Integration and returning SEIRPQ values.

4.3.2   LSTM Model

4.3.2.1   Data Pre-Processing

Data pre-processing is required to train any model to make sure that the training process behaves better by improving the numerical condition of the optimizer. This will also ensure that the various initializations are made appropriately [10]. LSTM networks are very sensitive to the scaling and the min max scaler works best for the LSTM network. This normalization will also help in removing unnecessary bias to the training and validation data [10]. The min max scaler equation is as shown in Equation (4.4):

$$X_{scaled} = \frac{X - X_{min}}{X_{max} - X_{min}} \tag{4.4}$$

where X is the data set and the X_{scaled} is the normalized data set.

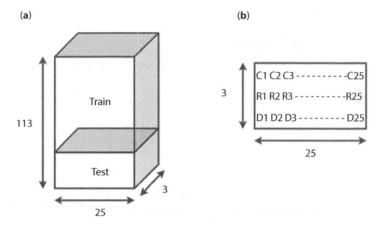

Figure 4.5 (a) Arrangement of data set in 3D tensor. (b) Mapping of the 3D and 2D tensors.

4.3.2.2 Data Shaping

The designed LSTM model takes input of 25days data (window = 25) and predicts the 26th day's data. The cumulative number of confirmed, recovered, and death cases for each day and predict the number for the next day is compiled. In the proposed work, data of 138 days from 16th of March 2020 to 31st of July 2020 is used for training and testing of the model. The number of training to testing ratio is 80:20. Since we have window of 25, the total number of data set generated is 138 − 25 = 113. These data are arranged in 3D numpy array as shown in Figure 4.4 since the LSTM model demands the data to be in 3D tensor with shape (number of data set, time stamp, input features) = (113, 25, 3) [11]. This 3D array is divided into training and testing data, training data input shape = (90, 25, 3) and testing data input shape = (23, 25, 3), each of these data will have the label as the next day's data; therefore the output will be (90, 3) and (23, 3), respectively.

The 3D tensor is as shown in Figure 4.5a. The ith row of the 3D tensor will have a 2D tensor as shown in Figure 4.5b, where $C_{k=25}$ denotes the confirmed cases, $R_{k=25}$ denotes recovered cases, and $D_{k=25}$ denotes the number of deaths.

4.3.2.3 Model Design

The deep learning model is designed with LSTM which takes 25 timestamped input to predict the number of cases for the next day. The model is designed with two hidden layers with each consisting of 45 hidden units. These hidden layers output is then connected to the output dense layer

Table 4.1 Model summary.

Model: "sequential"		
Layer (type)	Output shape	Param #
lstm (LSTM)	(None, 25, 45)	8,820
dropout (Dropout)	(None, 25, 45)	0
lstm_1 (LSTM)	(None, 45)	16,380
dropout_1 (Dropout)	(None, 45)	0
dense (Dense)	(None, 3)	138
Total Params: 25,338 Trainable params: 25,338 Non-Trainable params: 0		

with three units. These three units are confirmed, recovered, and death cases, respectively. The summary of the model is as shown in Table 4.1[8].

The model is regularized using L1_L2 kernel regularization; L2 bias regularization and a dropout of 0.2 to reduce the overfitting of the model.

The model is trained with a batch size of 32 by using an Adam optimizer with performance measuring loss function of root mean square logarithmic error (RMSLE) function defined by Equation (4.5).

$$RMSLE = \sqrt{\frac{1}{N} \sum log\left(\frac{P+1}{A+1}\right)^2} \qquad (4.5)$$

where N is the total number of predicts, P is the predicted value, and A is the actual value.

The reason for using RMSLE as a loss function over other functions is that in presence of outliers other function might explode but RMSLE does not, also RMSLE as a unique property of measuring the relative error. Also, it penalizes the underestimation of the actual value more severely than it does for the overestimation.

The significance of using loss function in the deep learning algorithm is to measure how well the algorithm is implemented in the model. For the model to train well, the error between the actual and the predicted

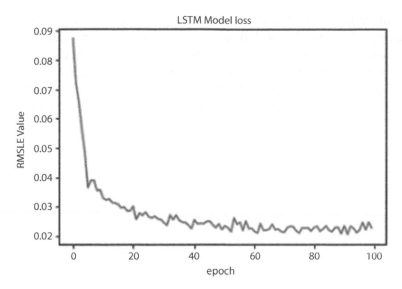

Figure 4.6 RMSLE value vs. number of epochs.

values should be less. So, the process of training any model is to reduce this error. In the process the loss function fluctuates a lot which needs a suitable optimization. With the help of Adam optimizer, the RMSLE loss function will reduce the error in prediction and tries to smoothen the loss function curve. The loss function curve over the epoch is as shown in Figure 4.6.

The model is then trained with the learning rate of 0.001. However, a reduce learning on plateau is used as a callback to vary the learning rate accordingly [14].

4.4   Experimental Results

4.4.1   Modified SEIR Model

The time series results are obtained by the standard deterministic approach for SEIR mode. Data is analyzed for Karnataka framework at a regional scale, and the results are computed. The interpretation of the Karnataka situation according to the deterministic solver shows the trends given in Figure 4.7. The plot indicates confirmed cases (infection), active cases, recovered, and death cases with respect to the number of days.

The sum of the active cases, recovered, and death cases gives the confirmed cases at that date. The model is trained with the given data by considering the following six parameters: infectious rate, recovery rate, death rate, protection rate, quarantine rate, and average latent time by using optimization function and curve fit function. For verifying the actual working of the model, 80% data is used for the training and 20% data is considered as testing data to minimize the error and fit the data. One hundred thirty-eight data samples are considered starting from March 16, 2020 to July 31, 2020. From this, 111-day data was used for training of our SEIR model. Test case data fitting in SEIR model is shown in Figure 4.8.

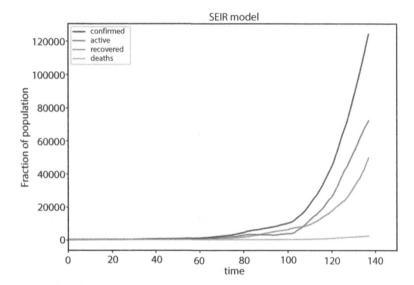

Figure 4.7 Cases in Karnataka.

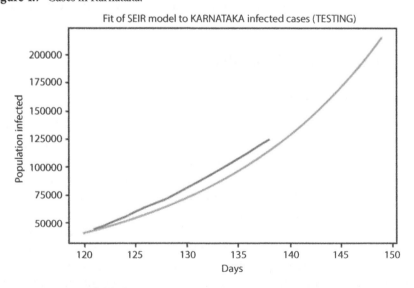

Figure 4.8 SEIR Model fit for test cases.

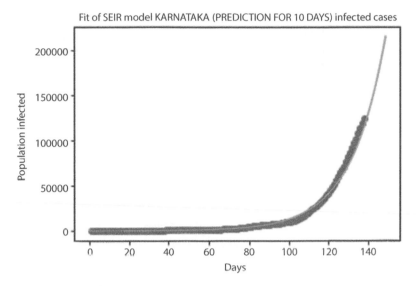

Figure 4.9 Cases predicted for next 10 days.

The orange and blue lines represent the fitted curve and actual curve, respectively. From Figure 4.7 the curve is approximately fitted with the RMSLE of 0.0304. If we increase the data training state and consider other factors such as medical facility available, medications, and hygiene factors in the mathematical modeling, then the exact curve fitting is achieved. In this context, six different parameters of infectious rate, recovery rate, death rate, protection rate, quarantine rate, and average latent time are considered to estimate the infection in the next 10 days using SEIR model that is as shown in Figure 4.9.

From the graph, we estimate that the cases after next 10 days will be around 18.8 lakhs.

4.4.2   LSTM Model

The LSTM is a neural network model which consists of the layers of neurons connected to each other and has associated parameters. These parameters are obtained through a better training of the model. The LSTM network could have captured the growth of the epidemic with better RMSLE when provided with the larger number of data (big data). The validation results obtained after training the LSTM model with the mentioned parameters are computed [16]. The graph plotted with actual and predicted number of cases for test data set is as shown in Figure 4.10. From Figure 4.10, the curve is approximately fitted with the RMSLE as 0.05438.

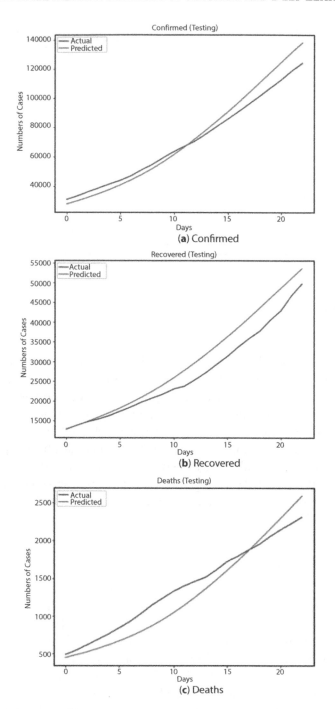

Figure 4.10 Testing results.

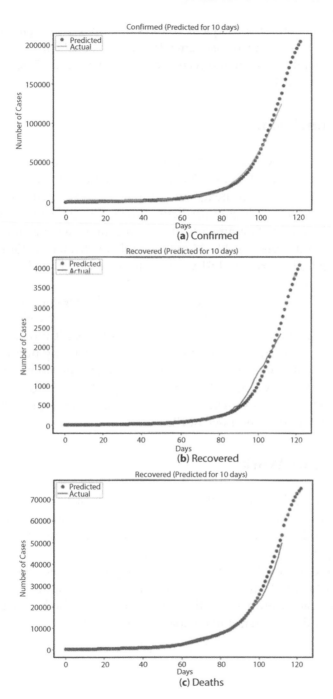

Figure 4.11 Next 10 days Prediction using LSTM model.

The prediction for subsequent 10 days is as shown in Figure 4.11. It is found that the confirmed cases after 10 days, i.e., on 11th of August 2020 may be around 2.12 lakh and recovered may be around 77,000 and there might be around 4,200.

4.5   Conclusion

The modified SEIR and LSTM model discussed in the paper is used to forecast the number of cumulative, recovered, and death cases in the state of Karnataka. In this context, the parameters considered are not time dependent leading to higher prediction error. The error in the SEIR will increase the values of parameters such as infectious rate, death rate, latent time, quarantine rate. The LSTM model implemented has RMSLE of 0.017 which implies less error in LSTM which leads to closer prediction toward the actual value.

Table 4.2 indicates the error in the LSTM model does not change much. The error in prediction from SEIR model varies linearly with increase in number of predictions days. This implies that the SEIR model cannot be used for the prediction of the epidemic data after a long period of time, whereas LSTM works effectively even for a longer duration when compared with the SEIR model. The variation of prediction error with respect to the number of days shown in Figures 4.12 and 4.13 implies that LSTM performs better than modified SEIR.

4.6   Future Work

The SEIR model can be further optimized such that the error does not increase with increase in number of days of predictions also the neural network model can be optimized and can also be tried on other networks and compare the performance of each network on same data. As the deep learning models are data hungry models and presently, the model has been tried on data of 138 days, which is not that sufficient to optimize the model. The model can be reworked with increased data and also be tried on other networks and optimizers and compare each of them.

Table 4.2 Predicted data.

Date	Actual	Modified SEIR		
		Predicted	**RMSLE**	**% Error**
01-08-2020	129287	120832	0.029372	−6.54
02-08-2020	134819	127985	0.022591	−5.07
03-08-2020	139571	135562	0.012657	−2.87
04-08-2020	145830	143588	0.006728	−1.54
05-08-2020	151449	152089	0.0018313	0.42
06-08-2020	158254	161093	0.0077219	1.79
07-08-2020	164924	170630	0.0147714	3.46
08-08-2020	172102	180731	0.0212466	5.01
09-08-2020	178087	191431	0.031379	7.49
10-08-2020	182354	202764	0.0460753	11.19
11-08-2020	188611	214768	0.0564022	13.87
Date	**Actual**	**LSTM**		
		Predicted	**RMSLE**	**% Error**
01-08-2020	129287	148020	0.0587651	14.49
02-08-2020	134819	155899	0.0630917	15.64
03-08-2020	139571	163532	0.0688071	17.17
04-08-2020	145830	170832	0.0687219	17.14
05-08-2020	151449	177725	0.0694816	17.35
06-08-2020	158254	184156	0.0658307	16.37
07-08-2020	164924	190088	0.0616704	15.26
08-08-2020	172102	195506	0.0553738	13.6
09-08-2020	178087	200410	0.0512868	12.53
10-08-2020	182354	208744	0.0586984	14.47
11-08-2020	188611	212229	0.0512374	12.52

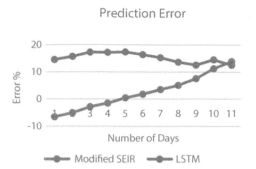

Figure 4.12 Prediction error curve.

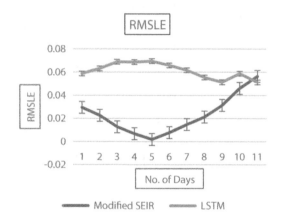

Figure 4.13 Prediction error and RMSLE curve.

References

1. Health and Family welfare Department, Government of Karnataka, Karnataka, 2020, COVID19 data: https://covid19.karnataka.gov.in/english.
2. COVID-19 dynamics with SIR model. Stochastic Epidemic Models with Inference, Springer 1st edition, 2019, https://www.lewuathe.com/covid-19-dynamics-with-sir-model.html.
3. Yang, Z., Zeng, Z., Wang, K., Wong, S.S., Liang, W., Zanin, M., Liu, P., Cao, X., Gao, Z., Mai, Z., Liang, J., Liu, X., Li, S., Li, Y., Ye, F., Guan, W., Yang, Y., Li, F., Luo, S., Xie, Y., Liu, B., Wang, Z., Zhang, S., Wang, Y., Zhong, N., He, J., Modified SEIR and AI prediction of the epidemics trend of COVID-19 in China under public health interventions. *J. Thorac. Dis.*, 12, 3, 165–174, 2020.
4. Calafiore, G.C., Novara, C., Possieri, C., A Modified SIR Model for the COVID-19 Contagion in Italy. *Computational Engineering,Finance, and*

Science (cs.CE); Social and Information Networks (cs.SI); Systems and Control (eess.SY), arXiv:2003.14391, 31 Mar 2020.

5. Tiwari, A., Modelling and analysis of COVID-19 epidemic in India, *J. Safety Sci. Resilience,* 1, 2, 135–140, Dec 2020. medRxiv 2020.04.12.20062794; https://doi.org/10.1101/2020.04.12.20062794.

6. OlahLSTM-NEURAL-NETWORK-TUTORIAL-15. Understanding LSTM Networks, 27 August 2015, https://web.stanford.edu/class/cs379c/archive/2018/ class_messages_listing/content/Artificial_Neural_Network_Technology_ Tutorials/OlahLSTM-NEURAL-NETWORK-TUTORIAL-15.pdf

7. Yudistira, N., COVID-19 growth prediction using multivariate long short-term memory, *J. Latex Class Files,* 14, 8, August 2015, arXiv: 2005.04809v2.

8. Sujath, R., Chatterjee, J.M., Hassanien, A.E., A machine learning forecasting model for COVID-19 pandemic in India. *Stoch. Environ. Res. Risk Assess.,* 34, 959–972, 2020, https://doi.org/10.1007/s00477-020-01827-8.

9. Mollalo, A., Rivera, K.M., Vahedi, B., Artificial Neural Network Modeling of Novel Coronavirus (COVID-19) Incidence Rates across the Continental United States,. *Int. J. Environ. Res. Public Health,* 17, 12, June 2020.

10. ftp://ftp.sas.com/pub/neural/FAQ2.html 11 October 2002.

11. Verma, S., Understanding Input and Outputshape in LSTM (Keras). *Towards Data Science,* 2019, https://mc.ai/understanding-input-and-output-shape-in-lstm-keras/.

12. SEIR Modeling of the Italian Epidemic of SARS-CoV-2 Using Computational Swarm Intelligence. *Int. J. Environ. Res. Public Health,* 17, 10, May 2020.

13. https://github.com/anasselhoud/CoVid-19-RNN

14. MATLAB code for SEIR model. Mathworks, 2020, https://in.mathworks.com/ matlabcentral/fileexchange/74545-generalized-seir-epidemic-model-fitting-and-computation.

15. Karnataka COVID19 timeline, https://en.wikipedia.org/wiki/COVID-19_ pandemic _in_ Karnataka, Wikipedia, 2020.

16. https://github.com/Aveek-Saha/CovidAnalysis/blob/master/LSTM_modeling.ipynb

5

The Significance of Feature Selection Techniques in Machine Learning

N. Bharathi[1], B.S. Rishiikeshwer[2], T. Aswin Shriram[2],
B. Santhi[2]* and G.R. Brindha[2]†

[1]*Department of CSE, SRM Institute of Science and Technology, Vadapalani,
Chennai, Tamil Nadu, India*
[2]*School of Computing, SASTRA Deemed University, Thanjavur, Tamil Nadu, India*

Abstract

Current digital era with tons of raw data and extracting insight from this is a significant process. Initial significant step is to pre-process the available data set. The pre-processed input is to be fed to the proper Machine Learning (ML) model to extract the insight or decision. The performance of the model purely depends on the features given to the model. Without the knowledge of feature selection process, perfect model building will be a question mark. Proper selection of feature is essential for building precise model. Plethora of techniques are available in the literature for feature extraction and feature selection. Irrelevant features may drastically decrease the performance of the model and increase the complexity. Though features are describing the record in an effective way, by representing the record with lesser number of features through optimal approach for predicting unseen record precisely is a complex task. To handle such complexities, appropriate feature selection methods are used. Hence, this chapter concentrates on different feature selection techniques with its merits and limitations. The discussion is supported with case study using python. Using the essence of this chapter, as plug and play tool, the model builder can design a precise model.

Keywords: Feature selection, pre-processing, machine learning, deep learning, dimension reduction, attribute subset selection

Corresponding author: shanthi@cse.sastra.ac.in
†*Corresponding author*: brindha.gr@ict.sastra.ac.in

Pradeep Singh (ed.) Fundamentals and Methods of Machine and Deep Learning: Algorithms, Tools and Applications, (121–134) © 2022 Scrivener Publishing LLC

5.1   Introduction

Machine learning algorithms use data set from different modalities with labels and without labels. With labels are used by supervised learning algorithms in which data set is viewed as independent variable (input) and dependent variable (output). Algorithm maps the relationship between the independent and dependent variables (features/attributes/characteristics). Performance of this algorithm depends on the proper selection of input variables.To extract the most relevant attributes, the selection of feature selection method should be compatible with chosen machine learning algorithm related to an application. Since the feature selection has significant contribution toward the precise outcome of the application, the focused attention to this area is inevitable. The selected features are validated through proper metrics by observing the model performance. ML models attempt to determine construction in the data, predictive relationship between the dependent and independent variables. Traditional algorithm trusted on handcrafted features but in deep learning architecture itself is having capacity to extract features from the data. In this chapter, several feature extraction methods, selection methods and its evaluation metrics are discussed. Challenges in pattern recognition applications are selecting the attributes from the different modalities which are relevant for classification. In the classification problem, records are collection of attributes in high dimension. Generally, for any applications, the part of the features is directly relevant to the class and some features can be transformed to relevant set by applying transformation techniques. The remaining features are irrelevant. Classifiers are designed to decide the related attributes automatically but this requires domain knowledge. Most of the time, this depends on the pre-processing stage. Proper features are used by ML to build the proper models which achieves proper objective.

5.2   Significance of Pre-Processing

Nowadays, enormous data sets are available in open source. However, most of the data sets require pre-processing before using them for model building. Multifaceted data investigation and analysis on large amounts of data consumes more time, making such analysis unfeasible or impracticable. The dimensionality of a data set is the number of input variables or features in the data set. The considerable increase in the number of input features leads to increase in difficulty level of the development of predictive models and this conceptual challenge is generally referred to as the curse of dimensionality. More numbers of input features than necessary may cause deprived performance when applying to ML algorithms. Though the data set may contain large number of input features, it can be reduced to an optimized set of features to yield better results in ML algorithms. Dimension reduction is a technique that reduces the number of input features in a data set. It is often used in the visualization of data and also in ML approaches to make the further processing simpler such as classification and regression.

5.3   Machine Learning System

Input to the ML algorithm should be treated before feeding it to the algorithm. Missing value is the major issue in ML models. Researchers advise many imputation techniques.

5.3.1   Missing Values

Removing missing value row from data set affect the model performance in case of smaller data set. In such cases, replacement of processed values is needed. Some of such processes are as follows:

- Numerical data values: filling all missing values with 0 or mean of the column/median of the column.
- Categorical data values: filling with maximum frequency value is replaced.
- Goal of imputation is to infer missing values suitable to the nature of data type, which is referred as matrix completion procedure.

5.3.2   Outliers

Outlier detection is another challenge. Detection of outliers using statistical methods and visualization is available. Using box plot (five-point summary), outliers are easily detected. Success of ML method depends on feature selection techniques. Model of an application is as good as its features. Extracting discriminative information from the given data set for the application is laborious task. Earlier to the application of ML method, it is suggested to perform exploratory data analysis for the given data set to visualize the nature of the data by plotting it.

When we prepare a flexible ML model for an application, we need to concentrate on the overfitting concept. The gap between training error and testing error is called overfitting. To handle this challenge, regularization techniques are applied. We should avoid every minor variation in the input.

5.3.3   Model Selection

Different algorithms are applied with given data set for preparing model for an application. A variety of models with different complexity are constructed for selecting suitable appropriate model through the computation of misclassification rate. Model is memorizing the data and getting minimal error on the training set. So, best model focuses on to minimizing the generalization error. Misclassification rate is minimum on large independent test set. Correct model complexity is selected through validation set. Based on "no free lunch" theorem, the set of assumptions in model preparation is well-suited for one domain, but may work poorly in another domain. Devising suitable model depending upon the nature of selecting appropriate feature using feature engineering is the backbone of the model building.

5.4   Feature Extraction Methods

The reduction in dimension of data set can be done through removing irrelevant, less relevant, and redundant input data or variables from the data set. The feature extraction improves the performance of predictive models by reducing the dimension through extracting salient features from data set [1, 2]. It is highly increasing the training speed and also infers the outcome soon. Various methods of feature extraction exist and new features are produced by transformations and manipulations on the original input set [3–5]. Example is the extraction of features from the images like color, texture, shape, and pixel value.

The various broad categories of feature extraction which is shown in Figure 5.1 based on data reduction are dimensionality reduction, parametric reduction, non-parametric reduction, and data compression. The dimensionality reduction has three types, and it essentially transforms the data set onto a lesser space to make the processing and manipulation easier. Among the three types, wavelet transforms and principal component analysis (PCA) map the data set onto the lesser dimension, whereas the third type attribute subset selection leads to removal of existing irrelevant and redundant data from data set.

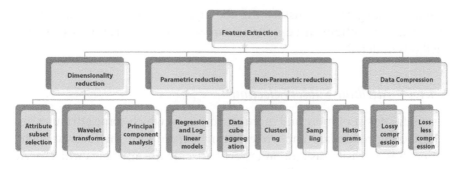

Figure 5.1 Classification of feature extraction methods.

Parametric reduction generates a model to estimate the data set, and hence, storage of model and data parameters is only required than the entire data. Non-parametric reductions are used to store the visual representations such as histograms and reduced representations such as clustering, sampling, and data cube aggregation. Data compression techniques involve the reduction of data by applying aggregation techniques and reconstructed through approximation techniques. Reconstructing the data, if any data loss exists, is called lossy compression. Whereas, if there is no data loss during reconstruction, then it is called lossless compression. The further discussion digs deeper into the dimensionality reduction, parametric, and non-parametric reductions.

5.4.1 Dimension Reduction

Dimension reduction is a basic technique which is often used in various ML applications to reduce the number of input features. It is more common and depends on the nature of the data alone and not specific to which application the data is used for. As an example, dimensionality reduction leads to the projection of data into a smaller dimension space and this may help or not to a ML application.

Data reduction is achieved by obtaining the reduced data set comparatively very less volume than the original data set and also maintaining the integrity of the actual data set [6, 7]. The manipulation and visualization of data with the reduced data set is efficient and also generate the same or almost same outcomes. Dimension reduction is categorized into two types based on the reduction procedure on input variables. Feature selection and feature extraction are the categories in which former simply includes or excludes the given features without modifying the input variables.

The latter category is transforming the input features into lesser dimension. Further sections discuss the feature selection and feature extraction methods in detail.

5.4.1.1   Attribute Subset Selection

Data sets consist of more and more attributes, in which some attributes are contributing redundant and irrelevant information for the focused application. It is an easier task for an expert to decide the attributes which need to be included in the prediction. However, it is time-consuming process when the nature of the data is not known. The attribute subset selection is to identify the minimum number of attributes that contributes closer to the probability distribution of the original data set. The possible subsets of attributes with n number of attributes in the original data set are 2n. The exhaustive approach is time-consuming and costlier to determine the optimal subset of attributes [8]. Hence, the heuristic approach is followed which provides closer accuracy with the original data set [9, 10]. General methods of the heuristic approach are forward selection, backward elimination, combination of both, and decision trees induction. For feature construction and selection process, PCA and K means methods are used respectively.

5.4.1.1.1   Forward Selection Method

Forward selection method has empty set initially and proceeds by adding the best attributes one by one from the actual data set to form the reduced data set. Adding the best attributes from the remaining data set is continued till the model reaches the optimum level in producing the model with best accuracy.

5.4.1.1.2   Backward Elimination Method

Backward elimination method works with the full set of attributes initially and proceeds by eliminating the worst attributes one by one from the full set of attributes which eventually results in the best predictive model. The combination of forward selection and backward elimination combines the benefits of both methods.

5.4.1.1.3   Decision Tree Induction Method

Decision tree induction method constructs a tree-like structure in which the non-leaf internal nodes indicate the decision assessment on the attribute, the branches indicate the inference of the assessments, and the leaf nodes indicates the prediction class. Also, in the attribute subset selection, the new attributes can be constructed from the existing attributes to improve the accuracy. The threshold to stop the iterations in the above methods may vary based on the method chosen and the application focused.

5.4.2   Wavelet Transforms

The data set is transformed using the discrete wavelet transform (DWT) in which the data vector is mapped to another vector of wavelet coefficients. Though the length of each vector is same, the application of DWT on the data set will considerably reduce the number of data to a small proportion. The wavelet coefficients larger than the predefined threshold alone is stored and others are set to zero resulting in a sparse data set. Obviously, the sparse data set takes less computation time in wavelet space and also reduced memory storage with optimization techniques. Also, this transform removes the noise and ensure to proceed for the efficient data cleaning process.

The regeneration of data set by applying inverse of the DWT is also achieved with good results in comparison with discrete Fourier transform (DFT) in regaining the data as well as the compressed data set occupies less space. Also, a family of DWT such as Haar, Daubechies, Symlets, Coiflets, Biorthogonal, Gaussian, Mexican hat, Shannon, etc., is available for transforming the data set unlike DFT which has only one. The python package and retrieving the python supported wavelets by using *pywt, pywt. families()*. The DWT is applied on a data set using hierarchical pyramid algorithm which reduces the data set by half of its number in each iteration of execution. The DWT can be applied to the hypercubes generated with multidimensional data. The process of applying is so simple by transforming each dimension at a time and proceed to next dimension.

5.4.3   Principal Components Analysis

Maximum variance is preserved by PCA and segregates the features into orthogonal components. It projects on the principal eigenvectors from the covariance matrix of the data set.

The n-dimensional data set is reduced into k n-dimensional vectors that are orthogonal and optimal representation of the data set with k < n. The dimensionality reduction is achieved by projection of the large data set into smaller space with principal components. The optimal combination of variables and the extraction of its essential features reduce the dimension [11]. The relationship even which are not suspected previously is revealed by PCA. The steps involved in data reduction using PCA are as follows:

Step 1: Normalize the input data and ensure the participation of all attributes in data reduction.

Step 2: Identification of principal components which are unit vectors in each dimension and they possess the orthonormality among themselves.

Step 3: Sort the principal components in decreasing order of their contribution to the variance on the data.

Step 4: Eliminate the weaker components with respect to the required reduced data size.

Step 5: Use the principal components to regenerate the original data and check the accuracy of the PCA.

5.4.4   Clustering

The tuples in the data set are considered as objects and partitioned into groups called clusters. The clustering techniques are based on how likely the objects are related to each other. A distance function is used to calculate the similarity between objects. The clusters are described by its largest distance between the objects, cluster diameter, cluster core object, attributes, etc. The distance between the multiple cluster centers called centroids also serves as a cluster quality. The data reduction is performed by representing clusters instead of the data in the clusters. The efficiency of the clustering techniques depends on the nature of the data in the data set.

The clustering techniques are categorized into four different methods. They are (i) partition methods, (ii) hierarchical methods (iii), density-based methods, and (iv) grid-based methods. Partition methods are formed by mutually exclusive objects with distance functions. This method works well in medium and smaller data set. Hierarchical methods constitute multiple levels with splits from top to bottom and merge from bottom to top like a tree structure. Density-based clustering methods are based on the regions where the objects are closely related or very rare as outliers. Grid-based methods use grid data structure to form the clusters and it involves fast processing time.

5.5   Feature Selection

It is very rare to find all variables in a data set which are useful to build a model. Adding redundant values reduces the capability of model to generalize and reduce overall accuracy. Adding more variables to a model increases the complexity of the model [12–14]. Every feature of the given data set does not need to be used for creating an algorithm. The feature selection methods are majorly classified into supervised [15] and unsupervised [16–18]. Feature selection enables faster training, reduces the complexity of the model, improves accuracy, and reduces overfitting.

The goal of feature selection is to find the best set of features to build useful models that could apply for various applications [19–21]. Different techniques classified under supervised are as follows:

- Filter methods
- Wrapper methods
- Embedded methods

5.5.1   Filter Methods

Filter methods are faster, less complex, and much cheaper than other methods. This method is generally used as a pre-processing step [22, 23]. It uses univariate statistics instead of cross validation performance. Features are selected based on the various statistical test scores. There are different techniques in filter methods like information gain, Chi-square test, fishers score, ANOVA, and LDA. These filter methods do not remove multicollinearity which makes the user to deal with it before training the models. It is very rare for the data sets to be exactly collinear but if it happens; there are methods to remove the similar data sets before training.

5.5.2   Wrapper Methods

Wrapper methods usually give better accuracy than filter methods. It requires some method to search for all possible subsets. Based on the results we get from the previous model; the user decides to add or remove features from the subset. Boruta package is one the best ways to implement this. It adds randomness to the data and creates copies of all features (shadow features). Then, it applies random forest and checks for the important features in the data set based on scores. If the real feature has higher Z-score than shadow feature, Boruta package removes the unimportant features. At last, the algorithm stops at specified random forest runs or when every feature gets evaluated. There are techniques under wrapper methods like forward feature selection, backward feature selection, exhaustive feature selection, and recursive feature selection.

5.5.3 Embedded Methods

This method brings the benefits of both filter and wrapper methods under one single umbrella by including feature interactions and keeping the computational costs under check. It takes care of the iteration of the model and carefully analyses and extracts those features which play major part for a particular iteration [24]. To analyze the significance of feature set, techniques such as decision tree and random forest are used.

Random forest is a tree-based ML algorithm that leverages the power of multiple decision trees for making decisions. Random forest combines the output of individual decision trees to generate the final output. In terms of final coding output, random forest outperforms decision tree due to the ensemble nature of random forest. Decision tree model gives high importance to particular feature set, whereas random forest chooses random features during the process. Therefore, the random forest trumps over decision trees in generalization of data. This makes random forest more accurate than its counterpart.

Imagine that a teacher has to segregate students into star category as 1 star, 2 stars, and 3 stars based on academic performance. Consider the basic and important feature as the start of decision tree, Grade Score (GS)—dividing the tree as students who have good GS and bad GS. The second feature to consider is research papers, where if a student has good GS and good research papers then he gets 3 stars, whereas good GS with no research papers gets 2 stars. Student who has bad GS and good research papers gets 2 stars, whereas bad GS with no research papers gets 1 star. As you can see in this decision tree, the primary priority is given to the GS for the first branching to happen; this clearly tells us that decision tree always gives priority to a particular set of features. Having said that, a combination of GS and research papers defines the star rating of the students in the class, which ultimately is the result of this decision tree. This is the process behind one decision tree and randomly combines the result of many similar decision trees to give out the final output.

Features are considered as telescopes through which nature of data can be visualized. "Features are work horses of Machine Learning"; hence, the relevant features can be evaluated by constructing models using different set of features and can be finalized through metrics of models.

Individual merits of features are evaluated through filter approach and sets of features are evaluated by wrapper approach.

5.6 Merits and Demerits of Feature Selection

A healthier approach is to estimate the same transform and model with different size of feature set and pick the number of features which results in the best average performance. For a given data set and model, best input features are picked using PCA or other dimensionality reduction methods. To demonstrate the merits of PCA, let us consider 2,000 random numbers with 30 features. The PCA components of the given data are fed to the logistic regression. The cross validated results are visualized using box plot. The model is run for 30 iterations and the optimum number of components is identified through the consistent best accuracy value. For this simulated 2,000 samples with 30 features, accuracy ranges from 0.504 (first component) to 0.864 (25th component). The consistency is from 25th iteration onward. Hence, the first 25 components are enough to get best accuracy for this data set.

Even though feature selection techniques are having high impact on ML modeling area, the limitations also exist. There is no general feature selection method which suits to all data sets in real time. Based on the nature of data, whether it is noisy or unstructured, apply suitable pre-processing techniques earlier to the feature selection/extraction methods. The selection method depending on the data set (input) and its corresponding expected output (target).

Feature selection method also depends on the data type of features. For numeric data, feature selection such as PCA or correlation coefficient can be used and for categorical data, Chi-square or mutual information statistics can be applied. For the Breast cancer data from UCI repository, the model built using logistic regression. When all features are used, the accuracy is 75.79%, and by applying chi-squared four features out of nine yields 74.74%, using mutual information statistics with top four features, the accuracy is 76.84%.

5.7 Conclusion

Effective ML algorithms lead to important application in the active research area. This chapter gave the pavement to improve the learning process by focusing on feature engineering concept by borrowing fruitful idea from different studies. Sparse coding techniques are reducing high-dimensional data into small numbers of basic methods and projecting into the lower dimension space. In spite of the numerous open research challenges, the enhancement made undoubtedly fine tune the future of ML and AI system. Method such as Filter feature selection employ a statistical measure to allot score to each feature. The features are ranked using score. Based on the score selection of features or rejection is decided. Wrapper methods apply searching techniques to select set of features. Through the search, different combinations are prepared and compared based on evaluation of model. Yet, adding or eliminating features from the data create model and evaluate on the validation set, become very time-intensive and costly. Regularization methods (penalization methods) come under embedded methods that host additional constraints into the optimization of a predictive algorithm that bias the model toward lower complexity. Feature learning algorithms identify a common pattern which is essential to discriminate between the class labels.

References

1. Zhang, L., Frank, S., Kim, J., Jin, X., Leach, M., A systematic feature extraction and selection framework for data-driven whole-building automated fault detection and diagnostics in commercial buildings. *Build. Environ.*, 186, 107338, 2020 Dec 1.

2. Sharma, G., Umapathy, K., Krishnan, S., Trends in audio signal feature extraction methods. *Appl. Acoust.*, 158, 107020, 2020 Jan 15.

3. Lu, J., Lai, Z., Wang, H., Chen, Y., Zhou, J., Shen, L., Generalized Embedding Regression: A Framework for Supervised Feature Extraction. *IEEE Trans. Neural Networks Learn. Syst.*, 1–15, 2020 Nov 4.

4. Sarumathi, C.K., Geetha, K., Rajan, C., Improvement in Hadoop performance using integrated feature extraction and machine learning algorithms. *Soft Comput.*, 24, 1, 627–36, 2020 Jan 1.

5. Marques, A.E., Prates, P.A., Pereira, A.F., Oliveira, M.C., Fernandes, J.V., Ribeiro, B.M., Performance Comparison of Parametric and Non-Parametric Regression Models for Uncertainty Analysis of Sheet Metal Forming Processes. *Metals*, 10, 4, 457, 2020 Apr.

6. Zebari, R., Abdulazeez, A., Zeebaree, D., Zebari, D., Saeed, J., A Comprehensive Review of Dimensionality Reduction Techniques for Feature Selection and Feature Extraction. *J. Appl. Sci. Technol. Trends*, 1, 2, 56–70, 2020 May 15.

7. Li, M., Wang, H., Yang, L., Liang, Y., Shang, Z., Wan, H., Fast hybrid dimensionality reduction method for classification based on feature selection

and grouped feature extraction. *Expert Syst. Appl.*, 150, 2020, https://doi.org/10.1016/j.eswa.2020.113277.

8. Rouzdahman, M., Jovicic, A., Wang, L., Zucherman, L., Abul-Basher, Z., Charoenkitkarn, N., Chignell, M., Data Mining Methods for Optimizing Feature Extraction and Model Selection, in: *Proceedings of the 11th International Conference on Advances in Information Technology*, 2020 Jul 1, pp. 1–8.

9. Mutlag, W.K., Ali, S.K., Aydam, Z.M., Taher, B.H., Feature Extraction Methods: A Review. *J. Phys.: Conf. Ser.*, 1591, 1, 012028, 2020 Jul 1, IOP Publishing.

10. Koduru, A., Valiveti, H.B., Budati, A.K., Feature extraction algorithms to improve the speech emotion recognition rate. *Int. J. Speech Technol.*, 23, 1, 45–55, 2020 Mar.

11. Garate-Escamilla, A.K., Hassani, A.H., Andres, E., Classification models for heart disease prediction using feature selection and PCA. *Inf. Med. Unlocked*, 27, 100330, 2020 Apr.

12. Al-Tashi, Q., Abdulkadir, S.J., Rais, H.M., Mirjalili, S., Alhussian, H., Approaches to Multi-Objective Feature Selection: A Systematic Literature Review. *IEEE Access*, 8, 125076–125096, 2020.

13. Toğaçar, M., Cömert, Z., Ergen, B., Classification of brain MRI using hyper column technique with convolutional neural network and feature selection method. *Expert Syst. Appl.*, 149, 113274, 2020 Jul 1.

14. Haider, F., Pollak, S., Albert, P., Luz, S., Emotion recognition in low-resource settings: An evaluation of automatic feature selection methods. *Comput. Speech Lang.*, 1, 101119, 2020 Jun.

15. Wu, X., Xu, X., Liu, J., Wang, H., Hu, B., Nie, F., Supervised feature selection with orthogonal regression and feature weighting. *IEEE Trans. Neural Networks Learn. Syst.*, 32, 1831–1838, 2020 May 14.

16. Martarelli, N.J. and Nagano, M.S., Unsupervised feature selection based on bio-inspired approaches. *Swarm Evol. Comput.*, 52, 100618, 2020 Feb 1.

17. Pandit, A.A., Pimpale, B., Dubey, S., A Comprehensive Review on Unsupervised Feature Selection Algorithms, in: *International Conference on Intelligent Computing and Smart Communication*, Springer, Singapore, pp. 255–266, 2020.

18. Zheng, W. and Jin, M., Comparing multiple categories of feature selection methods for text classification. *Digit. Scholarsh. Humanit.*, 35, 1, 208–24, 2020 Apr 1.

19. Açıkoğlu, M. and Tuncer, S.A., Incorporating feature selection methods into a machine learning-based neonatal seizure diagnosis. *Med. Hypotheses*, 135, 109464, 2020 Feb 1.

20. Al-Kasassbeh, M., Mohammed, S., Alauthman, M., Almomani, A., Feature Selection Using a Machine Learning to Classify a Malware, in: *Handbook of Computer Networks and Cyber Security*, pp. 889–904, Springer, Cham, 2020.

21. Zheng, W., Zhu, X., Wen, G., Zhu, Y., Yu, H., Gan, J., Unsupervised feature selection by self-paced learning regularization. *Pattern Recognit. Lett.*, 132, 4–11, 2020 Apr 1.
22. Bommert, A., Sun, X., Bischl, B., Rahnenführer, J., Lang, M., Benchmark for filter methods for feature selection in high-dimensional classification data. *Comput. Stat. Data Anal.*, 143, 2020, https://doi.org/10.1016/j.csda.2019.106839.
23. Alirezanejad, M., Enayatifar, R., Motameni, H., Nematzadeh, H., Heuristic filter feature selection methods for medical datasets. *Genomics*, 112, 2, 1173–81, 2020 Mar 1.
24. Elhariri, E., El-Bendary, N., Taie, S.A., Using Hybrid Filter-Wrapper Feature Selection With Multi-Objective Improved-Salp Optimization for Crack Severity Recognition. *IEEE Access*, 8, 84290–315, 2020 May 1.

6

Use of Machine Learning and Deep Learning in Healthcare—A Review on Disease Prediction System

Radha R.[1]* and Gopalakrishnan R.[2]

[1]*Anna University, Chennai, Tamil Nadu, India*
[2]*K. S. Rangasamy College of Technology, Tiruchengode, Tamil Nadu, India*

Abstract

The practice of adapting Machine Learning (ML) and Deep Learning (DL) methodologies for the exploration and identification of biomedical and health related issues has established unmatched response in the last few decades. A number of unearthing features that are meaningful are being recorded using these branches of Artificial Intelligence (AI) to achieve the difficult tasks that stood as challenge to human experts. The treatment processes, the devices used in treating patients, and the applications used are all capable in generating alarming amount of information. These information are technical data in the form of images, graph, test, and audio files; processing and getting the valuable insights from these data is a tedious task. The invention of ML and, lately, DL have paved way to access and analyze these data from the big data era in a smooth manner to predict, diagnose, and treat diseases effectively to save valuable lives of millions. DL, which has deeper (or more) hidden layers cascaded functions of similar quality, forms a network that is capable enough to dissect any magnetic resonance image in faster and accurate manner. The chapter discusses the basics related to DL and Ml methodologies and the related works where the impact of the same are high solicited. The implementation highlights of ML and DL are also presented with respect to pre- and post-treatment through healthcare systems. DL and ML find its application in every aspect of biological system, electronic health records related to patients, and image modalities as well. In addition to the above-mentioned, the chapter

---

Corresponding author: radhadoss25@gmail.com

Pradeep Singh (ed.) Fundamentals and Methods of Machine and Deep Learning: Algorithms, Tools and Applications, (135–152) © 2022 Scrivener Publishing LLC

presents the inherent challenges of ML and DL affecting the medical domain as well the research scope on improving healthcare systems with focus to promote and improve health management system.

Keywords: Machine learning, deep learning, artificial intelligence, public health monitoring and reporting, storing, retrieval

6.1   Introduction to Healthcare System

The healthcare system is an essential component in the life of every citizen in every country. The healthcare policies in different countries have different rules and regulations incarnated into it. The needs of people in rural and urban areas differ and their by the policies related to healthcare system differs. A healthcare system that is universal faces many discrepancies in terms of quality treatment and medical coverage of a patient or the likely disease. The difference between urban and rural background paves way for many dissimilarities in handling and treating a patient. The natives of rural areas suffer a lot due to lack of physicians in required numbers for proper and timely treatment; they are the ones who access the healthcare system infrequently. Although the public healthcare system is prevailing the expanse of these fail to compete with the private healthcare providers. The cost and time taken to diagnosis a disease and treat the same differs from one provider to another. The advancement in technology is combined to provide a better treatment for anyone irrespective of the service providers.

Growing need and increasing challenges faced by the enormous population on mother earth presents the need for more healthcare professionals. Apart from this, the low insurance dispersion, insufficient access, and increasing deadly disease threats also add up to the need for a better healthcare system. Traditional healthcare systems or providers failed to provide the required necessities to general public in large scale. Technological advancement leads to expansion of infrastructure, process improvements, accessibility, storage, and retrieval process and also to provide timely decision. The need to access and store digital data related to a treatment or invention provided the opportunity to join hands with Artificial Intelligence (AI). With AI, the information related to a patient is extracted to the core which aids in better understanding and thus leads to a better treatment plan. A better healthcare system makes medical services understandable, cost effective, and accessible. The usefulness of a healthcare system is undermined, and there are various reasons behind the failure of this life saving mechanism.

6.2   Causes for the Failure of the Healthcare System

One among the major reasons for failure in healthcare system usage in decision-making is characterized by mistrust, antagonism, and mostly skewed motivations. The consumers of the healthcare diagnostic system show an exemplified need for more facilities or features with less expenditure [1–3]. The concept behind using a system that could effectively treat a disease is diluted by the vicious notion of consumers to pay less and get more concepts. The concept of better tomorrow could be made possible only if the basic alterations are made in the healthcare culture. One other cause for failure is imparting the required knowledge among healthcare professionals as well. The motivation behind the usage of healthcare system should be care for patients rather than care for business.

The quality of such healthcare system has to be improved which was tempered by the overuse and misuse of such system by limiting the integration of structural design of such systems. One other cause of failure of any healthcare system is due to the inability in handling voluminous data generated in the form of digital facts and figures. With the ever increasing speed of data generation in the digital era, the need for a more accurate and fast diagnostic system is of high demand.

Limitation in data access and inadequate adoption to data in the form of electronic records and a proper data format to store them are also causes for the failure in healthcare system. The complex nature of healthcare system triggered another process, namely, evidence generation which become an acute task. The critical activities in healthcare units needed a wide range help from data analytics, engineers through the support from engineering principles. The point of focus here is right amount of knowledge at the correct time delivered to the right human to proceed further in assisting the right person with health related issues. All healthcare units either public or private need a sophisticated system that can provide the accurate and timely handover of potential knowledge about patient across healthcare units.

The most important factor that is a major reason behind the failure of healthcare predictive system is communication [4, 5]. The interpretation of patients' opinion about the health concern or experience is intervened by the opinion of doctors which greatly influence the result or outcome of healthcare systems. Failure occurs in every step in providing treatment to a patient but the primary concern is with the fault in interpretation, interaction/communication between primary, as well as secondary healthcare units and with the specialists. The lack of information flow from primary to secondary health unit is also a cause of concern. The inadequacy in knowledge sharing about the diagnosis, treatment, and post-monitoring plans between hospitals is also a cause for failure of healthcare predictive systems. Elderly patients are the most who suffer from these inadequate communications between primary and secondary healthcare units and their lack of language compatibility [6].

The major criticism thrown on most of the primary healthcare unit and their supporting system is insufficient details available with respect to disease their causes, impediments their diagnosis and treatment when an alternate is required. These inefficiency leads to refusal of patient needs which makes them move from public service to private service. While with secondary healthcare units, their services are blamed because of inaccurate prognosis which focuses on acquiring an efficient healthcare support system. Because of their lack of accurate diagnostic report, they suffer from insufficiency in terms of information to be supplied to specialists.

The overall problem or failure in healthcare system which is used for identifying or predicting a disease is lack of proper communication between patient and the specialist/doctor [7–9]. The doctors, though try, may not be able to identify or gather the details with respect to the symptoms, its severity level, disorientation in sleep pattern identification, drug usage level monitoring, life style quality, and the lack of ability to overlook the patients' incorrect way of projecting the cause, diagnosis, and post- and pre-treatment.

The health services like critical surgery with respect to life threatening diseases which happens at the disbursement of communication and followed through by clinical assistance post-surgery suffer a lot due to miscommunication. The routine questionnaires do identify the quality of the disease will also provide assistance in treating a patient again this causes issue if there is a language barrier [10]. The knowledge provided to patient with respect to the side effects of medication or surgery or treatment serves as a major cause of failure in healthcare service sector.

6.3   Artificial Intelligence and Healthcare System for Predicting Diseases

AI is a concept that made it possible to simulate the capabilities and behaviors of human in a machine. The voluminous data generated in this technological era made it difficult for humans to analyze these enormous data to provide insight about them. In a field where data are generated in exabytes, it needs a constant monitoring which is highly becoming an impossible activity for any human and the errors in prediction is also a major concern. The areas of critical activity like medicine, nuclear power plant activities, and forecast of disasters require accurate prediction. The advances in AI and its subsets made life more flexible and faster than ever; Siri in Apple, Cortana, and Alexa are smart enough to predict and provide the user with their needs in an interactive manner. These advances are utilized in the life saving industry to ease the diagnosis and treatment phase in terms of computational cost and time.

With advances in AI, the machines were able to handle things effectively like human beings but the concept of learning or gaining knowledge from data gathered was achieved only through Machine Learning (ML). AI is a field which works to make a system smart and intelligent and covers wide range of scope. ML is a subset of the above mentioned term AI, which focuses on enabling a system to forecast and make decision for a specific domain based on the knowledge gained through past data. ML focuses on learning and self-correction, while AI focuses on the above along with reasoning.

To outdo human understanding in terms of interpreting, analyzing, and comprehending complex medical prognosis and medical data, AI-based algorithms are most pursued. AI is also pursued to eliminate the costly backend process related to management tasks and is used to cease the inefficiencies as well. It is used to drastically eliminate the 51% load of the medical staff who assist the physicians and remove nearly 16% load off physician activities. AI-based healthcare systems are widely appreciated and mostly look up for stream lining administrative activities as well as clinical care system.

While ML is a subcategory of AI, Deep Learning (DL) is a subsection of ML. DL mimics human brain by implementing the complicated nervous system of human being in assisting the decision-making or predictive system. DL procedures has a motivation on analyzing and identifying patterns with respect to information ingrained in the data collected with respect to medical images. These procedures recognise the patterns in the similar ways as how human brains processes the information provided based on already acquired knowledge. The moment from ML to DL helps process the enormous data generated on daily basis and also to prepare themselves on self-learning objective as well. Figure 6.1 provides the relationship between AI, ML, and DL.

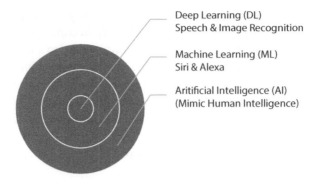

Deep Learning (DL)
Speech & Image Recognition

Machine Learning (ML)
Siri & Alexa

Aritificial Intelligence (AI)
(Mimic Human Intelligence)

Figure 6.1 Relationship between AI, ML, and DL.

6.3.1   Monitoring and Collection of Data

The regular activity of collecting data on appropriate modules of health and the elements responsible for it is Public Health Monitoring and Reporting (PHMR). These activities are considered essential in a wide population or in a sample space, which are considered important to address the major health issues with respect to pattern, trends, topological cover, and number of occurrence in the geographical location along with its impact. The relationship between the elements responsible for outbreak of a pandemic and its health issues helps us in considering the contrivances of health and disease.

Without a proper health report, these public health monitoring activities are useless. Primary aim of public health recording is to support and to communicate the state of health of general public. These are also used to prepare the evaluation modules of policy making of healthcare plans. Data collection is an ongoing process of systematic collection, scrutinizing, and elucidation of innumerable types of information from countless sources. The accuracy of information is considered as a powerful tool not only to improve commerce but rather it is used to highly influence the decisions made. Most prevention strategies depend on these powerful tools [11–13].

Data pursuing and scrutiny are considered to change the universe for better in the healthcare industry. Reduction of workload, profit increase of medical agency and efficiency in the process of predicting epidemic outbreak, as well as providing the proper treatment plan for existing diseases are the merits of data collection. With AI in picture, a better view of affected persons' interpretation of symptoms is achieved. Personalized treatments, advanced treatments, and improved communications between healthcare providers and disease affected persons and enhanced healthcare results are the boon of data collection.

Technological advances have enabled various modes of information collection from affected persons through wearable gadgets in collaboration with sensor devices. The information is processed by AI-based systems and ML algorithm to gain access to correlation between various data and is used to provide support to decision-making activity of physicians. In certain cases, these information services are based on predicting presence and absence of critical illnesses, and in some other cases, it predicts the possibility of occurrence of a disease or side effect of a treatment or relapse of an existing illness.

Chat bot therapy is used to collect the data of mentally instable person and their behavior; it is also used in the care taking process of elderly person by monitoring and understanding their daily routine. Use of AI in healthcare industry is the need of the hour but to make it possible enormous amount of information has to be gathered. The data collection comes with its own price in the form of privacy violation of a patient and is yet to find publicity in the society. The process of restructuring and implementing AI-based healthcare systems faces lots of hurdles due to lack of real-time data, since patients are not open minded in sharing their personal details related to treatment or causes or diagnosis.

6.3.2   Storing, Retrieval, and Processing of Data

In today's world, the management of storage of medical record and the management of data stored in those records are the tedious activities. The healthcare sector is flooded with enormous volumes of data. The internet data center reveals that, in 2014, the amount of healthcare data generated was in terms of 153 exabytes, and now, in 2020, this has escalated to 2,314 exabytes. These data that are collected are in the form of structured, unstructured, and semi-structured data.

The data collected from various sources are put together in a single space and they need to be formatted in such a way that, when accessed from anywhere, they should provide the required information. In addition, 80% of these data are in unstructured format and considered a pressing issue in larger healthcare units where petabytes of such information are stored, processed, and maintained. Now, with advances in technology, these varied data can be stored in various locations using the organization strategies like Flash and Block chain even though cloud is considered the most widely used choice. The security and secrecy of the information stored in these locations are the major concern, which, in some cases, many healthcare units bend to comply with the legal mandatories of every country. Apart from storage of electronic health records (EHR), x-rays, and other imaging modalities, the process of retrieval of these data from storage unit also plays an important role in accurate and quick prediction of disease pattern [14, 15].

The storage location from fire proof, secure, and easy access and proper backup facilities in case of natural disaster must also be concerned. The medical care unit has a constant need of updating in terms of securing this information with minimal cost. The concern with space, cost, etc., can be overcome by usage of cloud services. Now, cloud is being replaced slowly by Flash storage technology which is viable alternative. These offers low delay in retrieval of information, and it provides instant access as well. Uptime with respect to these is also highly recommendable upto 100% and loss of data access is also negligible. Another technology is block chain, which address the interoperability and data exchange which are the two prominent challenges of healthcare industries.

Pre-processing of data is again a challenging activity since these data are in different format; the need to define a unique format is a need. The data are to the structured in a way which makes it feasible to be accessed across hospitals or any medical unit. AI-based system will be able to gain proper information through these data more easily when it is structured. Most of the medical data are in the form of images, the quality of the images depends or highly influenced by the environment in which they are obtained or acquired. The quality of the image has to be improved so as to find the defect or hidden information from these images.

The resolution, color contrast, and noise removal are some of the pre-processing activities related to the image medical data. In case of data stored in the form of text and numerical format, redundancy and incomplete data are of great concern. The text data are processed using NLP (Natural Language Processing) technique which is one of the extensions of AI. This helps in translating the regional language information related to patients and diseases in to another language so as to assist the physician in identifying the cause, symptom, and treatments provided to a patient. Language barrier is broken using these AI and ML advancement. Further, it aids in communication between patient and physician even without worrying about language barrier. The chat bots are trained in such a way that it identifies the language of the patient and raises question in their native language to assist the patient upon analyzing their previous medical records.

6.4   Facts Responsible for Delay in Predicting the Defects

The facts responsible for delay in prediction systems are used earlier are non-AI based, which purely rely on the observations of the radiologists. The true state of the distribution of radiologist per 1,000 patient ratio is not convincing, thus resulting in delay in predicting the disease or the spread of an existing ailment. The delay in the prediction is deadly in critical diseases; in rural areas, the places where the medical facilities or staffing are insufficient and these delay are always blamed for high death rate in these regions. With the use of AI- and ML-based prediction system, the possibility with increase in speed of detecting the disease is high.

Communication is also a barrier which is yet another root cause for the failure of these systems. The lack of information related to a particular disease, its origin, symptoms, severity, and speed of spread are also missing in most cases which makes it difficult in designing and training an AI-based healthcare system. The AI system depends on the past history and ML learns from these previous data to train itself to handle the new incoming data, so the data shortage is also a major drawback.

Connectivity is also to be considered; the internet access in rural area is also a bottleneck in delay in predicting the disease or pattern. The images taken from patients in rural areas could be compared with existing images to find a match in them to identify the disease when a proper network supply is available within seconds. In most of developing countries where the population in rural areas suffer mostly with lack of facilities for testing and knowledge sharing among medical practitioners is limited could also be taken into consideration for delay in diagnosis of diseases.

6.5   Pre-Treatment Analysis and Monitoring

AI-induced predictive systems provide more information to clinicians with an abundance of insight about patient and the root cause of the disorders experienced by the patients. The AI-based systems help immensely to assist physicians in making accurate decisions in terms of diagnosis and also in planning the treatment. There are many systems effectively designed for treatment assistance for patients of need used in many healthcare units, but the most sought among them is the system for cancer detection. ML approaches are used in application including analysis of various image modalities for effective identification of presence of cancer cells, type of cancer, area of spread, and, in some cases, the remaining life of an organ [16, 17].

The pre-treatment process involves analyzing the image which involves pre-processing like enhancing the image quality and segment the image, finding the region of interest, and identifying the presence of cancer cell and cancer type by training the system. The pre-treatment process reduces the false positive or false negative issues faced during manual evaluation and could also be used in reducing the (invasive) testing done on patients. There are many advancements and systems designed for the purpose of assisting the physicians like VIZ which recognizes difference in the image modalities related to brain. The brain health is evaluated based on AI- and ML-enabled system neural analytics (robotics). The diseases like cardio-vascular diseases, lung disorders to eye disorders are identified through Voxel cloud, a computer aided detection system. Many such startup systems showing interest in AI enabled development in these areas like Nines, Botkin.AI, Prognica and Jiva.ai are to name few.

For example in pre-treatment phase of brain tumor, the detection process that uses ML- and DL-based computer-aided diagnostic (CAD) system plays a vital role in identifying the tumor region successfully than the radiologist with minimal time duration. Here, the image of the patient is fed to the system which pre-processes the image to enhance its contrast to define the boundaries of the components of the brain cavity. Upon enhancement, the image is fed to segmentation approach that sections various regions of the brain cavity based on the intensity of pixel value. Figure 6.2 shows the flow of the segmentation process flow of the computer-aided system using DL and ML [18–20]. The segmented image is then further processed to identify the features that are vital to indicate the incidence or non-appearance of tumor using various classification algorithms [21].

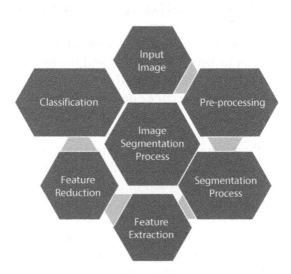

Figure 6.2 Image segmentation process flow.

6.6   Post-Treatment Analysis and Monitoring

DL approaches benefit most of the post-treatment analysis process of patients and helps reduce the time spent on patient analysis almost upto 15% from the physician end. The cut down of man power invested by physician on understanding and analyzing the background of their patient history and getting knowledge from the current image modalities of the patients help radiologist to a great extent. The images are analyzed by the DL-enhanced system and these procedures gets an insight about the image and assists the clinicians in determining the amount of radiation to be provided or the extend of exposure or the area to be re-operated in case of relapse in cancer patients. DL and ML being subsets of AI help in developing expert systems that questions patients and able to remotely access any patient's data similar to it, thus making the required suggestions to doctors in attending to the patient. The insight about the previous treatment provided for a similar kind of disease may help to treat the patient more accurately and quickly thus time and cost are optimized to a maximum.

Expert systems designed based on AI or computer-aided healthcare systems based on DL or ML are designed in such a way that they acquire the knowledge from the clinicians and train themselves based on those stored data. During treatment of critical illnesses, the dosage of medicine recommended for any patient is monitored and along with other vital information or fed to these systems which monitors to find the possibilities of occurrence of any other ailment during the post-treatment phase. These above activities require constant man power monitoring and increasing the expense on medicines as well, thus contributing to increase in the cost of treatment. The design of effective post-treatment procedures based on AI, ML, or DL could be employed to bring down the cost considerably. Thus, an effective healthcare system in rural areas of developing countries around the world is provided.

6.7   Application of ML and DL

6.7.1   ML and DL for Active Aid

Elderly people mostly rely on the support of others to meet their daily activities; AI provides an answer to overcome this dependency in the form of AI-based Active Aid. This is powered by the concepts and technologies like robotics and NLP. AI-based applications to help support these elderly people through home smart automation software, which uses the data generated by sensors along with wireless sensor network and some of the data mining tools is presented in [25] recently. Moreover, a part of AI, which is Neural Networks, is trained with specific input image modalities to identify the expressions displayed by humans in various scenarios and the modulations in their voices. These NNs are capable to interact with the humans and help them with their needs specifically for specially abled persons and persons affected by paralysis. These neural networks further assists people using wheelchair to monitor and control its moments without any gadgets mounted on them [26].

The AI-based RUDO helps blind people to have a comfortable work life along with others even in the field of electronics as well as informatics [27]. The system based on AI to detect fall and categorize them to identify the complication level in elderly people helps immensely in treatment plan. The activities of elderly people who are on their own in any environment can be monitored and the details are recorded, these records serve to identify a possible disorder that may cause an alarming situation [28]. The above-mentioned devices, tools, and software based on ML and DL help in improving the life style of differently abled person to a great extent. Many researches have collected enormous amount of information from the environment as well as from the users to device expert system that interacts with the radiologist or with the physicians to assist them in planning the treatment (post or pre), the systems are trained in such a way that they monitor the side effects of the medication based on the pathology report of any patient as well [29].

ML and DL cover wide range of applications in the medical domain. Processing of signals from various sensors and the image produced by various imaging techniques used to project the anatomy of human being for diagnosis or prediction of diseases uses these technologies that bubbled out from AI. They are widely used because of their capability to identify interlink between the factors and the diseases caused by these factors [30]. The issues related with enormous data that are generated on daily basis suffer with quality issues, inconsistency, as well as incompleteness along with ethical issues. Accessing these data from various domain and coming out with a meaningful insight is a complex task by itself. These technologies address all the disease related issues but still they majorly focus on data from three important domains: cancer [31], neurology [32], and cardiology [33]. Figure 6.3 shows the flow of data generation from clinical observations to NLP data and its enhancement which boost the analytics process done using ML and DL approaches.

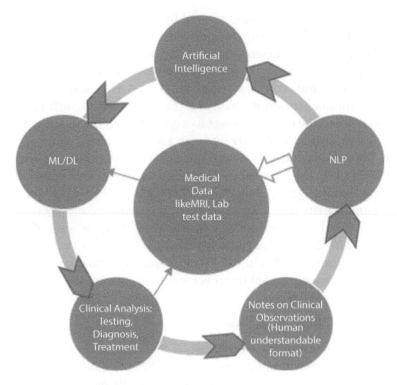

Figure 6.3 The visual representation of clinical data generation to natural language processing data enhancement, to machine learning data analysis, and to clinical decision-making.

The following sections describe few typical case studies, which enlightens the usage of ML and DL in medical domain.

6.7.1.1   Bladder Volume Prediction

The failure of bladder activities like urination and storage is prominent in many patients suffering from spinal cord injuries or by other diseases caused by neurological ailments. The bladder activity is regained by medicines in some cases and in many usages of sensors to monitor and trigger alarm to indicate the need to empty it is achieved. The data from these sensors in the form of digital values are processed along with the other factors recorded and observed in any patients body is processed by smart neuroprostheses. These are composed of two components, internal unit available inside the patients' body, and external unit is a wearable one. The internal unit records signals and these are processed by external unit with complex algorithms to activate the simulation commands related to the required neurological activity [34].

The existing mechanism is improved by including the activities of the external unit into the implantable device (internal unit), for this pressure sensor along with volume sensors are used. The ML-based quantitative and qualitative are used to achieve the required outcome. The neural activities are recorded, identified, and categorized as level 1, 2, and 3. The use of ML-based mechanism greatly reduced the cost involved with hard used and also reduced the usage of power to a great extent. The quantitative and qualitative mechanisms initially undergo a learning phase while in offline mode; the sensors learn to detect the factors responsible for real-time monitoring [35]. The learning phase deals with digital data conditioning, matching the closely related neural activity with that of the bladder status, background activity monitoring, volume curve analysis, and pressure prediction. In this, linear regression is used in predicting the level of bladder status as 1, 2, or 3, as well as regression method is used to analysis volume and pressure estimation. On-the-fly spike sorting algorithm is used on DSP which shows significant improvement than existing works.

6.7.1.2   Epileptic Seizure Prediction

As a neurodegenerative disease, Epilepsy is characterized by sudden, unpredictable and almost instantaneous seizures [22, 23]. Long-term intake of medicines or surgery is the solutions to control this degenerative disease. Surgery is still considered less as an option since it has a marginal success rate; this motivated the researchers to find a better practice. The earlier works were not able to present the region of onset of seizures. The AI-based approach made it possible to withstand the skewness in data distribution. One of the major issues in identifying seizures is the high density analyses required to be performed on iEEG signals. The spectrum-weighted adaptive directed transfer function (swADTF) [24] based on ML concepts helps in identifying generators of seizures and sinks. Further research in prediction of seizures is carried out in tracking features that enhances the outcome along with ML and DL techniques.

6.8   Challenges and Future of Healthcare Systems Based on ML and DL

Like any other expertise, ML and its subset also faces numerous bottlenecks and challenges. Enormous high quality dataset is the challenging requirement of these healthcare systems. Even though amplification of these data sets are done to increase size of the existing data reserve and by allowing the new images to maintain their original attributes helps to some extent. These new data are considered as training sets by these complicated neural networks.

Every medical image has many underlining information hidden init. A radiologist may view a medical image and identify many findings and produce different diagnosis report based on the image, but a CAD system will provide insight with respect to a specific focus only. A need for multi-purpose algorithm that effectively identifies multiple defects in a single image is the greatest expectation from the on lookers. These procedures are not generalized (one algorithm for all disease diagnosis) as well as they are not equipped to provide the underlining reasons for the incidence like a radiologist.

Lack of usage of 3D image is still a great issue while proceeding with DL approaches as well standardization of data format used while collecting data is still a challenge. Large data set processing needs more precise training along with specific algorithm to provide accurate outcome. These enormous data sets make these procedures more problematic and delicate. The wrong interpretation leads to legal issues is also a major concern.

The future healthcare system based on AI and its subsets will render a path that makes it possible to diversify hospitals as one place to treat critical illnesses while clinic are used to treat less urgent cases. A centralized hub of data is connected to all units irrespective to location but they are connected with respect to expertise in the treatment and disease domain, thus directing the patients to the exact service provider and practitioner for quick and accurate treatment with common to all payment schemes.

These procedures help clinicians as well by reducing the rate of burnout they face while attending to patients with minimal resources to dispense. These improve the workflow and work pattern by cutting down the human effort required in the administrative sector. The knowledge acquired with respect to disease symptoms, pattern, diagnosing procedure, and treatment plan provided to every individual, the models train themselves to assist the clinicians as well as patients, too.

6.9   Conclusion

An innovative approach to decipher medical data and understand the information provided by those modalities as well as statistical data AI provides a better path. With the benefits, there comes the bottleneck with these approaches which are to be tackled effectively in future to make human life better than the existing one. Proper training and by providing adequate knowledge to clinicians in terms of AI will provide a better network to handle these medical data. In future, data from various foundations will be used to uncover similarity factors in identifying diseases, and it will be used to predict the risk value of any individual, reduce waiting time for patients, and thus increase productivity in hospitals and healthcare systems. The healthcare systems are equipped in such a way that they predict risk development in a human being before it gets worse. These predictions will be projected not only based on health records of an individual rather based on the demographic details; thus, it helps to break the notion of SDOH (Social Determinants of Health). Networking models based on DL with generalized algorithm to analyze any kind of data to predict any type of disease is the need of the hour.

References

1. Lundell, L., Attwood, S., Ell, C., Fiocca, R., Galmiche, J.P., Hatlebakk, J., Lind, T., Junghard, O., Comparing laparoscopic antireflux surgery with esomeprazole in the management of patients with chronic gastrooesophageal reflux disease: a 3-year interim analysis of the LOTUS trial. *Gut*, 57, 1207–1213, 2008.

2. Liker, H.R., Ducrotte, P., Malfertheiner, P., Unmet medical needs among patients with gastroesophageal reflux disease: a foundation for improving management in primary care. *Dig. Dis.*, 27, 62–67, 2009.

3. Jones, R., Armstrong, D., Malfertheiner, P., Ducrotte, P., Does the treatment of gastroesophageal reflux disease (GERD) meet patients' needs? A survey-based study. *Curr. Med. Res. Opin.*, 22, 657–662, 2006.

4. Nocon, M., Labenz, J., Jaspersen, D., Leodolter, A., Richter, K., Vieth, M., Lind, T., Malfertheiner, P., Willich, S.N., Health-related quality of life in patients with gastro-oesophageal reflux disease under routine care: 5-year follow-up results of the ProGERD study. *Aliment. Pharmacol. Ther.*, 29, 662–668, 2009.

5. Olberg, P., Johannessen, R., Johnsen, G., Myrvold, H.E., Bjerkeset, T., Fjosne, U., Petersen, H., Long-term outcome of surgically and medically treated patients with gastroesophageal reflux disease: a matched-pair follow-up study. *Scand. J. Gastroenterol.*, 40, 264–274, 2005.

6. Dent, J., El-Serag, H.B., Wallander, M.A., Johansson, S., Epidemiology of gastrooesophageal reflux disease: a systematic review. *Gut*, 54, 710–717, 2005.

7. Kripalani, S., LeFevre, F., Phillips, C.O., Williams, M.V., Basaviah, P., Baker, D.W., Deficits in communication and information transfer between hospital-based and primary care physicians: implications for patient safety and continuity of care. *JAMA*, 297, 831–841, 2007.

8. Jiwa, M., Coleman, M., McKinley, R.K., Measuring the quality of referral letters about patients with upper gastrointestinal symptoms. *Postgrad. Med. J.*, 81, 467–469, 2005.

9. Garasen, H. and Johnsen, R., The quality of communication about older patients between hospital physicians and general practitioners: a panel study assessment. *BMC Health Serv. Res.*, 7, 133, 2007.

10. Halpern, R., Kothari, S., Fuldeore, M., Zarotsky, V., Porter, V., Dabbous, O., Goldstein, J.L., GERD-related healthcare utilization, therapy, and reasons for transfer of GERD patients between primary care providers and gastroenterologists in a US managed care setting. *Dig. Dis. Sci.*, 55, 328–337, 2010.

11. Jones, R. and Ballard, K., Healthcare seeking in gastro-oesophageal reflux disease: a qualitative study. *Eur. J. Gastroenterol. Hepatol.*, 20, 269–275, 2008, http://www.biomedcentral.com/1472-6963/11/111 Page 5 of 6.

12. McColl, E., Junghard, O., Wiklund, I., Revicki, D.A., Assessing symptoms in gastroesophageal reflux disease: how well do clinicians' assessments agree with those of their patients? *Am. J. Gastroenterol.*, 100, 11–18, 2005.

13. Flook, N.W. and Wiklund, I., Accounting for the effect of GERD symptoms on patients' health-related quality of life: supporting optimal disease management by primary care physicians. *Int. J. Clin. Pract.*, 61, 2071–2078, 2007.

14. Tytgat, G.N., McColl, K., Tack, J., Holtmann, G., Hunt, R.H., Malfertheiner, P., Hungin, A.P., Batchelor, H.K., New algorithm for the treatment of gastrooesophageal reflux disease. *Aliment. Pharmacol. Ther.*, 27, 249–256, 2008.

15. Tandel, G.S., A review on a deep learning perspective in brain cancer classification. *Cancers*, 11, 1, 111, 2019.

16. Bauer, S., Wiest, R., Nolte, L.-P., Reyes, M., A survey of MRI-based medical image analysis for brain tumor studies. *Phys. Med. Biol.*, 58, 13, R97, 2013.

17. Menze, B.H., The multimodal brain tumor image segmentation benchmark (BRATS). *IEEE Trans. Med. Imaging*, 34, 10, 1993, 2015.

18. Giulia Clementi, D.S., Paoluzzi, A., Università Roma Tre, Scorzelli, G., Pascucci, V., Progressive extraction of neural models from high-resolution 3D images of brain, in: *Proceedings of CAD'16*, pp. 348–351, 2016.

19. Talo, M., Baloglu, U.B., Yıldırım, Ö., Acharya, U.R., Application of deep transfer learning for automated brain abnormality classification using MR images. *Cognit. Syst. Res.*, 54, 176–188, 2019.

20. Emblem, K.E., Predictive modeling in glioma grading from MR perfusion images using support vector machines. *Magn. Reson. Med.*, 60, 4, 945–952, 2008.

21. Marshkole, N., Singh, B.K., Thoke, A., Texture and shape based classification of brain tumors using linear vector quantization. *Int. J. Comput. Appl.*, 30, 11, 21–23, 2011.

22. Wiebe, S., Eliasziw, M., Bellhouse, D.R., Fallahay, C., Burden of epilepsy: the-Ontario health survey. *Can. J. Neurol. Sci.*, 26, 4, 263–70, 1999.

23. Fisher, R.S., van Emde Boas, W., Blume, W., Elger, C., Genton, P., Lee, P. *et al.*, Epilepticseizures and epilepsy: definitions proposed by the international

leagueagainst epilepsy (ILAE) and the international bureau for epilepsy (IBE). *Epilepsia*, 46, 4, 470–2, 2005.

24. Bou Assi, E., Rihana, S., Nguyen, D.K., Sawan, M., Effective connectivityanalysis of iEEG and accurate localization of the epileptogenic focus atthe onset of operculo-insular seizures. *Epilepsy Res.*, 152, 42–51, 2019.

25. Dahmani, K., Tahiri, A., Habert, O., Elmeftouhi, Y., An intelligent model of homesupport for people with loss of autonomy: a novel approach, in: *Proceedings of 2016 International Conference on Control, Decision and Information Technologies*, St. Julian's, Malta, 2016 Apr 6–8, pp. 182–5, 2016.

26. Rabhi, Y., Mrabet, M., Fnaiech, F., A facial expression controlled wheelchair forpeople with disabilities. *Comput. Methods Programs Biomed.*, 165, 89–105, 2018.

27. Hudec, M. and Smutny, Z., RUDO: a home ambient intelligence system for blindpeople. *Sensors*, 17, 8, 1926, 2017.

28. Wu, Q., Zhang, Y.D., Tao, W., Amin, M.G., Radar-based fall detection based onDoppler time–frequency signatures for assisted living. *IET Radar Sonar Nav.*, 9, 2, 164–72, 2015.

29. Lloret, J., Canovas, A., Sendra, S., Parra, L., A smart communication architecture forambient assisted living. *IEEE Commun. Mag.*, 53, 1, 26–33, 2015.

30. García-Vázquez, J.P., Rodríguez, M.D., Tentori, M.E., Saldaña, D., Andrade, ÁG, Espinoza, A.N., An agent-based architecture for developing activity-awaresystems for assisting elderly. *J. Univers. Comput. Sci.*, 16, 12, 1500–20, 2010.

31. Esteva, A., Kuprel, B., Novoa, R.A. *et al.*, Dermatologist-level classification of skin Cancer with deep neural networks. *Nature*, 542, 115–8, 2017.

32. Bouton, C.E., Shaikhouni, A., Annetta, N.V. *et al.*, Restoring cortical control of functional movement in a human with quadriplegia. *Nature*, 533, 247–50, 2016.

33. Marr, B., First FDA approval for clinical Cloud-Based Deep Learning in Healthcare, 2017, https://www.forbes.com/sites/bernardmarr/2017/01/20/first-fda-approval-for-clinical-cloud-based-deep-learning-in-healthcare/?sh=2b55eea161c8

34. Mendez, A., Sawan, M., Minagawa, T., Wyndaele, J.J., Estimation of bladder volume from afferent neural activity. *IEEE Trans. Neural Syst. Rehabil. Eng.*, 21, 5, 704–15, 2013.

35. Mendez, A., Belghith, A., Sawan, M., A DSP for sensing the bladder volume through afferent neural pathways. *IEEE Trans. Biomed. Circuits Syst.*, 8, 4, 552–64, 2014.

7

Detection of Diabetic Retinopathy Using Ensemble Learning Techniques

Anirban Dutta, Parul Agarwal*, Anushka Mittal, Shishir Khandelwal and Shikha Mehta

Jaypee Institute of Information Technology, Noida, India

Abstract

Reliable detection of Diabetic Retinopathy (DR) in digital fundus images still remains a challenging task in medical imaging. Early detection of DR is essential to save a patient's loss as it is an irreversible loss. Premature symptoms of DR include the growth of features like hemorrhages, exudates, and microaneurysms on the retinal surface of the eye. The primary focus of this paper is on the detection of the severity of DR by considering the individual and the combined features. Image processing techniques are applied for the automated extraction of the retinal features. Machine learning algorithms along with ensemble learning techniques are used on these features for further detection of DR. In medical imaging, where the available data is highly imbalanced, specifically designed ensemble learning techniques are proved to be very helpful. In this paper, three ensemble learning algorithms—AdaNaive, AdaSVM, and Adaforest—are developed and compared with machine learning algorithms for binary and multi-classification of DR. Experimental results reveal that proposed algorithms outperform existing algorithms.

Keywords: Diabetic Retinopathy, machine learning, ensemble learning techniques, binary classification, multiclass classification

7.1 Introduction

As reported by international diabetes federation (IDF), in 2019 approximately 460 million adults in the age of 20–80 years are suffering from

---

*Corresponding author: cs.er.parul@gmail.com

Pradeep Singh (ed.) Fundamentals and Methods of Machine and Deep Learning: Algorithms, Tools and Applications, (153–176) © 2022 Scrivener Publishing LLC

diabetes and the number is expected to rise to 800 million by 2050. Due to high blood glucose levels, diabetic people are relatively more prone to serious health problems that affect heart, eyes, kidneys, nerves, and teeth. It is also one of the major causes of blindness, cardiovascular disease, kidney failure, and lower limb amputation. Diabetic Retinopathy (DR), a retinal vascular disease is the most common cause of losing vision and blindness among working-age adults. It is caused due to the damage of the blood vessels of an individual's light-sensitive tissue located at the back of the eye (retina) [1]. The longer a person suffers from diabetes and the less controlled the blood sugar level is, the more likely the person is to develop this eye disease. DR progresses through four stages. The first stage DR is Mild Non-proliferative Retinopathy which is characterized by the balloon-like swelling in the blood vessels of the retina. These are called microaneurysms and these vessels can leak into the eyes. The second stage is the Moderate Non-proliferative Retinopathy in which blood vessels nourishing the retina swell and may even get blocked. The third stage is the Severe Proliferative Retinopathy. In this stage, growing blood vessels may get blocked. As a result, the retina is informed to produce new blood vessels. The fourth and last stage is Proliferative DR. New blood vessels will start growing in retina, which are abnormal and delicate. These blood vessels can easily leak which causes blurred vision. Scary tissue formation causes retinal detachment and may lead to spotty vision and severe vision loss [2]. Successful classification of DR is very important to save the patient from vision loss. Therefore, accurate estimation of this disease is critical for timely prevention and care interventions.

With the exponential increase in healthcare data, interdisciplinary research is gaining huge attention among the researchers. ML algorithms are playing a leading role in discovering useful patterns from the existing health records by providing useful insights to medical practitioners which aid in the diagnosis of various disorders. Understanding and analyzing healthcare data is a sensitive issue as it deals with the life of human beings. Accuracy of prediction is very critical as false positives and false negatives both are life threatening. In literature, DR is considered as both a binary classification problem and multiclass classification problem. Binary classification only indicates whether a person is suffering from the diseases or not and multiclass classification helps in identifying the stage of DR in the patients. Thus, to predict the stage of DR, all the features need to be extracted from their specific location. Extraction of features and then further classification is a highly time-consuming task and hence requires automation [3]. A significant amount of work has been done by researchers on this automation using various ML algorithms like KNN and SVM [4–6].

In this paper, all the individual features are extracted from the retinal images using image processing techniques like Canny Edge Detection and Histogram equalization. ML and ensemble learning techniques are applied for binary and multiclass classification. This paper proposes three ensemble models for prediction of DR. The performance of these models is compared to its various existing algorithms. It is observed from experimental results that proposed ensemble techniques give better accuracy as compared to conventional algorithms. ROC curves are plotted for the same to ensure the efficacy of developed techniques. The workflow of this paper is described as follows. Section 7.2 describes the overview of the related work. Sections 7.3 and 7.4 describe the methodology and proposed system of our work. Section 7.5 describes the experimental results and analysis. Section 7.6 concludes the paper with future work.

7.2   Related Work

Table 7.1 depicts the literature of DR with the algorithm developed and limitations.

The various studies discussed above very limited feature analysis are done on extracted and combined features together for both binary and multiclass classification. Also, the accuracy achieved by algorithms on multiclass classification is less than 50%. This forms the motivation to develop new ensemble techniques.

7.3   Methodology

The proposed work is mainly divided into three phases—pre-processing, extraction, and classification of the disease. The pre-processing steps are necessary so as to make the images more uniform for classification. The dataset used is highly imbalanced, so before applying classification models, the count of all the levels should be made equal for more accurate results. Important features like exudates, hemorrhages, and microaneurysms are then extracted from these pre-processed images and passed on to the classifying algorithms [18].

7.3.1   Data Pre-Processing

Pre-processing of the images is important to remove the noise levels in the dataset as well as enhancing the image quality. Images are of varying

Table 7.1 Literature survey of Diabetic Retinopathy.

	Year	Paper reference	Method/algorithm	Drawback
1.	2020	[7]	• Ensemble-based techniques consisting random forest, KNN, decision trees, and logistic regression. • Diabetic Retinopathy dataset. • When the individual machine learning algorithms were compared with ensemble techniques, results showed that ensemble techniques give much better results than these individual algorithms.	Testing is done on a small dataset with very limited number of images.
2.	2017	[8]	• Bagging ensemble classifier was developed. • Approach involved feature extraction. In the first stage, important retinal features are extracted using machine learning techniques. In the second stage, these extracted features are used for further applying ensemble techniques like voting for final classification. • Results show that ensemble techniques outperform individual algorithms.	Image datasets with relatively small size were used for experiments. Scope for more combinations of algorithms for developing ensemble approaches.

(Continued)

Table 7.1 Literature survey of Diabetic Retinopathy. (*Continued*)

	Year	Paper reference	Method/algorithm	Drawback
3.	2016	[9]	• Focused on detection of bright and dark lesions for the early diagnosis of Diabetic Retinopathy. • The classification system is built using algorithms like Naive Bayes and SVM yielding considerable accuracy.	Focused only on certain types of lesions, limited features extracted. Only limited machine learning algorithms are used which can be further extended.
4.	2016	[10]	• Forward search and backward search method are the two proposed techniques used to select the best ensemble system.	The proposed model makes binary classification only. Feature extraction can be improved to get better accuracy.
5.	2015	[11]	• The work uses an approach which involves features subset selection using the lasso along with ensemble learning techniques such as RUSboost and AdaBoost followed by 10-fold cross-validation	The work uses the NHANES dataset - which relies on patient questionnaires, making it prone to poor data quality. There is a scope to improve the dataset using additional clinical data.

(*Continued*)

Table 7.1 Literature survey of Diabetic Retinopathy. (*Continued*)

	Year	Paper reference	Method/algorithm	Drawback
6.	2014	[12]	• The work focuses on combining several base classifiers like KNN, AdaBoost, random forest, SVM into ensemble techniques with a precisely designed strategy. • This paper presents an accuracy of 90% on the MESSIDOR dataset.	The analysis and the results obtained are binary class classification. The study revolves around image processing algorithms rather than reliable machine learning techniques.
7.	2014	[13]	• The paper shows the relationship between the bias-variance trade-off and the feature extraction, ensemble algorithms, and post-classification processing. • Ensemble learning techniques like bagging and random forests are used and experimental results show the effectiveness of the approach followed.	Focus on feature extractions, feature selections are missing. The overall accuracy can be further improved by using a larger dataset with higher resolution fundus images.

(*Continued*)

Table 7.1 Literature survey of Diabetic Retinopathy. (*Continued*)

	Year	Paper reference	Method/algorithm	Drawback
8.	2014	[14]	• Classification of retinopathy on the MESSIDOR dataset has been done through the analysis of classifiers such as support vector machines, K-nearest neighbors, AdaBoost, and Gaussian Mixture model.	Dataset employed for the purpose is highly imbalanced. The study revolves around whether the extracted spots are lesions or not, i.e., Binary classification.
9.	2013	[15]	• Support vector machine classifiers are used to test whether the patients are severely affected or moderately affected and this information helps in a much clearer diagnosis of Diabetic Retinopathy.	The proposed work has been conducted on 5 images. The research should have been conducted on larger datasets. The accuracy of the proposed work has not been reported.
10.	2012	[16]	• Author reviews state of art ensemble techniques for class imbalanced datasets. • The ensemble techniques (bagging or boosting) combined with sampling techniques like under-sampling or SMOTE gives better results and also eliminates the need for data pre-processing.	Classification algorithms are compared only on the basis of ROC curves. Some internal measures like Silhouette index, DB index can be used.

(*Continued*)

Table 7.1 Literature survey of Diabetic Retinopathy. (*Continued*)

	Year	Paper reference	Method/algorithm	Drawback
11.	2012	[17]	• The paper proposes an approach that involves gathering close microaneurysm candidates and applying a voting scheme on them to overcome the difficulty caused due to different algorithms extracting microaneurysms with different approaches. • A framework to build Micro Aneurysms based on the internal components of the detector has been proposed. • The Micro aneurysms detector proposed use pre-processing methods and candidate extractors.	In spite of an innovative approach, the system misclassified certain cases where serious cases of DR are present. Important factors such as the presence or lack of DR-specific lesions, the recognition of anatomical parts, quality of image are vital in a clinical setting have been ignored by the author. The proposed method has been tested only on the MESSIDOR dataset.

brightness levels so all the images must be brought to a usable format for training the model. The images used had only a certain portion of useful data, with the rest being just black background. So these images are cropped and rescaled to 256*256 pixels. The dataset used is highly imbalanced and hence needs to be balanced before further use. Balancing is done by the augmentation of the images (rotating and cropping). This also improves the localization ability of the network.

7.3.2   Feature Extraction

From each image different features are then extracted by using various image processing techniques. The features extracted from each retinal image are Blood Vessels, Exudates, Hemorrhages, and Microaneurysms [19]. We are proposing a way to use a mix of traditional and modern image processing techniques followed by morphological changes to extract these features.

These individual features are being passed to the training models and for the first time, a physician will be able to determine as to which component of the eye is causing the problem and prescribe accordingly.

7.3.2.1   Exudates

To extract the exudates (as shown in Figure 7.1), CLAHE (Contrast Limited Adaptive Histogram Equalization) technique is used to process the green Channel of the image, followed by modification using Image Blur, Erosion, and Dilation to get appropriate shapes. Other modifications are done using built-in OpenCV tools [20].

7.3.2.2   Blood Vessels

To extract the Blood vessels (Figure 7.2), Canny Edge Detection technique is used against the main challenge to differentiate between actual blood vessels and small noise portions in the images. For the small noise which could be mislabeled as blood vessels due to the sensitive nature of the Canny algorithm - Histogram equalization technique, CLAHE is being used. Masking techniques are being employed to remove smaller blood vessels which are not important to DR [21].

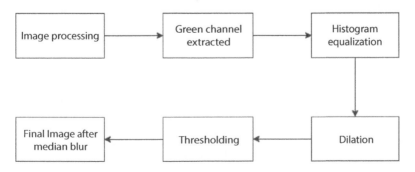

Figure 7.1 Extraction of exudates.

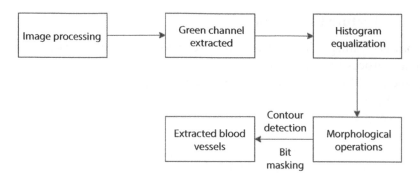

Figure 7.2 Extraction of blood vessels.

7.3.2.3 Microaneurysms

To extract the microaneurysms (Figure 7.3), the first different sets of shapes that could be identified as blob are generated using the blob detection algorithms. The algorithms are then applied after applying an edge detection algorithm on the isolated green channel of the images followed by several rounds of erosion and dilation. Not all the shapes in the set are appropriate with respect to DR, so some have been left out [22].

7.3.2.4 Hemorrhages

For the extraction of hemorrhages (Figure 7.4), a large number of parameters of the blob detection algorithms are experimented on until finally arriving at a set of parameters that is able to detect the features accurately in maximum number of images. Masking is being used extensively to

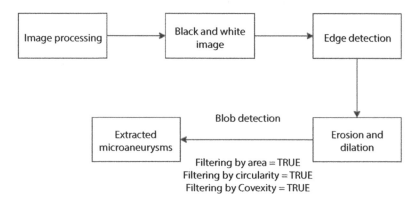

Figure 7.3 Extraction of microaneurysms.

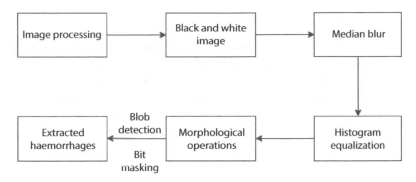

Figure 7.4 Extraction of hemorrhages.

draw the extracted features on a black image. Canny is being used for edge detection before masking out the blood vessels [23].

7.3.3   Learning

After the extractions are completed, the learning models are trained on the images. Ensemble learning techniques such as AdaBoost, AdaNaive, and AdaSVM are used after splitting the dataset into training and testing sets. These ensemble methods can potentially provide better accuracy for the dataset as they employ a strong predictor which is built by repeatedly calling the weak learner on different distributions over the training samples. Furthermore, support vector machines (SVMs), K-nearest neighbors (KNN), and random forest classifiers are also used to train the model.

7.3.3.1   Support Vector Machines

SVM is a supervised learning model that analyzes the data and recognizes patterns used for further classification [16]. When provided with different training instances with each belonging to its output category, this model would classify the images into its corresponding output stage. Initially, binary classification is made where we classify the images into two stages, DR and non-DR [24].

7.3.3.2   K-Nearest Neighbors

The KNN algorithm is based upon classifying the input sample by looking at its nearest neighbors. The Euclidean distance is used to identify the nearest neighbors and the majority output class of these neighbors is assigned to the sample [25].

7.3.3.3   Random Forest

Random forests are an ensemble learning technique that takes in several decision trees at training time and outputs the result class which occurs the greatest number of times out of all the output classes from individual trees [26]. The main idea is to make a strong learner out of the weak learners and reduce overfitting by the large numbers through the introduction of a degree of randomness. It also mitigates the problem of high variance and high bias by the use of averaging. It, therefore, produces a reasonable model fast and efficiently.

7.3.3.4   AdaBoost

Ensemble methods have the ability to improve the accuracy as we combine various classifiers. The final classification result is made by combining the results obtained from different classifiers used. Further accuracy of such ensemble technique can be improved by the boosting method. One such boosting algorithm used is AdaBoost. It is a model which helps us achieve accuracy just above the random chance on a classification problem. Specifically used with the weak learners. The most common classification technique used with AdaBoost is one level decision trees. This algorithm is also the default base learner while using AdaBoost. Every instance in the training dataset is initially uniformly weighted. But for the further trainings, the instances which fail to correctly get classified are the ones which are assigned more weight. Hence, a strong classifier or a predictor is built by repeatedly calling the weak learners with different weight distributions over the training data. This is the main reason why we are able to observe an increase in the accuracy [27]. Figure 7.5 below depicts the working of general AdaBoost model.

7.3.3.5   Voting Technique

One of the simplest techniques for combining the classification results from multiple ML algorithms is voting. We pick up two or more individual models for training the dataset. Then the voting technique can be combining the models and average the predictions obtained from different sub models to give a new result. The predictions obtained from individual classifiers can be weighted, but specifying the accurate weights for the models is a difficult task. Hence, more advanced models have been built which can learn how to give the best weights to the predictions from the sub models.

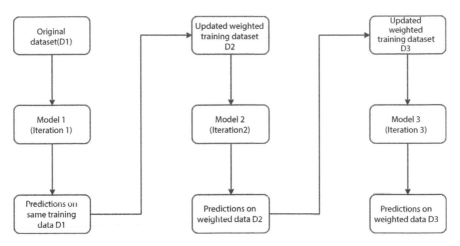

Figure 7.5 Working of AdaBoost model.

7.4   Proposed Models

In general, ensemble techniques are known to improve the accuracy and computation time of any classification problem. One great example of such a technique is the AdaBoost algorithm. Previous work that has been done on the detection of DR using ensemble techniques presents the usage of standard AdaBoost technique, which by default uses decision trees as the base algorithm. In this paper, we have proposed a new technique of using different classifiers such as naive Bayes, SVM as the base classifiers for this algorithm. It is observed that this technique is highly successful in obtaining a much higher accuracy as compared to the standard technique.

7.4.1   AdaNaive

AdaNaive is an ensemble learning method for classification that is built by keeping the Naive Bayes algorithm as the base estimator while defining the parameters for the AdaBoost algorithm. Its working is similar to that of an AdaBoost classifier where the objective is to build a predictor by combining multiple poorly performing classifiers so that they can together work as a better classifier which gives much higher accuracy, the higher accuracy is due to the estimator being set to Naive Bayes instead of the None. Figure 7.6 below depicts the working of the AdaNaive model.

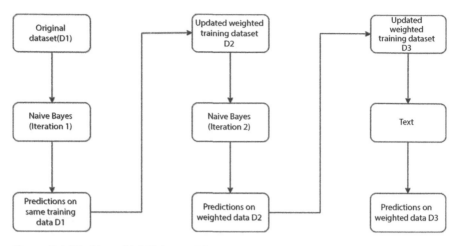

Figure 7.6 Working of AdaNaive model.

7.4.2   AdaSVM

In this algorithm, the base estimator used for the AdaBoost algorithm is the SVM model. AdaSVM classifier produces better results as compared to the default AdaBoost classifier. Working of AdaSVM is presented in Figure 7.7.

7.4.3   AdaForest

In this algorithm, the base estimator used for the AdaBoost algorithm is the Random Forest model. The random forest itself being an ensemble of

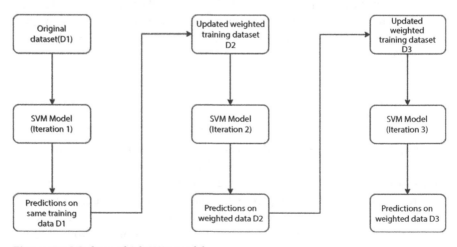

Figure 7.7 Working of AdaSVM model.

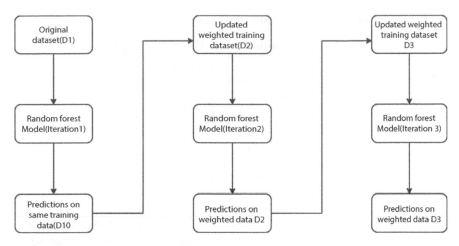

Figure 7.8 Working of AdaForest model.

many decision trees gives better classification accuracy for this model as compared to the standard technique where a single decision tree is used as the base classifier. Working of AdaForest is shown in Figure 7.8.

7.5 Experimental Results and Analysis

7.5.1 Dataset

The images for DR Detection were obtained from the Kaggle dataset of 35,000 images with 5 output classes. Dataset consists of colored fundus images varying in size (height and width). Also, the count of images of different levels is highly non-uniform with the non-DR images accounting for 75% of the total dataset. Hence, the dataset used is highly imbalanced and at the same time contains a lot of un-interpretable images. All the images are labeled with the subject id as well as the left or right forex (1_left.jpeg means the left eye of the first patient.) Table 7.2 describes the distribution of various levels in the dataset [28].

7.5.2 Software and Hardware

The Kaggle dataset consists of about 35,000 images while we have worked on a patch of 1,500 images for training proposed algorithms like AdaSVM,

Table 7.2 Retinopathy grades in the Kaggle dataset.

Level	Condition	Count of images
0	No DR	25,810
1	Mild DR	2,443
2	Moderate DR	5,292
3	Severe DR	873
4	End Stage	708

AdaForest, AdaNaive, and other conventional algorithms. The computation time of these classifiers is significantly high; hence, Google Collaboratory, a Google Cloud Service with free GPU, is used. A significant reduction in execution time is seen.

7.5.3   Results

The aim of our DR system is to grade the severity of the disease by using proposed classification algorithms. Retinal images without lesions are classified as normal and the abnormal images (with lesions) are further classified as mild, moderate, severe, and end-stage DR [19] as shown in Figure 7.9. A comparative analysis of the algorithms is done on our extracted feature set discussed in Section 7.3. Figures 7.1 to 7.4 depict the features extracted through image processing techniques.

Performance of Proposed Models for Binary Classification: Table 7.3 portrays the accuracies obtained in binary classification using proposed ensemble techniques in contrast to ML algorithms. Cumulatively, AdaNaive has provided results with high accuracies among all classifiers. AdaBoost accuracy is also very close to AdaNaive. In a feature wise binary classification, AdaNaive gives highest accuracy as compared to other

Class 0   Class 1   Class 2   Class 3   Class 4

Figure 7.9 Representative retinal images of DR in their order of increasing severity.

Table 7.3 Accuracy for binary classification using machine learning techniques.

Features	Random forest	KNN	AdaBoost	SVM	Voting technique	AdaForest	AdaNaive	AdaSVM
Blood vessels	78.125	82.000	81.250	84.375	81.5	84.400	**89.500**	89.200
Microaneurysms	84.375	81.000	84.375	81.250	69.4	79.900	**87.300**	85.200
Hemorrhages	83.330	73.300	80.000	83.300	68.7	80.100	**86.000**	83.000
Exudates	85.100	85.210	86.000	82.750	72.5	87.300	**92.200**	91.800
Combined features	63.300	61.672	75.000	67.600	63.2	69.000	**76.500**	71.800

learning algorithms. In blood vessels, AdaNaive accuracy is improved by 14.56%, 9%, 10%, 6%, and 10% from random forest, KNN, AdaBoost, SVM, and voting techniques, respectively. Random forest and AdaBoost have depicted similar results while classifying microaneurysms. SVM and random forest have provided an accuracy of 83% to classify hemorrhages. Random Forest and KNN have provided an accuracy of 85% in exudates classification. AdaNaive, AdaSVM, and AdaForest outperform all ML classifiers. In the case of combined features, AdaNaive and AdaSVM give accuracies of 76% and 72%, respectively. Percentage improvement in accuracy of AdaNaive from random forest, KNN, AdaBoost, SVM, and voting techniques are 20.8%, 24.2%, 2%, 13.2%, and 20%, respectively. Overall it can be deduced from Table 7.3 that AdaNaive gives highest accuracy and takes over all the other ensemble and machine learning algorithms.

Performance of Proposed models for Multiclass Classification: Table 7.4 illustrates the accuracies obtained in multiclass classification using proposed ensemble techniques in contrast to ML algorithms. On individual extracted features, say blood vessels, AdaNaive and AdaSVM perform similarly and provide an accuracy of 54%. Percentage improvement in accuracy of AdaNaive is 35.2%, 84.7%, 5%, and 37.2% from random forest, KNN, AdaBoost and SVM. In microaneurysms, AdaNaive and Adaforest provide similar accuracies of 56% and 55%. AdaNaive and AdaSVM provide an accuracy of approximately 58% while detecting hemorrhages. AdaForest performs well by providing an accuracy of 59% while detecting exudates. In combined features, AdaNaive gives highest accuracy as compared to other algorithms. AdaNaive accuracy is increased by 42%, 66.8%, 6.8%, 146%, and 25.6% from random forest, KNN, AdaBoost, SVM, and voting techniques.

We observe that the algorithms AdaNaive, AdaSVM, and AdaForest provide the highest accuracies in both binary and multiclass classification. For a better study and evaluation of the classifiers, we have plotted the Receiver operating characteristic curve or ROC curve comparing the performance of the algorithms in binary classification on the original images as shown in Figure 7.10. ROC curve is a probability curve and it shows how much the model is capable of distinguishing between classes. It is plotted between True Positive Rate (TPR) and False Positive Rate (FPR) where TPR is on the Y-axis and FPR is on the X-axis.

$$Accuracy = \frac{TP + TN}{TP + FP + TN + FN} \tag{7.1}$$

Table 7.4 Accuracy for multiclass classification using machine learning techniques.

Features	Random Forest	KNN	AdaBoost	SVM	Voting technique	AdaForest	AdaNaive	AdaSVM
Blood vessels	40.311	29.500	52.000	39.600	49.434	51.555	**54.500**	53.350
Microaneurysms	41.250	43.500	55.350	41.000	45.444	55.000	**56.540**	52.400
Hemorrhages	44.450	36.500	54.330	38.222	52.700	57.333	58.500	**58.600**
Exudates	42.500	40.100	56.250	39.300	55.500	**59.450**	58.750	57.500
Combined features	40.12	34.180	53.250	21.100	45.333	45.666	**56.950**	54.500

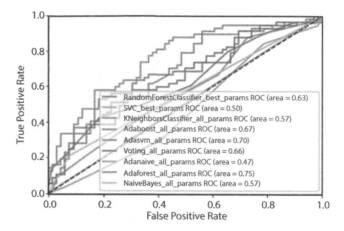

Figure 7.10 Comparison of classifiers using ROC curve (Binary classification).

The contribution of ensemble techniques in providing great results is quite significant as they outperform all the ML algorithms. Within ensemble algorithms, the proposed techniques of AdaNaive, AdaSVM, and AdaForest give the best results for both binary and multi-classification as shown in Figure 7.11 and 7.12 respectively. In multi-classification, the highest accuracy is achieved by the AdaForest algorithm for exudates. While in binary classification, AdaNaive performs the best. Also, from the results, it is quite evident that these algorithms are more effective in classifying the extracted features

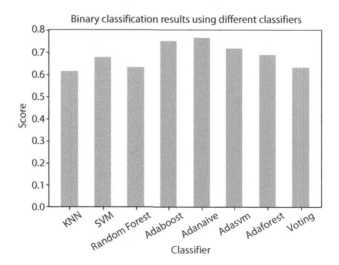

Figure 7.11 Comparison of classifiers (Binary Classification).

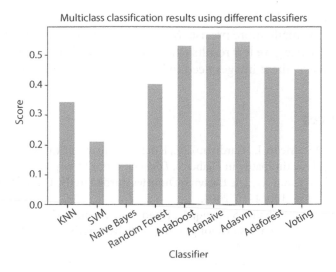

Figure 7.12 Comparison of classifiers (Multi Classification).

as compared to the combined ones. Hence, the extraction of these individual features plays a major role in the accurate classification of the disease.

7.6   Conclusion

With a humongous population of diabetic patients and the occurrence of DR among them, demand for such automated systems for DR detection is increasing. Several achievements have been made and acceptable outcome have been attained in feature extraction and detection of DR severity. Nevertheless, these results obtained are mostly on smaller datasets and are far away from the real-world applications. We have worked on a dataset that is moderate in size and classified with a labelling scheme that is more useful for clinical practice. This system extracts retinal features such as exudates, hemorrhages, and microaneurysms which help in better prediction of the severity of the disease. Various ML algorithms combined with ensemble techniques are then employed on these extracted features. We have developed three ensemble learning techniques, i.e., AdaNaive, AdaSVM, and AdaForest. These are developed by changing the base classifier of AdaBoost from Decision Tree to Naive Bayes, SVM, and Random Forest which brought significant change in terms of accuracy. AdaNaive gives better accuracy in contrast to majority of algorithms on binary and multiclass classification. AdaForest and AdaSVM give similar kind of performances to AdaNaive in multiclass classification. In the future, the dataset can be made more precise. Many images in the dataset are of poor quality and hence gave low results when extraction techniques were applied to them. Hence, these images need to be handled in a precautious manner.

References

1. Fong, D.S., Aiello, L., Gardner, T.W., King, G.L., Blankenship, G., Cavallerano, J.D. *et al.*, Retinopathy in Diabetes. *Diabetes Care*, 27, suppl 1:s84–s87, 2004.
2. Health N, Exam- N. The Evolving Diabetes Burden in the United States. *Ann. Intern. Med.*, 140, 4–10, 2004.
3. Akram, M.U., Khalid, S., Tariq, A., Khan, S.A., Azam, F., Detection and classification of retinal lesions for grading of diabetic retinopathy. *Comput. Biol. Med.*, 45, 161–71, 2014.
4. Williamson, T.H., Gardner, G.G., Keating, D., Kirkness, C.M., Elliott, A.T., Automatic detection of diabetic retinopathy using neural networks. *Investig. Ophthalmol. Vis. Sci.*, 37, 940–4, 1996.
5. Zohra, B.F. and Mohamed, B., *Automated diagnosis of retinal images using the Support Vector Machine(SVM)*, Fac Des Sci Dep Informatique, USTO, Alger, 2009.
6. R.P. and P.A., Diagnosis of Diabetic Retinopathy Using Machine Learning Techniques. *ICTACT J. Soft Comput.*, 3, 563–75, 2013, https://doi.org/10.21917/ijsc.2013.0083.
7. Saha, R., Chowdhury, A., Banerjee, S., Diabetic Retinopathy Related Lesions Detection and Classification Using Machine Learning Technology. *Artificial Intelligence and Soft Computing*, pp. 734–745, 2016.
8. Reddy, G. *et al.*, a Learning model for Diabetic Retinopathy Classification. *2020 International Conference on Emerging Trends in Information Technology and Engineering (ic-ETITE)*, 2020.
9. S.S.K. and A.P., A Machine Learning Ensemble Classifier for Early Prediction of Diabetic Retinopathy. *J. Med. Syst.*, 41, 12, 1–12, 2017.
10. Bhatia, K., Arora, S., Tomar, R., Diagnosis of diabetic retinopathy using machine learning classification algorithm. *Proc. 2016 2nd Int. Conf. Next Gener. Comput. Technol. NGCT 2016*, no. October, pp. 347–351, 2017.
11. Ogunyemi, O. and Kermah, D., Machine Learning Approaches for Detecting Diabetic Retinopathy from Clinical and Public Health Records. *AMIA ... Annu. Symp. proceedings. AMIA Symp.*, vol. 2015, pp. 983–990, 2015.
12. Antal, B. and Hajdu, A., An ensemble-based system for automatic screening of diabetic retinopathy. *Knowl.-Based Syst.*, 60, January, 20–27, 2014.
13. Tradeoff, B., Merentitis, A., Debes, C., Member, S., Heremans, R., Ensemble Learning in Hyperspectral Image Classification: Toward Selecting a Favorable. *IEEE J. Sel. Top. Appl. Earth Obs. Remote Sens.*, 7, 4, 1089–1102, 2014.

14. Roychowdhury, S., Koozekanani, D.D., Parhi, K.K., DREAM: Diabetic Retinopathy Analysis Using Machine Learning. *IEEE J. Biomed. Health Inform.*, 18, 5, 1717–1728, 2014.
15. Gandhi, M. and Dhanasekaran, R., Diagnosis of diabetic retinopathy using morphological process and SVM classifier. *Int. Conf. Commun. Signal Process. ICCSP 2013 – Proc.*, pp. 873–877, 2013.
16. Galar, M., Fernandez, A., Barrenechea, E., Bustince, H., Herrera, F., A review on ensembles for the class imbalance problem: Bagging-, boosting-, and hybrid-based approaches. *IEEE Trans. Syst. Man Cybern. Part C Appl. Rev.*, 42, 4, 463–484, 2012.
17. Antal, B. and Hajdu, A., An ensemble-based system for microaneurysm detection and diabetic retinopathy grading. *IEEE Trans. Biomed. Eng.*, 59, 6, 1720–1726, 2012.
18. Walter, T., Klein, J.C., Massin, P., Erginay, A., A contribution of image processing to the diagnosis of diabetic retinopathy - Detection of exudates in color fundus images of the human retina. *IEEE Trans. Med. Imaging*, 21, 1236–43, 2002, https://doi.org/10.1109/TMI.2002.806290.
19. Panchal, P., Bhojani, R., Panchal, T., An Algorithm for Retinal Feature Extraction Using Hybrid Approach. *Proc. Comput. Sci.*, 79, 61–8, https://doi.org/10.1016/j.procs.2016.03.009, 2016.
20. Biran, A. and SobheBidari KR, P., Automatic Method for Exudates and Hemorrhages Detection from Fundus Retinal Images. *Int. J. Comput. Electr. Autom. Control Inf. Eng.*, 9, 1443–6, 2016.
21. Soomro, T.A., Paul, M., Gao, J., Zheng, L., Retinal blood vessel extraction method based on basic filtering schemes. *Proc - Int Conf Image Process ICIP 2018*, 2017–Septe, pp. 4422–6, https://doi.org/10.1109/ICIP.2017.8297118.
22. Akram, M.U., Khalid, S., Khan, S.A., Identification and classification of microaneurysms for early detection of diabetic retinopathy. *Pattern Recognit.*, 46, 107–16, https://doi.org/10.1016/j.patcog.2012.07.002, 2013.
23. Bae, J.P., Kim, K.G., Kang, H.C., Jeong, C.B., Park, K.H., Hwang, J M., A study on hemorrhage detection using hybrid method in fundus images. *J. Digit. Imaging*, 24, 394–404, https://doi.org/10.1007/s10278-010-9274-9, 2011.
24. Hearst, M.A., Dumais, S.T., Osuna, E., Platt, J., Scholkopf, B., Support vector machines. *IEEE Intell. Syst. App.*, 13, 18–28, 1998.
25. Zhang, M.-L. and Zhou, Z.-H., A k-nearest neighbor based algorithm for multi-label classification. *IEEE Int. Conf. Granul. Comput.*, vol. 2, pp. 718–721, 2005, https://doi.org/10.1109/grc.2005.1547385.
26. Liaw, A. and Wiener, M., Classification and Regression by random Forest. *R News*, 2, 3, 18–22, 2003.
27. Rätsch, G., Onoda, T., Müller, K.R., Soft margins for AdaBoost. *Mach. Learn.*, 42, 287–320, 2001, https://doi.org/10.1023/A:1007618119488.
28. *Diabetic Retinopathy Detection*, n.d. https://www.kaggle.com/c/diabetic-retinopathy-detection/data, 2015.

8

Machine Learning and Deep Learning for Medical Analysis—A Case Study on Heart Disease Data

Swetha A.M., Santhi B.* and Brindha G.R.

SASTRA Deemed University, Thanjavur, Tamil Nadu, India

Abstract

Cardiovascular diseases (CVDs) encompass a variety of heart problems ranging from vascular disorders like coronary heart diseases and peripheral arterial disorders to morbid cardiac diseases like heart failure (or myocardial infarction) and cardiomyopathy, to name a few. These diseases often occur as repercussions of low cardiac output and decreased ejection factor, usually exacerbated by vascular blockages. With the increasing severity of CVDs, a need for predicting heart failures is on the rise, but the traditional methods employed for CVD-related event prediction, unfortunately, have failed to achieve the acme of accuracy. Given a set of medical records as datasets, Machine Learning (ML) can be employed to achieve high accuracy in the prediction of patient survival and also in determining the driving factors that increase mortality among CVD patients. The medical records that provide the necessary data for prediction form a basic framework that divulges inconspicuous consistencies of patient's data which along with an appropriate ML algorithm confute the traditional methods thereby providing a strong base for determining the feature that contributes the most for the risk factor. The proposed model uses various feature selection techniques to extract those features in particular that highly contributes to the prediction of the target attribute and exploits the application of ML and Deep neural classifier algorithms to predict possibilities of CVD development among patients. Our results show that follow-up time, ejection fraction, and serum creatinine as the most significant features that affect the survival rate of the heart failure patient when compared to other features giving an accuracy of 99.1% using XGBoost.

---

*Corresponding author: swetha.ambley@gmail.com

Pradeep Singh (ed.) Fundamentals and Methods of Machine and Deep Learning: Algorithms, Tools and Applications, (177–210) © 2022 Scrivener Publishing LLC

Keywords: Cardiovascular diseases, heart failure, ejection fraction, serum creatinine, feature selection

8.1   Introduction

Cardiovascular diseases (CVDs) [25] have become more prevalent in recent times with mortality rates counting as high as 15–17 million per year, which is about 30%–31% of the total deaths worldwide according to the WHO reports. Myocardial infarction, coronary heart diseases, and arrhythmia are some of the most common CVDs. The precarity of CVD makes it one of the most treacherous diseases that prevail presently in society. What accounts for this unpredictability is the diversity of contributing features that range from inevitable factors like inheritance, age, gender to avoidable ones like alcohol abuse and tobacco consumption. Recent medical reports reveal that about 80% of the patients who die premature (below the age of 70) fall under the elderly category and about 25% of the remaining are middle-aged women. Though these factors (age and sex of the patient) are not the best way to discern the worst of the cases, they cannot be entirely disregarded. Other clinical factors like the concentration of serum creatinine and ejection fraction play more prominent roles in patients' survival prediction, especially for those that have been receiving treatment over a period of time.

Considering the diversity of causal factors associated with CVDs, it remains a challenge to sort out the significant features that may aid in timely prediction of a patient's survival. Filtering the prominent factors requires careful perusal through different medical records to note the degree of influence a specific factor exerts on the patient's survival.

Hence, to ensure high efficacy and maximum accuracy, Machine Learning (ML) models could be exploited, as have been in the proposed model. ML models can be used for meticulous prediction of the target variable (which in this case is the survival rate of a patient) by taking into account several affecting features. The affecting features, however, could be a mix of both important as well as less-influential factors. Hence, to overcome this challenge, the proposed model employs feature selection methods.

The dataset used to train and test the ML models was obtained from live medical records [22] collected at the Faisalabad Institute of Cardiology and at the Allied Hospital in Faisalabad (Pakistan) from April to December 2015. The dataset contains the records of 299 heart failure patients, about

105 of which are women and whose age ranges from 40 to 95 years. All the patients listed in the records had suffered left ventricular dysfunction and had a history of cardiac arrests and fall under class III and IV of heart failure stages as deemed by New York Heart Association (NYHA) [7].

The dataset, which entails these live medical records, is normalized to treat outliers and other noise that may interfere with the model's predictive potential and also oversampled as the data showed conspicuous imbalance between classes.

Feature selection methods, like Extra Tree Classifiers, Pearson Correlation, Forward Selection, and Chi-square tests, were performed to sort out the most prominent features. Serum creatinine concentration, ejection fraction, age of the patients, and the duration of treatment were proved to have maximum influence on the patients' death event and were hence used as cardinal predictive variables in the model. Doing this increased the model's prediction accuracy to about 75%.

The proposed model constitutes several ML algorithms like SVM, CNN [26], and other ensemble methods that are trained on the set of medical records. These algorithms were weighed individually based on their accuracy score for different sets of features. The models were trained over three different studies: one with follow-up time, creatinine level, and ejection fraction as major factors, another with age instead of follow-up time and the third over the entire set of features available in the dataset.

8.2   Related Works

Chronic cardiac failure occurs when the fluid accumulates around the heart, causing it to pump insufficiently for the body to function normally. There are two types of chronic cardiac failure based on left ventricular function: systolic heart failure (reduced ejection fraction HFrEF) and diastolic heart failure. For normal people, the percentage of blood that is pumped out by the left ventricle in each contraction is 50%–70%. The reduced ejection fraction [18] is a case which occurs if the ejection fraction is below 40% without much effective contraction by the heart muscles. The causes of HFrEF are Ischemic cardiomyopathy and dilated cardiomyopathy. The diastolic heart failure [19] occurs when there is a normal contraction in heart muscles but no relaxation in ventricles during ventricular filling. With the increasing severity of CVDs, a need for predicting heart failures is on the rise but the traditional methods employed for CVD-related event prediction, unfortunately have failed to achieve the acme of accuracy.

Given a set of medical records as datasets, ML can be employed to achieve high accuracy in the prediction of patient survival and also in determining the driving factors like ejection fraction and serum creatinine [8] that increase mortality among CVD patients.

According to the NYHA, the heart failure is classified into four classes [5] based on the heart failure symptoms. Class I is where the patient experiences asymptomatic left ventricular dysfunction with normal physical activities, Class II with slight symptoms and limited physical activities, Class III with modest symptoms and very few physical activities, and Class IV with severe symptoms on complete rest. The dataset used in this analysis consists of 299 patients with left ventricular dysfunction belonging to Class III or IV [7].

The survival rate and the heart failure hospitalizations of patients suffering from heart failure due to preserved ejection fraction [6] using various ML models like logistic regression, SVM, random forest, and gradient descent boosting are predicted. Lasso regression and forward selection feature selection techniques [4] were used to find that blood urea nitrogen levels, cardiomyopathy questionnaire subscore, and body mass index are the most significant features affecting the survival rate of the patients. The random forest is found to be the best model for predicting the survival rate of the HFpEF patient with an AUC of 0.76.

The decision tree boosting model is trained using 5822 records of the patients in the UCSD Cohort [1, 9] with eight clinical features: diastolic blood pressure, creatinine, blood urea nitrogen, hemoglobin, white blood cell count, platelets, albumin, and red blood cell distribution width. The decision tree is the best classifier with AUC of 0.88. The Cox regression model [2] predicts that age is the most significant feature that affects the survival rate of the patient and with an increase in each year the mortality rate increases by 4%. The next most significant features are ejection fraction and serum creatinine with a p-value of 0.0026, and it is evident that the rate of survival decreases doubly with a one-unit increase in serum creatinine. Serum sodium and anemia were also significant with a p-value of 0.0052 and 0.0096, respectively. Other features like gender, smoking creatinine phosphokinase, and platelets were not significant for predicting the survival rate as these parameters may be significant at the initial stage of heart failure but this analysis contains patients at stage III or IV of heart failure.

The preceding studies presents finding the significant features using statistical methods, which leaves a plenty of space for various ML-based feature selection methods in healthcare services. The aim of this study is to

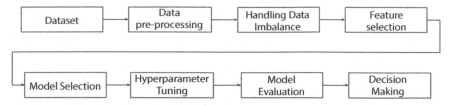

Figure 8.1 Workflow model of proposed system.

address the issue of efficiency using various feature selection methods to rank the importance of the features in predicting the survival rate. Figure 8.1 shows the workflow model of the proposed methodology.

8.3   Data Pre-Processing

Data pre-processing [3] is a cardinal method in data mining technique as it involves cleaning and organizing the data before being used. Processing of data is crucial as it may contain undesirable information such as outliers, noise, duplicate data, and, sometimes, even wrong data which might be misleading. In order to service these complications, data needs to be processed prior to its utilization. Sometimes, data may contain non-numeric and null values or missing attribute values along with imbalanced data. These issues can also be resolved using data pre-processing techniques. The most common procedures involved are data normalization, data wrangling, data resampling, and binning.

8.3.1   Data Imbalance

The distribution of data equally among the classes in the classification problem is one of the most important issues to be addressed to avoid misclassification due to severely skewed classes. There are various techniques to encounter class imbalance problems in the dataset. One of the techniques used for this analysis is Synthetic Minority Oversampling TEchnique (SMOTE).

SMOTE [27] is an oversampling method which is used to scale up the minority class in the dataset. A minority class is a class that is undersampled or in other words has significantly less data samples that fall under it. The presence of such imbalance may cause the training model to often overlook the minority classes; since training models have the propensity to consider the majority classes due to the considerable amount of training data they happen to possess. SMOTE is one of the techniques used to resample the minority classes to achieve equal proportions of data samples as is distributed among other classes. In SMOTE, the oversampling (or resampling) is achieved by considering all the data points that fall under the minority class and connecting each point to its k-nearest homologous neighbors. After repeating this for all the data points, the model artificially synthesizes or creates sample points that lie on the lines joining the original data points. The resampling is done until the data becomes balanced. ADAptive SYNthetic (ADASYN) imbalance learning technique is similar to SMOTE when it comes to the initial oversampling procedures. The data points are connected to each of their k-nearest neighbors and sample points are created on those connecting lines. But in ADASYN, the points are instead placed closer to those lines as opposed to on them, thereby inducing variation in the data samples.

8.4 Feature Selection

Feature selection or variable selection is a cardinal process in the feature engineering technique [14] which is used to reduce the number of dependent variables by picking out only those that have a paramount effect on the target attribute (survival rate in this case). By employing this method, the exhaustive dataset can be reduced in size by pruning away the redundant features [17] that reduces the accuracy of the model. Doing this will help curtail the computational expense of modeling and, in some cases, may also boost the accuracy of the implemented model [13].

The feature selection models applied herein to achieve maximum accuracy in target prediction encompass the following:

1) Extra Tree Classifier
2) Pearson Correlation
3) Forward selection
4) Chi-square
5) Logit (logistic regression model)

The features that recurred in at least three of the above-mentioned models were assumed as having maximum impact on the target variable and were accordingly classified to fit into the employed ML model.

8.4.1 Extra Tree Classifier

The Extra Tree Classifier or the Extremely Random Tree Classifier [21] is an ensemble algorithm that seeds multiple tree models constructed randomly from the training dataset and sorts out the features that have been most voted for. It fits each decision tree on the whole dataset rather than a bootstrap replica and picks out a split point at random to split the nodes. The splitting of nodes occurring at every level of the constituent decision trees are based on the measure of randomness or entropy in the sub-nodes. The nodes are split on all variables available in the dataset and the split that results in the most homogenous sub-childs is selected in the constituent tree models. But unlike other tree-based ensemble algorithms like random forest, an Extra Tree Classifier does not choose the split that results in most homogeneity; instead, it picks a split randomly from the underlying decision tree framework. This lowers the variance and makes the model less prone to overfitting.

8.4.2   Pearson Correlation

Pearson Correlation is used to construct a correlation matrix that measures the linear association between two features and gives a value between -1 and 1, indicating how related the two features are to one another. Correlation is a statistical metric for measuring to what degree two features are interdependent and by computing the association between each feature and the target variable, the one exerting high impact on the target can be picked out. In other words, this model helps determine how a change in one variable reflects on the outcome. The measure of linear association between the features is given by the Pearson Correlation Coefficient which can be computed using the equation:

$$r = \frac{\sum_{i-1}^{n}(x_i - \underline{x})(y_i - \underline{y})}{\sqrt{\sum_{i-1}^{n}(x_i - \underline{x})^2(y_i - \underline{y})^2}}$$

where x_i is the ith value of the variable x, $\underline{x}$ is the average value of sample attribute x, n is the number of records in the dataset, and x and y are the independent and target variables. A value of 1 indicates positive correlation, -1 indicates negative correlation, and 0 indicates no correlation between the features.

8.4.3   Forward Stepwise Selection

Forward selection is a wrapper model that evaluates the predictive power of the features jointly and returns a set of features that performs the best. It adds predictors to the model one at a time and selects the best model for every combination of features based on the cumulative residual sum of squares. The model starts basically with a null value and with each iteration the best of the attributes are chosen and added to the reduced list. The addition of features continues so far as the incoming variable has no impact on the model's prediction and if such a variable is encountered it is simply ignored.

8.4.4   Chi-Square Test

A chi-square test is used in statistical models to check the independence of attributes. The model measures the degree of deviation between the expected and actual response. Lower the value of Chi-square, less dependent the variables are to one another and higher the value more is their correlation. Initially the attributes are assumed to be independent which forms the null hypothesis. The value of the expected outcome is computed using the following formula:

$$E_i = P(x_i \cap y_i) = P(x_i) \times P(y_i)$$

Chi-square is obtained from the expression that goes as follows:

$$\chi^2 = \Sigma_{i=1}^n \frac{O_i - E_i}{E_i}$$

where i is in the range (1, n), n is the number of dataset records, O_i is the actual outcome, and E_i is the expected outcome.

8.5   ML Classifiers Techniques

Classification models predict the classes or categories of given features using a variety of ML models. The classification algorithms can be classified into different models.

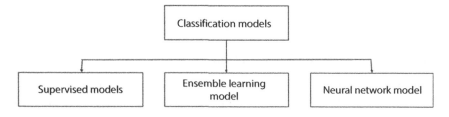

8.5.1   Supervised Machine Learning Models

Supervised learning is a branch of ML wherein a model is trained on a labeled dataset to deduce a learning algorithm. This is achieved by allowing the model to make random predictions and to correct and teach itself using the labels available. This happens iteratively until the learning algorithm specific to the data has been deduced and the model has achieved considerable accuracy. Supervised learning is a powerful technique in training ML models and is predominantly used. It can be classified into regression and classification based on whether the data is continuous or categorical.

8.5.1.1   Logistic Regression

As opposed to its name, a logistic regression model is a binary classification algorithm used when the target variable is categorical, or in other words when the target variable could be grouped into two different classes. The prediction is done by fitting the data to an activation function (a sigmoid logistic function) which returns a value between 0 and 1. The returned value determines how strongly a data entry belongs to one of the binary classes. This approach not only helps achieve higher accuracy but also ensures great precision, which makes it an ubiquitous, fundamental, and handy algorithm for binary classification. This statistical model can be mathematically formulated as follows:

$$y = \sigma\left(\sum_{i=0}^{n} x_i \theta_i \right)$$

where σ is the logistic function applied to a weighted sum of independent variables x_i: $i \in (0, n)$, where n is the total number of data entries available in the dataset. Conventionally, x_0 is assigned the value of 1 which leaves just θ_0 in the sum, which is considered as a bias. A bias term is included so that even when the model is applied over no independent variable or the sum merely cancels all the terms (positive and negative) the final result does not come to be 0. This makes sense because $\sigma(0)$ returns 0.5 which is ambiguous since class prediction becomes vague at that point.

8.5.1.2   SVM

Support Vector Machines (SVM) is a classification algorithm that introduces a best suited decision boundary which splits the dataset accordingly. It is generally used for binary classification but can also be extended to multi-class classification. SVM relies on Support Vectors, which are the data points that are closest to the hyperplane used to classify the dataset. For datasets that cannot be split using a decision boundary, an SVM model uses kernels to extend the data points to a higher dimension and by constructing a hyperplane to separate the classes. The kernels used are of two types: polynomial and radial. SVM models have higher accuracy even when fit to smaller data samples and in some cases may also outperform neural networks.

8.5.1.3   Naive Bayes

Naive Bayes is a fast learning classification algorithm based on Bayes' theorem. The reason it is called naive is because the algorithm supposes the independence of the predictor variables. Or in other words, it assumes that a particular feature is not affected by the presence of other features. For each data point, the algorithm predicts the probability of how related the feature is to that class and the class for which the probability ranks highest is chosen as a probable class [23].

Bayes' theorem can be given as follows:

$$P(c|x_i) = \frac{P(x_i|c)P(c)}{P(x_i)}$$

where $P(c|x_i)$ denotes the conditional probability that the data point may belong to class c provided it belongs to the feature x_i, $i \in (1, n)$, n is the number of data entries.

8.5.1.4   Decision Tree

Decision tree is a classification algorithm that splits the dataset into homogenous classes based on the most significant features [16]. With every split, the resulting sub-node is more homogeneously classified than the previous level. As the name suggests, the algorithm uses a tree-like structure to split the datasets. The best split is identified by a series of computations that include several other methods like Gini score, Chi-square, and Entropy, each of which return a value between 0 and 1. Higher the value of Gini and chi-square and lower the value of entropy, more is the resultant class homogeneity among the sub-nodes when split using that particular feature. However, the downside of this algorithm is that it is sensitive to over-fitting. But even this can be overcome by appropriate measures like setting height or node constraints and tree pruning.

8.5.1.5   K-Nearest Neighbors (KNN)

KNN is used to classify a data point based on the influence exerted upon it by the k neighboring data points. Here, k is a value often input explicitly which denotes the minimum number of neighbors that influence the class that the data point may belong to. The choice of k should not be too low nor too high as it may result in overfitting and data underfitting, respectively. If the value of k is given as 1, then the model is most likely to overfit since the closest point of influence to a particular data point will be the point itself. Such overfitting increases the variance of the model, thereby deeming it unfit for class prediction. Hence, an optimum k value can be computed by plotting the validation error curve. The k value corresponding to the local (or global) minima of the curve can be chosen since it indicates an optimum number of neighboring class influences that will aid the classification of the data point with maximum accuracy.

8.5.2   Ensemble Machine Learning Model

Ensemble learning is a learning algorithm in which multiple models are constructed and combined into one powerful predictive model [24]. Pooling of models into the ensemble helps achieve maximum accuracy than is often obtained from individually trained models. An ensemble aggregates the result of the models based on which it builds a powerful classifier which has low variance and high accuracy. An ensemble can be used to supplement for weaker models that are prone to overfit. Common ensemble methods involve bagging, boosting, and stacking.

8.5.2.1   Random Forest

Random forest classifier is an ensemble tree algorithm which can be applied for both categorical as well as continuous valued data. The "Forest" in the name implies that multiple trees are seeded and grown to the maximum depth, each on a different bootstrap replica of the dataset. Each tree classifier is grown on a randomly selected subset of features from the original dataset and is given the choice to vote for a significant feature. The random forest classifier selects the most-voted class. This algorithm can be extended to both regression as well as classification based models and is prone to outliers and noise in the dataset. While versatile, this algorithm is considered a black-box algorithm due to the fact that most of the random classification, data distribution and "voting" techniques are obscure.

8.5.2.2   AdaBoost

AdaBoost is a boosting algorithm that is used to convert weaker classifiers to strong classifiers. It calculates the weighted sum of all the weak classifiers. The weak classifiers are fit to the dataset and the one that gives the least classification error is chosen. Using this, the weight is calculated and it is updated for every data point. The classifier equation is as follows:

$$F(x) = (+|-)\left(\sum_{i=1}^{n} \theta_i f_i(x) \right)$$

where $f_i(x)$ is the weak classifier and θ_i denotes the calculated weight.

8.5.2.3   Bagging

Bagging is again a tree-ensemble algorithm. It grows decision tree CART models on a subset of the data sample. The decision trees are grown parallely to maximum height and are not pruned. Hence, every tree grown as a part of the ensemble model has high variance and low bias. The CART models vote for a class and the most popular class is chosen. The reason the trees are grown deeper is that the concern of overfitting is less in the bagging algorithm. Therefore, presence of noise does not affect the models performance. The data samples used for growing the trees are randomly selected from the dataset so that the data samples are independent of each other. These are called the bootstrap replica. Fitting these bootstrap samples instead of the entire dataset to the trees increases independence of the sample subsets and thereby decreases output variance.

8.5.3   Neural Network Models

Neural network architecture is collection of interconnected nodes/neurons distributed among different layers like Input layer, hidden layer, and output layer. Based on the number of hidden layers in the architecture the neural network is classified as shallow and deep neural networks. The shallow networks consist of a single hidden layer, whereas deep neural networks consist of two or more hidden layers.

8.5.3.1   *Artificial Neural Network (ANN)*

ANN [11] is a fundamental model in neural networks which works on the basic concepts of Multi-Level Perceptron (MLP). ANN has a series of inputs (continuous or categorical) each with a designated weight. Each of these weighted inputs are summed over multiple latent layers and finally passed through an activation function that generates an output between 0 and 1 or −1 and 1 depending on the function chosen. An ANN is called a Universal Function Approximator due to its potential to fit any non-linear data. Every layer of the network is densely connected, i.e., every neuron is connected to every other neuron and the inputs are processed only in the forward direction; hence, it is also a Feed-Forward Network. The capability to fit any non-linear model is introduced by the activation function, which helps the network uncover complex associations between the input and the output. But ANN is not suitable for back-propagation, in which the weights of the inputs can be altered to minimize the error function at any layer by propagating back.

8.5.3.2   *Convolutional Neural Network (CNN)*

CNN [15] is a neural network model usually used for visual image classification but can also be extended to fit other categorical data as well. A CNN consists of a series of densely connected latent layers of weights and filters between the input and the output. As in a regular neural network, the process involves the element-wise dot product of the input with a set of two-dimensional array of weights, called filter. The result obtained as a result of this weighted sum is a two-dimensional feature map. The elements of the feature map are applied to an activation function (ReLU or softmax), which returns a dichotomous result of 0 or 1 indicating the class to which the particular data belongs [20].

8.6   Hyperparameter Tuning

Hyperparameters are external model configurations that are used to estimate model parameters that cannot be directly estimated. Hyperparameter tuning is a method used to choose the best set of values for the model parameters in order to achieve better accuracy. In grid search tuning [10] method, the method is built over a range of parameter values that is specified explicitly by the practitioner in a grid format. It goes over every combination of model parameter values (each given as a list or an array) and picks out the one that has better performance than the rest.

Since it builds and evaluates the model over every possible parameter combination, grid search tuning is exhaustive and deemed computationally expensive.

In contrast, random search randomly picks out points from the hyperparameter grid and evaluates the model. Also, the number of iterations or the number of combinations to be tried out can be specified externally. This reduces time and the expense of computational power. The best score returned by the random search is based on the randomly chosen hyperparameter grid values, yet this method outperforms Grid Search with comparable accuracy in less time.

8.6.1   Cross-Validation

Cross-validation is a resampling algorithm used to compare different ML models or to find the best tuning parameter for a model. Basically, the dataset is divided into k blocks where k is provided externally, and every block is tested with other blocks as the training set. This is done iteratively for different models [12]. Cross-validation then returns the model that performed the best and with high accuracy. This method helps figure out the best algorithmic model for a given dataset. It is also used in SVM kernels and other similar models for finding hyperparameters.

8.7   Dataset Description

For this study, we used a heart failure clinical dataset containing medical records of patients who had left ventricular systolic dysfunction and with a history of heart failure. The dataset consists of 300 patient's records from Faisalabad Institute of Cardiology, from April to December 2015.

About 64% of the patients in the dataset are Male and the rest 36% are female patients, with their ages ranging between 40 to 95 years old. There are 13 features for each patient in the dataset, out of which 6 features are the clinical variables of the patient like the level of serum creatinine, serum sodium, creatinine phosphokinase, ejection fraction, blood platelets count, and the medical follow-up period of the patients. The target variable in this dataset is the death event feature with binary label, survived patient (death event = 0) and deceased patient (death event = 1). Table 8.1 shows the attributes in the dataset, and Table 8.2 shows the sample dataset taken for analysis.

Table 8.1 Description of each feature in the dataset.

Feature	Description	Measurement
Age	Age of the patient	Years
Anemia	Decrease of hemoglobin	Boolean
High blood pressure	If a patient is hypotensive	Boolean
Creatinine phosphokinase (CPK)	Level of CPK enzyme in the blood	mcg/L
Diabetes	If a patient is diabetic	Boolean
Ejection fraction (EF)	Percentage of blood leaving heart at each contraction	Percentage
Sex	Woman or man	Boolean
Platelets	Blood Platelets	Kiloplatelets/ mL
Serum creatinine	Level of creatinine in blood	mg/dL
Serum sodium	Level of sodium in blood	mEq/L
Smoking	If the patient smokes	Boolean
Time	Follow-up time of the patient	Days
Death event	If the patient died during the follow-up time	Boolean

Table 8.2 Sample dataset.

Age	Anemia	Creatinine_ phosphokinase	Diabetes	Ejection_ fraction	High_ blood_ pressure	Platelets	Serum_ creatinine	Serum_ sodium	Sex	Smoking	Time	Death event
75	0	582	0	20	1	265,000	1.9	130	1	0	4	1
55	0	7,861	0	38	0	263,358.03	1.1	136	1	0	6	1
65	0	146	0	20	0	162,000	1.3	129	1	1	7	1
50	1	111	0	20	0	210,000	1.9	137	1	0	7	1
65	1	160	1	20	0	327,000	2.7	116	0	0	8	1

8.7.1   Data Pre-Processing

In this study, the goal is to predict the survival rate of a patient with a history of heart failure and Figure 8.2 shows the complete architecture of the proposed system. There is a moderate class imbalance in these data; only 33% of the records contain information about the deceased patients as shown in Figure 8.3. This imbalance in classes will generate a biased model impacting the analysis. To address the class imbalance problem, we applied SMOTE to increase the number of records in the death event attribute.

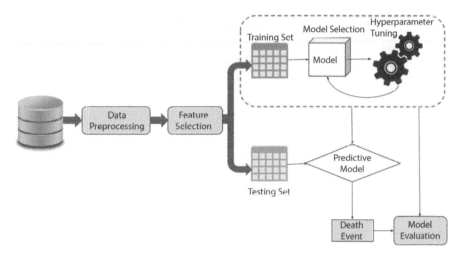

Figure 8.2 Architecture of proposed system.

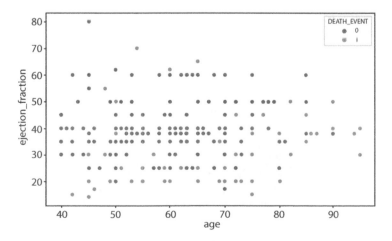

Figure 8.3 Original dataset distribution.

After applying sampling techniques, the number of records is increased to 406 with 203 numbers of entries for each class. Figure 8.4 shows how different SMOTE-based resampling techniques work out to deal with imbalanced data.

Figure 8.5 shows the distribution of target class (DEATH_EVENT) and it is evident from the plot that class 0 is the majority class and class 1 is minority class. After applying SMOTE resampling technique the classes are balanced with 203 records under each class as shown in Figures 8.4 and 8.6.

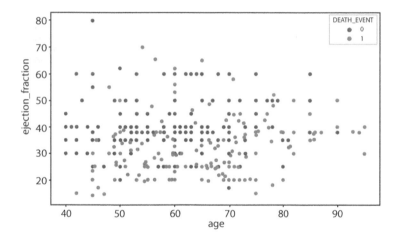

Figure 8.4 Resampling using SMOTE.

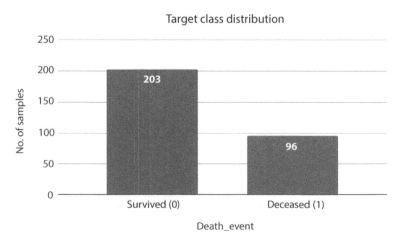

Figure 8.5 Target class distribution.

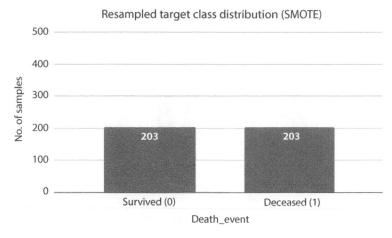

Figure 8.6 Resampled distribution applying SMOTE.

8.7.2 Feature Selection

The dataset consists of 13 attributes of which 3 most relevant features are selected using various feature selection algorithms, Extra Tree Classifier, Forward selection, Chi-square, Pearson Correlation, and Logit model. The Extra Tree Classifier generates the follow-up time, ejection fraction, and serum creatinine as the most important features that influence the survival rate of the heart failure patient as shown in Figure 8.7. Forward feature selection results show that age, ejection fraction, and serum creatinine as the top features.

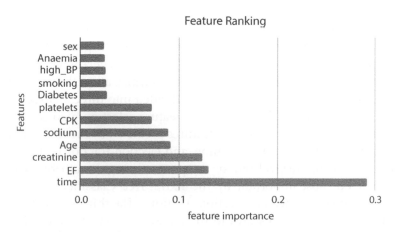

Figure 8.7 Feature ranking using Extra tree classifier.

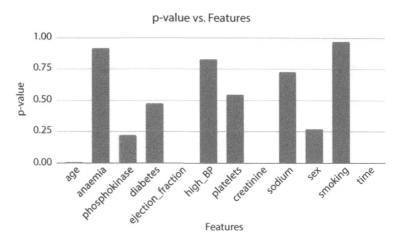

Figure 8.8 p-values of the features.

From Extra Tree Classifier, Pearson Correlation, and Logit model, the hypothesis suggests that time, ejection fraction, and serum creatinine as the top three most significant features. Whereas the other models, Forward Selection and Chi-Square generate that age, ejection fraction, and serum creatinine as the three most significant features. The p-values of ejection fraction, serum creatinine, and time are 0.0 (as shown in Figure 8.8) and are the most significant factors affecting the survival rate of the heart failure patient.

8.7.3   Model Selection

For the analysis, the dataset was split into 80% and 20% of the data as training and testing samples respectively. The model is trained for a two-class problem where the patient's survival rate is predicted given the medical parameters of the patient. The patient is classified as deceased or survived based on the most important medical features which affect the survival rate of the heart failure patient. The study is divided into three analyses based on the features selected by the various feature selection algorithms. The first study considers the important features predicted by the forward selection algorithm (age, serum creatinine, and ejection fraction). The second study predicts the survival rate of the patient using the attributes which are predicted most important by the Extra Tree Classifier and p-value (time, serum creatinine, and ejection fraction). The third study trains the ML model using all 13 features in the dataset to predict the death event of the patient. The dataset is trained on different ML models and neural networks, Logistic regression, Naive Bayes, SVM, Decision tree, Random forest, K-nearest neighbors, Bagging, AdaBoost, XGBoost, ANN, and Convolutional Neural Network. The hyperparameters of the models are tuned during the learning process using Grid Search and cross-validation techniques to optimize the model and minimize the loss by providing better results. For models such as SVM, neural networks, random forest, and decision trees where hyperparameter tuning is applied, the dataset is split into 70% of training samples, 15% of validation samples, and 15% as testing samples.

8.7.4 Model Evaluation

The classification model can be evaluated with the N × N confusion matrix, where N is the number of classes. The matrix compares the predicted variables and the actual variable to evaluate how well the model performs.

The 2 × 2 matrix contains four values: True Positive (TP), True Negative (TN), False Positive (FP), False Negative (FN). The rows and columns of the matrix represent the actual and predicted values. The confusion matrix for the target variable (Death_Event) is found, and the performance of the supervised models trained is quantified using classification evaluation metrics accuracy and F1-score.

8.8 Experiments and Results

In this section, we elucidate the results obtained for the prediction of survival rate using the three parameters: follow-up time, ejection fraction, and serum creatinine, the results of prediction using age, ejection fraction, and serum creatinine as the dependent features, and the results of prediction using all the features in the clinical records (Table 8.3).

Table 8.3 Experiments description.

Study	Selected features
1	All features
2	Age, ejection fraction, and serum creatinine
3	Time, ejection fraction, and serum creatinine

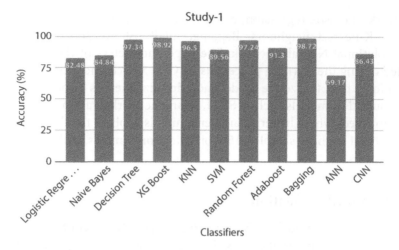

Figure 8.9 Performance evaluation of models under study 1 with dataset size = 1,000.

8.8.1   Study 1: Survival Prediction Using All Clinical Features

The dataset is preprocessed with various pre-processing techniques like applying SMOTE to handle the imbalance in the classes, logarithmic transformations to remove outliers in the features, and applying one hot encoding on the categorical variables to convert them into numerical values. All 12 attributes in the dataset are considered for training them in various ML and DNN classifiers. The prediction shows (Figure 8.9) that XGBoost is the best classifier with 98% accuracy and also correctly predicts the majority of the positive class with accuracy of 94% on the positive class. ANN is the least classifier among all the classifiers with F1-score of 0.60. CNN is found to perform better than ANN which is not the case in the previous study. Table 8.4 shows the accuracy scores of the classifiers that are trained on different sample sizes of dataset. The models show better performance when the data size is upsampled as 1,000 for analysis.

8.8.2   Study 2: Survival Prediction Using Age, Ejection Fraction and Serum Creatinine

The feature age is identified as one of the important features by forward selection feature selection algorithm and chi-square test. The chi-square test exhibits age, ejection fraction, and serum creatinine as the significant features with p-value close to 0. The ML and neural network classifiers are trained with the clinical parameters that are found significant by the

Table 8.4 Accuracy scores (in %) of all classifiers on different data size.

Classifiers	Data size = 200	Data size = 500	Data size = 1,000
Logistic Regression	77.3	81.51	82.48
Naive Bayes	79.52	82.87	84.84
Decision Tree	86.2	89.97	97.34
XG Boost	88.7	91.7	98.92
KNN	65.76	81.33	96.5
SVM	74.83	85.2	89.56
Random Forest	88.16	89.87	97.24
AdaBoost	86.9	85.2	91.3
Bagging	86.43	88.64	98.72
ANN	60.91	84.84	69.17
CNN	78.66	80.3	86.43

chi square test as the predictor variable to predict the survival rate. The performance metrics (Figure 8.10) shows that Bagging is the best classifier for predicting deceased patients with the leading accuracy of 98% and F1-score of 0.97 for data size = 1,000. Among neural network classifiers, outperforms CNN with the accuracy score of 82%, while ANN is the least classifier among all the algorithms with the accuracy score of 77.8%. Table 8.5 shows the accuracy scores of classifiers on different sizes of data and can be interpreted that the performance is increased with increase in size of the dataset.

8.8.3 Study 3: Survival Prediction Using Time, Ejection Fraction, and Serum Creatinine

The follow-up time, ejection fraction, and serum creatinine were obtained as the top three important features that affect the survival rate of the heart failure patient using extra tree classifier. The statistics of logit model is also used to find the feature importance with respect to the response variable. The logit statistics test showed that the p-value is close to 0 for time, ejection fraction, and serum creatinine. These three features are used as the

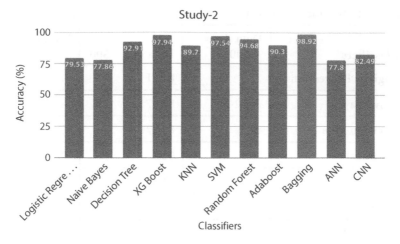

Figure 8.10 Performance evaluation of models under study 2 with data size = 1,000.

Table 8.5 Accuracy scores (in %) of all classifiers on different data size.

Classifiers	Data size = 200	Data size = 500	Data size = 1,000
Logistic Regression	73.87	69.1	79.53
Naive Bayes	73.67	72.47	77.86
Decision Tree	80.3	82.49	92.91
XG Boost	79.6	84.85	97.94
KNN	79.79	80.1	89.7
SVM	79.08	84.44	97.54
Random Forest	81.25	86.03	94.68
AdaBoost	77.1	77.8	90.3
Bagging	80.52	88.57	98.92
ANN	77.08	63.4	77.8
CNN	62.6	74.93	82.49

predictor variables in predicting the death event of the patient. The dataset is balanced using the SMOTE algorithm and then trained using various ML models. For models such as SVM, decision tree, CNN, ANN, KNN, and random forest, the dataset is split into 70% for training, 15% for validation,

Table 8.6 Accuracy scores (in %) of all classifiers on different data size.

Classifiers	Data size = 200	Data size = 500	Data size = 1,000
Logistic Regression	73.87	81.51	82.48
Naive Bayes	73.67	82.87	84.55
Decision Tree	80.3	89.97	96.65
XG Boost	79.6	91.7	99.11
KNN	79.79	81.33	92.7
SVM	79.08	85.2	97.44
Random Forest	81.25	89.87	95.96
AdaBoost	77.1	85.2	90.3
Bagging	80.52	88.64	98.92
ANN	77.08	84.84	85.5
CNN	62.6	80.3	88.16

and 15% for testing. The hyperparameters for these models are selected using the Grid Search algorithm in order to get the optimized result. For other models like Naive Bayes, XGBoost, AdaBoost, Bagging, and logistic regression classifiers, the data is split into 80% for training and 20% for testing.

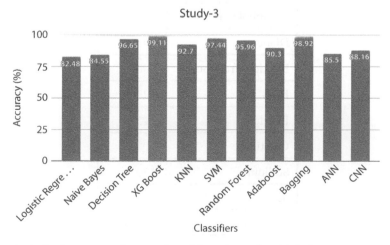

Figure 8.11 Performance evaluation of models under study 3 With dataset size = 1,000.

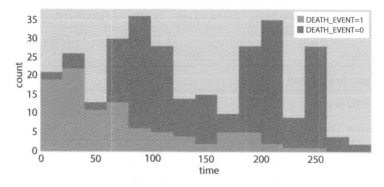

Figure 8.12 Correlation between follow-up time and death event.

Among the ML models (Table 8.6), XGBoost classifier and Bagging classifier outperform other models with highest accuracy of 99% and top F1-score of 0.96 when the dataset size is 1,000. Naive Bayes achieved a top accuracy of 92% and correctly classified the majority of the survived patients (49/53) than any other classifier. Random forest predicts correctly the majority of the patients who have less chance of survival achieving an accuracy of 82% on the positive class. The Convolution Neural Network

Table 8.7 Logit model statistical test.

Features	p-value
Age	0.07
Anemia	0.39
Phosphokinase	0.04
Diabetes	0.98
Ejection_fraction	0.00
High_BP	0.27
Platelets	0.15
Creatinine	0.00
Sodium	0.20
Sex	0.96
Smoking	0.86
Time	0.00

Table 8.8 Chi-square test.

Features	p-value
Age	0.000
Anemia	0.9178
Phosphokinase	0.2203
Diabetes	0.4751
Ejection_fraction	0
High_BP	0.8282
Platelets	0.545
Creatinine	0.0001
Sodium	0.7225
Sex	0.2727
Smoking	0.9677
Time	0.007

and ANN obtain the accuracy of 80% and 84%, respectively. The ANN is the least performing classifier with an accuracy of 85%. Figure 8.11 shows the performance metrics comparison among all the models which are trained with sample size of 1,000 records.

Though the classifiers perform well given time, ejection fraction, and serum creatinine as the medical features for predicting the survival rate, the correlation between the follow-up time and the patient's survival rate is investigated. Figure 8.12 shows that, as the follow time increases, the patients who have deceased (Death_event = 1) is very minimum compared to the patients at the initial trial of medication. Even though there is no complete linear correlation between the follow-up time and the survival rate, it is one of the important parameters and cannot be eliminated completely. The p-values obtained using statistical Logit model is shown in Table 8.7 and chi-square test values for study-2 is depicted in Table 8.8.

8.8.4 Comparison Between Study 1, Study 2, and Study 3

Supervised models like Logistic regression, Naive Bayes, Decision Tree, KNN, and SVM perform better when extra tree classifier is used for feature selection (study 3) compared to the other two studies (Figure 8.13).

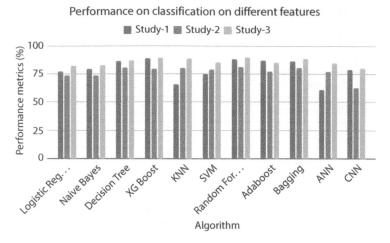

Figure 8.13 Performance evaluation of models on different classifiers.

Among neural network classifiers, ANN performs least when all features are considered for training, and the highest performance is seen in the study 3, while CNN is the least performer in the study 2 but brings about comparatively better results in study 1 and study 3. Ensemble models like XGBoost, Random Forest, and Bagging show a best performance for all the three studies irrespective of the features considered for training. Overall, all models used for prediction perform extremely well when they are trained with time, ejection fraction, and serum creatinine as the predictor variables. In most of the cases, the models do not perform well when age is considered as one of the features. The findings from the statistical and performance analysis show that age may not be a significant factor which affects the survival rate of the patient. Also, other factors like cholesterol, high blood pressure, and smoking are not found to be significant factors that affect the survival rate of the heart failure patient. One of the ground causes of this may be these factors are basically the features which influence heart failure at the early stage, but this study is concerned with the patients at the advanced level of heart failure. The first study, i.e., the one with follow-up time, serum creatinine, and ejection fraction, showed maximum accuracy thereby implying the influence of these factors on a CVD patient's survival.

8.8.5 Comparative Study on Different Sizes of Data

To analyze how the size of the dataset affects the model performance, the initial dataset containing 299 records is upsampled to 508 and 1,000 using upsampling technique to account for the problem of data imbalance.

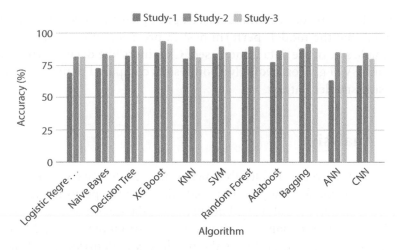

Figure 8.14 Performance evaluation of models on dataset size = 508.

Figure 8.14 shows that there is a significant increase in the accuracy of the trained models when the dataset is increased to 508. XGBoost ensemble model which outperforms in the previous analysis (Figure 8.13) shows the same nature when the dataset size is increased with the accuracy score elevating to 93%. In neural network classifier models, there is an increase in trend when the dataset size is increased. To further improve the quality and precision of the model, the sample size is increased to 1,000. Figure 8.15 shows the accuracy results obtained by all the classification algorithms on the three different studies when trained with

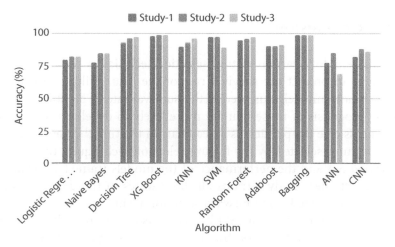

Figure 8.15 Performance evaluation of models on dataset size = 1,000.

the number of records in the dataset upsampled to 1,000 records. It is observed that the models perform best in precision and accuracy when the sample size of the data is increased. Classifiers like decision tree, bagging, and SVM give exceedingly good results compared to previous analysis using smaller dataset.

8.9   Analysis

There is no universal model that performs best for the whole pool of datasets available for analysis. The prediction and the performance of the model depend on the nature and quality of the dataset on which the model is trained. From our analysis, it shows that the ensemble models XGBoost and random forest out performs the baseline ML algorithms and neural networks for the considered dataset. The tree-based model gives a decent result in a fast manner, whereas neural networks lack the one reason for this contusion that is the size of the data. Neural networks like CNN require a large and feature engineered dataset to train on and hypertuned parameters to outperform in the evaluation. With increasing dataset, the performance of CNN is also observed to be increasing, but XGBoost gives the desired results with 1,000 records itself and further increasing the dataset samples may cause the ML models to overfit even though neural networks may see an increasing trend. Hence, ensemble and ML classifier models are adequate for the prediction of survival rate of the heart failure patient with minimum resources and reduced time complexity.

8.10   Conclusion

Our work employs various feature selection techniques and classification algorithms to predict the survival rate of the heart failure patient. This approach not only helps us predict the survival rate of a patient but also in early prognosis of those that are more likely to develop CVDs and in that process give the physicians a headstart in treating the patients. Based on the features selected by the feature selection techniques, three studies are carried out and the performance of the models trained are evaluated for all the studies. Study 1 trains all the features in the dataset. Study 2 uses features selected using forward selection techniques: age, serum creatinine, and ejection fraction. Study 3 consists of features follow-up time, serum creatinine, and ejection fraction selected using extra tree classifier. The classification models are applied on the features selected in each study.

From the results obtained in the study, it is interpreted that XGBoost and random forest from the ensemble model are the overall best performers in all three studies for the given heart failure dataset. Study 3 which applies time, serum creatinine, and ejection fraction as the most important features performs best on all classification models compared to other two studies. Furthermore, to enhance the performance of the classifiers, all three studies are repeated on different dataset sizes, and it is observed that XGBoost performs well in this case also.

This work concentrates on the static data of heart failure patients collected from the clinical trial; furthermore, this work can be extended to real-time monitoring of patients using mobile application. Real-time monitoring of patient's clinical features using wearable devices can be a supportive technology for doctors with less experience in that subject matter and also for the patients and their family for the early detection of heart failure.

References

1. Adler, E.D., Voors, A.A., Klein, L., Macheret, F., Braun, O.O., Improving risk prediction in heart failure using machine learning. *Eur. J. Heart Fail.*, 22, 1, 139–147, 2020, 10.1002/ejhf.1628.
2. Ahmad, T., Munir, A., Bhatti, S.H., Survival analysis of heart failure patients: A case study. *PLoS One*, 12, 7, 2017.
3. Alasadi, S.A. and Bhaya, W.S., Review of data pre-processing techniques in data mining. *J. Eng. Appl. Sci.*, 12, 16, 4102–4107, 2017, 10.3923/jeasci.2017.4102.4107.
4. Angraal, S., Mortazavi, B.J., Gupta, A., Khera, R., Ahmad, T., Desai, N.R., Jacoby, D.L., Machine Learning Prediction of Mortality and Hospitalization in Heart Failure With Preserved Ejection Fraction. *JACC: Heart Fail.*, 8, 1, 12–21, 2020, 10.1016/j.jchf.2019.06.013.
5. Bennett, J.A., Riegel, B., Bittner, V., Nichols, J., Validity and reliability of the NYHA classes for measuring research outcomes in patients with cardiac disease. *Heart Lung: J. Acute Crit. Care*, 31, 4, 62–70, 10.1067/mhl.2002.124554.
6. Borlaug, B.A., Evaluation and management of heart failure with preserved ejection fraction. *Nat. Rev. Cardiol.*, 17, 9, 559–573, 2020, 10.1038/s41569-020-0363-2.
7. Charlene, B., Margherita, M., Alexander, K., Rafael, A.-G., Lorna, S., New York Heart Association (NYHA) classification in adults with congenital heart disease: Relation to objective measures of exercise and outcome. *Eur. Heart J. - Qual. Care Clin. Outcomes*, 4, 1, 51–58, 2018, 10.1093/ehjqcco/qcx031.

8. Chicco, D. and Jurman, G., Machine learning can predict survival of patients with heart failure from serum creatinine and ejection fraction alone. *BMC Med. Inf. Decis. Making*, 20, 1, 2020, 10.1186/s12911-020-1023-5.

9. Chiew, C.J., Liu, N., Tagami, T., Wong, T.H., Heart rate variability based machine learning models for risk prediction of suspected sepsis patients in the emergency department. *Med. (United States)*, 98, 6, 2019.

10. Hatem, F.A. and Amir, A.F., Speed up grid-search for parameter selection of support vector machines. *Appl. Soft Comput. J.*, 80, 202–210, 2019, 10.1016/j.asoc.2019.03.037.

11. Javeed, A., Rizvi, S.S., Zhou, S., Riaz, R., Khan, S.U., Kwon, S.J., Heart risk failure prediction using a novel feature selection method for feature refinement and neural network for classification. *Mob. Inf. Syst.*, 2020, 2020, 10.1155/2020/8843115.

12. Mary, B., Brindha, G.R., Santhi, B., Kanimozhi, G., Computational models for predicting anticancer drug efficacy: A multi linear regression analysis based on molecular, cellular and clinical data of Oral Squamous Cell Carcinoma cohort. *Comput. Methods Programs Biomed.*, 178, 105–112, 2019, 10.1016/j.cmpb.2019.06.011.

13. Nithya, R. and Santhi, B., Comparative study on feature extraction method for breast cancer classification. *J. Theor. Appl. Inf. Technol.*, 31, 2, 220–226, 2011.

14. Nithya, R. and Santhi, B., Mammogram classification using maximum difference feature selection method. *J. Theor. Appl. Inf. Technol.*, 33, 2, 197–204, 2011.

15. Nithya, R. and Santhi, B., Breast cancer diagnosis in digital mammograms using statistical features and neural networks. *Res. J. Appl. Sci. Eng. Tech.*, 4, 24, 5480–5483, 2012.

16. Nithya, R. and Santhi, B., Decision tree classifiers for mass classification. *Int. J. Signal Imaging Syst. Eng.*, 8, 1–2, 39–45, 2015, 10.1504/IJSISE.2015.067068.

17. Nithya, R. and Santhi, B., Application of texture analysis method for mammogram density classification. *J. Instrum.*, 12, P07009–P07009, 2017, 10.1088/1748-0221/12/07/P07009.

18. Packer, M., What causes sudden death in patients with chronic heart failure and a reduced ejection fraction. *Eur. Heart J.*, 41, 18, 15229645, 2020.

19. Pfeffer, M.A., Shah, A.M., Borlaug, B.A., Heart Failure with Preserved Ejection Fraction in Perspective. *Circ. Res.*, 124, 11, 1598–1617, 2019, 10.1161/CIRCRESAHA.119.313572.

20. Rishiikeshwer, S., Shriram, T., Raju, J., Hari, M., Santhi, B., Brindha, G.R., Farmer-Friendly Mobile Application for Automated Leaf Disease Detection of Real-Time Augmented Data Set using Convolution Neural Networks. *J. Comput. Sci.*, 16, 158–166, 2020, 10.3844/jcssp.2020.158.166.

21. Saeys, Y., Abeel, T., Van De Peer, Y., Robust feature selection using ensemble feature selection techniques. *Lect. Notes Comput. Sci. (including subseries Lecture Notes Artificial Intelligence and Lecture Notes in Bioinformatics)*, 5212 LNAI, PART 2, 313–325, 2008, 10.1007/978-3-540-87481-2_21.

22. Shakthi, K.P.A., Brindha, G.R., Bharathi, N., Enhanced classification through improved feature selection technique. *Int. J. Mech. Eng. Technol.*, 8, 10, 342–351, 2017.
23. Suresh, A., Aashish, S., Santhi, B., Multi classifier analysis using data mining classification algorithms. *Int. J. Appl. Eng. Res.*, 9, 22, 13047–13060, 2014.
24. Taha, K., An Ensemble-based approach to the development of clinical prediction models for future-onset heart failure and coronary artery disease using machine learning. *J. Am. Coll. Cardiol.*, 75, 11, 2046, 2020.
25. Timmis, A., Townsend, N., Gale, C., Torbica, A., Lettino, M., European society of cardiology: Cardiovascular disease statistics 2019. *Eur. Heart J.*, 41, 1, 12–85, 2020, 10.1093/eurheartj/ehz859.
26. Wang, Z., Zhu, Y., Li, D., Yin, Y., Zhang, J., Feature rearrangement based deep learning system for predicting heart failure mortality. *Comput. Methods Programs Biomed.*, 191, 2020, 10.1016/j.cmpb.2020.105383.
27. Yan, Y., Liu, R., Ding, Z., Du, X., Chen, J., Zhang, Y., A parameter-free cleaning method for SMOTE in imbalanced classification. *IEEE Access*, 7, 23537–23548, 2019, 10.1109/ACCESS.2019.2899467.

9

A Novel Convolutional Neural Network Model to Predict Software Defects

Kumar Rajnish*, Vandana Bhattacharjee and Mansi Gupta

Department of CSE, BIT Mesra, Ranchi, India

Abstract

Machine learning (ML) is becoming increasingly important as a research tool due to its various frameworks and learning approaches. With the ever-increasing scale of software, reliability has become a crucial issue and software defect prediction is utilized to assist developers in finding potential defect and allocating their testing efforts. Traditional methods of software defect prediction mainly focus on designing static code metrics which are fed into ML classifiers to predict defects in the code. Even with the same ML techniques, many researchers apply statistical approaches to classify software modules and decide whether each module is defect prone or not and, accordingly, train their model. Deep neural network (DNN) and convolutional neural network (CNN) models built by the appropriate design decisions are crucial to obtain the desired classifier performance. This is especially significant when predicting fault proneness of software modules. When correctly identified, this could help in reducing the testing cost by directing the efforts more toward the modules identified to be fault prone. This paper proposed a **Novel CNN** (NCNN) model to predict software defects. The framework used is Python Programming Language with Keras and TensorFlow. A comparative analysis with ML algorithms [such as Random Forest (RF), Decision Trees (DT), and Naïve Bayes (NB)] and DNN model in terms of F-measure (known as F1-score), recall, precision, and accuracy has been presented from four NASA system data sets (KC1, PC1, PC2, and KC3) selected from PROMISE repository. The experimental results indicated that NCNN model was comparable to the existing classifiers and outperformed them in most of the experiments.

*Corresponding author: krajnish@bitmesra.ac.in

Pradeep Singh (ed.) Fundamentals and Methods of Machine and Deep Learning: Algorithms, Tools and Applications, (211–236) © 2022 Scrivener Publishing LLC

Keywords: Machine learning, software defect prediction, CNN model, deep learning, metrics

9.1 Introduction

The increasing complexity of modern software has raised the importance of software reliability. Building highly reliable software requires a substantial amount of testing and debugging. Due to limited budget and time, these efforts must be prioritized for better efficiency. As a result, software defect prediction methods, which predict the occurrence of defects, have been widely used to assist developers in prioritizing their testing and debugging efforts [1].

Software defect prediction [2–5] is the process of building classifiers to predict defects that occur in a definite area of source code. The prediction results can contribute developers in ordering their testing and debugging efforts. From the viewpoint of prediction hardness, software defect prediction can include method-level, class-level, file-level, package-level, and change-level defect prediction. In this research, we focused on file-level defect prediction. Typical software defect prediction [6] relies on extracting features from software artifacts and building classification models using various machine learning (ML) algorithms for training and validation.

Previous research on software defect prediction methods initially used code metrics or simply software metrics and statistical approach for fault prediction. Thereafter, the focus shifted to soft computing and ML techniques which took over all the prediction techniques [7]. In software code metric–based methods, internal attributes of the software were measured for fault prediction. The commonly used software metrics suites were QMOOD metric suite [8], Chidamber and Kemerer (CK) metric suite [9], MOOD metric suite [10], etc. From the perspective of ML, fault prediction comes under classification task in which it discriminates faulty and non-faulty modules [11]. Some representative ML methods are Ensemble, Support Vector Machine (SVM), Naïve Bayes (NB), Logistic Regression, Decision Table, etc., and a review of such techniques applied to software fault prediction is given in [12].

For this study, we proposed NCNN model for software defect prediction. The role of number of layers, nodes in each layer, learning rate, loss function, optimizer, and regularization methods have been studied. We evaluate NCNN model on four NASA system data sets (KC1, PC1, PC2, and KC3) are selected from PROMISE repository [13] to confirm that proposed NCNN model was comparable to or better than existing state-of-the-art models [such as Random Forest (RF), Decision Tree (DT), and NB] [12] and Deep Neural Network (DNN) [14] in terms of F-measure (known as F1-score), recall, precision, and accuracy. The experimental results indicated that NCNN model was comparable to the existing classifiers and outperformed.

The rest of the sections in this paper are organized as follows: Section 9.2 presents the related work. Section 9.3 gives the theoretical background on convolutional neural network (CNN) and software defect prediction. Section 9.4 presents the experimental setup. Section 9.5 gives the results and analysis. Finally, Section 9.6 concludes the paper.

9.2 Related Works

This section presents the literature review of research papers on software defect prediction based on deep learning, defect prediction based on deep features, and deep learning in software engineering.

9.2.1 Software Defect Prediction Based on Deep Learning

Singh *et al.* [15] used public data set AR1 for predicting fault proneness of modules. They compared logistic regression technique with six ML classifiers (DT, group method of data handling polynomial method, artificial neural network (ANN), gene expression programming, SVM, and cascade correlation network). The performance was compared by computing the area under the curve using Receiver Operating Characteristic (ROC) analysis where it was concluded that the value generated by DT was 0.865 which outperformed regression and other ML techniques. Dejaeger *et al.* [16] considered 15 distinct Bayesian Network (BN) classifiers and comparison was done with ML techniques. For the purpose of feature selection, Markov blanket principle was used. AUC and H-measure was tested using statistical framework of Demšar. The result showed that simple and comprehensible networks having a smaller number of nodes can be constructed using BN classifiers other than the NB classifier. Kumar *et al.* [17] experimented on 30 open-source projects to build a ML-based model for software fault prediction model using Least Square SVM (LSSVM). They applied 10 distinct feature selection techniques. Their prediction model was only appropriate for project with faulty classes less than the threshold value. B. Twala [18] performed software fault prediction on four NASA public data sets using DT, SVM,

K-Nearest Neighbor, and NB. He concluded that NB classifier was most robust and DT classifier the most accurate.

9.2.2   Software Defect Prediction Based on Deep Features

S. Wang *et al.* [19] proposed a representation learning algorithm using Deep Belief Network (DBN) which helps in learning semantic program representation directly from source code. They worked on 10 open-source projects and showed that directly learned semantic features considerably improve both within- and cross-project defect prediction (WPDP and CPDP). On an average, WPDP was improved by 14.2% in F1, 11.5% in recall, and 14.7% in precision. CPDP approach beats TCA+ having traditional features by 8.9% in F1. Miholca *et al.* [20] proposed HYGRAR, a non-linear hybrid supervised classification method for software fault prediction. HYGRAR combined relational association rule mining and ANNs to distinguish between faulty and non-faulty software objects. For experiment purposes, they used 10 open-source data sets and validated the outstanding performance of the HYGRAR classifier. J. Li *et al.* [21] proposed a framework called Defect Prediction via CNN (DP-CNN) that used deep learning in order to effectively generate features. On the bases of program's Abstract Syntax Trees (ASTs), they initially extracted token vectors and then encoded them as numerical vectors with the help of the process of word embedding and word mapping. Then, these numerical vectors were fed into CNN that automatically learnt structural and semantic program features. After this, for perfect software fault prediction, they combined traditional hand-crafted features with the learnt features. The experiment was conducted on seven open source project data. The measurement was done on the basis of F-measure. The final results showed that DP-CNN improves the state-of-the-art method by 12%. Cong Pan *et al.* [22] proposed an improved CNN model for WPDP and compared their results to existing CNN results and an empirical study. Their experiment was based on a 30-repetition holdout validation and a 10 * 10 cross-validation. Experimental results showed that their improved CNN model was comparable to the existing CNN model, and it outperformed the state-of-the-art ML models significantly for WPDP. Furthermore, they defined hyperparameter instability and examined the threat and opportunity it presents for deep learning models on defect prediction.

9.2.3   Deep Learning in Software Engineering

Apart from software defect prediction, deep learning models have been used in software maintenance [23], code clone detection [24], defect detection [25], and other areas. Guo *et al.* [23] used a Recurrent Neural Network (RNN) model in software maintenance to create links between requirements, design, source code, test cases, and other artifacts. Li *et al.* [24] proposed a deep learning-based clone detection approach. In their paper, they used ASTs tokens to represent method-level code clones and non-clones to train a classifier, and classifier used to detect code clones. Their methods accomplished similar performance with low time cost. Nguyen *et al.* [25] in defect prediction used DNN for bug localization. Their model aim was to solve lexical mismatch problem, and pointed out that the terms used in bug report are different from the terms and code tokens used in source files. Their model achieved 70% accuracy with five recommended files.

Other software engineering areas influenced by deep learning are source code organization [26], run-time behavior analysis [27], feature position [28], vulnerability analysis [29], and code novelist identification [30].

9.3 Theoretical Background

9.3.1 Software Defect Prediction

Figure 9.1 presents a typical file level defect prediction process based on ML concepts, which is adopted by many researchers in most recent studies. From Figure 9.1, the first step of the procedure is to extract program modules (i.e., source files) from the repositories. The second step is to cate gorized program modules defect (i.e., buggy) or no-defect (i.e., clean). The categorization is based on post-release defects collected from PROMISE repository (i.e., NASA Metrics Data Program). The third step is to extract features from the categorized program modules to form training instances. The features consist of code and design metrics. The fourth step is to build

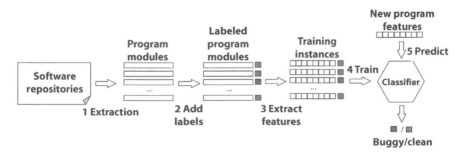

Figure 9.1 File level defect prediction process.

a classification model and use training instances to train the model. In our case, we had selected three ML models (RF, DT, and NB) as well as DNN for comparative analysis with our proposed NCNN model. The last step is to feed new program feature instances into the trained classifier to predict whether a source file is defective or non-defective (Buggy/Clean).

9.3.2   Convolutional Neural Network

CNN is a special kind of neural network which is used to process data and has a recognized, grid-like topology [31] such as one-dimensional (1D) time series data and 2D image data. CNN has been extremely successful in practical applications, with speech recognition [32], image classification [33], and natural language processing [34, 35]. In our work, we influenced our proposed model to extract features from software repositories (i.e., source files).

Figure 9.2 demonstrates a basic CNN architecture. It consists of convolutional layers, pooling layers, and a simple fully connected network, along with a dense network. Neuron units are also connected to all neuron units of its neighboring layers. Even neural units connected to these two layers are sparsely connected, which is determined by kernel size and pooling size. The architecture represents the two features of CNN: sparse connectivity and shared weights, which allows CNN to capture local structural information of inputs.

The sparse connectivity property means that each neuron is connected to only a limited number of other neurons, and in CNN, it is controlled by kernel size and pooling size. From Figure 9.2, if we take node V_3 and kernel size 3, it only affects three nodes in convolutional layer, i.e., h_1, h_2, and h_3, whereas node h_4 is not affected by V_3. Each subset acts as a local filter

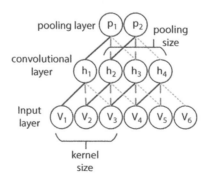

Figure 9.2 A basic convolutional neural network (CNN) architecture.

connecting to the next layer in CNN which produce strong responses to a spatially local input pattern. To find the output to the next layer, each local filter will multiply by outputs from the previous layer, then add a bias and perform a non-linear transformation. From Figure 9.2, it is observed that the ith neuron in the mth layer (convolutional layer) as h_i^m, the weights of the ith neuron in the $(m-1)^{th}$ layer as W_i^{m-1}, the bias in the $(m-1)^{th}$ layer as b^{m-1}, and, in our work, we use rectified linear units (RELUs) which were recently shown to give a better performance in many neural network classifications tasks. The out can be calculated as follows:

$$h_i^m = ReLU(W_i^{m-1} * V_i^{m-1} + b^{m-l})$$ (9.1)

To produce values from output layer, Softmax activation function is used which is also a type of sigmoid function. Softmax normalizes each neuron's output to a range 1 and 0. It is non-linear in nature. It is usually used when we are trying to handle multiple classes.

The mathematical expression for Softmax activation function is as follows:

$$\sigma(z)_i = \frac{e^{zi}}{\sum_{j=1}^{K} e^{zj}}$$ (9.2)

where

z: The input vector to the softmax function.

zi: All the zi values are the elements of the input vector to the softmax function, and they can take any real value, positive, zero, or negative.

e^{zi}: The standard exponential function is applied to each element of the input vector. This gives a positive value above 0, which will be very small if the input was negative, and very large if the input was large.

$\sum_{j=1}^{K} e^{zj}$: The term on the bottom of the formula is the normalization term. It ensures that all the output values of the function will sum to 1 and each be in the range (0, 1), thus constituting a valid probability distribution.

K: The number of classes in the multi-class classifier.

Shared weight means filter shares the same parameterization (weight vector and bias). From Figure 9.2, connecting the input layer and convolutional layer indicated by all the solid black lines which share the same parameters. The same is also true for the blue sparse-dotted lines and the orange dense-dotted lines. This concept of share weights allows a CNN to capture features that are self-determining their positions and efficiently diminish model capacity.

Another significant concept of CNN is max-pooling, which partition the output vector into several non-overlapping subregions, and outputs the maximum value of each sub-region. This keen concept of reducing the dimensionality of in-between representations provides additional robustness to our defect prediction.

The efficacy of CNNs largely works in an empirical manner, with the researcher tuning her models as per the application domain and the data available. Thus, parameter tuning is a key to train a successful CNN. We will discuss in Section 9.4 how to set these parameters in our proposed model.

9.4   Experimental Setup

9.4.1   Data Set Description

There are a number of open-source data sets available online for the analysis of defect prediction models. For the study, four NASA system data sets (KC1, PC1, PC2, and KC3) are selected from PROMISE repository [13] which is freely available as public data sets. The selected data sets are of different sizes and different number of set of metrics, i.e., KC1, have 22 attributes with 2,109 instances, PC1 have 22 attributes with 1,109 instances, PC2 have 37 attributes with 745 instances, and KC3 have 40 attributes with 194 instances. These data sets contain software metrics like Halstead and McCabe metrics and a Boolean variable that indicates defect or no-defect proneness of a module. Table 9.1 displays characteristics of the NASA data sets (PC1, PC2, KC1, and KC3).

The WEKA (Waikato Environment for Knowledge Analysis) tool was used for the statistical output processing of data sets. WEKA is open-source software that gives the user the power of pre-processing, implementation of well-known ML algorithms, and conception of their data so that one can develop ML techniques and apply them to real-world data problems. The data was analysed i.e., the accuracy of different data sets was calculated using various classifiers, namely, RF, DT, NB [12], and DNN [14]. The results of these classifiers were then compared with the results generated by our proposed NCNN model.

Moreover, in this data set, we are provided with 21 traditional defect prediction features for each source file, including Lines of Code (LOC), McCabe complexity measures, Halstead base measure, and derive measure. The 21 traditional features are carefully extracted from PROMISE Software Engineering Repository [13]. We list the detailed description about the 21 features in Table 9.2.

Table 9.1 Characteristics of the NASA data sets.

Data set	Project	Number of attributes	Number of instances	Number of defective entities	Number of non-defective entities
NASA	PC1	22	1109	77 (6.9%)	1,032 (93.05%)
NASA	PC2	37	745	16 (2.10%)	729 (97.90%)
NASA	KC1	22	2109	326 (15.45%)	1,783 (84.54%)
NASA	KC3	40	194	36 (18.6%)	158 (81.4%)

9.4.2 Building Novel Convolutional Neural Network (NCNN) Model

This section presents our proposed NCNN model based on 1D CNN model. The overall network architecture of NCNN is shown in Figure 9.3. NCNN model consisted of two convolutional layers, two max-pooling layers to extract global pattern, a flattening layer and two dense layers to generate deep features and help better simplification, and, finally, a convolutional linear sequential model classifier to predict whether a source file was defect.

Other details about NCNN architecture are mentioned below:

✓ For the proposed NCNN model's modeling, Python 3.5.2 is used. With the help of Keras pre-processing (version: 1.1.2), which is a neural network library written in Python and which is also capable of running on top of TensorFlow (version: 2.3.1), the NCNN related results were generated. The experiment was executed using the system having 64-bit operating system, x64 processor with 16 GB RAM.

✓ For predicting software defects convolutional linear sequential model classifier is proposed which is implemented in Keras. After pre-processing of labeled source files, we split data set into training set and test set with split ratio [75:25]. We fed our training data to our NCNN model, both weights and bias are fixed, and then for each

Table 9.2 Attribute information of the 21 features of PROMISE repository [13].

Attribute information	Symbol
McCabe's line count of code	loc
McCabe "cyclomatic complexity"	v(g)
McCabe "essential complexity"	ev(g)
McCabe "design complexity"	iv(g)
Halstead total operators + operands	n
Halstead "volume"	v
Halstead "program length"	l
Halstead "difficulty"	d
Halstead "intelligence"	i
Halstead "effort"	e
Halstead	b
Halstead's time estimator	t
Halstead's line count	lOCode
Halstead's count of lines of comments	lOComment
Halstead's count of blank lines	lOBlank
Halstead lines of code and comment	lOCodeAndComment
Unique operators	uniq_Op
Unique operands	uniq_Opnd
Total operators	total_Op
Total operands	total_Opnd
The flow graph	branchCount

file in the test set, we fed it into defect prediction model to get our prediction results. The obtained result is in the form of 0 and 1 and based on which we predicted a source file as defective or non-defective. If the result was above

Figure 9.3 Overall network architecture of proposed NCNN model.

    0.5, then it is considered as defective, otherwise it was considered as non-defective.

✓ Since we use two convolutional layers, two max-pooling layers, two dense layers, and a flattening, as increasing more depth of deep models, we might get better outcomes.

✓ Input layers and hidden layers used a RELU activation function and last layer which used the SoftMax function for classification.

✓ We used Adam optimizer, as an optimization function in order to update the weight of the network after every single iteration. We used binary cross-entropy as the loss function.

9.4.3   Evaluation Parameters

This section presents the effectiveness of our NCNN by comparing its F-measure and accuracy on defect prediction with other state-of-the-art methods such as RF, DT, and NB [12] and DNN [14]. We also explain some basic terminologies associated with software defect prediction. A *training set* refers to a set of instances used to train a model, whereas a *test set* refers to a set of instances used to evaluate the learned model. When applying defect prediction, the training set and the test set come from the same source file. In the field of ML and, specifically, the problem of statistical classification, a confusion matrix, also known as an error matrix is used. A confusion matrix is a summary of prediction results on a classification problem. The number of correct and incorrect predictions are summarized with count values and broken down by each class. This is the key to the confusion matrix. The confusion matrix shows the ways in which classification model is confused when it makes predictions. It gives us insight not only into the errors being made by a classifier but more importantly the types of errors that are being made. Figure 9.4 shows the description regarding the confusion matrix.

Class 1: False

Class 2: True

Where the above terms are defined as follows:

1. True: Observation is true.
2. False: Observation is not true.
3. True-Positive (TP): Observation is true, and is predicted to be true.
4. False-Negative (FN): Observation is true, but is predicted false.

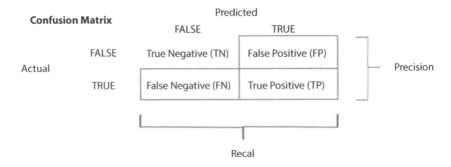

Figure 9.4 Description regarding confusion matrix.

5. True-Negative (TN): Observation is false, and is predicted to be false.
6. False-Positive (FP): Observation is false, but is predicted true.

The other evaluation parameters used in this research work are TP Rate (TPR), TN Rate (TNR), FN Rate (FNR), and FP Rate (FPR), precision, recall, F-measure (also called F1-score), and accuracy.

TPR is when it is actually positive, how often does it predict positive?

$$TPR = \frac{TruePositive\,(TP)}{TruePositive\,(TP) + FalseNegative\,(FN)}$$

TNR is when it is actually negative, how often does it predict negative?

$$TNR = \frac{TrueNegatives\,(TN)}{TrueNegatives\,(TN) + FalsePositives\,(FP)}$$

FPR is when it is actually negative, how often does it predict positive?

$$FPR = \frac{FalsePositives\,(FP)}{FalsePositives\,(FP) + TrueNegatives\,(TN)}$$

FNR is proportion of positive which yield negative test outcomes with the test?

$$FNR = \frac{FalseNegatives\,(FN)}{FalseNegatives\,(FN) + TruePositive\,(TP)}$$

Precision (P) measures the number of positive class predictions that belong to the positive class.

$$(P) = \frac{TruePositive(TP)}{TruePositive\,(TP) + FalsePositives\,(FP)}$$

Recall measures the number of positive class predictions made out of all positive examples in the data set.

$$(R) = \frac{TruePositive\,(TP)}{TruePositive\,(TP) + FalseNegatives\,(FN)}$$

F-measure offers a single score that balances both the concerns of precision and recall in one number.

$$(FM) = 2 * \frac{Recall\,(R) * Precision\,(P)}{Recall\,(R) + Precision\,(P)}$$

Whereas the accuracy is the total number of correct predictions divided by the total number of predictions made for a data set.

$$(A) = \frac{TruePositive(TP) + TrueNegatives(TN)}{TP + TN + FP + FN}$$

9.4.4   Results and Analysis

For the final analysis, we computed the performance measures for all the five classification techniques used in the study. The results were based on the values of precision, recall, F-measure, and accuracy. Mentioned below are the tables and graphs of our study for four NASA system data sets (KC1, PC1, PC2, and KC3) that are selected from PROMISE repository [13] which is freely available as public data sets.

The observations from the tables and graphs are as follows:

✓ For better performance, TPR and TNR should be high, and FNR and FPR should be low. From Table 9.7, it is observed that NCNN classifier predicts TPR and TNR greater than all ML classifier (RF, DT, and NB) and DNN classifier in the data sets KC1, KC2, and PC2 except in PC1 TPR of NCNN is lower than NB classifier but greater than RF, DT, and DNN classifiers but TNR of NCNN in case of PC1 is greater than all other classifiers. It is also observed that NCNN predicts FNR and FPR well; it is lower than all the data sets except in KC3 and PC1 where FPR of DNN is lower than NCNN and FNR of NB is lower than NCNN. This observation predicts that NCNN model outperformed in confusion rate analysis for the all data sets. This shows that NCNN model is not in underfit or overfit.

✓ From Figure 9.5, it is found that NCNN predicts more faults than RF, DT, NB, and DNN (162 faults in case of KC1 data set, 33 faults in case of KC3 data set, and 14 faults in case of PC2 data set), but in case of PC1 data set, NCNN predicts more faults than DNN, RF, and DT but lesser than NB as NB predicts 23 faults and NCNN predicts 20 faults.

✓ Figure 9.6 represents model accuracy and model loss for the data sets (KC1, KC3, PC1, and PC2). Accuracy and loss are two well-known metrics in ML and neural networks. Splitting data set will use at every epoch and used Adam optimizer, as an optimization function in order to update the weight of the network. Binary cross-entropy used as the loss function, so that we can get better model performance. Accuracy is a method for measuring a classification model's performance and naturally expressed as a percentage. It is the count of predictions where the predicted value is equal to the true value and a loss function taken into consideration

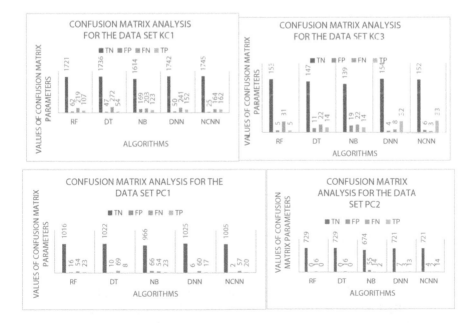

Figure 9.5 Confusion matrix analysis for the data sets (KC1, KC3, PC1, and PC2).

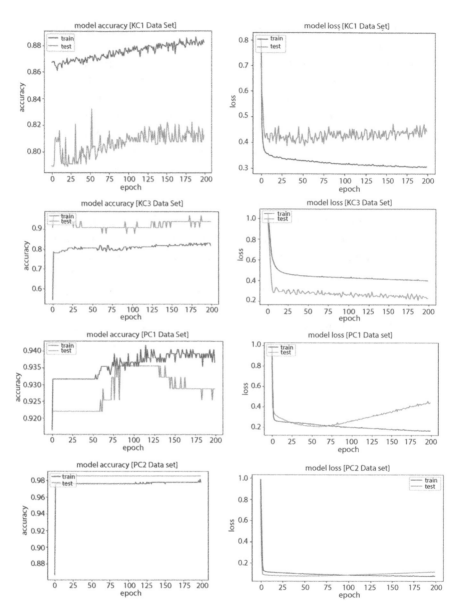

Figure 9.6 Model accuracy and model loss analysis for the data sets (KC1, KC3, PC1, and PC2).

the probabilities of a prediction based on how much the prediction varies from the true value. This gives us a clearer view how well the model is performing. The lower the loss the better a model to the training data. The loss is calculated on training and validation and its interpretation is how well the model is doing for the data sets. Unlike accuracy, loss is not a percentage. From the plot of model accuracy, we can see that the model could possibly be trained a little more as the trend for accuracy on KC1 data set, KC3 data set, and PC2 data set is rising for the middle and last few epochs except in PC1 data set where, in the middle and last epochs, it slightly moves up and down. From the plot of model loss, we can see that the model has comparable performance on both train and validation data sets (labeled test). If these equivalent plots start to depart constantly, then it might be a sign to stop training at an earlier epoch. For the data sets KC1, KC3, and PC2 model loss has comparable performance on both train and validation data sets except in PC1 data set where in the last few epochs it drastically increasing.

✓ To evaluate prediction accuracy F-measure (also called a F1-score), precision, and recall were used. Usually, there are adjustment between precision and recall. As for example, by predicting all the test files as defective, we will get a recall values as 1 and a very low precision. So, F-measure is the better prediction performance representation which is a compound of precision and recall and falls in the range [0, 1].

✓ Figure 9.7 shows the performance comparison in terms of F-measure, recall, and precision of different models for software defect prediction for the data sets (KC1, KC3, PC1, and PC2). From Figure 9.7, it is observed that F-measure of NCNN is 5% higher than DNN, 9.3% higher than NB, 7.4% higher than DT, and 6.5% higher than RT for the data set KC1. For the data set KC3, F-measure of NCNN is 1% higher than DNN, 10.9% higher than NB, 8.1% higher than DT, and 8.5% higher than RF. For the data set PC1, F-measure of NCNN is 1.8% higher than NB and equal to RF and DT but 1% less than DNN. The reason may be that the training set of PC1 is relatively small. Similarly, for the data set PC2 F-measure of NCNN is 1% higher than DNN, 3.9% higher than NB, 1% higher than DT, and 1% higher than RF. Almost in all the data sets, NCNN outperformed the other state-of-the-art models of ML and DNN in terms of F-measure for software defect prediction.

✓ From Tables 9.3 to 9.6 and Figure 9.8, we examined the accuracy value for the data sets KC1, KC3, PC1, and PC2.

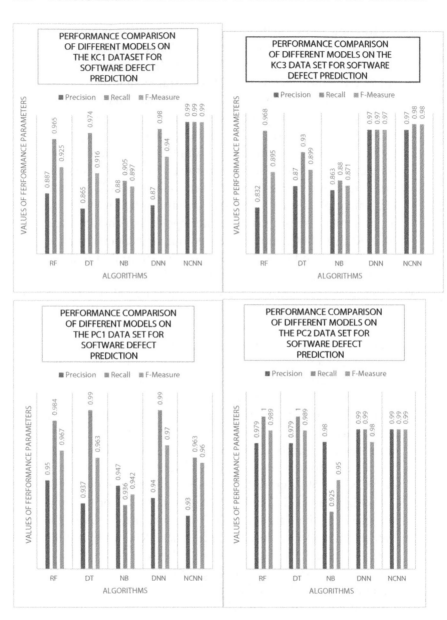

Figure 9.7 Performance comparison of different models for software defect prediction for the data sets (KC1, KC3, PC1, and PC2).

Table 9.3 Performance comparison for the data set KC1.

KC1				
Algorithm	**Precision**	**Recall**	**F-Measure**	**Accuracy**
RF	0.887	0.965	0.925	86.67
DT	0.865	0.974	0.916	84.87
NB	0.888	0.905	0.897	82.36
DNN	0.87	0.98	0.94	88.57
NCNN	0.99	0.99	**0.99**	**88.76**

Table 9.4 Performance comparison for the data set KC3.

KC3				
Algorithm	**Precision**	**Recall**	**F-Measure**	**Accuracy**
RF	0.832	0.968	0.895	81.44
DT	0.87	0.93	0.899	82.99
NB	0.863	0.88	0.871	78.87
DNN	0.97	0.97	0.97	87.88
NCNN	0.97	0.98	**0.98**	**96.97**

Table 9.5 Performance comparison for the data set PC1.

PC1				
Algorithm	**Precision**	**Recall**	**F-Measure**	**Accuracy**
RF	0.95	0.984	0.96	**93.68**
DT	0.937	0.99	0.96	92.87
NB	0.947	0.936	0.942	89.17
DNN	0.94	0.99	**0.97**	**94.65**
NCNN	0.93	0.93	0.96	93.16

Table 9.6 Performance comparison for the data set PC2.

PC2				
Algorithm	Precision	Recall	F-Measure	Accuracy
RF	0.979	1	0.989	97.85
DT	0.979	1	0.989	97.85
NB	0.98	0.925	0.951	90.73
DNN	0.99	0.99	0.98	98.66
NCNN	0.99	0.99	**0.99**	**98.71**

From analysis, we found that NCNN has higher accuracy for the data set KC1 (88.76), for the data set KC3 (96.97), and for the data set PC2 (98.71). For the data set PC1, NCNN has less accuracy (93.16) than DNN (94.65) and RF (93.68) but higher than DT and NB.

✓ From the above analysis, it reflects that the proposed NCNN model outperforms well for all four NASA system data sets from PROMISE repository [13] with other ML classifier and neural network classifier in terms of F-measure, recall, precision, and accuracy and through confusion matrix analysis and confusion rate analysis for the software defect prediction.

9.5   Conclusion and Future Scope

In this paper, an attempt has been made to propose a NCNN model to predict software defects. The framework using Python Programming Language with Keras and TensorFlow was used to implement our NCNN model. A comparative analysis with ML algorithms (such as RF, DT, and NB) and DNN model in terms of F-measure (known as F1-score), recall, precision, and accuracy has been presented from four NASA system data sets (KC1, PC1, PC2, and KC3) selected from PROMISE repository. From Table 9.7, we observed that NCNN classifier predicts TPR and TNR greater than all ML classifier (RF, DT, and NB) and DNN classifier almost in all the data sets. Even, NCNN predicts FNR and FPR well, it is lower almost in all the data sets. From Tables 9.3 to 9.6 and Figures 9.7 and 9.8, we examined (F-measure, recall, precision, and accuracy). From Figure 9.7, we observed that NCNN predicts software

Table 9.7 Confusion matrix analysis for the KC1, KC3, PC1, and PC2 data sets (TPR, True Positive Rate; TNR, True Negative Rate; FPR, False Positive Rate; FNR, False Negative Rate).

Algorithm	KC1				KC3				PC1				PC2			
	TPR	TNR	FPR	FNR	TPR	TNR	FPR	FNR	TPR	TNR	FPR	FNR	TPR	TNR	FPR	FNR
RF	0.33	0.96	0.04	0.67	0.14	0.97	0.03	0.86	0.29	0.98	0.015	0.70	0	1	0	1
DT	0.17	0.97	0.03	0.83	0.38	0.91	0.07	0.61	0.10	0.99	0.009	0.89	0	1	0	1
NB	0.38	0.90	0.07	0.62	0.38	0.90	0.12	0.61	0.29	0.93	0.06	0.70	0.13	0.92	0.07	0.88
DNN	0.47	0.98	0.02	0.53	0.88	0.83	0.02	0.11	0.22	0.994	0.005	0.77	0.81	0.990	0.009	0.19
NCNN	0.50	0.99	0.01	0.50	0.91	0.82	0.03	0.08	0.25	0.998	0.001	0.74	0.87	0.994	0.005	0.13

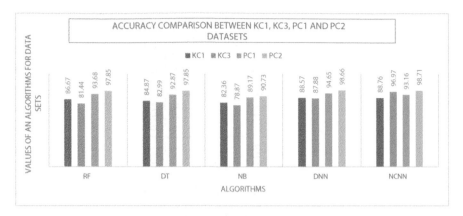

Figure 9.8 Model accuracy analysis for the data sets (KC1, KC3, PC1, and PC2).

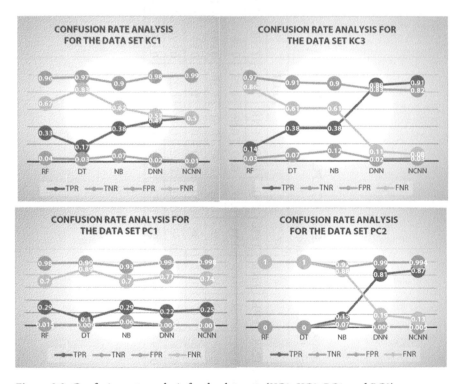

Figure 9.9 Confusion rate analysis for the data sets (KC1, KC3, PC1, and PC2).

defects in terms of F-measure which is higher than all other classifiers (DNN, RF, DT, and NB) for the data sets KC1, KC2, and PC2 except in PC1 where it is lower than DNN. From Table 9.3 to 9.6 and Figure 9.8, we found that NCNN has higher accuracy for the data set KC1 (88.76), for the data set KC3

(96.97), and for the data set PC2 (98.71). For the data set PC1, NCNN has less accuracy (93.16) than DNN (94.65) and RF (93.68) but higher than DT and NB. Thus, it is shown that the proposed NCNN model outperformed the other algorithm models in most cases. In terms of future scope, we will present a deep learning outline which automatically obtains syntactic and semantic features from the source code and yields key features from them for accurate software defect prediction. We believed to apply an open-source python packaged name *javalang* which helps to parse Java source code into ASTs, which offers a lexical analyzer and parser based on the Java language specification which helps to construct ASTs of the Java source code. From Figure 9.9, it is observed that NCNN classifier predicts TPR and TNR greater than all ML classifier (RF, DT, and NB) and DNN classifier in the data sets KC1, KC2, and PC2 except in PC1 TPR of NCNN is lower than NB classifier but greater than RF, DT, and DNN classifiers but TNR of NCNN in case of PC1 is greater than all other classifiers. It is also observed that NCNN predicts FNR and FPR well; it is lower than all the data sets except in KC3 and PC1 where FPR of DNN is lower than NCNN and FNR of NB is lower than NCNN. This firmly belief that NCNN model outperformed in confusion rate analysis for the all-data sets and it is not underfit or overfit.

References

1. Menzies, T., Milton, Z., Turhan, B., Cukic, B., Jiang, Y., Bener, A., Defect prediction from static code features: Current results, limitations, new approaches. *Autom. Software Eng., 17*, 375–407, 2010.
2. Moser, R., Pedrycz, W., Succi, G., A comparative analysis of the efficiency of change metrics and static code attributes for defect prediction, in: *Proceedings of the 30th International Conference on Software Engineering*, Leipzig, Germany, 15 May 2008, p. 181.
3. Tan, M., Tan, L., Dara, S., Mayeux, C., Online Defect Prediction for Imbalanced Data, in: *Proceedings of the 2015 IEEE/ACM 37th IEEE International Conference on Software Engineering (ICSE)*, Florence, Italy, 16–24 May 2015, pp. 99–108.
4. Nam, J., Pan, S.J., Kim, S., Transfer defect learning, in: *Proceedings of the International Conference of Software Engineering*, San Francisco, CA, USA, 18–26 May 2013.
5. Nam, J., *Survey on Software Defect Prediction*. Ph.D. Thesis, The Hong Kong University of Science and Technology, Hong Kong, China, 3 July 2014.
6. Lyu, M.R., *Handbook of Software Reliability Engineering*, vol. 222, IEEE Computer Society Press, Washington, DC, USA, 1996.
7. Rathore, S.S. and Kumar, S., A decision tree logic-based recommendation system to select software fault prediction techniques. *Computing*, 99, 3, 255–285, Mar. 2016.

8. Malhotra, R. and Jain, A., Fault Prediction Using Statistical and Machine Learning Methods for Improving Software Quality. *J. Inf. Process. Syst.*, 8, 2, 241–262, Jun. 2012.

9. He, P., Li, B., Liu, X., Chen, J., Ma, Y., An empirical study on software defect prediction with a simplified metric set. *Inf. Software Technol.*, 59, 170–190, Mar. 2015.

10. Elish, O.M., Al-Yafei, H.A., Al-Mulhem, M., Empirical comparison of three metrics suites for fault prediction in packages of object-oriented systems: A case study of Eclipse. *Adv. Eng. Software*, 42, 10, 852–859, Oct. 2011.

11. Peng, Y., Kou, G., Wang, G., Wu, W., Shi, Y., Ensemble Of Software Defect Predictors: An Ahp-Based Evaluation Method. *Int. J. Inf. Technol. Decis. Mak.*, 10, 01, 187–206, Jan. 2011.

12. Malhotra, R., A systematic review of machine learning techniques for software fault prediction. *Appl. Soft Comput.*, 27, 504–518, Feb. 2015.

13. http://promise.site.uottawa.ca/SERepository/datasets-page.html.

14. Gupta, M., Rajnish, K., Bhattacherjee, V., Impact of parameter tuning for optimizing deep neural networks models for predicting software faults. *Sci. Program.*, Hindawi, 2021, 1–17, 12th June, 2021 (Page No:234) [communicated].

15. Singh, Y., Kaur, A., Malhotra, R., Prediction of Fault-Prone Software Modules using Statistical and Machine Learning Methods. *Int. J. Comput. Appl.*, 1, 22, 8–15, Feb. 2010.

16. Dejaeger, K., Verbraken, T., Baesens, B., Toward Comprehensible Software Fault Prediction Models Using Bayesian Network Classifiers. *IEEE Trans. Software Eng.*, 39, 2, 237–257, Feb. 2013.

17. Kumar, L., Sripada, K.S., Sureka, A., Rath, K.S., Effective fault prediction model developed using Least Square Support Vector Machine (LSSVM). *J. Syst. Software*, 137, 686–712, Mar. 2018.

18. Twala, B., Predicting Software Faults in Large Space Systems using Machine Learning Techniques. *Def. Sci. J.*, 61, 4, 306–316, Jul. 2011.

19. Wang, S., Liu, T., Tan, L., Automatically learning semantic features for defect prediction. *Proceedings of the 38th International Conference on Software Engineering - ICSE '16*, 2016.

20. Miholca, L.D., Czibula, G., Czibula, G.I., A novel approach for software defect prediction through hybridizing gradual relational association rules with artificial neural networks. *Inf. Sci.*, 441, 152–170, May 2018.

21. Li, J., He, P., Zhu, J., Lyu, R.M., Software Defect Prediction via Convolutional Neural Network. *IEEE International Conference on Software Quality, Reliability and Security (QRS)*, Jul. 2017.

22. Pan, C., Lu, M., Xu, B., Gao, H., An Improved CNN model for within project software defect prediction. *Appl. Sci.*, 9, 2138–216, 2019.

23. Cheng, J., Guo, J., Cleland-Huang., J., Semantically Enhanced Software Traceability Using Deep Learning Techniques, in: *Proceedings of the 2017 IEEE/ACM 39th International Conference on Software Engineering (ICSE)*, Buenos Aires, Argentina, 20–28 May 2017, pp. 3–14.

24. Li, L., Feng, H., Zhuang, W., Meng, N., Ryder, B., CC Learner: A Deep Learning-Based Clone Detection Approach, in: *Proceedings of the IEEE International Conference on Software Maintenance and Evolution (ICSME)*, Shangai, China, 17–24 September 2017, pp. 249–260.

25. Lam, N.A., Nguyen, A.T., Nguyen, H.A., Nguyen, T.N., Bug localization with combination of deep learning and information retrieval, in: *Proceedings of the 2017 IEEE/ACM 25th International Conference on Program Comprehension (ICPC)*, Buenos Aires, Argentina, 22–23 May 2017, pp. 218–229.

26. Reyes, J., Ramirez, D., Paciello, J., Automatic Classification of Source Code Archives by Programming Language: A Deep Learning Approach, in: *Proceedings of the International Conference on Computational Science and Computational Intelligence (CSCI)*, Las Vegas, NV, USA, 15–17 December 2016, pp. 514–519, 2016.

27. Zekany, S., Rings, D., Harada, N., Laurenzano, M.A., Tang, L., Mars, J., Crystal Ball: Statically analyzing runtime behaviour via deep sequence learning, in: *Proceedings of the 2016 49th Annual IEEE/ACM International Symposium on Microarchitecture (MICRO)*, Taipei, Taiwan, 15–19 October 2016, pp. 1–12.

28. Corley, C.S., Damevski, K., Kraft, N.A., Exploring the use of deep learning for feature location, in: *Proceedings of the 2015 IEEE International Conference on Software Maintenance and Evolution (ICSME)*, Bremen, Germany, 29 September–1 October 2015, pp. 556–560.

29. Pang, Y., Xue, X., Wang, H., Predicting Vulnerable Software Components through Deep Neural Network, in: *Proceedings of the 2017 International Conference on Deep Learning Technologies*, Chengdu China, 2–4 June 2017, pp. 6–10.

30. Bandara, U. and Wijayarathna, G., Deep Neural Networks for Source Code Author Identification, in: *Proceedings of the 20th International Conference*, Daegu, Korea, 3–7 November 2013, pp. 368–375.

31. Goodfellow, I., Bengio, Y., Courville, A., *Deep learning Nature*, 2021, 1–17, 12th June, 2021 (Page No:234).

32. Abdel-Hamid, O., Mohamed, A.R., Jiang, H., Penn, G., Applying Convolutional Neural Networks concepts to hybrid NN-HMM model for speech recognition, in: *Proceedings of the 2012 IEEE International Conference on Acoustics, Speech and Signal Processing (ICASSP)*, Kyoto, Japan, 25–30 March 2012, pp. 4277–4280.

33. Krizhevsky, A., Sutskever, I., Hinton, G.E., Image net classification with deep convolutional neural networks, in: *Proceedings of the Advances in Neural Information Processing Systems*, Lake Tahoe, NV, USA, 3–8 December 2012, pp. 1097–1105.

34. LeCun, Y., Bottou, L., Bengio, Y., Haffner, P., Gradient-based learning applied to document recognition. *Proc. IEEE, 86*, 2278–2324, 1998.

35. Zhang, X., Zhao, J., LeCun, Y., Character-level Convolutional Networks for Text Classification, in: *Proceedings of the Advances in Neural Information Processing Systems*, Montreal, QC, Canada, 7–12 December 2015.

10

Predictive Analysis of Online Television Videos Using Machine Learning Algorithms

Rebecca Jeyavadhanam B.[1], Ramalingam V.V.[2]*, Sugumaran V.[3] and Rajkumar D.[4]

[1]Department of Computer Applications, Faculty of Science and Humanities, SRMIST, Kattankulathur, India
[2]Department of Computer Science and Engineering, College of Engineering and Technology, SRMIST, Kattankulathur, India
[3]SMBS, VIT Chennai Campus, Chennai, India
[4]Department of BCA, Faculty of Science and Humanities, SRMIST, Ramapuram, India

Abstract

In recent years, intelligent machine systems promote different disciplines and facilitate reasonable solutions in various domains. Machine learning offers higher-level services for organizations to build customized solutions. Machine learning algorithms are widely integrated with image, video analytics, and evolving technologies such as augmented and virtual reality. The advanced machine learning approach plays an essential key role in handling the huge volume of time-dependent data and modeling automatic detection systems. The data grows exponentially with varying sizes, formats, and complexity. Machine learning algorithms are developed to extract meaningful information from huge and complex datasets. Machine learning algorithms or models improve their efficiency by the training process. This chapter commences with machine learning fundamentals and focuses on the most prominent machine learning process of data collection, feature extraction, feature selection, and building model. The significance and functions of each method on the live streaming television video dataset are discussed. We addressed the dimensionality reduction and machine learning incremental learning process (online). Finally, we summarized the performance assessment

*Corresponding author: ramalinv@srmist.edu.in

Pradeep Singh (ed.) Fundamentals and Methods of Machine and Deep Learning: Algorithms, Tools and Applications, (237–258) © 2022 Scrivener Publishing LLC

of decision tree, J48 graft, LMT tree, REP tree, best first (BF), and random forest algorithms based on their classification performance to build a predictive model for automatic identification of advertisement videos.

Keywords: Machine intelligent, machine learning, prediction, dimensionality reduction, feature extraction, feature selection, decision tree

10.1   Introduction

There is a need to develop customized and cognitive solutions in various fields in a service-driven generation. Cognitive solutions where the system could listen, respond, and recognize things and learning from the interactions. Machine learning is a subdivision of artificial intelligence (AI) in which we need efficient algorithms to process and analyze the huge volume of data. It aims to extract meaningful information such as features or patterns from a huge volume of data. There is a critical step to derive meaningful information as the feature which helps as the intelligent learning agent. Feature extraction is where would give the attention to extracting the useful data. Feature selections are the optimal subset of input variables to the learning algorithms. In other words, dimensionality reduction is necessary to choose the best performing features from the larger dataset. Significantly, it improves the performance of the learning algorithms. Choosing suitable algorithms and techniques on the training data gives a better prediction model. Training is the iterative process to reach the correct prediction goal and evaluate its performance using F1 score, precision, and recall. Evaluation of a model is a measure of success rate. If the evaluation process gets successful, then the next step is to proceed with the parameter tuning, where we can regularize the mode, scaling up, and tuning parameters. Prediction is the final process to consider the model to be ready for real-time applications. A well-built and executed machine learning model can improve the decision-making process for the respective domains. As an outcome, human resource is unbound from the encumbrance of processing the information and decisions. Brezeal *et al.* discussed a detailed survey for automatic video classification techniques and low level features. The statistical approach has been explained and helps the reader to enhance their works [1]. Qi *et al.* illustrated the SVM classifier and its classification performance on news stories [2]. Many research works have concentrated on television videos. CBIR (content-based image retrieval) framework for categorical-based searching has been proposed using machine learning methods for image pre-filtering, similarity matching with statistical distance measures and relevance feedback schemes. This approach has performed better than the traditional and it captures the variation of attributes in semantic categories. This system can be used as a front-end search application for medical images [3]. A combined fuzzy learning approach for a relevant feedback-based CBIR system for image search is proposed using both short term technique [fuzzy support vector machine (FSVM)] and long-term learning technique (novel semantic clustering technique). The results have shown the best retrieval accuracy compared to all its equivalent alternate methods and it occupies less space, increased scalability to larger databases [4]. A generic framework for analyzing large scale diverse sports videos with three different video analyses incoherent and sequential order is proposed [5]. Encouraging results of about 82.16% in genre categorization using KNN classifier, 82.86% using supervised SVM and 68.13% using unsupervised PLSA for average classification accuracy, and 92.31 by unsupervised PLSA and 93.08% by supervised SVM for structure prediction are achieved. Performance evaluation of various classifiers is reported and the decision tree algorithm (C4.5) finds good attributes to categorize video genre [6]. A study on pilot behaviors and their mood-based TV programmer classification has illustrated broadly. The video clips were labeled as happy, serious, and exciting for mood classification. Since it is a pilot study, a small dataset was used. Mel-Frequency Cepstral Coefficients (MFCCs) were used on audio, and phase correlation was used on video for feature classification and it produced an average of 75% to 100% accuracy on 3-minute clips when using two mood axes and 70% to 76% accuracy when all three mood axes were used [7]. A new algorithm for incremental feature learning in restricted Boltzmann machines is proposed to reduce the model complexity in computer vision problems as hidden layer incremented. There are two tasks defined as determining the incrimination necessity of neurons and the second, to compute the added attributes for increment. The results have shown that this approach has incremental RBM archives comparable reconstruction and classification errors than its non-comparable RBMs [8]. A video classification method is proposed to classify videos into different categories. This method aims at generic classification, namely, specific video classifier and generic video classifier, and it exploits motor information and cross-correlation measure for classification. Experiments were conducted on four popular video genres: cartoon, sports, commercial, and news, which yielded a good classification accuracy of 94.5% [9]. High-resolution video frame is a great challenge to process and discriminate their attributes. A learning-based technique has been used to enhance the super resolution of video frames exploit Artificial Neural Network (ANN). The method has been developed based on the edge properties and the spatial and temporal information has properly been utilized [10]. The simulation results show improvement in average PSNR and perceptual quality of the super-resolved frame. A finger joint detection method to measure modified total sharp (MTS) using SVM is proposed for the early detection of Rheumatoid Arthritis (RA), which increased by 30,000 patients annually. The experiments performed on 45 RA patients showed its early detection with an accuracy of 81.4% [11]. Content-based automatic video genre classification system exploits low-level audio and visual features and combines them with cognitive structural information. In web videos, the meta-information is also used for classification and this method is runs on YouTube videos. An accuracy of 99.2% on RAI dataset and 94.5% on Quareo 2010 evaluation dataset under TV programs and 89.7% on YouTube videos is measured [12]. A dataset DEAP (Database for Emotion Analysis using Physiological Signals) has developed a 3D emotional model. EEG signals were used to extract the features for their experimental study [13]. The authors discussed a systematic, comprehensive review and the advantage of neural networks. Image and video compression is done in three ways: excellent adaptability and leveraging samples from the far distance and texture and feature representation [14]. New objectives are used to evaluate the performance of the techniques [15]. Low level visual features were used to analyze the satellite images due to the different colors and textural variations. A multimodal feature learning mechanism based on deep networks for video classification is proposed through two-stage learning frameworks using intra-modal and inter-modal semantics. Compared to other deep and shallow models, experimental results show improvements in our approach in video classification accuracy [16]. A rule-based video classification method is suitable for online and offline study which helps in various video genre. Rule-based method is the better approach to classify the basket clips with increased accuracy [17]. The labeling problem is a significant one to consider in the classification approach. A semi-supervised learning technique has been used in vehicle classification and fused with an unsupervised graph which combines multiple feature representations under different distance measures [18]. The affinity between instances becomes more reliable, facilitating the vehicle type label propagation from labeled instances to their unlabeled ones when tested on BIT vehicle dataset. Classification of various video summarization techniques used to compress video files is carried out. A comparison chart of various techniques adopted in video summarization is discussed, and the usage of techniques adopted along with its dataset applied strengths, and weaknesses is presented [19]. Suggestions on how can use network techniques like CNN and RNN for video summarization is also suggested. A new method temporal-space-smooth warping (TSSW) is proposed to solve low temporal coherence in synthesized videos during its editing process [20]. This method produces a result with advantages like robustness to temporal coherence and preserves the temporal coherence and spatial smoothness, and effortless video editing options make this method a practically preferred method for video editing. A novel graph-based SSL framework structure sensitive anisotropic manifold ranking (SSAniMR) is proposed by studying the connections between graph-based SSL and PDE-based diffusion [21]. Experiments conducted on the TRECVID dataset have demonstrated that this framework outperforms the existing graph-based methods and is effective for semantic video annotation. In this work, the effective features of the furniture style. A three-way classification strategy is used to compare handcrafted classification and learning-based classification. Machine learning techniques like SVM and CNN are used for training and learning. According to the experimental results, the combinations of both handcrafted classification and learning-based classification can achieve state-of-the-art performance in labeling and detecting furniture's style [22, 23].

This chapter is intended to provide the fundamental concepts of machine learning techniques for readers who are primarily familiar with image processing and machine learning. We described elaborately the feature extraction, feature selection, and classification techniques. Also, the performance evaluation of various classifiers is presented in the following sections.

10.1.1 Overview of Video Analytics

In image and video processing technology, video analytics has become used to process digital video signals to achieve many security goals and provide robust solutions in various domains. Video analytics technology has scaled with advances in machine learning, AI, multi-lingual speech recognition, and rules-based decision engines. Prescriptive analytics is mostly required in real time. YouTube and television videos contain rich content information. In contemporary applications, image or video plays a critical role in low and high resolution and bandwidth communication. High resolutions are required at the user end display system. In surveillance video, television videos, medical images, and satellite images have significantly gained the focuses on high resolutions. Resolutions greatly influence in the viewing experience and better quality. Video resolution mainly depends on the number of pixels in a frame. Pixels combine RGB values as the smallest unit, making a picture in a video frame. Possibly,

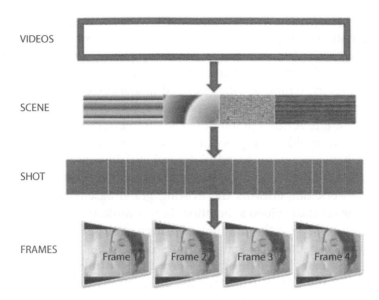

Figure 10.1 Hierarchical video representation.

the more pixels of the images present, the better clarity of the image. Therefore, to process the live streaming television videos, spatial information of the current frame and the next frame's temporal information must be considered. In television, the broadcast videos are in different genres such as news, music, sports, cartoon, movie, and commercials are supposed to build the model. Generally, the video contains scenes, shots, and frames, respectively. Figure 10.1 shows the hierarchical representation of the videos.

10.1.2   Machine Learning Algorithms

To examine the consistency of various machine learning algorithms, we used the five other television video genre. Predictive accuracy criteria estimate the efficiency of the classifiers. Various machine learning algorithms such as C4.5, J48 graft, logistic model tree (LMT), random tree, best fit (BF) tree, reduced error pruning (REP) tree, and random forest (RF) are evaluated similarly on same attributes consistently. Each algorithm is illustrated below.

10.1.2.1   Decision Tree C4.5

Presentation of decision tree J48 has been assessed and contrasted and different calculations. Grouping calculations consistently discover standard rules to speak to the information and arranged to groups. DT is a famous and straight forward structure that utilizes a "partition and overcome" strategy to separate a non-predictable dynamic cycle into an assortment of basic choices. The decision tree system is straightforward and, in this manner, giving an interpretable arrangement. Given an information base $D = \{t1, t2, ..., tn\}$ where $ti = \{ti1, ti2, ..., tih\}$ and the information base composition contains the qualities $\{A1, A2, A3, ..., Ah\}$. It is additionally given a bunch of classes $C = \{1, ..., m\}$.

A decision tree computational model related to D that has the accompanying properties:

- Each interior hub is named with a quality, simulated intelligence.
- Each bend is named with a predicate that can be applied to the parent's quality.
- Each leaf hub is marked with a class, Cj.

Given a bunch of classes $C = \{1, ..., m\}$ with an equivalent likelihood of the event, the entropy is $-p1\log 2p1 - p2\log 2p2 ... - pm\log 2pm$ where pi is the likelihood of even to fI. A property with the most minimal entropy is chosen as part of the standards for the tree. It is utilized to advance the forecast and grouping exactness of the calculation by limiting over-fitting problem.

10.1.2.2   J48 Graft

J48 graft is an efficient technique suggested to escalation the prospect to classify the objects exactly. J48 graft algorithm creates a single tree which aids in reducing the prediction error. J48 grafting algorithm is inherently generated from J48 tree algorithm. The main advantage of J48 graft is used to increase the probability of correctly predicted attributes. The grafting system is an inductive method and inserts nodules to trees to decrease prediction errors. The J48 grafting algorithm gives a good prediction accuracy on selected attributes of the training process.

10.1.2.3   Logistic Model Tree

A LMT comprises of a typical choice with strategic relapse capacities at the leaves. The LMT covers a tree like structure consisting of many internal or non-terminal bunch of nodes and end hubs. The LMT calculation formulates a tree with double and multi-class marked factors, like "numeric" and "missing abilities". LMT is a mix of acceptance trees and calculated relapse. LMT utilizes cost-unpredictability trimming. Execution capability is slower in nature when compared with other techniques.

10.1.2.4   Best First Tree

In BF decision tree calculation, the tree grows by choosing the hub, which boosts the contamination decrease all the current hubs to part. In this calculation, the contamination could be estimated by the Gini index as well as information gain. BF trees are developed in a separation vanquish technique like the standard profundity first DT. The important guidelines for building the BF tree is as follows:

- Select a characteristic to put at the root hub and make a few branches for this trait dependent on certain measures.
- Split preparing occasions into sub group, one branch inherited from root hub.
- The building measure proceeds until all hubs are unadulterated or a particular value of extensions is arrived.

10.1.2.5   Reduced Error Pruning Tree

REP tree is the easiest and reasonable strategy in choice tree pruning. It is a quick choice tree student, which constructs a choice or a relapse tree utilizing data pick up as the parting basis and prunes it and using decreased blunder pruning. Utilizing REP calculation, the tree crossing has performed from base to top and afterward checks for each interior hub and supplants it with most of the time class with the most worry about the tree exactness, which should not diminish. This method will proceed until any further pruning reduces the proficiency.

10.1.2.6   Random Forest

RF tree is an effective calculation for building a tree with K irregular highlights at every hub. The irregular tree is a tree drawn indiscriminately from a bunch of potential trees. Irregular trees can be created effectively, and the blend of huge arrangements of arbitrary trees prompts precise models. Irregular tree models have been widely evolved in AI to fabricate a reasonable and solid video order model.

10.2   Proposed Framework

Detection of the unique video is a popular yet challenging task in learning and intelligence, including various internet, YouTube, and television videos. Commercial monitoring systems brought a ground-breaking revolution in the internet, television, and smart-phones. Commercial videos are a good idea which spreads and communicates quickly to the targeted customers. However, the television video system faces two challenges nowadays: on the one hand, the growing number of television viewers and, on the other hand, increasing the advertisement channels. Hence, there is a great demand on smart remote sensing enabled device to facilitate happy timing for the homemakers and working peoples. It also provides a beneficial strategy for business sectors to promote their products in the competitive world. Hence, it is essential to identify a particular video genre for all kinds of multimedia applications. However, few observations have been noticed to carry out in the proposed work. Identifying a common feature among various videos, differentiating a particular video genre from others and identifying the commercial videos from the non-commercial videos are significant challenges. This chapter gives a concise and insightful analysis of commercial videos using a machine learning approach. Finding the unique features from the commercial frames can be utilized to classify accurately using spatial and temporal techniques. Temporal consistency gives valuable clues to derive most prominent features from the video-frames. Spatial information of the video frames provides the visual contents, giving a better prediction using machine learning techniques. In this chapter, there are two orthogonal views of features extraction techniques using spatial-temporal information: selection of best performing features and the classification results analysis are described elaborately to understand the importance of machine learning techniques in a better way. This chapter aims to help the researchers learn more and understand the machine learning and AI concepts aids of video classification developed model as depicted in Figure 10.2. We elaborately discussed the feature extraction techniques, feature selection process, and the machine learning classification methodology.

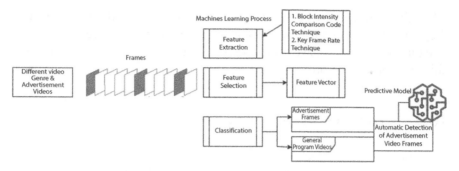

Figure 10.2 Overall architecture of the proposed framework.

10.2.1 Data Collection

The quality of data defines the accuracy of the model. Pre-processing is an essential step to removing the duplicates, handling the missing values, normalization, and data type conversion.

However, the collection dataset of the real-time video is an excellent challenging task to extract useful information. Data are extracted from five different video genres like news, music, sports, movie, and commercial videos in this framework. The dataset is categorized into two levels: advertisement videos and it is labeled as ADD class and other videos are labeled as NADD class. All commercial videos are taken in the ADD category and news, music, sports, and movie videos come under NADD category. We have extracted 20,000 individual frames for extracting the spatial and temporal features for ADD and NADD categories, respectively. The proposed algorithm extracted the frames at a rate of 25 FPS. Among 20,000 frames, 8,000 were taken for the test data. In a large scale dataset, robustness and efficiency are the most important concern in machine learning models.

10.2.2 Feature Extraction

In a typical feature extraction process, the low-level features are extracted from the spatial information and high-level features are generated from the temporal information. Here, we used the Block Intensity Comparison Code (BICC) to mine the spatial relevance objects. Key Frame Rate (KFR) technique has been used to generate high-level visual features to obtain the ADD and NADD frames' likeness and variance. The experiment was conducted to identify the best promising block size such as 2×2, 3×3,

$4 \times 4, 5 \times 5, 6 \times 6, 7 \times 7, 8 \times 8, 9 \times 9$, and 10×10 [23]. Block size 8×8 has selected as the promising block size, and then, the BICC feature extraction technique has applied to generate the feature vector to carry out the experimental procedures. Next, the KFR feature extraction technique was used to extract the high-level feature to differentiate the ADD and NADD frames.

To increase the classification efficiency, accuracy, and effectiveness, we applied machine learning techniques and incorporated the feature extraction techniques such as BICC and KFR to produce a better predictive model to identify the commercial videos from another video genre. A brief description of the two advanced feature extraction techniques is discussed below to grab the machine learning process' insightfulness of feature extraction techniques.

10.2.2.1   Block Intensity Comparison Code

Application of block pattern yields the proof of changes between the present frame and the adjacent frame. In each block of the frame, the average is calculated and compared with all other blocks. BICC feature vector has generated using the different phases are as follows.

Phase 1: Apply various blocking patterns on the frames.
Phase 2: Choosing the prominent block size.
Phase 3: Computing the average intensity value for each block.
Phase 4: Comparison of average values.
Phase 5: Constructing a feature vector.

Algorithm Implementation:

Step 1: Divide the Image (M) into $K \times K$ blocks, whereas $K = 2$ to 10; $M/K \times N/K$.
Step 2: Block Size: 8×8 and Image Size: 320×240. Find Average Intensity of each block.
Step 3: Construction of Feature Dataset: $Y = [((i - 1) * M) + 1: ((i * M), (j - 1)*N) + 1):(j * N)]$,
Step 4: Iterate step 2 and step 3.
Step 5: Assume the Feature Set $= V = \{f_1, f_2, ..., f_n\}$.

Blocking pattern of BICC technique is shown in Figure 10.3. BICC feature extraction technique is significant proof for the images' static and dynamic properties and improvises the learning and intelligent process.

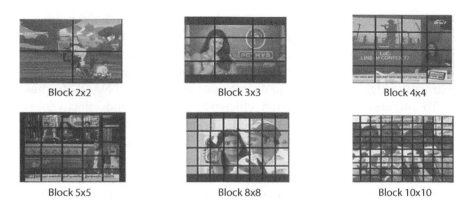

Figure 10.3 Blocking pattern.

10.2.2.2   Key Frame Rate

To calculate the frame rate of the online streaming television videos, it is essential to choose the key frame for various applications like video searching, retrieval, efficient browsing, content-based retrieval, and query-based search and classification. KFR feature extraction technique reduces the flaws in high-level semantic features and low-level features. From the literature study, most of the research works focused only on two methods to choose the key frames from the sequence of video images, such as uniform key frame collection and random key frame selection. However, rapid changes are occurring more in all commercial videos than in other videos. Therefore, the variations that might be occurred two selected key frames at a specific interlude is supposed to be dissimilar in the advertisement video frames (ADD Frame) than the other frames (NADD frames). In the proposed work, we have considered the key frames in the three different equal intervals of frames like 8, 12, and 16, as shown in Figure 10.4. The motion acceleration of the frames can calculate frame rate. Furthermore, KFR feature gives a progressive incline nearly in all multimedia applications. Different phases are carried out to generate the feature vector using the KFR feature extraction technique.

Phase 1: Shot segmentation: Input video shots are processed and segmented.
Phase 2: Key frames are collected in the equal interval of frames.
Phase 3: Divided the key frames into sixteen macro blocks to calculate frame rate.
Phase 4: Construct the feature vector.

Figure 10.4 Key frame extraction.

Algorithm Implementation:
Step 1: Let us consider the Video frames $X = \{F_1, F_2, F_3, ..., F_n\}$
Step 2: Key Frames Set $X1 = \{KF\ i{:}j;$ where $j = 8, 12$ and $16\}$
Step 3: Select key frames and compute average $K = \{k_1, k_2, k_3, ..., k_n\}$
Step 4: Assume T is a threshold value.
    Apply the condition:
    If $T \geq$ average intensity;
    ADD frames
    Else
    NADD frames.

Motion information can be considered through the sequential manner of the frame arrangements in the video. Hence, we utilized this KFR feature for insightful component extraction dependent on machine learning strategy.

10.3   Feature Selection

A machine learning technique plays a critical role in building a model with the dataset for automation anywhere. In a well-defined dataset, all the variables are participating in a useful way. The redundant variables' presence always reduces the efficiency of the model and it might reduce the accuracy of the classifier. Moreover, involving more variables increases the complexity and decreases the capacity of the model. Therefore, feature selection identifies the best performing input variables in building the predictive model. Microscopic analysis of every variable in the dataset is not feasible for larger datasets. It is important to diminish the number of variables that cause a great impact on the computational cost of a model and increase the model's performance. However, dimensionality reduction is a sensible method when dealing with a huge volume of high dimensional data. Dimensionality techniques would handle the space and time complexity effectively. In this work, we employed C4.5 algorithm for the feature selection process. Using BICC feature with 8 × 8 block size, 64 features were extracted and pruned after, 19 features are selected as best features (h1, h5, h8, h10, h15, h20, h27, h31, h39, h42, h47, h50, h52, h54, h55, h56, h57, h58, and h61) out of 64 features. The rest of the features were ignored sensibly.

In KFR technique, the experiments were carried out with the ratio of 1:4, 1:8, and 1:12 from each shot. Further, the frames weredividedinto16 macro blocks, which reduces of the temporal redundancy. However, the well-performing feature were identified as feature1 (f1), feature2 (f2), feature3 (f3) up to feature16 (f16) and 12 features selected as best attributes. We compared the two key frames concerning the ratio of 1:12 and, if the average is greater than the threshold value, the frame rate is high and it means that the frame belongs to ADD and it is lesser than the threshold value, it is NADD frames.

10.4   Classification

In this section, the classification performance of various machine learning algorithms and experimental breakthroughs are discussed elaborately in section 2.4. Owing to the prediction of ADD and NADD frames, the given datasets are split into 80% of training dataset and 20% for testing dataset. The algorithms' classification accuracy is compared with their predictive accuracy, robustness, and scalability and interpretability criteria. Finally, decision treeJ48, J48 graft, LMT, RF, and REP tree classifiers are applied along with AI to predict whether the input frame is ADD frames or NADD frames. Table 10.1 shows the classifiers classification accuracy using BICC and KFR features, and it gives evidence to prove that RF with their "k" values achieved 99.50% of classification accuracy.

The most important factors are training and testing, which affect the success rate of machine learning. The quality of the built model depends

Table 10.1 Classifiers vs. classification accuracy.

Classifiers	Variable parameters	Classification accuracy (%)	
		BICC Feature	KFR
Decision Tree J48	Minimum Number of Objects	83.69	60.94
J48 Graft	Minimum Number of Objects	83.69	62.08
LMT	Minimum Number of Instances	91.34	71.01
Best First (BF Tree)	Minimum Number of Objects	83.51	62.28
REP Tree	Minimum Total Weight of Instances	80.64	59.11
Random Forest	K values	99.50	71.9

on an efficient training process. Figure 10.5 shows the proposed developed model and the dataset divided into two parts for the training and testing process. The training and testing sets are considered in the ratio of 60% to 40% for the proposed model development. However, iteration of the training process could increase the success rate of the classifiers performance and the process flow is shown in Figure 10.5.

10.5   Online Incremental Learning

Incremental and online machine learning attracts more attention with respect to learning real-time data streams, in disparity with conventional assumptions of the available data set. Though various approaches exist, it is unclear to choose the suitable one for specific work. Instant or online-based incremental learning is that the model could learn each attribute as it receives. Traditional machine learning techniques access the data concurrently fail to meet the actual requirements to handle the huge volume of complete data set within the stipulated time. It leads more unprocessed accumulated data. Moreover, the existing approaches do not integrate and

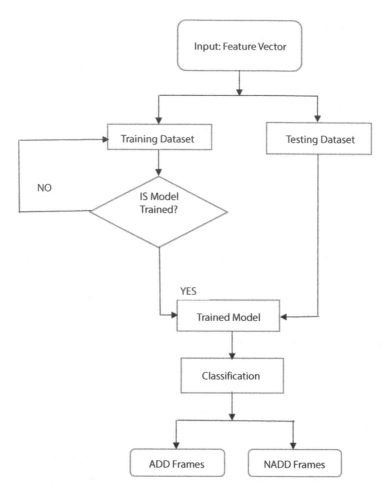

Figure 10.5 Training and testing process.

update new incremental information into the existing built models instead it reconstructs new-fangled models from the mark. It is a time-consuming process as well as potentially outmoded. Hence, there is a need for a paradigm change to sequential data processing for the video streaming system to overcome this state of concerns.

Challenges of Incremental Learning Algorithms:

1. Incremental learning algorithms are limited in run time and model complexity.
2. Long term leaning with a device and restricted resources.

3. Adaptation of model without retraining process.
4. Conservation of earlier assimilated knowledge and without any impact of **catastrophic failure**.
5. Limited number of training attributes is allowed to be upheld.

Here, few algorithms are recommended for the online incremental learning process in the perspective of concept gist as given below:

- Incremental Support Vector Machine (ISVM)
- LASVM is an online approximate SVM
- Online Random Forest (ORF)
- Incremental Learning Vector Quantization (ILVQ)
- Learn++ (LPPCART)
- Incremental Extreme Learning Machine (IELM)
- Naive Bayes (NBGauss)
- Stochastic Gradient Descent (SGDLin)

The evaluation process of these algorithm allows the interpretation of various aspects concerning to the algorithmic performance and provide deeper insight.

10.6   Results and Discussion

In this experimental analysis, we investigated the arrangements of spatial and temporal information of advertisement videos and Non-advertisement videos for recognizable ADD frames and NADD frames aided with AI concepts. Optimization and tuning of the parameters were executed and run on the Waikato environment–Weka tool and all other windows operating systems applications. The classifiers' performance is estimated, and the video frames are analyzed in terms of F1 score, precision, and recall sores. Results and outputs of the video frames are analyzed and shown in Table 10.2.

Referring to Table 10.3, the predicted number of frames is shown in the confusion matrix. The confusion matrix is used to explore the performance of the classifiers based on the prediction like True Positive (TP), False Positive (FP), True Negative (TN), and False Positive (FN). From the confusion matrix given, one can understand that there commended RF classifier correctly predicted 9,515 ADD frames and the rest of 485 frames are misclassified as NADD frames. However, these frames belong

Table 10.2 Performance metrics of the recommended classifier.

TP rate	FP rate	Precision	Recall	F-Measures	ROC area	Class
0.951	0.10	0.896	0.951	0.922	0.95	ADD
0.88	0.048	0.983	0.88	0.917	0.95	NADD
0.920	0.078	0.921	0.920	0.920	0.95	Weight Avg.

Table 10.3 Confusion matrix.

Class	ADD	NADD
ADD	9,514	486
NADD	1,097	8,903

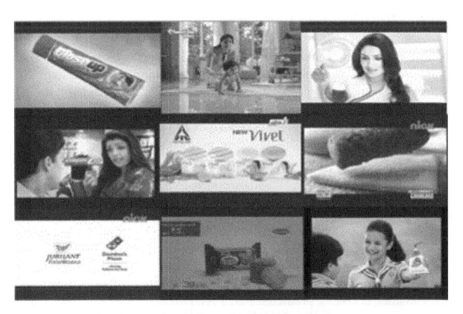

Figure 10.6 Predicted output frames from advertisement videos.

Figure 10.7 Predicted output frames from non-advertisement videos.

to ADD frames. Similarly, RF correctly classified 8,902 NADD frames and 1,098 frames are misclassified as ADD frames. The predicted resultant video frames of ADD and NADD frames are shown in Figures 10.6 and 10.7.

10.7   Conclusion

The importance is given for plausible experiment methodology to analyze online television streaming videos to classify commercial videos using a machine learning approach. Machine learning is imperative to classify the video genre and identify the advertisement videos from other videos like news, music, sports, and movie videos for the proposed work. The finding of this work is mainly utilized for quick access and various multimedia applications. Experiment results are based on the fusion of machine learning and AI. The recommended model for classification of the advertisement video frames is proficient with an accuracy of 99.50%. Recall score with the precision score is verified with advertisement frames. Hopefully, the present findings and verified methodology help the researchers better understand machine learning techniques for versatile approaches. Hence, the machine learning model is the best tool and achieves better decisions with minimum effort. The study will extend the investigation on various methods to get the optimal classification performance. Probable future directions in online incremental algorithms are appropriate for learning new information instantly enabling devices to adapt the environments.

References

1. Brezeale, D. and Cook, D.J., Automatic video classification: A survey of the literature. *IEEE Trans. Syst. Man Cybern. Part C Appl. Rev.*, 38, 3, 416–430, 2008.

2. Qi, W., Gu, L., Jiang, H., Chen, X.R., Zhang, H.J., Integrating visual, audio and text analysis for news video. *IEEE Int. Conf. Image Process.*, 3, 520–523, 2000.

3. Rahman, M.M., Bhattacharya, P., Desai, B.C., A framework for medical image retrieval using machine learning and statistical similarity matching techniques with relevance feedback. *IEEE Trans. Inf. Technol. Biomed. Publ. IEEE Eng. Med. Biol. Soc.*, 11, 1, 58–69, Jan. 2007.

4. Barrett, S., Chang, R., Qi, X., A fuzzy combined learning approach to content-based image retrieval, in: *2009 IEEE International Conference on Multimedia and Expo*, pp. 838–841, 2009.

5. Zhang, N. *et al.*, A generic approach for systematic analysis of sports videos. *ACM Trans. Intell. Syst. Technol.*, 3, 3, 1–33, 2012.

6. Jeyavadhanam, R., Mohan, S., Ramalingam, V.V., Sugumaran, V., Performance Comparison of Various Decision Tree Algorithms for Classification of Advertisement and Non Advertisement Videos. *Indian J. Sci. Technol.*, 9, 1–10, Dec. 2016.

7. Eggink, J., Allen, P., Bland, D., A pilot study for mood-based classification of TV programmes. *Proc. ACM Symp. Appl. Comput*, pp. 918–922, 2012.

8. Yu, J., Gwak, J., Lee, S., Jeon, M., An incremental learning approach for restricted boltzmann machines. *ICCAIS 2015 - 4th Int. Conf. Control. Autom. Inf. Sci.*, pp. 113–117, 2015.

9. Kandasamy, K. and Subash, C., Automatic Video Genre Classification. *Int. J. Eng. Res. Tech. (IJERT)*, 2, 5, 94–100, 2014.

10. Cheng, M.H., Hwang, K.S., Jeng, J.H., Lin, N.W., Classification-based video super-resolution using artificial neural networks. *Signal Process.*, 93, 9, 2612–2625, 2013.

11. Morita, K., Tashita, A., Nii, M., Kobashi, S., Computer-aided diagnosis system for Rheumatoid Arthritis using machine learning, in: *2017 International*

Conference on Machine Learning and Cybernetics (ICMLC), vol. 2, pp. 357–360, 2017.

12. Liu, Y., Feng, X., Zhou, Z., Multimodal video classification with stacked contractive autoencoders. *Signal Process.*, 120, 761–766, 2016.

13. Dabas, H., Sethi, C., Dua, C., Dalawat, M., Sethia, D., Emotion classification using EEG signals. *ACM Int. Conf. Proceeding Ser.*, pp. 380–384, 2018.

14. Ma, S., Zhang, X., Jia, C., Zhao, Z., Wang, S., Wang, S., Image and Video Compression with Neural Networks: A Review. *IEEE Trans. Circuits Syst. Video Technol.*, 30, 6, 1683–1698, 2020.

15. Asokan, A. and Anitha, J., Machine Learning based Image Processing Techniques for Satellite Image Analysis -A Survey. *Proc. Int. Conf. Mach. Learn. Big Data, Cloud Parallel Comput. Trends, Prespectives Prospect. Com. 2019*, pp. 119–124, 2019.

16. Zhou, W., Vellaikal, A., Kuo, C.C.J., Rule-based video classification system for basketball video indexing. *Proc. 2000 ACM Workshops Multimed.*, 213–216, 2000.

17. Sun, M., Hao, S., Liu, G., Semi-supervised vehicle classification via fusing affinity matrices. *Signal Process.*, 149, 118–123, 2018.

18. Basavarajaiah, M. and Sharma, P., Survey of compressed domain video summarization techniques. *ACM Comput. Surv.*, 52, 6, 1–29, 2019.

19. Li, X., Liu, T., Deng, J., Tao, D., Video face editing using temporal-spatial-smooth warping. *ACM Trans. Intell. Syst. Technol.*, 7, 3, 1–29, 2016.

20. Tang, J., Qi, G.J., Wang, M., Hua, X.S., Video semantic analysis based on structure-sensitive anisotropic manifold ranking. *Signal Process.*, 89, 12, 2313–2323, 2009.

21. Hu, Z. *et al.*, Visual classification of furniture styles. *ACM Trans. Intell. Syst. Technol.*, 8, 5, 1–20, 2017.

22. Ramalingam, V.V. and Mohan, S., Prosthetic Arm Control with Statistical Features of EEG signals using K-star Algorithm. *J. Appl. Sci.*, 16, 4, 138–145, 2016.

23. Vadhanam, B.R.J., Mohan, S., Sugumaran, V., Ramalingam, V.V., Exploiting BICC Features for Classification of Advertisement Videos Using RIDOR Algorithm, in: *2016 International Conference on Micro-Electronics and Telecommunication Engineering (ICMETE)*, pp. 247–252, 2016.

11

A Combinational Deep Learning Approach to Visually Evoked EEG-Based Image Classification

Nandini Kumari*, Shamama Anwar and Vandana Bhattacharjee

Department of Computer Science and Engineering, Birla Institute of Technology, Mesra, Ranchi, India

Abstract

Visual stimulus evoked potentials are neural oscillations acquired, from the brain's electrical activity, evoked while seeing an image or video as stimuli. With the advancement of deep learning techniques, decoding visual stimuli evoked EEG (electroencephalogram) signals has become a versatile study of neuroscience and computer vision alike. Deep learning techniques have capability to learn problem specific features automatically, which eliminates the traditional feature extraction procedure. In this work, the combinational deep learning–based classification model is used to classify visual stimuli evoked EEG signals while viewing two class images (i.e., animal and object class) from MindBig and Perceive dataset without the need of an additional feature extraction step. To achieve this objective, two deep learning–based architecture have been proposed and their classification accuracy has been compared. The first proposed model is a modified convolutional neural network (CNN) model and the other one is hybrid CNN+LSTM model which can better classify and predict the EEG features for visual classification. The raw EEG signal is converted to spectrogram images as CNN-based networks learn more discriminating features from images. The proposed CNN+LSTM-based architecture uses a depthwise separable convolution, i.e., Xception Network (Extreme inception network) with a parallel LSTM layer to extract temporal, frequential and spatial features from EEG signals, and classify more precisely than proposed CNN network. The overall average accuracy achieved are 69.84% and 71.45% on CNN model and 74.57% and 76.05% on combinational CNN+LSTM model on MindBig and Perceive dataset, respectively, which shows better performance than CNN model.

Corresponding author: missnandinikumari@gmail.com

Pradeep Singh (ed.) Fundamentals and Methods of Machine and Deep Learning: Algorithms, Tools and Applications, (259–276) © 2022 Scrivener Publishing LLC

Keywords: Electroencephalogram, visual stimuli, convolutional neural network, long short-term memory, Xception, depthwise separable convolution, spectrogram

11.1   Introduction

Deep learning is a sub-field of artificial intelligence which endeavors to learn significant layerwise abstracted patterns and information by using deep network models. It is an arising approach and has been broadly applied in conventional decision reasoning and machine learning areas, for example, semantic parsing [9], natural language processing [39], transfer learning [13, 46], computer vision [33], and some more. Three most significant explanations behind the booming of deep learning today: the significantly expanding and high processor abilities (e.g., GPU units), the low expense of computing hardware, and the extensive advancement of machine learning algorithms [17]. Recently, diverse deep learning strategies have been broadly implemented and examined in many application areas such as self-driving cars [25], news aggregation and fraud news detection [57], natural language processing [31], virtual assistants entertainment [30], visual recognition [50], fraud detection [47], healthcare [21], and many more. Deep learning is widely being accepted for computer vision tasks as it has shown near-human or even better capabilities to perform numerous tasks, such as object detection and sequence learning. As opposed to deep learning, traditional machine learning approaches for classification tasks require hand-crafted discriminating features which essentially contribute to design a system, for example, linear discriminant analysis (LDA), or support vector machine (SVM). The hand-crafted feature extraction techniques require detailed information of the problem domain for discovering exceptionally expressive features in complex tasks, for example, computer vision and natural language processing. Additionally, the large dimension of extracted features also prompts the curse of dimensionality. Deep learning is the best approach to move toward these complex issues. The different layers in a deep learning model reveals the complex features by progressively learning theoretical portrayals in the first few layers and more specific qualities in the accompanying layers [22]. Deep networks have been exposed to be effective for computer vision tasks such as visual recognition, object recognition [18], motion tracking [19], action recognition [36], human pose estimation [53], and semantic segmentation [37]. Since, they can separate suitable features while simultaneously performing classification or detection tasks. Through the ImageNet LargeScale

Visual Recognition Challenge (ILSVRC) competitions [1], deep learning techniques have been generally embraced by various analysts and accomplished highest accuracy scores. Recently, deep learning strategies have found applications in more innovative and promising areas of research dealing with human perception. As vision is one of the main component in the human perception system, it has great potential to find applications based on deep learning techniques. At the point when the eyes get visual instigation, neural spikes are conveyed to the brain. The analysis of these neural spikes is turning into a fascinating research subject in the field of computer vision. Even though deep learning mechanism [35], for example, CNN, has accomplished a great improvement in the image classification tasks [26, 43], computer vision is as yet unapproachable with of the extent of the actual human vision. Alternatively, extricating discriminating component relying upon the train dataset, the visual stimuli evoked recognition in a human's mind includes intellectual hypotheses as well as perceptive process [7], i.e., how the visual stimulus such as images and video invigorate the human's brain with respect to color shading and shape, and which parts of mind visual cortex can offer reaction to them. Some intellectual neuroscience researches investigated that while recording the brain's electrical activity when a person is seeing an image, there are some explicit pattern about visual evoked image categories produced in the brain [45]. The human cerebrum has the capacity to arrange visual improvements depending on the common and frequent patterns. This grouping and categorizations of these frequent patterns is fast and shows up in millisecond time scales [10]. Because of the splendid temporal resolutions of the electroencephalogram (EEG) signals, the visual object's images can be successfully perceived utilizing explicit patterns generated from EEG signals that are captured when images are shown on screen before the subjects [56]. EEG signals have been used to investigate and analyze the complexity of EEG signal for object detection and for classification tasks using machine learning methods [6].

Recently, the accessibility of huge EEG datasets and advancement in machine learning techniques have both motivated the implementation of deep learning tools, particularly in analyzing EEG signals and in perceiving the brain's functionality. At present, deep learning has likewise attracted lot of consideration in the field of EEG classification research. A few researchers have attempted to apply the deep learning strategy to EEG in order to accomplish good accuracy [15]. But deep learning strategies ar still challenging when applied to the EEG-based BCI framework because of different affecting factors, for example, the relationship among channels, artifacts, and noise while EEG recording and the high-dimensional EEG

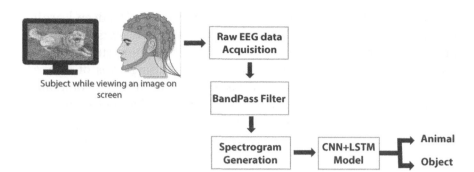

Figure 11.1 Flowchart of proposed architecture.

information. To address all these challenges mentioned above, the effective implementation of deep learning strategies for the characterization of EEG signals is a serious accomplishment.

This paper aims at providing a CNN- and LSTM-based framework for classification of visually evoked stimuli. Figure 11.1 describes the overall workflow of the proposed architecture. As a very initial step, we have explored the utilization of CNNs for multi-class classification of EEG signals recorded while a subject is viewing image from animal (i.e., cat, dog, panda, capuchin, and elephant) and object (i.e., mug, bike, airliner, broom, and phone) category. In the second step, the acquired EEG signals are then pre-processed using basic filtering process in order to remove artifacts, followed by a Short-Time Fourier Transform (STFT) implementation so as to get the spectrogram images of the EEG signals. Finally, these images are then used as input to the proposed CNN model for a binary classification task representing the two categories, i.e., animal and object. The paper also presents accuracy results of the implemented CNN network designed to classify stimuli evoked EEG recordings along with a comparative study of some past outcomes from CNN and combinational CNN+LSTM-based classifiers. The result shows that the proposed CNN+LSTM-based model provides better accuracy compared to some of the existing work. The following sections of the paper presents an extensive literature review, followed by the methodology section including dataset description, the proposed architecture and the implementation of the model. At last, the results are documented followed by the conclusion section.

11.2   Literature Review

There are various innovative researches based on feature extraction and machine learning techniques [14]. Priorly, the time-recurrence examination [23], nonlinear elements, unpredictability, synchronization, and additions of collected vitality [28] techniques were utilized as feature extraction strategies. Additionally, the machine learning classifier also incorporates naive Bayes, conventional neural network system, SVM, random forest classifiers [24]. Indeed, feature extraction strategies have been utilized effectively in EEG classification tasks. In past studies, different feature extraction techniques for retrieving EEG complex information have been proposed [5]. Existing strategies for the discovery of complex pattern uses hand-crafted procedures for extraction of prominent features from EEG signals, then the chosen features must be able to characterize EEG signals by utilizing a wide range of classifiers, for example, SVM, KNN, principal component analysis, independent component analysis, and LDA [51] using FFT-based dual tree complex wavelet transform [11].

Most of the literature on the traditional approaches extract features from EEG for different application domains. This results in a 1D vector representation of the extracted features and this representation may loose some of the discriminating and prominent features. Therefore, few researcher have used methods to represent an EEG signal using a 2D representation before applying a deep learning framework. In [16], STFT was used to transform time-frequency features of EEG data into 2D images. In some previous researches, feature extraction was not executed and the deep learning models were rather prepared with raw EEG signals [4, 29].

These images were then used as input neurons for two class motor imagery classifications by combining CNN and VAE (Variational Auto-Encoder) framework. Multiple motor imagery classification has also been implemented using two variant of CNN models, namely, monolithic (single CNN) and modular (four CNN) architecture by using Bayesian optimization technique. These two procedures uses features extracted by a variation of Discriminative Filter Bank Common Spatial Pattern (DFBCSP) [44].

Deep Learning techniques such as DBN (Dynamic Bayesian Network), RNN (Recurrent Neural Network), CNN (Convolutional Neural Network), LSTM (Long Short-Term Memory), SAE (Stacked Autoencoder), and hybrid deep networks have made noteworthy leaps in seizure and emotion detection, sleep scoring, motor imagery, event related potential detection, and visual stimuli–related image classification problem [15] and pattern recognition tasks [20, 32]. Recently, EEG information used in conjugation with facial expressions has been applied in persistent emotion recognition [49].

In [55], a new 3D CNN architecture to predict different stages of EEG data for epilepsy classification from multichannel EEG signals was discussed. Each EEG channel is converted into 2D images and are then combined to form 3D images which serve as input to a 3D CNN structure for classification. According to [59], frequency-based signals have greater potential than temporal signals for CNN applications; therefore, both frequency and time domain features for EEG classification were tested using the same CNN classification architecture. The EEG signal is also utilized to screen the brain's electrical activity to analyze diverse sleep disorders. Deep learning has been also applied for sleep disorder detection using single channel EEG [40] and speech recognition [42]. Decoding visual stimulus from EEG captured brain's activities is an interdisciplinary investigation of neuroscience and computer vision. Novel EEG-driven automatic visual classification and regeneration techniques have likewise been proposed. Ran Manor and Amir B. Geva have presented a CNN model for single-trail EEG classification of visually evoked potential tasks [38]. Similar tasks were performed for object classification using EEG signals evoked by stimulus-related potentials but with different CNN architecture [48]. Nicholas Waytowich proposed compact CNN to extract features from raw EEG signals automatically which can be used to decode signals from a 12 class visual evoked potential dataset [54]. The combination of CNN and LSTM has also been implemented for visual evoked classification. An automated model for visual classification in which LSTM is used to extract prominent feature representation from EEG signal and further that is fed to ResNet that leads to the improvement of classification performance [58]. A deep neural network (DNN) with RNN and CNN is trained for the EEG classification task by using video as visual stimuli [52]. In [8], authors proposed a deep learning model that uses a hybrid architecture based on CNN and RNN to classify visual evoked EEG signals and achieved better accuracy than CNN only as LSTM works well with temporal data as it helps to find the prominent features, and then, CNN architecture uses those features for improved classification. Despite many examples of impressive progress of deep network for visual stimuli evoked EEG signal classification, there is still room for considerable improved performance accuracy with hybrid deep structure.

11.3   Methodology

11.3.1   Dataset Acquisition

In this experiment, two publicly accessible open datasets; MindBig dataset [2] and Perceive lab dataset [3] are considered. Table 11.1 represents the overall description of both the datasets.

In this paper, for experimentation, the EEG signals are used from two categories of visual stimuli that is object and animals. Object class consists of the EEG signals recorded while seeing images of objects like mug, bike,

Table 11.1 Dataset description.

Dataset	MindBig dataset	Perceive dataset
No. of subject	1 subject	6 subjects
No. of images used as stimulus	569 image class from ImageNet ILSVRC2013 train dataset (14,012 images)	40 image class from ImageNet ILSVRC2013 train dataset (2,000 images)
Available data	Raw EEG data available	Raw EEG data available
Sampling rate	128 Hz	128 Hz
EEG headset	5-channel EEG Headset (Emotive Insight) used. Channel locations: AF3, AF3, T7, T8, Pz	128-channel EEG headset (actiCAP 128ch)

airliner, broom, and phone. Similarly, the animal class consists of EEG signals acquired when a subject is viewing the images of animals like cat, dog, panda, capuchin, and elephant.

11.3.2 Pre-Processing and Spectrogram Generation

The EEG signals acquired from the dataset can be decomposed into different frequency band powers, the range of which specifically depends on the motivation behind the research. A 50-Hz notch filter and a band-pass Butterworth filter between 14 and 71 Hz were set up; hence, the recorded EEG signals covered the Beta (15-31 Hz) and Gamma (32-70 Hz) frequency, as they carry information about the psychological cycles engaged with the visual recognition [41]. The time and spatial resolution of EEG data can be retained by converting the EEG data to an image like representation. Various techniques have been used to create a 2D image representation from 1D raw signals to handle classification tasks of a time series data using CNNs [27, 34]. Hence, to maintain both time and spatial resolution of the acquired EEG signal and to convert 1D EEG signals to 2D images, the STFT algorithm is applied to the filtered EEG signals. It produces a solitary 2D time-frequency domain spectrogram images for every EEG electrode position E. For instance, in this experiment, 128 EEG channels were used to create 128 2D spectrogram images.

The EEG signals in MindBig dataset were acquired from five electrode points; therefore, five 2D spectrogram images were generated for each image sample. Here, 1,250 spectrogram images with 64 × 64 image size is generated from 25 trails for each of the 10 images (5 from object group and 5 from animal group), i.e., 25 × 10 × 5 = 1,250 images. Similarly, the EEG signals from the Perceive dataset were acquired from 6 subjects with 128 electrode points; therefore, 128 2D spectrogram images can be generated of 5 trails for each of the 10 images, i.e., 10 × 10 × 128 = 12,800 images from 1 subject. A total number of 76,800 spectrogram images has been generated from 6 subjects using the STFT algorithm. The generated data was split into 80:20 ratio.

We have proposed two deep learning–based model to classify visual stimuli evoked EEG signal. The first architecture has been proposed using CNN model and then the hybrid architecture of CNN and LSTM has been proposed as hybrid deep learning model to achieve better performance. These models have been also compared with respect to accuracy, architecture, and its performance.

11.3.3   Classification of EEG Spectrogram Images With Proposed CNN Model

Since the objective is to classify spectrogram images which is generated from stimuli evoked EEG signals, a modified version of CNN model has been used to classify EEG spectrogram. The STFT generated 2D spectrogram images serve as an input vector to the CNN architecture. In this paper, the CNN architecture is composed of four Conv2D layers and one fully connected (FC) layers. All four layers use non-linear activation function ReLU (Rectified Linear Units) to convert the output between 0.01 and 1. In this paper, the CNN architecture is composed of four Conv2D layers and two FC layers. All four layers use non-linear activation function ReLU to convert the output between 0.01 and 1.

The first layer receives the spectrogram images of dimension 64 × 64 × 3 (3 represents RGB images) as input and outputs a 64 × 64 × 64 feature map by applying 64 kernels with kernel size 3 × 3 of stride 1. The second layer comprises of a pooling layer with stride 2 which has been applied to reduce the dimensionality of the 128 kernels with 3 × 3 kernel size and yields 62 × 62 × 128 feature map followed by a 2D Maxpooling layer with 2 stride rate which suppresses the output to 31 × 31 × 128. The third and fourth layers consist of 256 kernels with 3 × 3 kernel size which yields 29 × 29 × 256 feature maps. Again a 2D maxpooling layer is used to find the

Table 11.2 Architecture of proposed convolutional neural network.

Layer	Input	Operation	Filter size	Strides	Output
1	$64 \times 64 \times 3$	Conv2D + ReLU	$64 \times 3 \times 3$	1	$64 \times 64 \times 64$
3	$64 \times 64 \times 64$	Conv2D + ReLU	$128 \times 3 \times 3$	1	$62 \times 62 \times 128$
4	$62 \times 62 \times 128$	Maxpool	2×2	2	$31 \times 31 \times 128$
5	$31 \times 31 \times 128$	Conv2D + ReLU	$256 \times 3 \times 3$	1	$31 \times 31 \times 256$
6	$31 \times 31 \times 256$	Conv2D + ReLU	$256 \times 3 \times 3$	1	$29 \times 29 \times 256$
7	$29 \times 29 \times 256$	Maxpool	2×2	2	$14 \times 14 \times 256$
8	$14 \times 14 \times 256$	Flatten			50,176
9		Dense+ReLU	512		25,690,624
10		Dropout (0.5)			
11		Dense+Softmax	2		2×512

most relevant features with size $14 \times 14 \times 256$. Finally, the resultant feature map from the previous layer are FC with 2 dense layer of 512 and 2 outputs neurons and derive the probabilities for 2 classes, i.e., object and animal using 50% dropout and Softmax function. A brief explanation with number of layers, input and output size, different operation along with filter size implemented in CNN model is shown in Table 11.2. This architecture has been tested using both the datasets.

Additionally, this network was trained with batch size 32 and RMSprop (Root Mean Square Propagation), a widely known gradient descent optimizer was used for 100 epochs. For the RMSprop optimizer, a learning rate of 0.0001 and decay of $1e^{-6}$ was used. This architecture has been tested using the above described dataset and acquired results and further analysis is provided in Result and Discussion section.

11.3.4   Classification of EEG Spectrogram Images With Proposed Combinational CNN+LSTM Model

The proposed network consists of two different modules: a CNN module which uses the Xception model, pretrained on ImageNet dataset implemented by Keras and another independent module is LSTM module. Each one of these modules runs parallel to each other. The first module is a CNN-based architecture, i.e., Xception, which stands for "Extreme Inception". This is an extension of the Inception architecture which replaces the standard Inception modules with depthwise separable convolutions. The Xception architecture has 36 convolutional layers comprising the feature extraction unit of the network. The two spatial dimensions of width and height and the channel dimension helps the convolution layer to learn filters in a 3D space. Thus, the task of simultaneously mapping cross-channel features and spatial features rests with a single convolution kernel [12].

The EEG signals contain the temporal, frequential, and spatial features. These features should be extracted from the EEG signals as it consist important information regarding EEG signals. The conventional CNN do not perform convolution across all channels. That means the number of connections are fewer and the model is lighter and is unable to extract depthwise features. Therefore, we have implemented Xception network which can extract spatial features as it uses depthwise separable convolution. Initially, the entire network takes a RGB spectrogram image whose shape is $299 \times 299 \times 3$ and passed through the pretrained Xception model until it reaches the final convolution block which has the bottleneck features, which is of batch size 2,048. The second module, i.e., LSTM layer is used to extract the temporal relationship of the input spectrogram images generated from the input EEG signals.

On the LSTM module, the 299 × 299 × 3 image is converted to grayscale image of size 299 × 299 × 1 to be able to properly split it into chunks to feed it into the LSTM. Afterward, this 299 × 299 image is reshaped into (23, 3887), where 23 is the time-step and 3887 is the dimension of each time-step. These values were chosen because 23 × 3887 = 299 × 299. The reshaped image is then passed through two LSTM layers, each of which are of (batch size, 2,048) output. The Xception network yields the depthwise features using multiple feature extraction layers from EEG signals and the other independent LSTM model process the EEG signals to yield temporal features which when combined can help to recognize the overall pattern of EEG spectogram and can improve the classification results. Next, now that we have (batch size, 2,048) from both the CNN and LSTM modules, these two outputs are merged using elementwise multiplication. The output of this multiplication is then provided to the classification layer which consists of two nodes (two classes, i.e., object and animal) and a softmax activation. Figure 11.2 shows the architecture of proposed hybrid CNN+LSTM network, and Figure 11.3 depicts the overall architecture of original Xception network [12].

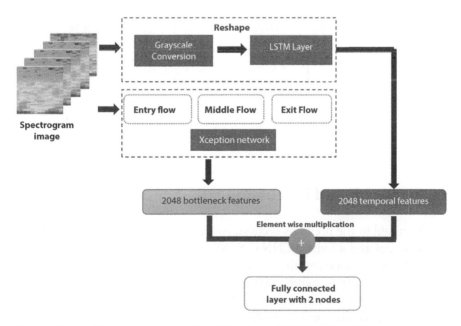

Figure 11.2 Architecture of proposed combinational CNN+LSTM model.

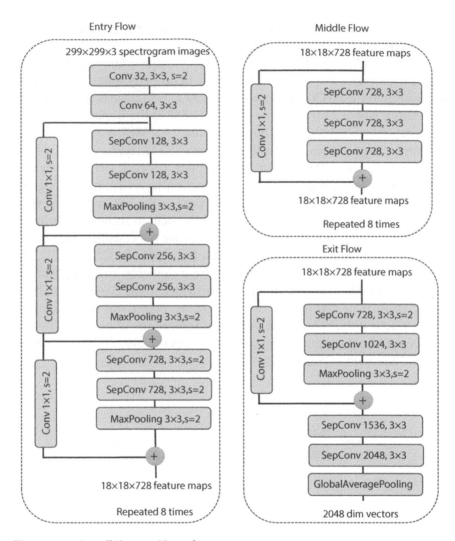

Figure 11.3 Overall XceptionNet architecture.

11.4   Result and Discussion

As discussed in the previous section, two different models, i.e., a modified CNN model and a hybrid CNN+LSTM model is implemented to classify the EEG-based spectrogam images. As described in dataset description section, two datasets, namely, MindBig and Perceive datasets, are used to train and test the proposed model. As clarified in the above sections, the raw EEG signals are converted into spectrogram images using STFT, which

Table 11.3 Classification accuracy (%) with two proposed models on two different datasets.

Model	MindBig dataset	Perceive dataset
CNN	69.84	71.45
CNN+LSTM	74.57	76.05

then serve as an input data for the proposed CNN- and CNN+LSTM-based techniques. Additionally, this method was processed in mini-batches of size 32 and Adam optimizer has been used for both datasets for 50 epochs. The overall accuracy for both models on both datasets are provided in Table 11.3. The proposed CNN model achieved 69.84% and 71.45% classification accuracy, and combinational CNN+LSTM model has performed better with classification accuracy of 74.57% and 76.05% on MindBig and Percieve datasets, respectively. In this current work, firstly, a CNN model was implemented but as the acquired accuracy was not very good, depthwise CNN architecture (Xception Network) with LSTM model was implemented to extract multilevel spatial and channelwise features as well as temporal and frequential features from LSTM layer which can help to improve classification accuracy. Figures 11.4a and 11.4b show the accuracy graph of training and testing of CNN model and Figures 11.5a and 11.5b present the proposed combinational CNN+LSTM model's training and testing accuracy.

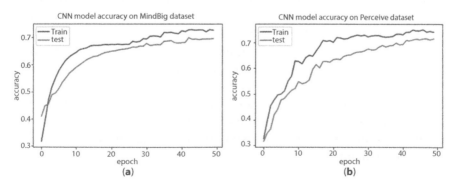

Figure 11.4 Proposed CNN model's accuracy graph on (a) MindBig dataset and (b) Perceive dataset.

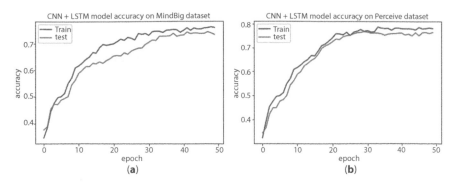

Figure 11.5 Proposed CNN+LSTM model's accuracy graph on (a) MindBig dataset and (b) Perceive dataset.

11.5   Conclusion

In this chapter, a visual classification system is proposed utilizing EEG signals, evoked from visual stimuli while seeing an image. A CNN-based model and combinational CNN+LSTM model has been proposed to classify the images based on the recorded EEG signals. The contribution of this work is in two essential viewpoints. The first is the utilization of the STFT strategy to transform the visually evoked 1D EEG signals into 2D spectrogram images for obtaining better results. Second, this paper provides the deep learning–based network model to accomplish the problem. This paper proposes a CNN-based model and a combinational CNN+LSTM model, which is used to classify the visual evoked EEG signal and recognizes the image an individual is seeing at the time of EEG recording procedure. The proposed CNN model was able to classify the spectrogram images as inputs extracted from the MindBigData to identify two different classes (animal and object) the subject was viewing while the EEG was captured. The CNN+LSTM-based model efficiency is evident from its accuracy in comparison to CNN model. A future extension to the work may include testing the model on other datasets acquired through different visual stimulus. This architecture can also be tested for multi classification using more image classes. Application wise, this technique can find varied implementations in the field of brain fingerprinting and also early abnormality detection in children by asking them to visualize any object that is shown to them on screen.

References

1. Imagenet dataset visual challenge ilsvrc, 2014, http://www.image-net.org/challenges/LSVRC/2014/results.
2. Mindbig dataset,http://opendatacommons.org/licenses/odbl/1.0/. Database Contents License: http://opendatacommons.org/licenses/dbcl/1.0/
3. Spampinato, C., Palazzo, S., Kavasidis, I., Giordano, D., Souly, N., Shah, M., Deep learning human mind for automated visual classification, in: *Proceedings of the IEEE conference on computer vision and pattern recognition*, pp. 6809–6817, 2017.
4. Acharya, U.R., Oh, S.L., Hagiwara, Y., Tan, J.H., Adeli, H., Deep convolutional neural network for the automated detection and diagnosis of seizure using EEG signals. *Comput. Biol. Med.*, 100, 270–278, 2018.
5. Acharya, U.R., Sree, S.V., Ang, P.C.A., Yanti, R., Suri, J.S., Application of non-linear and wavelet based features for the automated identification of epileptic EEG signals. *Int. J. Neural Syst.*, 22, 02, 1250002, 2012.
6. Ahmadi-Pajouh, M.A., Ala, T.S., Zamanian, F., Namazi, H., Jafari, S., Fractal-based classification of human brain response to living and non-living visual stimuli. *Fractals*, 26, 05, 1850069, 2018.
7. Alpert, G.F., Manor, R., Spanier, A.B., Deouell, L.Y., Geva, A.B., Spatiotemporal representations of rapid visual target detection: A single-trial EEG classification algorithm. *IEEE Trans. Biomed. Eng.*, 61, 8, 2290–2303, 2013.
8. Attia, M., Hettiarachchi, I., Hossny, M., Nahavandi, S., A time domain classification of steady-state visual evoked potentials using deep recurrent-convolutional neural networks, in: *2018 IEEE 15th International Symposium on Biomedical Imaging (ISBI 2018)*, IEEE, pp. 766–769, 2018.
9. Bordes, A., Glorot, X., Weston, J., Bengio, Y., Joint learning of words and meaning representations for open-text semantic parsing. In: *Artificial Intelligence and Statistics*, La Palma, Canary Islands, PMLR, 127–135, 2012.
10. Cecotti, H., Eckstein, M.P., Giesbrecht, B., Single-trial classification of event-related potentials in rapid serial visual presentation tasks using supervised spatial filtering. *IEEE Trans. Neural Networks Learn. Syst.*, 25, 11, 2030–2042, 2014.
11. Chen, G., Xie, W., Bui, T.D., Krzyżak, A., Automatic epileptic seizure detection in EEG using nonsubsampled wavelet–fourier features. *J. Med. Biol. Eng.*, 37, 1, 123–131, 2017.
12. Chollet, F., Xception: Deep learning with depthwise separable convolutions, in: *Proceedings of the IEEE conference on computer vision and pattern recognition*, pp. 1251–1258, 2017.
13. Cireşan, D.C., Meier, U., Schmidhuber, J., Transfer learning for Latin and Chinese characters with deep neural networks, in: *The 2012 international joint conference on neural networks (IJCNN)*, IEEE, pp. 1–6, 2012.
14. Cogan, D.L.C., *Multi extracerebral biosignal analysis for epileptic seizure monitoring*. ProQuest Dissertations Publishing, The University of Texas at Dallas, 2016.

15. Craik, A., He, Y., Contreras-Vidal, J.L., Deep learning for electroencephalo-gram (EEG) classification tasks: a review. *J. Neural Eng.*, 16, 3, 031001, 2019.

16. Dai, M., Zheng, D., Na, R., Wang, S., Zhang, S., EEG classification of motor imagery using a novel deep learning framework. *Sensors*, 19, 3, 551, 2019.

17. Deng, L., A tutorial survey of architectures, algorithms, and applications for deep learning. *APSIPA Trans. Signal Inf. Process.*, 3, 2014.

18. Diba, A., Sharma, V., Pazandeh, A., Pirsiavash, H., Van Gool, L., Weakly supervised cascaded convolutional networks, in: *Proceedings of the IEEE conference on computer vision and pattern recognition*, pp. 914–922, 2017.

19. Doulamis, N., Adaptable deep learning structures for object labeling/track-ing under dynamic visual environments. *Multimed. Tools Appl.*, 77, 8, 9651–9689, 2018.

20. Erfani, S.M., Rajasegarar, S., Karunasekera, S., Leckie, C., High-dimensional and large-scale anomaly detection using a linear one-class SVM with deep learning. *Pattern Recognit.*, 58, 121–134, 2016.

21. Faust, O., Hagiwara, Y., Hong, T.J., Lih, O.S., Acharya, U.R., Deep learning for healthcare applications based on physiological signals: A review. *Comput. Methods Programs Biomed.*, 161, 1–13, 2018.

22. Fedjaev, J., *Decoding EEG brain signals using recurrent neural networks*, 2017.

23. Fiscon, G., Weitschek, E., Cialini, A., Felici, G., Bertolazzi, P., De Salvo, S., Bramanti, A., Bramanti, P., De Cola, M.C., Combining EEG signal process-ing with supervised methods for Alzheimer's patients classification. *BMC Med. Inf. Decis. Making*, 18, 1, 35, 2018.

24. Fraiwan, L., Lweesy, K., Khasawneh, N., Wenz, H., Dickhaus, H., Automated sleep stage identification system based on time-frequency analysis of a sin-gle EEG channel and random forest classifier. *Comput. Methods Programs Biomed.*, 108, 1, 10–19, 2012.

25. Grigorescu, S., Trasnea, B., Cocias, T., Macesanu, G., A survey of deep learn-ing techniques for autonomous driving. *J. Field Rob.*, 37, 3, 362–386, 2020.

26. Gu, J., Wang, Z., Kuen, J., Ma, L., Shahroudy, A., Shuai, B., Liu, T., Wang, X., Wang, G., Cai, J. *et al.*, Recent advances in convolutional neural networks. *Pattern Recognit.*, 77, 354–377, 2018.

27. Ha, K.W. and Jeong, J.W., Motor imagery EEG classification using Capsule Networks. *Sensors*, 19, 13, 2854, 2019.

28. Hsu, Y.L., Yang, Y.T., Wang, J.S., Hsu, C.Y., Automatic sleep stage recurrent neural classifier using energy features of EEG signals. *Neurocomputing*, 104, 105–114, 2013.

29. Hussein, R., Palangi, H., Ward, R., Wang, Z.J., Epileptic seizure detection: A deep learning approach. *Signal Process.*, 1–12, 2018.

30. Iannizzotto, G., Bello, L.L., Nucita, A., Grasso, G.M., A vision and speech enabled, customizable, virtual assistant for smart environments, in: *2018 11th International Conference on Human System Interaction (HSI)*, IEEE, pp. 50–56, 2018.

31. Kamath, U., Liu, J., Whitaker, J., *Deep learning for (NLP) and speech recognition.* vol. 84, Springer, Switzerland, 2019.
32. Krizhevsky, A., Sutskever, I., Hinton, G.E., Imagenet classification with deep convolutional neural networks. In: *Advances in neural information processing systems*, vol. 25, 1097–1105, 2012.
33. Krizhevsky, A., Sutskever, I., Hinton, G.E., Imagenet classification with deep convolutional neural networks. *Commun. ACM*, 60, 6, 84–90, 2017.
34. Kwon, Y.H., Shin, S.B., Kim, S.D., Electroencephalography based fusion two-dimensional (2D)-convolution neural networks (CNN) model for emotion recognition system. *Sensors*, 18, 5, 1383, 2018.
35. LeCun, Y., Bengio, Y., Hinton, G., Deep learning. *Nature*, 521, 7553, 436–444, 2015.
36. Lin, L., Wang, K., Zuo, W., Wang, M., Luo, J., Zhang, L., A deep structured model with radius–margin bound for 3D human activity recognition. *Int. J. Comput. Vision*, 118, 2, 256–273, 2016.
37. Long, J., Shelhamer, E., Darrell, T., Fully convolutional networks for semantic segmentation, in: *Proceedings of the IEEE conference on computer vision and pattern recognition*, pp. 3431–3440, 2015.
38. Manor, R. and Geva, A.B., Convolutional neural network for multi-category rapid serial visual presentation BCI. *Front. Comput. Neurosci.*, 9, 146, 2015.
39. Mikolov, T., Sutskever, I., Chen, K., Corrado, G.S., Dean, J., Distributed representations of words and phrases and their compositionality, in: *Advances in neural information processing systems*, pp. 3111–3119, 2013.
40. Mousavi, S., Afghah, F., Acharya, U.R., Sleep EEGN: Automated sleep stage scoring with sequence to sequence deep learning approach. *PLoS One*, 14, 5, e0216456, 2019.
41. Niedermeyer, E., da Silva, F.L., *Electroencephalography: basic principles, clinical applications, and related fields.* Lippincott Williams & Wilkins, Lopes da Silva, F. H., 1, 2005.
42. Noda, K., Yamaguchi, Y., Nakadai, K., Okuno, H.G., Ogata, T., Audio-visual speech recognition using deep learning. *Appl. Intell.*, 42, 4, 722–737, 2015.
43. Ogawa, T., Sasaka, Y., Maeda, K., Haseyama, M., Favorite video classification based on multimodal bidirectional LSTM. *IEEE Access*, 6, 61401–61409, 2018.
44. Olivas-Padilla, B.E. and Chacon-Murguia, M.I., Classification of multiple motor imagery using deep convolutional neural networks and spatial filters. *Appl. Soft Comput.*, 75, 461–472, 2019.
45. Op de Beeck, H.P., Vermaercke, B., Woolley, D., Wenderoth, N., Combinatorial brain decoding of people's whereabouts during visuospatial navigation. *Front. Neurosci.*, 7, 78, 2013.
46. Ren, J., Xu, L., On vectorization of deep convolutional neural networks for vision tasks. In: *Proceedings of the AAAI Conference on Artificial Intelligence.* vol. 29, 2015.

47. Roy, A., Sun, J., Mahoney, R., Alonzi, L., Adams, S., Beling, P., Deep learning detecting fraud in credit card transactions. In: *2018 Systems and Information Engineering Design Symposium (SIEDS)*, Charlottesville, VA, USA, IEEE, 129–134, 2018.

48. Shamwell, J., Lee, H., Kwon, H., Marathe, A.R., Lawhern, V., Nothwang, W., Single-trial EEG RSVP classification using convolutional neural networks. In: *Micro-and Nanotechnology Sensors, Systems, and Applications VIII*. vol. 9836, Baltimore, Maryland, United States, International Society for Optics and Photonics, 2016, 983622.

49. Soleymani, M., Asghari-Esfeden, S., Fu, Y., Pantic, M., Analysis of EEG signals and facial expressions for continuous emotion detection. *IEEE Trans. Affect. Comput.*, 7, 1, 17–28, 2015.

50. Spampinato, C., Palazzo, S., Kavasidis, I., Giordano, D., Souly, N., Shah, M., Deep learning human mind for automated visual classification, in: *Proceedings of the IEEE conference on computer vision and pattern recognition*, pp. 6809–6817, 2017.

51. Subasi, A. and Gursoy, M.I., EEG signal classification using PCA, ICA, LDA and support vector machines. *Expert Syst. Appl.*, 37, 12, 8659–8666, 2010.

52. Tan, C., Sun, F., Zhang, W., Chen, J., Liu, C., Multimodal classification with deep convolutional-recurrent neural networks for electroencephalography, in: *International Conference on Neural Information Processing*, Springer, pp. 767–776, 2017.

53. Toshev, A. and Szegedy, C., Deeppose: Human pose estimation via deep neural networks, in: *Proceedings of the IEEE conference on computer vision and pattern recognition*, pp. 1653–1660, 2014.

54. Waytowich, N., Lawhern, V.J., Garcia, J.O., Cummings, J., Faller, J., Sajda, P., Vettel, J.M., Compact convolutional neural networks for classification of asynchronous steady-state visual evoked potentials. *J. Neural Eng.*, 15, 6, 066031, 2018.

55. Wei, X., Zhou, L., Chen, Z., Zhang, L., Zhou, Y., Automatic seizure detection using three-dimensional CNN based on multi-channel EEG. *BMC Med. Inf. Decis. Making*, 18, 5, 111, 2018.

56. Yu, R., Qiao, L., Chen, M., Lee, S.W., Fei, X., Shen, D., Weighted graph regularized sparse brain network construction for MCI identification. *Pattern Recognit.*, 90, 220–231, 2019.

57. Zhang, J., Cui, L., Fu, Y., Gouza, F.B., Fake news detection with deep diffusive network model. arXiv preprint arXiv:1805.08751, 2018.

58. Zheng, X., Chen, W., You, Y., Jiang, Y., Li, M., Zhang, T., Ensemble deep learning for automated visual classification using EEG signals. *Pattern Recognit.*, 102, 107147, 2020.

59. Zhou, M., Tian, C., Cao, R., Wang, B., Niu, Y., Hu, T., Guo, H., Xiang, J., Epileptic seizure detection based on EEG signals and CNN. *Front. Neuroinf.*, 12, 95, 2018.

12

Application of Machine Learning Algorithms With Balancing Techniques for Credit Card Fraud Detection: A Comparative Analysis

Shiksha

School of Computer Science and Mathematics, Liverpool John Moores University, Liverpool, United Kingdom

Abstract

This paper investigates the performance of the four supervised machine learning algorithms: logistic regression, support vector machine, decision tree, and random forest on the highly imbalanced ULB machine learning credit card fraudulent transaction dataset and a comparative analysis is performed. The major point that distinguishes this study from others is that this work is not only focused on the four supervised machine learning algorithms, rather than the permutation and combination of these methods with different balancing techniques are studied and analyzed for several evaluation metrics to obtain a better performance. In addition of the sampling techniques, one more method is used to balance the dataset by taking in account the balanced class weight at the modeling time. It is important to mention that the random forest with balanced class weight has shown the lowest false positive transactions with a value of only 3. The comparative results demonstrate that the random forest with SMOTE oversampling technique has output the best results in terms of all the selected metrics with accuracy of 99.92%, recall value of 81.08%, precision of 76.43%, F1-score of 78.69%, MCC of 0.79, AUC of 0.96, and AUPRC of 0.81.

Keywords: Supervised machine learning algorithms, logistic regression, SVM, decision tree, random forest, random undersampling technique, random oversampling technique, SMOTE

Email: shiksha13nov@gmail.com

Pradeep Singh (ed.) Fundamentals and Methods of Machine and Deep Learning: Algorithms, Tools and Applications, (277–310) © 2022 Scrivener Publishing LLC

12.1   Introduction

The credit card is one of the important financial product and a revolutionizing application of the technology evolution which is used widely to spend money easily [1]. The heavy usage of the credit cards has become one of the important application in the last 10 years [2]. As the credit card transactions are increasing, there is a high probability of identity theft and losses to customers and banks both [3]. The credit card fraud is the type of identity theft and it occurs when someone else than the assigned person uses the credit card or the credit account for making a transaction [4]. It is on the top rank in the identity theft and has increased by 18% in 2018 [4]. The credit card fraudulent transactions are increasing considerably with a huge loss every year. Credit Card Fraud Statistics show that more than 24 billion dollars were lost in 2018 due to the credit card fraud [4] and poses a serious threat as the individual information is being misused. Hence, prevention of the credit card fraud at the correct time is the need of the hour.

Fraud detection for the credit card is the process of distinguishing the successful transactions into two classes. It can be legitimate (genuine) or fraudulent transaction [5]. Hence, classifying the credit card fraud transactions is a binary classification problem whose objective is to classify the transaction as a legitimate (negative class) transaction or a fraudulent (positive class) transaction [6]. With the advancement of credit card fraud detection methods, there is also rise in the fraud practices to avoid the fraud detection; hence, the fraud detection methods for credit card also require continuous evolution [7]. There are few things that need to be considered during fraud detection. First is the quick decision; it means the credit card should be immediately revoked once the fraud is detected; second is the misclassification significance; and the third one is the issue related to the highly biased dataset [8]. Misclassification of a no-fraud transaction as a fraud one can be tolerated, since fraud transaction requires more investigation but, if a fraud transaction is considered as a genuine one, then it will certainly cause more problems [8]. For the fraud detection of the credit card, the main goal is to reduce the misclassification of the fraudulent cases and the secondary aim is to reduce the misclassification of the genuine cases [9]. It can also happen that a transaction identified as a fraud is actually a genuine transaction or a no-fraud transaction is actually a fraud case. So, a good performance of fraud detection requires less number of false positive and false negative [8].

The performance of the fraud detection system is extremely influenced by the imbalanced credit card transaction dataset which has a very less number of fraud cases compared to the genuine cases, and it makes detection of fraud transaction a cumbersome and uncertain process [7, 8]. Hence, a sampling technique is required to balance both types of transactions to get a good result. But, the method of balancing has been fixed even before the implementation in almost all reported works, which is the motivation of this work to explore the performance of different sampling techniques. One more technique (other than the sampling methods) has been used in this study to balance the dataset by accounting the balanced class weight at the modeling time. This technique is executed in this experiment to evaluate and compare its results with the performance of the sampling techniques used. Moreover, each machine learning algorithm provides the good result for different parameters. Hence, there is a need of permutation and combination of different algorithms with several result parameters along with different balancing techniques. The above-mentioned points are taken care in this work. Since the credit card fraud data is highly imbalanced, different balancing techniques are implemented to obtain the high performance. The rationale to explore the four techniques selected: logistic regression, support vector machine (SVM), decision tree, and random forest, is because of their performance values and advantages reported in the different literatures, and also as not many papers have compared the result of all these four techniques in a single work, so this work focused mainly on these four algorithms and the performance of the classifiers are evaluated based on accuracy, recall, precision, F1-score, MCC, AUC, and area under precision-recall curve (AUPRC). The main aim of this paper is to obtain a model to detect the credit card fraudulent transaction on an imbalanced dataset. Hence, the primary goal of this work is to reduce the misclassification of the fraudulent cases and the secondary goal is to reduce the misclassification of the genuine cases. The identification of the credit card fraud transaction using the well-studied techniques prevents recurrence of the fraud incidences and can save the revenue loss.

As seen in the several papers, all the works are either not using the sampling method or utilizing mostly one of the sampling technique for the credit card fraud detection which has been already fixed before implementing the model [2, 7–13]. Very few papers have compared the sampling techniques for a better performance; hence, this has motivated to go ahead in this work to compare different sampling techniques with different machine learning algorithms.

From the literature review, it is found that the highest accuracy of 99.95% is achieved for credit card fraud detection [5]. But as discussed in this paper, only the accuracy is not a sufficient measure for such a highly biased dataset, hence other parameters also should have maximum value along with accuracy [2, 6, 14–16]. Also, it is concluded that if sensitivity or specificity is increased, accuracy decreases, and as seen, for a high value of accuracy of 98.6%, only specificity of 90.5% is achieved; also, there is not any models which have high values for accuracy, sensitivity, specificity, and AUC [5]. The literature reviews done for this work showed that mostly the high performance metrics are given by models: random forest and logistic regression. Hence, the purpose of this study is to develop a model having better values for all the mentioned evaluation metrics compared to the results obtained in the literatures review and for this a comparative analysis of four supervised machine learning techniques: logistic regression, SVM, decision tree, and random forest, on the highly skewed real-time dataset will be done for better detecting the credit card fraudulent transaction and controlling the credit card fraud. The performance of the classifiers will be compared based on accuracy, recall, and precision, F1-score, Matthews's correlation coefficient (MCC), area under ROC curve (AUC), and AUPRC. As the credit card fraud data is highly biased, this work will enhance the handling of the highly biased credit card fraud dataset as presented in related papers by using different methods of sampling.

12.2   Methods and Techniques

Credit card fraud detection is the method to identify the transactions as legitimate or fraud. As discussed in this paper, the machine learning algorithms are categorized in supervised and unsupervised techniques where supervised learning algorithms require labeled output and unsupervised methods cluster the data into the similar class [17]. Several works have been presented for both types of techniques and showing the usage of supervised and unsupervised techniques for credit card fraud detection with a good performance for both. The supervised techniques are mostly used since it is trained using prior labeled data and the transaction class can be controlled using human interference [18]. Since this work is implemented using supervised machine learning techniques, so details regarding unsupervised methods are excluded and not presented in this paper. Among all the machine learning techniques, logistic regression and random forests are preferred due to the high performance measured in terms of accuracy, recall, and precision [2, 7, 12, 13, 19].

12.2.1   Research Approach

This section illustrates the approach designed for the research work of credit card fraud detection carried out in this paper, as shown in Figure 12.1

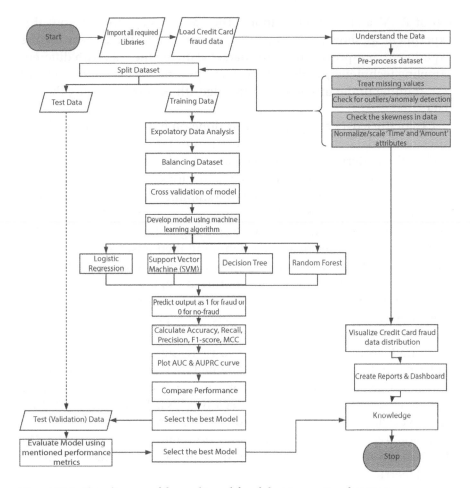

Figure 12.1 Flow diagram of the credit card fraudulent transaction detection.

including dataset, different balancing techniques, and the four machine learning algorithms: logistic regression, SVM, decision tree, and random forest classifiers.

In the pre-processing of the dataset, the data is imported, and it is checked for any missing values. Since the selected dataset is highly skewed, the balancing method is implemented on the prepared data to get the equal distribution of both the classes. In the training phase, machine learning algorithm is implemented on pre-processed data and then its performance is evaluated on basis of accuracy, recall, and precision, F1-score, MCC, AUC, and AUPRC.

The analysis of the ULB machine learning credit card dataset is done in Python 3 kernel using Jupyter Notebook on a Windows System of 8

GB of RAM and 1 TB of memory. The various steps to carry out this experiment as shown in Figure 12.1 are collecting the dataset for the experiment, pre-processing of the data, balancing the data with different sampling techniques, analyzing the data, splitting the data into train and test, training of the machine learning algorithm, and evaluating the test data.

Exploratory data analysis (EDA) is done on both: the individual features of the dataset, and with respect to the target variable (class), to outline the patterns in the dataset using visual methods. The dataset is analyzed without sampling techniques and with sampling techniques too for comparing the results. The different sampling techniques used for this experiment are Random Undersampling (RUS), Random Oversampling (ROS), and synthetic minority over sampling technique (SMOTE). One more technique, other than the resampling methods, has been used to balance the dataset by accounting the balanced class weight at the modeling time. This one technique has not been implemented in any of the known literatures for the credit card fraud detection hence it is implemented in this experiment to investigate if it is possible to obtain a good performance without using the sampling techniques. Four supervised machine learning algorithms: logistic regression, decision tree, SVM, and random forest have been implemented on the dataset. The different modelings are evaluated on basis of true positive (TP), false positive (FP), true negative (TN), and false negative (FN). These four metrics are used to calculate the performance for the different algorithms: accuracy, precision, recall, F1-score, MCC, confusion matrix, AUC, and AUPRC. The best model is selected on the basis of good performance for all the stated metrics.

12.2.2   Dataset Description

The dataset used in this experiment has been taken from [20] which was publically released by the ULB machine learning as a part of the research project [19]. This dataset consists of the credit cards transactions details for a duration of 2 days for European card holders in September 2013. The dataset has 31 variables, among these only three features: "Time", "Amount", and one target variable "Class" are in their original form, rest all features have been transformed using PCA due to the confidentiality issue to protect the customers' identities and sensitive details. The PCA transformed features are all numerical variables and known as principal components: V1, V2, …, V28. The description of the variables in the credit card dataset is shown in Table 12.1.

Table 12.1 Description of ULB credit card transaction dataset.

Variable name	Feature type	Description
Time	Original Feature	Time in seconds elapsed between each transaction and the first transaction
V1	PCA Transformed	1st Principal Component
V2	PCA Transformed	2nd Principal Component
V3	PCA Transformed	3rd Principal Component
------	------------	----------------------
V28	PCA Transformed	Last Principal Component
Amount	Original Feature	Transaction amount
Class	Target variable	Binary response: 1 for fraud and 0 for no-fraud transaction

A total of 284,807 transaction records have been provided in this dataset where the number of genuine (negative class) or legitimate transactions are 284,315, and fraud (positive class) transactions are only 492, accounting for just 0.172% of the total transactions. It can be inferred that the selected dataset is heavily skewed toward the legitimate transactions. There are 30 input variables to work with in this experiment. The target variable is "Class" having value 0 for genuine transactions and 1 for fraudulent transactions [20].

12.2.3   Data Preparation

In the data preparation step, the imported credit card dataset is transformed into the working format. The dataset is checked for the missing values (null values), outliers, and the skewness. There are no missing values in the dataset; hence, no treatment is required for null values handling. The variables "Time" and "Amount" are standardized in a similar way as other features (principal components) with a mean of 0 and standard deviation of 1 [5]. Robust Scaler is used to transform "Time" and "Amount" since it is less prone to the outliers. All other features (V1 to V28), principal components, have been transformed using Principal Component Analysis (PCA) to protect customers' identities and sensitive features. The number of transformed features in the dataset after PCA transformation is 28 which are the principal components, and all are numerical variables [5]. As the dataset is highly skewed, this paper focuses on the data level–based balancing techniques, and these techniques are utilized in the pre-processing of the dataset before training the data. EDA is being performed on the cleaned data before feeding it to the machine learning algorithms. The EDA is performed here on the features corresponding to the target variable "Class" and also among each other.

12.2.4   Correlation Between Features

The data needs to be examined first before starting the implementation for a better performance. All the features of the dataset are visualized using correlation (relationship) between them. The feature having a high correlation with target variable will have a significant effect in the training time. The correlation matrix for the selected dataset is shown in Figure 12.2.

It can be observed from the above correlation matrix that all the principal components: V1 to V28 have no correlation among themselves. This is due to the fact that PCA is already performed on these features hence no collinearity among them. But, the target variable "Class" has some correlation with few features which is investigated further.

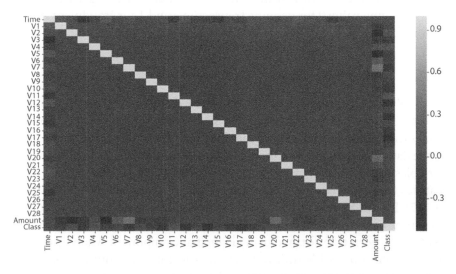

Figure 12.2 Correlation matrix for the credit card dataset showing correlation between features.

12.2.5   Splitting the Dataset

After EDA is done, the cleaned and transformed dataset is split into train and test data where 70% of the dataset is taken as training data and remaining 30% of the data as the test data. For train-test split, stratify = y is used to maintain the original rate of frauds and no-fraud cases for each set. The important thing to notice here is that the data needs to be split into train and test before using any balancing techniques so that the original test data can be used for testing; otherwise, the algorithms may use the test data in the training phase and lead to overfitting. Hence, the train data is used for different sampling techniques, hypeparameter tuning and the training of the different algorithms. The attribute "random state" for train-test split is specified to any random number (0 here) to ensure the same split to take place each time the code is executed.

12.2.6   Balancing Data

The main problem with the selected dataset is its high skewness which has been reported in many papers [2, 5, 13, 15, 16, 21]. As the dataset is biased toward the legitimate transactions; hence, this skewness needs to be corrected before implementing any model else the results for the training data will be good one but results will be poor for the unseen test data. The high bias in the dataset is reduced by using several methods. The most widely used technique for this is the resampling of the dataset to have a balanced class distribution. This work focuses on the balancing methods based on the data level and no changes are made to the algorithms, so the algorithmic level sampling techniques are eliminated and not investigated as a part of this study. The different resampling techniques used in several papers are under-sampling the majority class [22, 23], oversampling the minority class [24], hybrid of undersampling and oversampling, and SMOTE [24]. All these methods have been termed as rebalancing mechanisms in [22] since all these methods try to make the data relatively balanced. The credit card dataset is analyzed without using any sampling technique to check the performance of the models which will be used to compare the sampled models. Then, the dataset is analyzed using three sampling methods: RUS, ROS, and SMOTE. All these sampling methods have been implemented on the train data to get a balanced distribution. In addition of the sampling techniques, one more method (not resampling) is used to balance the dataset by taking in account the balanced class weight at the modeling time to evaluate the performance of the algorithms. These sampling techniques are briefly described below.

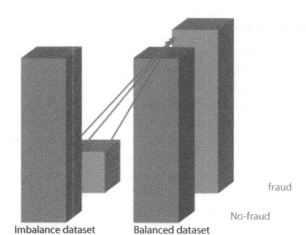

fraud

No-fraud

Imbalance dataset   Balanced dataset

■No-fraud ■fraud

Figure 12.3 Oversampling of the fraud transactions.

12.2.6.1   Oversampling of Minority Class

Oversampling of fraudulent class is done by producing more fraud (minority class) transactions as shown in Figure 12.3. It is a good option when there is less data to work with. One important thing here is that over-sampling technique can be carried on the data after the data is split into train and test else there are chances of overfitting [25].

12.2.6.2   Under-Sampling of Majority Class

Undersampling of legitimate (majority) class is done by removing the majority class transactions randomly as shown in Figure 12.4. This is one of the most common resampling techniques and works well with huge data giving better performance for models. The only drawback here is that some valuable information are removed, and there is a risk of underfitting [25].

12.2.6.3   Synthetic Minority Over Sampling Technique

This is a technique similar to oversampling where synthetic samples are created by using a nearest neighbor algorithm shown in Figure 12.5. It should also be implemented after the train-test split of the dataset to generalize the test data and to avoid overfitting [25, 26].

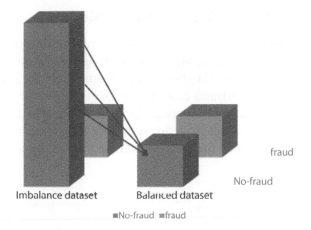

Figure 12.4 Undersampling of the no-fraud transactions.

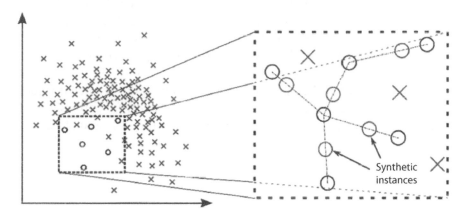

Figure 12.5 SMOTE [26].

12.2.6.4   Class Weight

In addition of the sampling techniques, one more method (not resampling) is used to balance the dataset by taking in account the class weight at the modeling time. It is an easy approach to account the class imbalance by providing the weights for all classes where minority class is given more importance so that the resulting model can learn from both the classes equally. The argument class_weight = "balanced" is used in the training phase to penalize the errors on the minority class which increases the classification cost for the minority class [27].

12.2.7   Machine Learning Algorithms (Models)

Classification problems are ones where the output is a categorical variable instead of numerical variable, such as 0 and 1, or Yes and No. Credit card fraud detection is a binary classification problem where the transaction is classified as fraud or no-fraud case [15]. As seen above, the performance of four supervised machine learning algorithms in predicting the credit card fraud transaction: logistic regression, SVM, decision tree, and random forest, is investigated for this work. These four techniques are briefly described below.

12.2.7.1   Logistic Regression

It is a supervised classification technique and a predictive analysis algorithm [28]. It results in the probability of the target (dependent) variable evaluated from the independent variables for the given dataset [13]. As the output variable for the selected credit card dataset is binary, logistic regression is the most commonly used algorithm as seen in Section 12.1 [7]. The logistic regression here will predict the output as 0 for non-fraud or 1 for fraud.

Logistic regression uses sigmoid function to map the predicted values to probabilities and the value can range between 0 and 1 [28]. The sigmoid function σ for the given input x is given in Equations (12.1) and (12.2):

$$(x) = \frac{1}{1+e^{-x}} \tag{12.1}$$

$$x = w_0 z_0 + w_1 z_1 + w_2 z_2 + \cdots + w_n z_n \tag{12.2}$$

$\sigma(x)$ is the sigmoid function, and x is the vector of input data. When the sigmoid value is more than 0.5, output label is 1; else, it is 0 [28].

12.2.7.2   Support Vector Machine

SVM is a popular advanced supervised machine learning technique for classification problem, and it belongs to the class of linear machine learning models same as logistic regression [13]. SVM is capable of dealing with quite complex problems too where models like logistic regression fails. It is a widely used algorithm for classification problems due to its higher accuracy and less computation [29]. They are computationally very efficient and very accurate models, and it can be extended to non-linear boundaries between classes. SVMs require numeric variables, if dataset has non-numeric variables, then it should be converted to numeric form in the pre-processing stage. Here, the data is trained first and then this model is used to make prediction on test data. There is a concept of hyperplane, a decision boundary, in SVM which separates the classes (data points) from each other and many hyperplanes can be present that separates the two classes of data points [29]. The main aim of SVM is to find that n-dimensional hyperplane (n is the number of variables) which can classify the data points efficiently with maximum distance between the points for the two classes as shown in Figure 12.6. This maximum distance between the data points is called maximum margin.

Many times, it can happen that data is intermingled; hence, it is not possible to find a hyperplane that can distinctly separate into classes; here comes the concept of support vector classifier (or soft margin classifier) which is a hyperplane that allows some data points to be deliberately misclassified and maximizes the margin as shown in Figure 12.7.

The mathematical function which all data points are required to satisfy for the soft margin classifier is given in Equation (12.3).

$$l_i \times (\vec{w}.\vec{y}_l) \geq M(1-\epsilon_i) \tag{12.3}$$

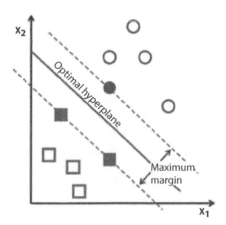

Figure 12.6 Optimal hyperplane and maximum margin [29].

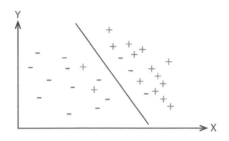

Figure 12.7 Support vector classifier.

$l_i \times (\vec{w}.\vec{y}_l)$ is the distance of the data point from the hyperplane, M is the margin, l_i = label, $\vec{w}$ = coefficients of the attributes, y_i = data points of all attributes in each row, and ϵ is the slack variable. The left-hand side function in Equation (12.3) is the classification confidence and its value ≥ 1 shows that the classifier has identified the points correctly while value lesser than 1 shows that points are not being classified correctly hence a penalty of ϵ_i is incurred [30].

12.2.7.3 Decision Tree

Decision tree is a supervised machine learning algorithm used for classification problems [31]. It uses a tree-like model to make predictions, and it resembles an upside-down tree. The objective of the decision tree is to split the data into multiple sets and then each set is further split into the subsets to make a decision.

Figure 12.8 shows a binary decision tree for a person is fit or not. It can be seen that the tree is split into sets, and again based on the questions, it is further split and this process continues till the final outcome is reached [31]. Every node will represent a test and those nodes which do not have descendants are called leaves. The decisions are lying at the leaves. For classification problem, every leaf will contain a class label.

A homogeneity measure (it gives measure how homogeneous a dataset is) is applied on a dataset and more homogeneous the dataset is, the less the variations among the labels for the different data points in the dataset and if the variations are more, the homogeneity will be less.

The objective of the decision tree algorithm is to generate partitions (by creating a test) in such a way which results in homogeneous data points with homogeneity as high as possible [32]. The working of decision tree is that one attribute is selected and data is split such that homogeneity

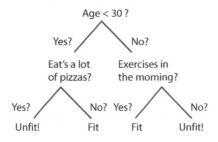

Figure 12.8 Binary decision tree [31].

increases after each split and it is continued till the resulting leaves are sufficiently homogeneous. The homogeneity is measured in terms of Gini Index, entropy, and information gain.

Entropy quantifies the degree of disorder in the data, and its value varies from 0 to 1. If a data set is completely homogenous, then the entropy of such dataset is 0, i.e., there is no disorder. The entropy for a dataset D is defined as follows:

$$Entropy \ \varepsilon[D] = -\sum_{i=1}^{k} P_i \log_2 P_i \tag{12.4}$$

where P_i is the probability of finding a point with label i and k is the number of different labels.

$$Entropy \ \varepsilon[D_A] = -\sum_{i=1}^{k} ((\frac{|D_A|}{|D|})_i \varepsilon[D_{A=i}]) \tag{12.5}$$

$\varepsilon[D_A]$ is the entropy of the partition after splitting on attribute A, $\varepsilon[D_{A=i}]$ is the entropy of partition where the value of attribute A for the data points has value i, and $D_{A=i}$ is the number of data points for which value of attribute A is i and k is number of different labels.

Information gain [Gain (D,A)] measures reduction in entropy for the dataset D after splitting on the feature A, that is it is the difference between the original entropy $\varepsilon[D]$ and entropy obtained after partition on A $\varepsilon[D_A]$.

$$Gain(D,A) = \varepsilon[D] - \varepsilon[D_A] = \varepsilon[D] - \sum_{i=1}^{k} ((\frac{|D_A|}{|D|})_i \varepsilon[D_{A=i}]) \quad (12.6)$$

12.2.7.4   Random Forest

Random forest is a popular supervised learning algorithm. It is a collection of decision trees and works on bagging technique which is an ensemble method [33]. In ensemble, instead of using an individual model, a collection of models is used to predict the output [34]. The most popular ensemble is the random forest which is a collection of many decision trees [7]. Bagging is the bootstrap aggregation where bootstrap refers to creating bootstrap samples for a given dataset containing 30% to 70% of the data and aggregation refers to aggregate the result of various models present in the ensemble [7]. It is a technique to select random samples from the dataset. Each of these samples is then used to train each tree in the forest.

The random forest is a classic ensemble technique which creates a collection of decision trees each of them built on different samples from the dataset, and it takes the majority score among these. A large number of trees as individual models ensures diversity that even if few trees overfit, the other trees in ensemble will take care of that and more diversity means the model is more stable. The independence among the trees results in a lower variance of the ensemble compared to a single tree which makes it computationally efficient. In this way, random forest controls the overfitting problem encountered with decision tree [13].

For a given dataset D with N attributes, each tree in the random forest can be created as: finding a bootstrap samples of D, then at each node selecting randomly a subset S from N attributes, evaluating the best split at each node from reduced subset of S features and growing the complete tree [7]. The total number of trees T and the attribute S at each node in the random forest are varied to have the best performance [7]. The error of the random forest is dependent on the correlation among the trees and the strength of the tree. If the correlation is less and strength high, then it results in low error. The low value of S implies low correlation and low strength between the trees, hence S is varied to obtain an optimal value [7]. The selection of features at each node is done majorly with Gini index. The outputs of each trees is then aggregated and the majority of the vote is used to predict the output case [7].

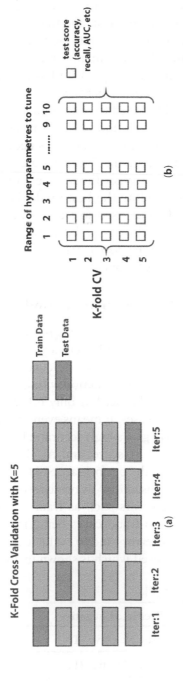

Figure 12.9 (a) Five-fold cross-validation technique and (b) GridSearchCV.

12.2.8   Tuning of Hyperparameters

Cross-validation technique is used to tune the values of hyperparameters. The data is first split into train and test, and then, the multiple models are trained by sampling the train set. In last, the test data is used to test the hyperparameter once. In this experiment, to avoid the overfitting problems, k-fold cross-validation technique with k = 5 is used to evaluate the fraud detection. Each time (for k = 5 here), k – 1 = 4 folds are used to build the model and the fifth fold is used to test the model. Figure 12.9a shows the five-fold cross-validation technique used for this experiment. The final result is then predicted from five trained models taking average from each subset and hence performance result gives accurate outputs.

As each machine learning algorithms have different hyperparameters, hence the search for finding the best model is completely different from each other. The technique used for tuning many hyperparameters at the same time is grid search cross validation, GridSearchCV, used in this experiment. The grid is a matrix (metrics such as accuracy and recall) which is populated on each iteration, as shown in Figure 12.9b.

12.2.9   Performance Evaluation of the Models

Different measures of classification performance are observed in Section 12.1. It is concluded that the overall accuracy is an insufficient performance measure for highly biased dataset because for all the transactions of majority class, even the default prediction will show a high performance [7]. The selected credit card dataset has only 0.172% fraud transactions with remaining as legitimate cases. It means even the classifier is not good enough, and then, also, it will give a high accuracy. Hence, other evaluation metrics like precision, recall, F1-score, and AUC should be investigated along with accuracy to check the performance of the models [7].

As the classification of transactions in two classes are being done, there are chances to incur some errors such as fraud cases being incorrectly classified as no-fraud and no-fraud cases being incorrectly classified as fraud cases. To capture these errors and to evaluate the performance of the model, confusion matrix is used which is shown in Table 12.2 [7].

Table 12.2 Confusion matrix [7].

	Predicted negative	**Predicted positive**
Actual Negative	True Negative (TN)	False Positive (FP)
Actual Positive	False Negative (FN)	True Positive (TP)

The confusion matrix shows four basic metrics: TP, TN, FP, and FN [7]. TP is the number of actual positive transactions predicted as positive; it means fraud cases are predicted as fraud. TN is the number of actual negative transactions predicted as negative; it means no-fraud transactions are predicted as genuine. FP is the number of actual negative transactions predicted as positive; it means no-fraud cases are predicted as fraud ones. FN is the number of actual positive transactions predicted as negative; it means fraud cases are predicted as no-fraud ones [35]. A good performance of fraud detection requires less number of FP and FN.

The performance of the logistic regression, SVM, decision tree, and random forest classifiers are evaluated based on accuracy, precision, recall, F1-score, MCC, AUC, and AUPRC [20].

$$Accuracy = \frac{TP + TN}{TP + FP + TN + FN} \tag{12.7}$$

$$Recall\ (or\ sensitivity) = \frac{TP}{TP + FN} \tag{12.8}$$

$$Precision = \frac{TP}{TP + FP} \tag{12.9}$$

$$F1 - score = \frac{2 * (Precision * Recall)}{(Precision + Recall)} \tag{12.10}$$

The simplest model evaluation metric for classification models is accuracy which is the percentage of correctly predicted labels [7]. Recall (or sensitivity) tells the accuracy for fraud (positive) cases. Precision tells the accuracy on transactions predicted as fraud (positive) [35]. It is difficult to select the best model between different models with low recall and high precision or vice versa, in that case F1-score (or F-measure), which is the harmonic mean of precision and recall, is used [36].

MCC is a balanced performance measure used for a binary class problem and provides the good measure even when the dataset is unbalanced [37]. It is calculated using true and false negatives and positives.

$$(MCC) = \frac{TP \times TN - FP \times FN}{\sqrt{(TP + FP)(TP + FN)(TN + FP)(TN + FN)}} \tag{12.11}$$
[37]

A value of +1 for MCC shows the perfect prediction and a value of −1 shows the complete difference [37].

$$True\ Positive\ Rate\ (TPR) = \frac{TP}{TP + FN} \tag{12.12}$$

$$False\ Positive\ Rate\ (TPR) = \frac{FP}{TN + FP} \tag{12.13}$$

TPR tells the number of correctly predicted positive (fraud) cases divided by total number of positives cases which is same as recall (sensitivity) [38]. Whereas FPR tells the number of FPs (0s predicted as 1s) divided by total number of negatives [38]. On plotting TPR and FPR, a graph is found which shows the trade-off between the both and this curve is called ROC curve as shown in Figure 12.10a [38]. The area under the ROC curve is called AUC. For a good model, TPR should be high and FPR should be low and for this cut-off should be high.

The AUPRC is an important evaluation metrics for binary classification with highly imbalanced dataset [38]. Since the precision and recall are mainly concerned for the minority cases (here fraud cases) which makes the area under the precision and recall curve an important performance metrics for highly biased dataset [40]. It is the plot of recall and precision for various probability threshold as shown in Figure 12.10b. The area under the precision recall curve is investigated for evaluating the performance of the classifier [40, 41].

Once the optimum hyperparameters after tuning is obtained for each machine learning algorithm, the model is built with those hyperparameters using the train data. Then, this built model is used to evaluate the performance on the test data. In this experiment, the performance of the models is evaluated on the basis of recall, precision, accuracy, F1-score, MCC, AUC, and AUPRC. Since this work is mainly focused on the fraud detection of the credit card, hence the primary goal is that the models should detect all fraudulent transactions and for that "recall" score should be maximum; hence, it is used as "score" in the GridSearchCV for maximizing. Also at the same time, the precision should also not be very low else the genuine transaction will be predicted as fraud which can impact the customers. The F1-score, which is the harmonic mean of precision and recall, is also a good performance metric for this experiment. The best

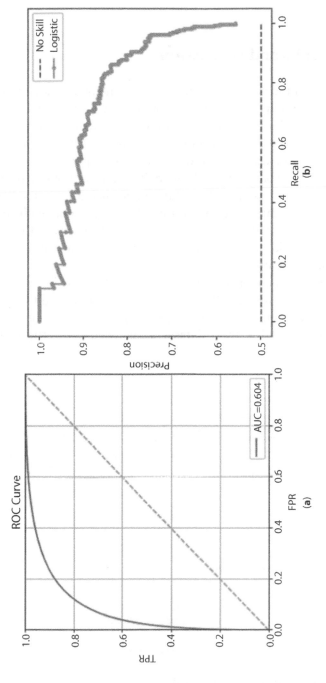

Figure 12.10 (a) ROC curve [39]. (b) Precision recall curve for no skill and logistic regression algorithms [40].

model is selected on the basis of good performance for all the above stated metrics.

12.3   Results and Discussion

The results from the analysis and models implementation are discussed in this section. The outline of "Results and Discussion" is shown in Figure 12.11.

The cleaned and transformed data after EDA is modeled using different sampling techniques. The important thing to observe here for a better performance is that the transformed data needs to be split into train-test data before applying any balancing technique. It is done for holding the original test data for testing else the algorithms might use it (if not split) in the training phase and can lead to overfitting. As it can be noticed from Figure 12.11, the first implementation is done without using any of the sampling technique, to check the performance of the machine learning algorithms on the unsampled data.

Four different balancing techniques: RUS, ROS, SMOTE, and balanced class weight (class_weight = "balanced") have been utilized to implement four machine learning techniques: logistic regression, decision tree, SVM, and random forest. The train dataset is modeled using the mentioned

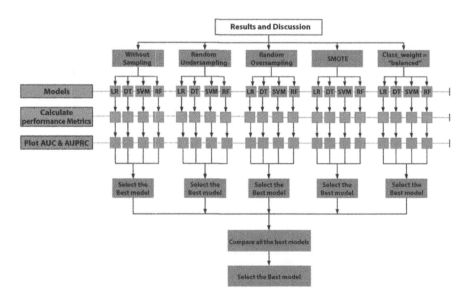

Figure 12.11 Outline of implementation and results.

algorithms. The best hyperparameters of each model is searched using GridSearchCV of five-fold cross-validation technique. The built model (using the best hyperparameters) is used to predict the output for the test data, and then, the different performance metrics are calculated for fraud and genuine transactions. This method is followed for each of the built models.

12.3.1 Results Using Balancing Techniques

In RUS technique, the train dataset is random undersampled in which the majority class data (genuine ones) is reduced such that both the classes have same number of records. Here, the no-fraud transactions have been randomly reduced to the number of transactions equal to the fraud ones, both having same number of records of 344 in their train data.

For random oversampled technique, the train dataset is random over-sampled in which the minority class data is increased such that both the classes have same number of records. Here, the fraud transactions have been randomly increased to the number of transactions equal to the no-fraud ones, both having same number of records of 199,020 in their train data.

For SMOTE technique, the minority class data is synthetically generated such that both the classes have same number of records. Here, the fraud transactions have been synthetically increased to the number of transactions equal to the no-fraud ones, both having same number of records of 199,020 in their train data.

The argument class_weight = "balanced" for balanced class weight is used for class imbalance problem. It penalizes the errors on the class having lower number of records by the same amount. It is used for all the four algorithms to check if any better performance value is obtained without using the sampling technique.

After using the balancing techniques, the implementations are done again using all the four machine learning algorithms for each of them.

12.3.2 Result Summary

The results for the implemented models have been collated here. In this experiment, total of 20 models have been implemented using permutation and combination of different balancing techniques with four machine learning algorithms. Table 12.3 summarizes the results for all the implemented models.

Table 12.3 Result summary for all the implemented models.

Algorithm	Sampling technique	Accuracy	Precision	Recall	F1-score	MCC	ROC	AUPRC
Logistic Regression	Without sampling	99.92%	86.11%	62.84%	72.66%	0.74	0.95	0.71
	RUS	97.43%	5.64%	87.84%	10.59%	0.22	0.97	0.66
	ROS	97.84%	6.65%	87.84%	12.36%	0.24	0.968	0.73
	SMOTE	97.78%	6.46%	87.84%	12.04%	0.23	0.965	0.74
	Balanced class weight	98.08%	7.33%	86.49%	13.52%	0.25	0.97	0.69
Decision Tree	Without sampling	99.93%	76.58%	81.76%	79.08%	0.79	0.935	0.74
	RUS	92.96%	2.20%	91.22%	4.29%	0.14	0.948	0.45
	ROS	99.15%	13.77%	74.32%	23.23%	0.32	0.87	0.7
	SMOTE	97.46%	5.19%	79.05%	9.74%	0.2	0.89	0.65

(Continued)

Table 12.3 Result summary for all the implemented models. (*Continued*)

Algorithm	Sampling technique	Accuracy	Precision	Recall	F1-score	MCC	ROC	AUPRC
	Balanced class weight	95.03%	2.96%	87.16%	5.72%	0.16	0.93	0.66
SVM	Without sampling	99.92%	78.47%	76.35%	77.40%	0.77	0.927	0.71
	RUS	96.77%	4.53%	87.84%	8.61%	0.2	0.969	0.67
	ROS	99.75%	37.21%	64.86%	47.29%	0.49	0.86	0.44
	SMOTE	99.64%	27.17%	65.54%	38.42%	0.42	0.957	0.44
	Balanced class weight	99.67%	29.34%	66.22%	40.66%	0.44	0.97	0.38
Random Forest	Without sampling	99.94%	92.37%	73.65%	81.95%	0.82	0.927	0.81
	RUS	97.49%	5.68%	86.49%	10.65%	0.22	0.967	0.69
	ROS	99.94%	87.02%	77.03%	31.72%	0.82	0.93	0.82
	SMOTE	**99.92%**	**76.43%**	**81.08%**	**78.69%**	**0.79**	**0.96**	**0.81**
	Balanced class weight	99.95%	97.27%	72.30%	82.95%	0.84	0.92	0.82

The intention of any credit card fraud detection is to identify the fraud cases correctly, i.e., to have a better value of the recall of the fraudulent transaction. Also, the fraudulent transaction dominates the credit card fraud detection; hence, a high recall value (accuracy on fraud cases) instead of overall accuracy is the requirement. As seen from the results in Table 12.3, all the machine learning algorithms without using any sampling technique have shown a low recall value and a high precision value. The research objective of this study is to obtain a suitable balancing technique to be applied on the highly skewed dataset for getting better performance of the models. Table 12.3 shows that all the models with RUS technique have resulted in a good recall but at the cost of very low precision and a low F1-score with low MCC and a low AUPRC value. The recall is increased using the ROS technique but even though the precision and F1-score with MCC and AUPRC are not in a good range. Only random forest model has performed well with ROS technique, whereas all other models have shown not so good results. SMOTE oversampling has performed well with the models and it has increased the recall for random forest resulting in better performance metrics compared to the other models. One important thing to notice here is that, without using any sampling technique for all the models and using the "balanced" class weight configuration for the machine learning algorithms, a good result (except low precision) is achieved for all the classifiers. Hence, it can be inferred that SMOTE over-sampling technique has provided a good result.

This work has started with a motive to get the better result for all the selected performance metrics: recall, precision, accuracy, F1-score, MCC, AUC, and AUPRC. On comparing the results in Table 12.3, it can be observed that the highest recall of 91.22% is obtained for the decision tree model with RUS technique. But this model has a precision of only 2.20%, F1-score of 4.29%, MCC of 0.14, and AUPRC of 0.45; hence, this cannot be considered as the best model. It can also be noticed from Table 12.3 that the random forest even without using any sampling technique has done well in terms of all the performance metrics compared to the other machine learning algorithms. It shows the strength of the ensemble model even with the imbalanced dataset. Also, the result for random forest with SMOTE technique is around the same using the "balanced" class weight configuration with recall value lower than SMOTE. As expected, the accuracy and AUC are not the accurate measures for the credit card fraud detection as it has approximately same values (greater than 90%) for all the implemented models.

As seen in other literatures, there is no fixed performance metrics for the fraud detection as it depends on the business requirement. But, what is important for the credit card fraud detection is that, if a fraud transaction is misclassified as a genuine one, it will definitely cause severe problems. At the same time, no one will want to misclassify a genuine transaction as a fraud one. Hence, a good performance of the fraud detection should have lesser number of FN and FP. Table 12.4 collates the result of confusion matrix of all the implemented models. It can be seen that the lowest value of FN, FN is 13 for decision tree model with RUS technique, but it has a high FP, FP cases with a value of 6,006 which is unacceptable. The random forest model with SMOTE oversampling has a less number of FN cases: 28 with less number of FP cases: 37 compared to the other models. It can also be noticed that the random forest model with class_weight = "balanced" has the lowest FP with a value of 3 and a lower FN cases as 41.

Comparing the results from Tables 12.3 and 12.4 for each of the machine learning algorithms, it can be deduced that the logistic regression model has given the best recall with SMOTE oversampling technique but not good values for other parameters. This model has shown lower FN cases of value 18 but higher FP cases as 1,881. The decision tree classifier has performed well with RUS technique giving the maximum recall obtained in this experiment but at lower values for all other performance metrics. Also, it has output in a high FP cases with value of 6,006 with low FN cases value of 13. SVM with RUS has given a good recall with a lower performance values for other parameters. This model has shown a low number of FN cases as 18 but with a higher FP cases with value of 2741. The random forest has performed great with SMOTE oversampling and balanced class weight technique both.

This work is focused on obtaining a model with good values for all the performance metrics rather than improving any one parameter and with a less number of FN and FP at the same time. Hence, the best model should not only give a high recall value, but a good value of precision, good accuracy, better F1-score, good MCC, high values of AUC and AUPRC. Comparing all the results from Tables 12.3 and 12.4, it can be seen that the random forest with balanced class weight has demonstrated a good result with the highest precision of 97.27%, the highest F1-score of 82.95% and the highest MCC value of 0.84 compared to all other models with AUC value of 0.92 and AUPRC of 0.82. But this model has shown a lower recall of 72.30%. Hence, it is concluded that the Random forest with SMOTE oversampling technique has provided the best result in terms of all the mentioned performance metrics with accuracy of 99.92%, recall value of 81.08%, precision of 76.43%, F1-score of 78.69%, MCC of 0.79, AUC of 0.96, and AUPRC as 0.81. It also has output the less number of FN transactions with value as 28 and less number of FPs with value as 37. Using

Table 12.4 Confusion matrix results for all the implemented models.

Algorithm	Sampling technique	TN (No-Fraud)	FP	FN	TP (Fraud)
Logistic Regression	Without sampling	85,280	15	55	93
	RUS	83,119	2,176	18	130
	ROS	83,470	1,825	18	130
	SMOTE	83,414	1,881	18	130
	Balanced class weight	83,677	1,618	20	128
Decision Tree	Without sampling	85,258	37	27	121
	RUS	79,289	6,006	13	135
	ROS	84,606	689	38	110
	SMOTE	83,157	2,138	31	117
	Balanced class weight	81,064	4,231	19	129
SVM	Without sampling	85,264	31	35	113
	RUS	82,554	2,741	18	130
	ROS	85,133	162	52	96
	SMOTE	85,035	260	51	97
	Balanced class weight	85,059	236	50	98
Random Forest	Without sampling	85,286	9	39	109
	RUS	83,168	2,127	20	128
	ROS	85,278	17	34	114
	SMOTE	**85,258**	**37**	**28**	**120**
	Balanced class weight	85,292	3	41	107

the best model of this random forest for SMOTE oversampled data, the features are ranked in order of importance and it is observed that feature V14 is the most important variable selected by this model followed by V10, V17, V11, and V4.

12.4   Conclusions

This paper researched how the balancing techniques along with different machine learning algorithms can be utilized to account the problem of credit card fraud detection and to obtain a better result. In particular, this work has tried to get a better performance for the model in terms of all the mentioned metrics rather than anyone of them. The random forest with SMOTE oversampling has provided the best result in terms of all the selected performance metrics with accuracy of 99.92%, recall value of 81.08%, precision of 76.43%, F1-score of 78.69%, MCC of 0.79, AUC of 0.96, and AUPRC of 0.81. It also has resulted in less number of FN transactions with value as 28 and less number of FPs with value as 37. The key point of this study is that, unlike other reported works, the balancing technique to handle the highly biased dataset is not fixed before implementing the model and all the balancing methods are implemented with all the classifiers to select the best one. In addition to the sampling techniques, this work has also used the balanced class weight at the modeling time for all the algorithms for considering the biased nature of the dataset. The contribution of this thesis toward credit card fraud detection is achieving a comparable result considering the balanced class weight and without using any sampling technique. The other major point that distinguishes this study from others is that this work is not only focused on the mentioned machine learning algorithms, rather than the permutation and combination of these methods with several result parameters and with different balancing techniques are studied and analyzed for several evaluation metrics to obtain a better outcome. As a result, total of 20 models have been implemented, compared and analyzed to get the best output.

12.4.1   Future Recommendations

In future, a cost-sensitive learning technique can be carried out on this study by evaluating the misclassification costs. The misclassification cost for a fraudulent transaction as a genuine one (FN) known as the fraud amount is higher than the misclassification cost for a genuine case as a fraudulent case (FP), and it is related to the cost for contacting and analyzing the customer. The machine learning techniques can be implemented considering these different costs of misclassifications and to evaluate the performance metrics. The algorithmic ensemble techniques can be used to balance the dataset and to evaluate the performance of the models implemented for this work. An ensemble technique combining the random forest (best model of this study) with neural networks can be implemented as a future work. As there is continuous evolution to avoid the fraud detection by the fraudsters, hence the non-stationary behavior of credit card fraud can be considered for the model building. Also, the hybrid approach of undersampling and oversampling technique along with other sampling techniques can be investigated as a future work.

References

1. Landes, H., *Credit Card Basics: Everything You Should Know*, Forbes, USA, 2013, [Online]. Available: https://www.forbes.com/sites/moneybuilder/2013/06/11/credit-card-basics-everything-you-should-know/#5f26b45d42c0.
2. Rajora, S. *et al.*, A comparative study of machine learning techniques for credit card fraud detection based on time variance. *Proc. 2018 IEEE Symp. Ser. Comput. Intell. SSCI 2018*, March 2019, pp. 1958–1963, 2019.
3. Rohilla, A. and Bansal, I., Credit Card Frauds : An Indian Perspective. *Adv. Econ. Bus. Manage.*, 2, 6, 591–597, 2015.
4. Seeja, K. R. and Zareapoor, M., FraudMiner: A novel credit card fraud detection model based on frequent itemset mining. *Sci. World J.*, 2014, 252797, 10, 2014. https://doi.org/10.1155/2014/252797.
5. Awoyemi, J.O., Adetunmbi, A.O., Oluwadare, S.A., Credit card fraud detection using machine learning techniques: A comparative analysis. *Proc. IEEE Int. Conf. Comput. Netw. Informatics, ICCNI 2017*, Janua, vol. 2017, pp. 1–9, 2017.
6. Seeja, K.R. and Zareapoor, M., FraudMiner: A novel credit card fraud detection model based on frequent itemset mining. *Sci. World J.*, 2014, 3–4, 2014.
7. Bhattacharyya, S., Jha, S., Tharakunnel, K., Westland, J.C., Data mining for credit card fraud: A comparative study. *Decis. Support Syst.*, 50, 3, 602–613, 2011.
8. Dal Pozzolo, A., Caelen, O., Le Borgne, Y.A., Waterschoot, S., Bontempi, G., Learned lessons in credit card fraud detection from a practitioner perspective. *Expert Syst. Appl.*, 41, 10, 4915–4928, 2014.
9. Sohony, I., Pratap, R., Nambiar, U., Ensemble learning for credit card fraud detection. *ACM Int. Conf. Proceeding Ser.*, pp. 289–294, 2018.
10. Sorournejad, S., Zojaji, Z., Atani, R.E., Monadjemi, A.H., A survey of credit card fraud detection techniques: Data and technique oriented perspective. 1–26, 2016. arXiv:1611.06439 [cs.CR].

11. Carcillo, F., Dal Pozzolo, A., Le Borgne, Y.A., Caelen, O., Mazzer, Y., Bontempi, G., SCARFF: A scalable framework for streaming credit card fraud detection with spark. *Inf. Fusion*, 41, 182–194, 2018.

12. Dal Pozzolo, A., Boracchi, G., Caelen, O., Alippi, C., Bontempi, G., Credit card fraud detection: A realistic modeling and a novel learning strategy. *IEEE Trans. Neural Networks Learn. Syst.*, 29, 8, 3784–3797, 2018.

13. Navanshu, K. and Saad, Y.S., Credit Card Fraud Detection Using Machine Learning Models and Collating Machine Learning Models. *J. Telecommun. Electron. Comput. Eng.*, 118, 20, 825–838, 2018.

14. Mekterović, I., Brkić, L., Baranović, M., A systematic review of data mining approaches to credit card fraud detection. *WSEAS Trans. Bus. Econ.*, 15, 437–444, 2018.

15. Puh, M. and Brkić, L., Detecting credit card fraud using selected machine learning algorithms. *2019 42nd Int. Conv. Inf. Commun. Technol. Electron. Microelectron. MIPRO 2019 - Proc.*, pp. 1250–1255, 2019.

16. Kumar, A. and Garima, G., Fraud Detection in Online Transactions Using Supervised Learning Techniques, in: *Towards Extensible and Adaptable Methods in Computing*, pp. 309–386, Springer, Canada, 2018.

17. Mittal, S. and Tyagi, S., Performance evaluation of machine learning algorithms for credit card fraud detection. *Proc. 9th Int. Conf. Cloud Comput. Data Sci. Eng. Conflu. 2019*, pp. 320–324, 2019.

18. Yee, O.S., Sagadevan, S., Malim, N.H.A.H., Credit card fraud detection using machine learning as data mining technique. *J. Telecommun. Electron. Comput. Eng.*, 10, 1–4, 23–27, 2018.

19. Dal Pozzolo, A., *Adaptive Machine Learning for Credit Card Fraud Detection Declaration of Authorship*, PhD Thesis, p. 199, December 2015.

20. Kaggle, 2018. [Online]. Available: https://www.kaggle.com/mlg-ulb/credit-cardfraud/data#creditcard.csv.

21. Wen, S.W. and Yusuf, R.M., Predicting Credit Card Fraud on a Imbalanced Data. *Int. J. Data Sci. Adv. Anal. Predict.*, 1, 1, 12–17, 2019.

22. Collell, G., Prelec, D., Patil, K.R., A simple plug-in bagging ensemble based on threshold-moving for classifying binary and multiclass imbalanced data. *Neurocomputing*, 275, 330–340, 2018.

23. Estabrooks, A., Jo, T., Japkowicz, N., A multiple resampling method for learning from imbalanced data sets. *Comput. Intell.*, 20, 1, 18–36, 2004.

24. Chawla, N.V., Bowyer, K.W., Hall, L.O., SMOTE: Synthetic Minority Oversampling Technique. *J. Artif. Intell. Res.*, 16, 1, 321–357, 2002.

25. Tara, B., *Dealing with Imbalanced Data*, towards data science, 2019, [Online]. Available: https://towardsdatascience.com/methods-for-dealing-with-imbalanced-data-5b761be45a18.

26. AnalyticsVidhya, *Imbalanced Data : How to handle Imbalanced Classification Problems*, Analytics Vidhya, Indore, 2017, [Online]. Available: https://www.analyticsvidhya.com/blog/2017/03/imbalanced-data-classification/.

27. elitedatascience, *How to Handle Imbalanced Classes in Machine Learning*, elitedatascience, 2019, [Online]. Available: https://elitedatascience.com/imbalanced-classes.

28. Ayush, P., *Introduction to Logistic Regression*, towards data science, 2019, [Online]. Available: https://towardsdatascience.com/introduction-to-logistic-regression-66248243c148.

29. Rohith, G., *Support Vector Machine — Introduction to Machine Learning Algorithms*, towards data science, 2018, [Online]. Available: https://towardsdatascience.com/support-vector-machine-introduction-to-machine-learning-algorithms-934a444fca47.

30. Misra, R., *Support Vector Machines — Soft Margin Formulation and Kernel Trick*, towardsdatascience, 2019, https://towardsdatascience.com/, [Online]. Available: https://towardsdatascience.com/support-vector-machines-soft-margin-formulation-and-kernel-trick-4c9729dc8efe#:~:text=how they work.-, Soft Margin Formulation, modifying the objective of SVM.

31. Mayur, K., *Decision Trees for Classification: A Machine Learning Algorithm*, Xoriant, 2017, [Online]. Available: https://www.xoriant.com/blog/product-engineering/decision-trees-machine-learning-algorithm.html.

32. Prince, Y., *Decision Tree in Machine Learning*, towards data science, 2018, [Online]. Available: https://towardsdatascience.com/decision-tree-in-machine-learning-e380942a4c96.

33. tutorialspoint, *Classification Algorithms - Random Forest*, tutorialspoint, 2019, [Online]. Available: https://www.tutorialspoint.com/machine_learning_with_python/machine_learning_with_python_classification_algorithms_random_forest.htm.

34. Tony, Y., *Understanding Random Forest*, towards data science, 2019, [Online]. Available: https://towardsdatascience.com/understanding-random-forest-58381e0602d2.

35. Awoyemi, J.O., Adetunmbi, A.O., Oluwadare, S.A., Credit card fraud detection using machine learning techniques: A comparative analysis. *Proc. IEEE Int. Conf. Comput. Netw. Informatics, ICCNI 2017*, Janua, vol. 2017, pp. 1–9, 2017.

36. Prabhu, *Understanding Hyperparameters and its Optimisation techniques*, towardsdatascience, 2018, [Online]. Available: https://towardsdatascience.com/understanding-hyperparameters-and-its-optimisation-techniques-f0debba07568#:~:text=What are Hyperparameters%3F, Model parameters vs Hyperparameters.

37. Randhawa, K., Loo, C.K., Seera, M., Lim, C.P., Nandi, A.K., Credit Card Fraud Detection Using AdaBoost and Majority Voting. *IEEE Access*, 6, 14277–14284, 2018.

38. Jason, B., *How to Use ROC Curves and Precision-Recall Curves for Classification in Python*, Machine Learning Mastery, 2018, [Online]. Available: https://machinelearningmastery.com/roc-curves-and-precision-recall-curves-for-classification-in-python/.

39. Nazrul, S.S., *Receiver Operating Characteristic Curves Demystified (in Python)*, towards data science, 2018, [Online]. Available: https://towardsdatascience.com/receiver-operating-characteristic-curves-demystified-in-python-bd531a4364d0.
40. Brownlee, J., *ROC Curves and Precision-Recall Curves for Imbalanced Classification*, Machine Learning Mastery, 2020, [Online]. Available: https://machinelearningmastery.com/roc-curves-and-precision-recall-curves-for-imbalanced-classification/.
41. Asare-Frempong, J. and Jayabalan, M., Predicting customer response to bank direct telemarketing campaign. *2017 Int. Conf. Eng. Technol. Technopreneurship, ICE2T 2017*, January, vol. 2017, pp. 1–4, 2017.

13

Crack Detection in Civil Structures Using Deep Learning

Bijimalla Shiva Vamshi Krishna[1], Rishiikeshwer B.S.[1], J. Sanjay Raju[1], N. Bharathi[2*], C. Venkatasubramanian[1†] and G.R. Brindha[1‡]

¹SASTRA Deemed University, Thanjavur, Tamil Nadu, India
²SRM Institute of Science and Technology, Tamil Nadu, India

Abstract

The safety monitoring process of the structure of any civil engineering work is the most significant task. The continuous monitoring for any abnormal state of the structure is predicted and severe damages can be prevented. It also depends on the other environmental parameters like load, nature of seasonal parameter, and soil type, not only in civil engineering, but also other industries, which makes efficient use of the technology. In mechanical engineering, internal parts have to be monitored and set alarm to give attention to prevent the major damage to the system. Flight internal engines, brake system in cars, etc., are monitored. The manual approach completely relies on the person's knowledge, experience, and skillset which obviously differs and always has the possibility of lacking objectivity in terms of quantitative analysis. The manual inspection can be replaced with automatic crack detection using ML and DL with computer vision. Currently, more powerful and fast image detection and recognition technologies are applied. The entire theme is all about providing the overview in brief and envisages the reader to analyze the crack detection using convolutional neural network (CNN) with real-time data.

Keywords: Crack detection, civil structure damages, deep learning, CNN, thermal imaging, computer vision, automation, monitoring process

---

*Corresponding author: bharathn2@srmist.edu.in
†Corresponding author: cv@civil.sastra.edu
‡Corresponding author: brindha.gr@ict.sastra.edu

Pradeep Singh (ed.) Fundamentals and Methods of Machine and Deep Learning: Algorithms, Tools and Applications, (311–326) © 2022 Scrivener Publishing LLC

13.1   Introduction

Automatic system by capturing the data from the structure dynamically and the CAD system is the need of the day. Plenty of models based on image processing, statistical-based, and machine learning (ML) algorithms are available in literature. Each method is having its own limitations. This aforesaid case imbibes the real-time images from surfaces and train them using CNN and compare it with performance metrics of existing methods.

Structure surface are very prone to cyclic loading, stress in the concrete surface engineering which leads to hairline cracks at the initial stage. Microscopic level cracks are common in structures like concrete and beams but often results in cracks. This occurs because the structures are not resistant to serious stress, cyclic loading which happens due to long term exposure. This diminishes local strength and reduction in stiffness and material degradation [1, 2]. Early findings allow us to initiate preventive measures to reduce damage and can arrest the possible failure [3]. The crack detection can be made in two ways such as destructive testing (DT) and non-destructive testing (NDT). The dimensional analysis of the cracks on the structural surface shows the initial degradation level and holding strength of the concrete structures [4]. It also further helps the reader to focus on choosing the input, pre-processing and enhancing the model with much more sophistication incorporated with fine tuning parameter. Recently, deep convolutional neural networks (DCNN) have been conceived to bestow a remedy that involves intensity along with geometrical information. This procedure really yields effective results in conventional computer vision problems like semantic segmentation which occurs because of the various levels of abstraction in tracing out images. Such encouraging results envisages to boost the application of deep learning (DL) for vision-based surface auditing by availing advantage of the mathematical similarity between image segmentation and crack detection. This chapter discusses the automation of crack detection through the thermal and digital images using CNN. OpenCV is a python library which is designed to solve computer vision problems. It supports multiple platforms by which the vision based surface detection is achieved rapidly.

13.2   Related Work

DL is the latest technique which tends to replace all the previous techniques and it emphatically focuses toward the study of image data, DCNNs. DCNNs are neural network classifiers, having only the raw image as the input. Hence, image processing and cumbersome feature extraction will no longer be required. At the time of learning of a DCNN, the bit loads of different convolution network (neurons and boundaries) are iteratively evolved to naturally get familiar with the convolutional invariant highlights of the given picture. The major obstacle is that the training set does not restrain adequate examples. The loss function is generally learning to reduce the error in prediction. Its minimization performed with SGD (stochastic gradient descent) can be laborious even with GPUs. DCNNs are congenitally image or image patch segregators. That is the reason why, in the majority of the works, the information picture is examined with a fix, and for each fixes the DCNN figures if it contains breaks (fix grouping level) [5, 6]. In [7], fundamental calculations are utilized to recognize patches containing moderately clear breaks, yet a colossal number of incorrect positives are identified. Authors in [8] have additionally included the test of bogus positives at the CNN yield; however, they can be disposed of utilizing a few casings in post-preparing. Authors in [5, 9] examine imperfect learning techniques. The structure of DCNNs can be improved to guarantee expectation as a probabilistic break forecast map (pixel characterization level and all the pixels are obviously named in, based on the relationship between pixels), it is additionally brought in the writing "semantic division picture". In [10], a completely convolutional network model (FCN) is encouraged to recognize breaks at the pixel level.

In initial DCNN application, the networks are a sequential model with fully connected layers at the end [11]. Such architecture needed ample of computational units, being most of the pixels in the image helps their weights on the speculation for every single pixel. The blurred output is due to loss function and the convolution layers are not related to the model parameters. This abstraction degrades the conservation of detailed patterns and, subsequently, may impact the accuracy of crack feature extraction. However, the upcoming hierarchical networks exhibited the improvement in arresting the degradation affect by the blurry effect. Thus, they have enormous scope of potentiality in all these tools for surface inspection and systematic health monitoring.

Researchers have developed an infrared (IR) thermography method on the basis of which IR image rectification happens [12, 13]. Crack description, size, and direction obtained from the extracted features. It further assists in evaluation of the structure of different cracks with a faster approach. Bahl *et al.* (1987) proposed the pre-processing technique and get geometric features of defect to enhance the classification accuracy [14]. The identification of cracks using the notches in the irregularities was propelled by [15]. It employs the IR thermography image rectification technique; cracks are being identified based on notches which differentiate as per the temperature.

Optically stimulated IR thermography is effectively used for the precise crack detection. PCA and pulse phase thermography are used for analysis [16]. Wavelet transform outperforms Fourier transform by removing more noise in the crack detection process.

13.3   Infrared Thermal Imaging Detection Method

The IR thermal imaging gentle testing technology is primarily handled by taking the peculiar conditions of the temperature variation at the crack level [17]. Cracks are depicted as hotspots or regions in the thermal camera, when the object temperature is higher than the surrounding temperature. When the area of interest has less temperature than the neighboring area, then cracks reveal themselves as cold spots. As per this approach, with the thermal images, the cracks will display vividly and can be able to magnify the variance high and low depth crack images [18, 19].

The heat is internally circulated when the temperature of the surface and the surrounding temperature are varied. In this chapter, focus will be mainly on cracks existing on the surface and the fabrication of heat buildup due to the pitfalls of crack defects. In local hot zone, the surface temperature is obviously high. The crack is found out by considering the thermal camera's output and it is judged by the change in characteristics of the IR thermography [4, 7, 17]. If there are inconsistent emission levels on the surface, then analysis of real cracks will get seriously hampered due to unusual variations in temperature and alterations in the thermal image gathered by the IR camera [20]. Surface of on and inside cracks can be shown by IR imaging technology. Gradient difference is identified in the area with normal and abnormal region, when the area is cooled or heated. The variations are displayed by noticeable cracks in the thermal images. For identifying cracks, thermal image temperature gradient difference is analyzed. Variations are calculated in the cooling and heating stages, by considering the direction of heat.

13.4   Crack Detection Using CNN

The stages of crack detection are depicted in this section through the workflow as shown in Figure 13.1. Initially, retrieving the image of the structure pertinent to the crack detection process captured by thermal camera or any

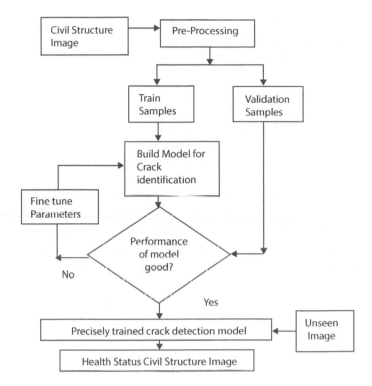

Figure 13.1 The architecture crack detection system.

other allied sources. From thermal camera, both thermal image and digital image can be obtained. Training the classifier with the DL techniques uses the thermal images collecting from real-time. In addition, 300 numbers of crack surface thermal images and 600 numbers of non-crack surfaces are obtained for this work. The sample data from input data set used in CNN is showed in Figure 13.2. By argumentation techniques (rotation, horizontal flip, and vertical flip), imbalanced data set is converted to a balanced one with 3,000 images in each class. The dataset is segregated into train and test

(a) (b) (c) (d)

Figure 13.2 (a) Thermal image. (b) Digital image. (c) Thermal image. (d) Digital image.

by the ratio of 80:20, by rescaling the images from [0, 255] range to [0, 1], training the classifier in Google Colab with open-source DL framework and Keras framework with TensorFlow backend.

13.4.1   Model Creation

With the advent of DL, separate feature extraction methods need not be applied, since the algorithm itself has the capacity to understand the data. Images obtained by the cameras are processed for getting useful insights. Convolutional neural network (CNN) extracts only those essential features, from the raw image data and learns to classify the status as shown in Figure 13.3. Using the trained model, CNN predicts the class that the images belong to, and if they are crack or non-crack. The images are loaded and inverted before they are fed into the model. In the model, the convolution layer is one of the most important primary layers that help in the feature extraction process. The convolution layer takes the image array and filter as input. The accuracy of the model is then improved by tuning the hyper parameters.

This combination of convolution and activation function such as ReLu, sigmoid, and SeLu is then passed on to the pooling layer where the dimensionality is reduced. The outputs are combined into a single neuron for the next layer. In the pooling layer, Max pooling is used to extract the largest element from the feature map. The convolution and pooling layer together form the hidden layers where the extraction of features from the image

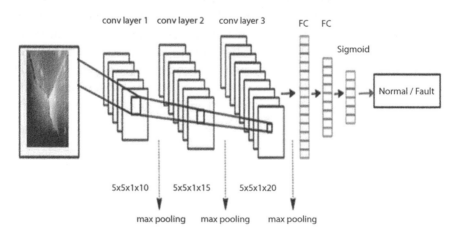

Figure 13.3 CNN layers in learning process.

takes place. There are totally five hidden layers used in the model that acts as an important parameter for the accuracy obtained. Sometimes, a number of layers improve the feature extraction that helps obtain better performance of the model, while at times increasing the layers would lead to deterioration in the model performance. Using these features extracted from the hidden layers, the task of image classification is performed.

13.4.2   Activation Functions (AF)

An AF shown in Table 13.1 is an indispensable component in the context of DL, as it is accountable for a neuron to be activated. AF controls the amount of information to be passed through the networks using nonlinear transformations of an input signal that helps to learn the complex mapping between the input and the output.

Table 13.1 Activation functions.

S. no.	Activation function	Description	Formula
1.	Rectified Linear Unit (*ReLU*)	• A non-linear transformation function with an output range of $[0, \infty)$. • It only activates a few neurons and computation is quicker if used.	$f(x) = \begin{cases} x, & x \geq 0 \\ 0, & x < 0 \end{cases}$
2.	Tanh	• A non-linear function which is symmetric over the origin with an output range of $(-1, 1)$. • Continuous and differentiable at all points and easy while performing backpropagation. • Approximately linear when x is very nearer to the origin.	$f(x) = \dfrac{2}{(1+e^{-2x})} - 1$

(Continued)

Table 13.1 Activation functions. (*Continued*)

S. no.	Activation function	Description	Formula
3.	*Linear (Identity activation function)*	• A linear transformation function having the output directly proportional to the input. • Activates multiple neurons at once and can be used to predict continuous values in the output range of $(-\infty, \infty)$.	$f(x) = x$
4.	Sigmoid	• A widely used non-linear function, symmetric about the line $y = 0.5$ with an output range of $(0, 1)$. • Continuous and differentiable at all points and easy while performing backpropagation. • When x is closer to 0, small changes in x translates to considerable changes in y, resulting in pushing values to the extreme ends.	$f(x) = \dfrac{1}{(1+e^{-x})}$
5.	Softsign	• A less popular non-linear function, with an output range of $(-1, 1)$. • Similar to tanh except it converges in a polynomial style and the gradient descent will not suffer vanishing or exploding gradient problem.	$f(x) = \dfrac{x}{(1+|x|)}$

Table 13.2 Optimizers.

S. no.	Optimizer	Description	Formula
1.	Gradient descent (GD)	• A parameter that was randomly initialized will be updated after every iteration until the minimum of the cost function is obtained. • Let a cost function be $J(\theta)$, where θ is the parameter, θ-learning rate	$\theta := \theta - \alpha.\dfrac{\partial J(\theta)}{\partial \theta}$
2.	Stochastic GD (SGD)	• In stochastic gradient descent, the parameter gets updated for every training sample in the dataset instead of every iteration.	$\theta := \theta - \alpha.\dfrac{\partial J(\theta)}{\partial \theta}$
3.	Momentum	• It is an augmented version of SGD, by accelerating the gradient descent in the relevant direction and diminishing the oscillations of parameters. • The new gradient is the weighted average of past gradients, resulting in better control of the optimization.	$\Delta\theta = \gamma.\Delta\theta - \alpha.\dfrac{\partial J(\theta)}{\partial \theta}$ $\theta := \theta + \Delta\theta$ $\Delta\theta - gradient\,update$ $\gamma - coefficient\,of\,momentum$

(Continued)

Table 13.2 Optimizers. (*Continued*)

S. no.	Optimizer	Description	Formula
4.	Adagrad	• The adaptive gradient algorithm modifies each of the parameters with different learning rates. This varying learning speed will enable faster convergence.	$\theta := \theta - \dfrac{\eta}{\sqrt{\varepsilon + G_{i,i}}} \cdot \dfrac{\partial J(\theta)}{\partial \theta}$ $G_{i,i} = \displaystyle\sum_{t=1}^{\tau} g_t g_t^T$ g_t – Gradient at iteration t $G_{i,i}$ – diagonal matrix of gradient vectors ε – Constant to avoid divide by 0 η – Initial learning rate

(*Continued*)

Table 13.2 Optimizers. (*Continued*)

S. no.	Optimizer	Description	Formula
5.	Adam	• The adaptive moment estimation algorithm, like Adagrad, adjusts different learning rates for every parameter. It has an additional term for moving average of second moments along with the average of the gradient, giving it a robust learning experience and rapid convergence.	$\theta := \theta - \dfrac{\hat{m}_\theta}{\sqrt{\hat{v}_\theta} + \varepsilon}$ $\hat{m}_\theta = \dfrac{m_\theta}{1 - \beta_1}$ $\hat{v}_\theta = \dfrac{v_\theta}{1 - \beta_2}$ $m_\theta := \beta_1 m_\theta + (1 - \beta_1)\dfrac{\partial J(\theta)}{\partial \theta}$ $v_\theta := \beta_2 v_\theta + (1 - \beta_2)\left(\dfrac{\partial J(\theta)}{\partial \theta}\right)^2$ β_1, β_2-Bias correlation constants m_θ – *First moment(mean) of the gradient* v_θ – *Second moment(variance) of the gradient*

13.4.3   Optimizers

Optimizers are used to minimize a cost function while learning the parameters of the model as shown in Table 13.2. They are accountable for quicker convergence of the solution to the optimization problem. In CNN, weights and bias are the learnable parameters and a suitable optimizer that determines the global minima value which, in turn, results in the lowest cost.

13.4.4   Transfer Learning

CNN is applied and the performance metrics are still to be improved. Hence, this case study applied the transfer learning concept. From the literature, the deeper CNN configuration like AlexNet, VGG16, Inception, and ResNet enhanced the performance of the crack detection system by adding the weight layers. The results proved that transfer learning is increased the accuracy and their detection system efficiency also increased effectively.

In the transfer learning concept, the pre-trained model is loaded first. Fully connected layers are customized and trained on the features. This output is flattened, and it is connected to the output layer with a single node and sigmoid activation is used to decide the output as 0 or 1 to indicate a crack or no-crack, respectively. Here, the model is trained with different combinations to pick the best performance metric. The three concepts are considered for this different case study. They are activation function, optimizer, and loss functions.

13.5   Results and Discussion

Using the given data set, CNN is applied and the model is built to predict the status of given civil structure image. To figure out the performance of the model, it is tested with a combination of different optimizers and activation functions. To enhance the performance further, transfer learning is applied. The trained model uses 50 epochs with batch size of 16 and the same is maintained in testing time also. The transfer learning with VGG16 yields good accuracy. In this work, the fully connected network encoder uses the pre-trained weights from standard VGG16. The decoder is replacing the final fully connected layers. Total images are split into training, testing, and validation test by the function. Learning rate of 10^3 and weight decay of $5 * 10^{-4}$. The model was trained with an Adam with a learning rate of 1e−3 for 50 epochs. The weights loaded at the end of the block result from a good run (based on validation score). The results tabulated with

Table 13.3 Performance: optimizer vs. activation functions.

Activation function / Optimizer	Accuracy in %			
	ReLu	Tanh	Softsign	Sigmoid
SGD	97.7	96.29	96.73	96.11
RMSprop	97.27	97.4	96.82	97.06
AdaGrad	96.61	95.58	95.77	95.29
Adam	98.46	98.17	96.99	97.62

different combinations in the Table 13.3. Of all the activation functions tested, ReLu was observed to have the highest accuracy. ReLu when tested with Adam as optimizer was observed to have an accuracy of 98.46%.

13.6 Conclusion

To ensure the safety of civil construction by detecting the cracks is a noteworthy challenge. From the state of the art, we inferred CNN achieves best performance in several applications like object recognition/detection and segmentation. The CNN has the special feature to aggregate visual levels in hierarchy. This motivates to apply CNN for crack detection. Hence, the challenges in civil structure are mitigated by designing a CNN framework to detect the cracks automatically. The conventional crack detection by experts with related instruments is time consuming procedure. Scarcity of experts and scanning huge and tall civil structures induced researchers to design automated crack detection system. It will assist users in early diagnosis and suggestion of precautionary maintenance for the civil structure in effective and efficient way. After detecting the crack, characteristics of cracks such as length, breadth, and depth can be measured.

References

1. Lawrence, S. *et al.*, Face recognition: A convolutional neural-network approach. *IEEE Trans. Neural Networks*, 8, 1, 98–113, 1997.
2. Liu B., Zhang W., Xu X., Chen D., Time delay recurrent neural network for speech recognition. In Journal of Physics: Conference Series (Vol. 1229, No. 1, p. 012078). IOP Publishing, 2019 May 1.

3. Mohan, A. and Poobal, S., Crack detection using image processing: A critical review and analysis. *Alexandria Eng. J.*, 57, 2, 787–798, 2018.

4. Ito, A., Aoki, Y., Hashimoto, S., Accurate extraction and measurement of fine cracks from concrete block surface image. *IEEE IECON 02*, pp. 2202–2207, 2002.

5. Hu, Y., Zhao, C.-x., Wang, H.-N., Automatic pavement crack detection using texture and shape descriptors. *IETE Techn. Rev.*, 27, 5, 398–405, 2010.

6. Kumar, A., Kumar, A., Jha, A.K., Trivedi, A., Crack Detection of Structures using Deep Learning Framework, in: *2020 International Conference on Intelligent Sustainable Systems*, 2020.

7. Prasanna, P., Dana, K., Gucunski, N., Basily, B., Computer vision based crack detection and analysis. *Proc. SPIE 8345, Sensors and Smart Structures Technologies for Civil, Mechanical, and Aerospace Systems*, 2012.

8. Fujita, Y. and Hamamoto, Y., A robust automatic crack detection method from noisy concrete surfaces. *Mach. Vis. Appl.*, 22, 2, 245–254, 2011.

9. Shahrokhinasab, E., Hosseinzadeh, N., Monirabbasi, A., Torkaman, S., Performance of Image-Based Crack Detection Systems in Concrete Structures. *J. Soft Comput. Civ. Eng.*, 4, 1, 127–39, 2020 Jan 1.

10. Yu, S.N., Jang, G.A., Han, C.S., Auto inspection system using a mobile robot for detecting concrete cracks in a tunnel. *Autom. Constr.*, 16, 3, 255–261, 2007.

11. Zhang, W., Zhang, Z., Qi, D., Liu, Y., Automatic crack detection and classification method for subway tunnel safety monitoring. *Sensors*, 14, 10, 19307–19328, 2014.

12. Rodríguez-Martín, M., Lagüela, S., González-Aguilera, D., Martínez, J., Thermographic test for the geometric characterization of cracks in welding using IR image rectification. *Autom. Constr.*, 61, 58–65, 2016.

13. Zhang, Q., Barri, K., Babanajad, S.K., Alavi, A.H., Real-Time Detection of Cracks on Concrete Bridge Decks Using Deep Learning in the Frequency Domain. *Engineering*, ISSN 2095-8099, 2020 Nov 19. https://doi.org/10.1016/j.eng.2020.07.026.

14. Bahl, L.R. *et al.*, Speech recognition with continuous-parameter hidden Markov models. *Comput. Speech Lang.*, 2, 3–4, 219–234, 1987.

15. Yang, J. *et al.*, Infrared Thermal Imaging-Based Crack Detection Using Deep Learning. *IEEE Access*, 7, 182060–18207755, 2019.

16. LeCun, Y. *et al.*, Handwritten digit recognition with a back-propagation network. *Adv. Neural Inf. Process. Syst.*, 2, 396–4045, 1989.

17. Fujita, Y., Mitani, Y., Hamamoto, Y., A method for crack detection on a concrete structure. *ICPR*, 2006.

18. Zhu, Z., German, S., Brilakis, I., Visual retrieval of concrete crack properties for automated post-earthquake structural safety evaluation. *Autom. Constr.*, 20, 7, 874–883, 2011.

19. Hutchinson, T.C. and Chen, Z., Improved image analysis for evaluating concrete damage. *J. Comput. Civ. Eng.*, 20, 3, 210–216, 2006.

20. Kapela, R. and all, Asphalt surfaced pavement cracks detection based on histograms of oriented gradients. *Proceedings of the 22nd International Conference Mixed Design of Integrated Circuits and Systems*, pp. 579–584, 2015.

14

Measuring Urban Sprawl Using Machine Learning

Keerti Kulkarni* and P. A. Vijaya

Dept of ECE, BNM Institute of Technology, Bangalore, India

Abstract

Urban sprawl generally refers to the amount of concrete jungle in a given area. In the present context, we consider a metropolitan area of Bangalore. The area has grown tremendously in the past few years. To find out how much of the area is occupied by built-up areas, we consider the remotely sensed images of the Bangalore Urban District. Each material on the earth's surface reflects a different wavelength, which is captured by the sensors mounted on a satellite. In short, the spectral signatures are the distinguishing features used by the machine learning algorithm, for classifying the land cover classes. In this study, we compare and contrast two types on machine learning algorithms, namely, parametric and non-parametric with respect to the land cover classification of remotely sensed images. Maximum likelihood classifiers, which are parametric in nature, are 82.5% accurate for the given study area, whereas the k-nearest neighbor classifiers give a better accuracy of 85.9%.

Keywords: Urbanization, maximum likelihood classifier, support vector machines, remotely sensed images

14.1 Introduction

Urbanization is a key deciding factor for the government to provide various infrastructure facilities. It is an indirect indication of the amount of population staying in the cities. Although the census report does provide this information, it is generally a very tedious process. Remotely sensed

Corresponding author: keerti_p_kulkarni@yahoo.com

Pradeep Singh (ed.) Fundamentals and Methods of Machine and Deep Learning: Algorithms, Tools and Applications, (327–340) © 2022 Scrivener Publishing LLC

images aid this kind of an analysis, wherein we try to classify the raw images and extract the built-up areas from it. Machine learning algorithms have been traditionally used for the classification of the land cover. We basically need the features depending on which the classification can be done. We also need distance measures, to calculate how far apart the features in the feature space are. In Section 14.2, a brief literature survey of the various methodologies used here is given. Section 14.3 describes the basics of remotely sensed images and the pre-processing done. The main emphasis is on the machine learning algorithms and not on the images themselves; hence, only basics related to these images are provided. Section 14.4 deals with features and their selection criteria. The different methods of calculating distances and similarities along with the equations are given, as these form a basis for feature selection. In Section 14.5, the emphasis is on the machine learning classifiers as applicable to the work. Section 14.6 details and compares the results obtained. We finally discuss the results and conclude in Section 14.7.

14.2   Literature Survey

The literature survey was undertaken on two levels. One domain is related to understand the remote sensing images, the band information, and the pre-processing that is required. The other relates to the various machine learning algorithms that can be used for the land cover classification.

Satellite images can be multispectral or hyperspectral. Hyperspectral images have a greater number of overlapping bands, whereas multispectral images have a smaller number of non-overlapping bands. Both the types can be used for wetland mapping [1]. This can be extended to the land use classification also. Pre-processing of the multispectral images, including atmospheric correction and enhancement techniques have been discussed by various authors [2, 3]. Geometric processing may also be required in certain datasets and applications [4]. The datasets which we use have been geometrically corrected.

The next literature survey was to analyze the pros and cons and comparisons of various machine learning algorithms [5, 6]. Maximum likelihood classifier (MLC) algorithm has been used and compared with regression trees for estimating the burned areas of the grassland [7]. MLC has been used for sea ice mapping of the polarimetric SAR images [8]. MLC has also been used to compare the outputs from two different datasets Landsat and SAR images [9] and land cover changes integrated with GIS [10]. Additional metadata or the Normalized Difference Vegetation Indices

(NDVI) is used with the classification algorithms to improve the accuracy of classification [11, 12]. Use of Normalized Difference Built-up Index (NDBI) for the calculation of urban sprawl is discussed by the authors in [13]. Urbanization is directly related to the land surface temperature [14, 15]. The land cover change can also be analyzed using Adaptive Neuro Fuzzy Inference Systems [16]. Object-based classification methods as compared to pixel-based classification have been discussed by various authors [17, 18]. The evaluation methods for the machine learning models have been discussed [19, 20].

14.3   Remotely Sensed Images

The images captured from the cameras mounted on a satellite are generally termed as remote sensing images. In this work, we have used the LANDSAT-8 images captured in 2019. The dataset is freely downloadable from the GloVis website. The Landsat images have nine spectral bands and two thermal bands. Out of these eight spectral bands have a resolution of 30 meters and one band (band 8) has a resolution of 15 meters. Two of the bands in the raw form, as downloaded, are shown in Figure 14.1. The thermal bands (Band 10 and Band 11) have a resolution of 100 meters. Out of these bands, we choose bands 2-7 as the features, because of their distinct spatial signatures. In other words, these bands used in different combination can easily distinguish between the different land cover classes. As an example, the band combination 3-4-6 is good for visualizing

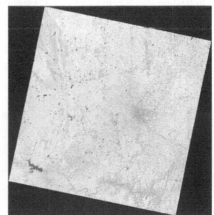

Figure 14.1 Raw images (Band 2 and Band 5, respectively).

urban environments. Here, the vegetation is shown in green, and water is dark blue or black. The built-up areas generally show up as brown. The band combinations are shown in Figure 14.2. Comparing Figures 14.1 and 14.2, we can make out how using a combination of the bands aids the visualization.

The images have to be preprocessed for atmospheric corrections before they can be further used. We have chosen only those image sets where the cloud cover is less than 10%. Hence, correction for cloud removal is not required. Further, atmospheric correction provides a kind of normalization of the spectral signatures, which makes them easily distinguishable in the feature space. Figure 14.3 shows the spectral signatures after the atmospheric correction.

Figure 14.2 Band combination 3-4-6 and 3-2-1, respectively.

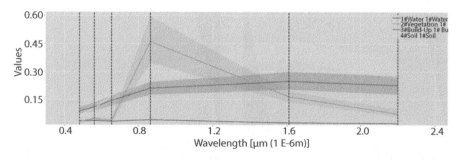

Figure 14.3 Spectral signatures after atmospheric correction.

14.4   Feature Selection

Feature selection is based on the spectral distances. Distance-based metrics as compared to similarity-based metrics are of better use for the selection of features. Similarity-based metrics give the degree of similarity between the vectors, whereas the distance-based metrics tell us how different the features are from each other.

14.4.1   Distance-Based Metric

The spectral distances evaluate the degree of separability between the spec tral signatures. The Euclidean distance is one of the simplest methods for calculating the separability. In its simplest form, the Euclidean distance gives the degree of separability in an N-dimensional vector space. The more the distance, the better is the separability. If the Euclidean distance is zero, then the spectral signatures are same and hence cannot be used as feature. The better the separability, the more will be the Euclidean distance. Mathematically,

$$d(x,y) = \sqrt{\sum_{i=1}^{n} (x_i - y_i)^2} \tag{14.1}$$

where
   x = first spectral signature vector;
   y = second spectral signature vector;
   n = number of image bands under consideration.

The other distance-based metric that can be used is the Manhattan distance, which is given as

$$d(x,y) = \sum_{i=1}^{n} |x_i - y_i| \tag{14.2}$$

Figure 14.4 shows the difference between the Euclidean distance and the Manhattan distance. The green line represents the Euclidean distance, and the red line represents the Manhattan distance. Manhattan distance is preferred when we have a high-dimensional dataset, where it gives better results compared to the Euclidean distance. As shows from the figure, the

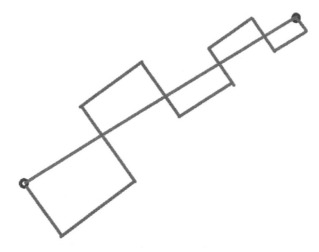

Figure 14.4 Pictorial representation of Euclidean and Manhattan distances.

Euclidean distance seems to be better suited for the application in hand; hence, we use it for feature selection.

14.5   Classification Using Machine Learning Algorithms

14.5.1   Parametric vs. Non-Parametric Algorithms

Parametric algorithms are the ones, which use a fixed set of parameters, and we assume that the data follows a specified probability distribution (e.g., MLC). Even if the training data is increased, there is no guarantee that the accuracy of the algorithm will improve. On the other hand, the complexity of a non-parametric [e.g., support vector machine, k-nearest neighbor (k-NN)] model will increase with number of parameters.

14.5.2   Maximum Likelihood Classifier

We have a large number of sample points available with us, since the dataset is really huge. Hence, the MLC works best according to literature. The likelihood function tells us how likely the observed pixel is as a function of the possible classes. Maximizing this likelihood outputs the class that agrees with that pixel most of the time. Mathematically, maximum likelihood algorithm calculates the probability distributions for the classes, related to Bayes' theorem, estimating if a pixel belongs to a land cover class. In order to use this algorithm, a sufficient number of pixels are required for each training area, allowing for the calculation of the covariance matrix. The discriminant function is calculated for every pixel as given in Equation (14.3):

$$g_k(x) = \ln p(C_k) - \frac{1}{2}\ln\left|\sum_k\right| - \frac{1}{2}(x - y_k)^t \sum_k^{-1}(x - y_k) \quad (14.3)$$

where
    C_k = land cover class k;
    x = spectral signature vector of an image pixel;
    $p(C_k)$ = probability that the correct class is Ck;
    $|\Sigma\, k|$ = determinant of the covariance matrix of the data in class Ck;

$$\sum_k^{-1}(x - y_k) = \text{inverse of the covariance matrix ;}$$

y_k = spectral signature vector of class k.
Therefore,

$$x \in C_k \leftrightarrow g_k(x) > g_j(x) \,\forall\, k \neq j \quad\quad (14.4)$$

Figure 14.5 shows the intuitive approach toward this kind of a classification. The two curves can be considered as two different classes with distinct discriminant functions. Here, since we have four classes, we will have four such distinct curves.

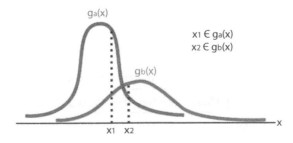

Figure 14.5 Discriminant functions.

14.5.3   k-Nearest Neighbor Classifiers

The k-NN algorithm simply considers all the sample points together and classifies them depending on the similarity measures. The similarity (or dissimilarity) measures can be calculated by using the Euclidean distance mentioned before in Section 14.3. The important parameter to be considered in the k-NN implementation is the value of k. The value of k decides how many neighbors we consider for the classification. For example, if we keep k = 5, then we consider the output from majority voting of 5 neighbors. A smaller value of k is susceptible to noise, whereas a larger value is computationally expensive. The value of k also depends on the training data size. Here, we have roughly 2,500 pixels belonging to different classes as a training data. Hence, we choose k = sqrt(2,500) = 50.

14.5.4   Evaluation of the Classifiers

The evaluation of both the algorithms is done by the chalking out the confusion matrix that represents the output of the classification algorithm. Generally, for a two-class problem, the confusion matrix looks as shown in Table 14.1.

The confusion matrix is used to indicate the performance of the model on the test data, for which the true values are known. Depending on these values, we obtain the precision, recall, and the F-score values for that model.

14.5.4.1   Precision

Precision expresses the proportion of pixels that the model says belongs to Class A, actually belongs to Class A. Referring to the confusion matrix in Table 14.1, mathematically,

$$precision = \frac{TP}{TP + FN} \tag{14.5}$$

Table 14.1 General confusion matrix for two class problems.

	Class 1 predicted	Class 2 predicted
Class 1 Actual	TP	FN
Class 2 Actual	FP	TN

14.5.4.2   Recall

Recall indicates the relevance of the pixels classified. In other words, it is a measure of the model's ability to identify true positives. It is also called as sensitivity or true positive rate.

$$recall = \frac{TP}{TP+TN} \qquad (14.6)$$

14.5.4.3   Accuracy

Using accuracy is intuitive. It is an indication of how correct the model is. In other words, all trues divided by all the values in the confusion matrix.

$$totalAccuracy = \frac{TP+TN}{TP+TN+FP+FN} \qquad (14.7)$$

14.5.4.4   F1-Score

There are certain instances, where the trade-off between precision and recall is required. In some other instances, both of them are actually important. In these cases, F1-score is a better measure. It is a harmonic mean of precision and recall.

$$F1 = 2*\frac{precision*recall}{precision+recall} \qquad (14.8)$$

14.6   Results

As mentioned previously, the remotely sensed images were preprocessed and then classified. Figure 14.6 shows the results of the MLC and Figure 14.7 shows the output of the kNN Classifier. Note then, the actual satellite image was very large. It has been clipped to show only the region of interest, in this case, the area in and around Bangalore. The red color shows the concentration of the urban or the built-up areas. Other land cover classes are indicated accordingly in the legend. The confusion matrices obtained from the MLC and the k-NN classifier are shown in Tables

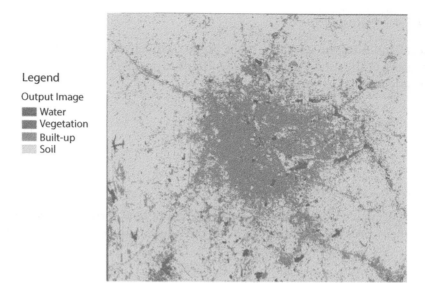

Figure 14.6 Result of ML classifier.

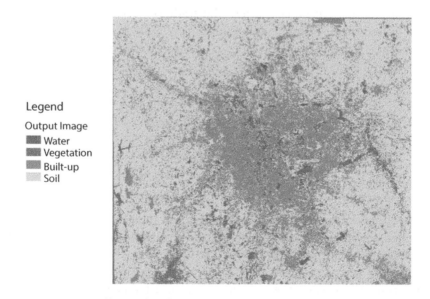

Figure 14.7 Result of k-NN classifier.

14.2 and 14.3, respectively. Table 14.4 shows the average precision, recall, F1-score, and accuracy of both the methods.

Observe that in both the cases, we get a better score for the precision, but the value for recall is less. There is always a trade-off between the two. Here, the precision is of more importance for which we get a value of 82% for the MLC and a value of 86% for the k-NN. Also, the accuracy of the k-NN is better (85.9%) compared to that of the MLC (82.5%).

Table 14.2 Confusion matrix for a ML classifier.

	Water	Vegetation	Built-up	Soil
Water	194	15	5	6
Vegetation	20	152	8	22
Built-Up	2	10	188	3
Soil	32	21	7	178

Table 14.3 Confusion matrix for a k-NN classifier.

	Water	Vegetation	Built-up	Soil
Water	200	14	2	8
Vegetation	20	162	2	12
Built-Up	8	6	195	4
Soil	20	16	9	185

Table 14.4 Average precision, recall, F1-score, and accuracy.

	Precision	Recall	F1-score	Accuracy
ML	0.826364	0.25	0.383366	0.825029
k-NN	0.861825	0.25	0.387078	0.859791

14.7   Discussion and Conclusion

As seen from Figures 14.6 and 14.7, both the classifiers give comparable results. The built-up part, which is shown in red color, is concentrated in the center of the city, which is justified since much of the urban activities are in and around this area. The MLC output shows continuous areas of red, whereas the k-NN output shows red areas interspersed with the yellow, blue, and green areas, especially in the middle part of the image. This indicates that the k-NN algorithm is capable of finer classification compared to the MLC. Comparison with the ground truth (survey maps) also ascertains this fact.

The complexity and the running time of the algorithm for the MLC are independent of the changes in any of the parameters (number of training pixels). The complexity and the running time of the k-NN increases with the increase in number of training pixels. This directly increases the k value and the algorithm has to look at a greater number of neighbors for the classification of the pixels. This increases the time taken for generating the model. On the plus side, a higher value of k generates a land cover map which is nearer to the ground truth.

We conclude by saying that the accuracy and the efficiency of the algorithms depend majorly on the feature set used. It also depends on the domain knowledge of the user and the dataset used for the classification. Choosing a proper machine learning algorithm to better suit the classification problem is a critical part of the entire process of classification.

As a future work, some more non-parametric classifiers like support vector machines and random forests can be explored. A still further extension can be the use of convolutional neural networks, which are patch-based, as opposed to pixel-based used here. This may further increase the accuracy.

Acknowledgements

The authors extend a heartfelt thanks to the management of BNM Institute of Technology, Bangalore, for providing us the infrastructure to carry out the research work on which this publication is based. The authors also sincerely thank Visveswaraya Technological University for providing the platform to do the research work.

References

1. Adam, E., Mutanga, O., Rugege, D., Multispectral and hyperspectral remote sensing for identification and mapping of wetland vegetation: A

review. *Wetl. Ecol. Manage.*, 18, 281–296, 2010, https://doi.org/10.1007/s11273-009-9169-z.

2. K. Themistocleous, D. G. Hadjimitsis, D. G. Hadjimitsis, and K. Themistocleous, The importance of considering atmospheric correction in the pre-processing of satellite remote sensing data intended for the management and detection of cultural sites: a case study, Proceedings of the 14th International Conference on Virtual Systems and Multimedia, pp 9–12, October, 2008.

3. Hanspal, R.K. and Sahoo, K., A Survey of Image Enhancement Techniques. *Int. J. Sci. Res.*, 6, 2467–2471, 2017.

4. Toutin, T., Geometric processing of remote sensing images: Models, algorithms and methods. *Int. J. Remote Sens.*, 25, 1893–1924, 2004, https://doi.org/10.1080/0143116031000101611.

5. Talukdar, S., Singha, P., Mahato, S., Shahfahad, Pal, S., Liou, Y.A., Rahman, A., Land-use land-cover classification by machine learning classifiers for satellite observations-A review. *Remote Sens.*, pp 1–24 12, 2020, https://doi.org/10.3390/rs12071135.

6. Nitze, I., Schulthess, U., Asche, H., Comparison of machine learning algorithms random forest, artificial neuronal network and support vector machine to maximum likelihood for supervised crop type classification. *Proc. 4th Conf. Geogr. Object-Based Image Anal. – GEOBIA 2012*, pp. 35–40, 2012.

7. Cabral, A.I.R., Silva, S., Silva, P.C., Vanneschi, L., Vasconcelos, M.J., ISPRS Journal of Photogrammetry and Remote Sensing Burned area estimations derived from Landsat ETM + and OLI data: Comparing Genetic Programming with Maximum Likelihood and Classification and Regression Trees. *ISPRS J. Photogramm. Remote Sens.*, 142, 94–105, 2018, https://doi.org/10.1016/j.isprsjprs.2018.05.007.

8. Dabboor, M. and Shokr, M., ISPRS Journal of Photogrammetry and Remote Sensing A new Likelihood Ratio for supervised classification of fully polarimetric SAR data : An application for sea ice type mapping. *ISPRS J. Photogramm. Remote Sens.*, 84, 1–11, 2013, https://doi.org/10.1016/j.isprsjprs.2013.06.010.

9. Ali, M.Z., Qazi, W., Aslam, N., The Egyptian Journal of Remote Sensing and Space Sciences A comparative study of ALOS-2 PALSAR and landsat-8 imagery for land cover classification using maximum likelihood classifier. *Egypt. J. Remote Sens. Space Sci.*, 21, S29–S35, 2018, https://doi.org/10.1016/j.ejrs.2018.03.003.

10. Mishra, P.K., Rai, A., Rai, S.C., Land use and land cover change detection using geospatial techniques in the Sikkim Himalaya, India. *Egypt. J. Remote Sens. Space Sci.*, 23, 2, 133–143, 2019, https://doi.org/10.1016/j.ejrs.2019.02.001.

11. Taufik, A., Ahmad, S.S.S., Ahmad, A., Classification of Landsat 8 satellite data using NDVI thresholds. *J. Telecommun. Electron. Comput. Eng.*, 8, 4, 37–40, 2016.

12. Wen, Z., Wu, S., Chen, J., Lü, M., NDVI indicated long-term interannual changes in vegetation activities and their responses to climatic and anthropogenic factors in the Three Gorges Reservoir Region, China. *Sci. Total Environ.*, 574, 947–959, 2017, https://doi.org/https://doi.org/10.1016/j.scitotenv.2016.09.049.

13. Krishna, H., Study of normalized difference built-up (NDBI) index in automatically mapping urban areas from Landsat TM imagery. *Int. J. Eng. Sci.*, 7, 1–8, 2018.

14. Guha, S., Govil, H., Gill, N., Dey, A., A long-term seasonal analysis on the relationship between LST and NDBI using Landsat data. *Quat. Int.*, 575–576, 249–258, 2020, https://doi.org/https://doi.org/10.1016/j.quaint.2020.06.041.

15. Debnath, M., Syiemlieh, H.J., Sharma, M.C., Kumar, R., Chowdhury, A., Lal, U., Glacial lake dynamics and lake surface temperature assessment along the Kangchengayo-Pauhunri Massif, Sikkim Himalaya, 1988–2014. *Remote Sens. Appl. Soc. Environ.*, 9, 26–41, 2018, https://doi.org/https://doi.org/10.1016/j.rsase.2017.11.002.

16. Sivagami, K.P., Jayanthi, S.K., Aranganayagi, S., Monitoring Land Cover of Google Web Service Images through ECOC and ANFIS Classifiers, 5, 8, 9–16 2017.

17. Rizvi, I.A. and Mohan, B.K., Object-based image analysis of high-resolution satellite images using modified cloud basis function neural network and probabilistic relaxation labeling process. *IEEE Trans. Geosci. Remote Sens.*, 49, 12, 4815–4820, 2011, https://doi.org/10.1109/TGRS.2011.2171695.

18. Qian, Y., Zhou, W., Yan, J., Li, W., Han, L., Comparing Machine Learning Classifiers for Object-Based Land Cover Classification Using Very High Resolution Imagery. 7, 153–168, 2015, https://doi.org/10.3390/rs70100153.

19. Deborah, H., Richard, N., Hardeberg, J.Y., A Comprehensive Evaluation of Spectral Distance Functions and Metrics for Hyperspectral Image Processing. *IEEE J. Sel. Top. Appl. Earth Obs. Remote Sens.*, 8, 3224–3234, 2015, https://doi.org/10.1109/JSTARS.2015.2403257.

20. Pontius, R.G. and Millones, M., Death to Kappa: Birth of quantity disagreement and allocation disagreement for accuracy assessment. *Int. J. Remote Sens.*, 32, 4407–4429, 2011, https://doi.org/10.1080/01431161.2011.552923.

15

Application of Deep Learning Algorithms in Medical Image Processing: A Survey

Santhi B.*, Swetha A.M. and Ashutosh A.M.

SASTRA Deemed University, Thanjavur, Tamil Nadu, India

Abstract

Deep learning (DL) in medical image processing (MIP) and segmentation for a long time and it continues to be the most popular and not to mention a powerful technique, given its exceptional capability in image processing and classification. From fledgeling DL models like convolutional neural networks (CNNs), which is, by far, the best rudimentary yet convoluted model for image classification, to complex algorithms like transfer learning which involves model construction on top of state-of-the-art pre-trained classifiers, DL has established itself as a capable and potential technique for medical imaging processing. Prior to the development of DL models, MIP or image processing, in general, was restricted to edge-detection filters and other automated techniques. But the advent of artificial intelligence (AI) and, along with it, the instances of ML and DL algorithms changed the facet of medical imaging. With adequate dataset and proper training, DL models can be made to perfect the task of analyzing medical images and detecting tissue damage or any equivalent tissue-related abnormality with higher precision.

This paper summarizes the evolution and contribution of various DL models in MIP over the past 5 years. This study extracts the fundamental information to draw the attention of researchers, doctors, and patients to the advancements in AI by consolidating 80 papers that categorize five areas of interest. This comprehensive study increases the usage of AI techniques, highlights the open issues in MIP, and also creates awareness about the state of the art of the emerging field.

Keywords: MIP, deep learning, classification, segmentation, feature engineering

---

*Corresponding author: shanthi@cse.sastra.ac.in

Pradeep Singh (ed.) Fundamentals and Methods of Machine and Deep Learning: Algorithms, Tools and Applications, (341–378) © 2022 Scrivener Publishing LLC

15.1   Introduction

In the emerging times, artificial intelligence (AI) has extended into all sectors of knowledge like government, security, medical, and agriculture through automations in different domains. AI was founded by a group of researchers in the early 1950s and has since gained popularity (after having faced inexorable winters), with the increase in technology. Machine learning (ML) and deep neural networks are the two branches of AI that have revolutionized AI.

Medical imaging refers to the myriad of procedures involved in procuring digital images of a subject's internal organs for the diagnosis of associated ailments and to also identify and detect changes in the functioning of inter tissues. With the advancements in the field of digital imaging, detailed multi-planar vision of the interiors of the human body with exceptional resolution has been made possible. Rapid developments in the domain of image processing including the development of techniques such as image recognition have enhanced the approach of studying and analyzing different body parts and diseases. The thriving domain of digital image processing has amplified the accuracy of diagnosing a disease and also in detecting the expanse of damage to tissues as a result of the ailment. Medical imaging uses non-invasive approaches to obtain segmented images of the body, which are transmitted to computers as signal and, are converted to digital images on reception for the detection of anomalies and defects.

Several techniques exist for medical imaging which include both organic as well as radiological imaging techniques together with thermal, magnetic, isotopic, and sonogram-based imaging among a few. Though the usage of ML in industries is increasing, deep learning (DL) being the subset of ML, outshines the traditional rule-based algorithms in extracting the features and domain expertise. In traditional algorithms, the features are identified by the experts to minimize the complexity of the intelligence. The DL algorithms achieve higher precision and accuracy by learning incrementally to pick out the important features in the enormous data for accurate predictivity analysis.

A parallel and profound development in the domain of DL has changed the way in which medical images are processed and analyzed. With the overwhelming inflow of DL algorithms, computer models are being trained to study and understand the subtleties of the human body. These DL models are trained on a set of available medical images [38] that gives the model a basic overview of the internal framework of the human body. Increasing advancements in DL algorithms have given birth to models that detect tissue damage and other internal ailments with exceptional accuracy and precision. These developments have reshaped the field of medicine and are crucial for better and early diagnosis.

15.2   Overview of Deep Learning Algorithms

The ML algorithms in medical image processing (MIP) can be classified as supervised and unsupervised deep neural networks.

15.2.1   Supervised Deep Neural Networks

A neural network is called supervised if the expected output is predefined and during the training phase the neurons in the networks are trained accurately with the target output. Regularization and back propagation can be used on the network to train the model so that the output is almost closer to the expected output with minimum error or loss. The most frequently used supervised deep neural networks in MIP are convolutional neural network (CNN), transfer neural network, and recurrent neural networks (RNNs).

15.2.1.1   *Convolutional Neural Network*

CNN [4] is the most commonly used composite deep feedforward neural network used in image classification and segmentation. CNN can extract higher level features from the image accurately which signifies that this model is the core component in image classification problems. CNN architecture consists of convolution layer, pooling layer, and fully connected layer.

Convolutional layer: This layer applies the convolution on the input image with filters to extract the feature map from the images, constructing an output feature map of the same size as the filter. The filter is moved over the image based on the stride assigned and the feature map of the entire image is calculated using convolution function.

The ReLU activation function is applied on the hidden layer neurons to impose nonlinearity in the model. The ReLU function is given by, $f(x) = max(0,x)$, for any positive value of x.

Pooling layer: This layer downsamples the feature map into lower dimension by preserving the important features in the input feature. The pooling can be divided as max pooling and average pooling, the former takes the high value in the window as the output feature and the later calculates the average of all the values in the window to be the output feature value.

Fully connected layer: The fully connected layer performs the classification based on the features extracted in the previous layers. The softmax activation function is applied on the output layer so that the output is classified in the probability space.

15.2.1.2   Transfer Learning

Models like CNN require a lot of data for training the model to get better accuracy, but in real-time medical applications, the publicly available data is very minimal which restricts the performance of a model that is built from scratch. In case of less training samples, models like transfer learning [75] can be trained since these models are already trained with the huge collection of data, reducing the training time of the model. The weights of the pre-trained models in transfer learning are loaded except the weights in the output layer. The model is trained by analyzing the patterns in the training data and the new custom layer can be added at the end of the model which best fits the classification or feature extraction problem. Some of the most high performance transfer learning networks are VGGNet, ResNet, AlexNet, DenseNet [65], Inception, and GoogleNet. These networks are the collection of series of CNN feedforward networks with a variable number of layers and parameters.

AlexNet consists of five convolutional layers while VGGNet and GoogleNet have 19 and 22 layers, respectively. However, transfer learning is simply not about stacking the layers to increase the network. As the depth of the network increases, there is a higher chance of degrading the performance of the model due to vanishing gradient problems. ResNet [19] circumvents the problem of vanishing gradients by skipping the intermediate connections and performing identity feature mapping with their outputs and the stacked layers.

15.2.1.3   Recurrent Neural Network

RNN [68] is a deep neural network that takes into consideration the historical information, i.e., in other words, it uses previous outputs as inputs while using the hidden states to produce a series of output vectors. RNN finds its purpose in image recognition, speech recognition, etc. Unlike a vanilla neural network, RNN remembers prior inputs that form its internal memory and is thereby best-suited for modeling sequential data. It copies the output from the previous information cycle and pushes it into the network along with the current input after assigning them weights. The weights are assigned through backpropagation and gradient descent. The disadvantage of RNNs is that it has a short-term memory which prevents proper tuning of weights via backpropagation. However, this disadvantage can be overcome using LSTM.

15.2.2   Unsupervised Learning

The neural network that performs some task without any pretext labels is called unsupervised learning. The images that are similar are grouped together into the same class. Some of the most frequently used unsupervised deep neural networks are autoencoders and generative adversarial networks (GANs).

15.2.2.1   Autoencoders

Autoencoder is an unsupervised neural network model that effectively compresses data and encodes it to fit the imposed network bottleneck, thereby providing a compressed representation of the input information. This encoded data can be decoded using the same technique to obtain a data representation that is as accurate as the input. An encoder has four stages namely encoder, bottleneck, decoder, and reconstruction error. The compressed data is its lowest possible dimensional representation. The reconstruction error is the difference between the decoded representation of the compressed data and the original one. This error factor helps the model to better adapt to the original data via backpropagation, thereby reducing the error margin. Autoencoders are used in image denoising, anomaly detection, noise reduction, etc.

15.2.2.2   GANs

GANs [31] are a class of powerful neural network models. They are used to generate example data when the dataset is too little to be used for model training, thereby increasing classifier accuracy. They are also used for increasing image resolutions and morphing audio from one speaker to another. GANs function with two sub-models called generators and discriminators. A generator is a model that generates examples that are drawn from the original data. A discriminator labels the generated examples as real or fake. Both the models are trained simultaneously and the generator is constantly updated on how well it performed. When a generator model fails to fool the discriminator, the model parameters of the generator are tuned to enhance its performance.

15.3   Overview of Medical Images

The medical images are the tasks that are used to create the images of different parts of the anatomy for the sake of treatment and diagnostics of the patient's health. Medical images help practitioners to view the biological changes in the patient's body and diagnose the condition with more accurate and suitable treatment decisions. Figure 15.1 shows various radiographic imaging techniques used in medical imaging.

15.3.1   MRI Scans

MRI (magnetic resonance imaging) [17] is a procedure used to visualize a detailed cross-section of the patient's body. The imaging technique uses powerful magnetic fields coupled with radio waves to generate a circumstantial image of the patient's internals, thereby making it easy to detect and locate abnormalities. The fluctuating magnetic field stimulates the

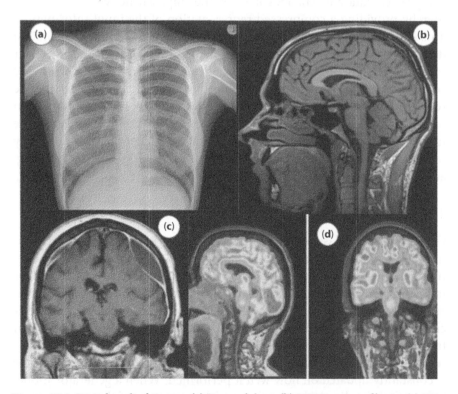

Figure 15.1 Digital medical images: (a) X-ray of chest, (b) MRI imaging of brain, (c) CT scan of brain, and (d) PET scan of brain.

protons found in the living tissue and aligns them along the field direction. The radio waves interact with these aligned protons and produce resonating signals which are tapped by the receiver to be displayed as computer-processed images of the body tissue. The MRI scan images show the desired body part with greater clarity accentuating the affected region. This makes it easy for physicians to locate any irregularity, which would have otherwise been difficult to detect.

15.3.2   CT Scans

CT (computed tomography) [13] scans use a rotating X-ray generator to generate a high-quality fragmented image of the body. This method is used to diagnose disorders associated with bone-marrow, blood vessels, and other soft tissues. The machine captures X-ray images of the body from different angles, which are later combined to produce a three-dimensional image of the body. CT scans also enable multiplanar views of the body of late, which helps us view reformatted images in traverse as well as the longitudinal plane. A patient is intravenously administered with contrast agents which enhances the contrast of body fluids. These agents are used to better visualize blood vessels. The threat associated with this technique is that it uses ionizing radiation which may prove to be carcinogenic.

15.3.3   X-Ray Scans

X-ray scans are critical for diagnosing bone-related injuries like fractures, dislocation, or misalignment, and tumors. An x-ray generator shoots high-frequency x-ray radiations which are received by the detector on the opposite end as it passes through the patient's body. Bones have high calcium density hence absorb most of the x-ray radiations while soft tissues allow the rays to pass through easily. This helps form a well-structured definition of the bone framework. To prevent undesirable radiation exposure some body parts can be covered with lead aprons. Apart from bone injuries x-rays are used to detect pneumonia and are used in mammograms to detect breast tumors.

15.3.4   PET Scans

PET (positron emission tomography) scans are used to check the viability and the functionality of living tissue. The patient is administered with a radioactive drug called tracer either orally or via injection. Organs that have abnormalities usually display high chemical activity. The tracer cumulates in these organs insinuating associated irregularities which help the physicians detect ailments even before it shows up on other scans.

15.4   Scheme of Medical Image Processing

The medical images of the human body that are collected from various radiographic imaging techniques are required to be handled and processed by computers so that the DL models can classify the images as normal or abnormal without any human intervention. The medical images processing encompasses five major areas [12]: image formation, enhancement, analysis, visualization, and management, as shown in Figure 15.2.

15.4.1   Formation of Image

To analyze the images quantitatively, a good understanding about the projection and digitalization of the images is very essential. There are different modalities of images for MIP like CT, PET, MRI, X-rays, and ultrasound, each of which has different qualities. The image formation involves acquisition of raw images and then digitalizing the images into matrix for further pre-processing and analysis.

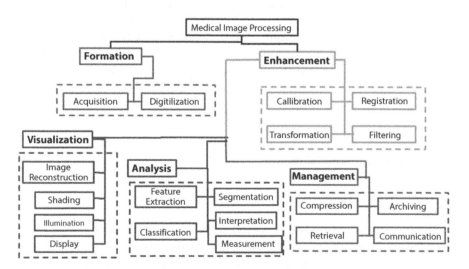

Figure 15.2 Scheme of image processing [12].

15.4.2   Image Enhancement

The main idea behind enhancement is to unwrap the hidden features in the images that are more suitable for classification. Image enhancement involves transforming the images into spatial or frequency domain in order to improve the interpretability of these images. The technique in which the pixels from an image are utilized to calibrate it is called spatial domain technique. For sharpening and smoothening the images, frequency domain technique is used. The images are aligned to analyze the temporal changes in multiple images in the image registration technique. These techniques allow elimination of noise and heterogeneity in the images by improving the most relevant features that are required for the analysis.

15.4.3   Image Analysis

Preliminary to image classification, the feature extraction and segmentation are the most important steps in analyzing the nature of the image for classification. Segmentation [3] is the partitioning of different anatomical structures into contours. The accuracy of the classification relies on accuracy of the segmentation. Feature extraction deals with extracting relevant attributes for image recognition and interpretation. The image classification is the procedure of designating labels to the object based on the information extracted from the image.

15.4.4   Image Visualization

This process renders the images from initial or intermediate steps for visualizing the anatomical images.

15.5   Anatomy-Wise Medical Image Processing With Deep Learning

MIP is important in diagnosis of the patient's health condition by the practitioners. The medical imaging can be of multiple modalities like CT, MRI, mammograms, X-rays, and ultrasound. Table 15.1 gives the summary of the datasets used in the anatomy-wise analysis of different papers. Analyzing these digital images can be beneficial in segregating the normal patients from the abnormal patients who need the attention in diagnosis of the medical condition. Some of the medical diagnoses that can be made by studying the scans of the patients' anatomical structure are detection

Table 15.1 Summary of datasets used in the survey.

S. no.	Dataset	Dataset abbreviation	Dataset description
Brain tumor			
1.	BRATS 2015	Multimodal Brain Tumor Image Segmentation (BRATS)	The Dataset is prepared from NIH Cancer Imaging Archive (TCIA) and contains 300 high- and low-grade glioma cases.
2.	T1 -W CEMRI	T1-weighted dynamic contrast-enhanced MRI (CEMRI)	The T1 weighted CEMRI dataset is obtained from the NBDC database archive and contains structural images involving clinical information on patients with unipolar and bipolar diseases and schizophrenia.
3.	FLAIR	Fluid-attenuated inversion recovery (FLAIR)	This dataset contains structural MRI images for medical image visualization and processing collected as part of a neurohacking course available in coursera consisting of 176 cases.
Lung nodule cancer dataset			
1.	LIDC/IDRI	Lung Image Database Consortium image collection (LIDC-IDRI)	The dataset comprises of CT scans with annotated lesions of Lung cancer thoracic regions.
2.	18F-FDG PET/CT	PET with 2-deoxy-2-[fluorine-18]fluoro-D-glucose integrated with computed tomography (18F-FDG PET/CT)	The dataset is the combined procurement of PET and CT scans of the thoracic region.

(Continued)

Table 15.1 Summary of datasets used in the survey. (*Continued*)

S. no.	Dataset	Dataset abbreviation	Dataset description
Breast cancer			
1.	DDSM	Digital Database for Screening Mammography (DDSM)	The DDSM dataset comprises 2,620 samples of mammogram images of the patients annotated as normal, benign and malignant.
2.	WBCD	Wisconsin Breast Cancer Dataset	The dataset consists of 701 instances of patients with solid breast mass.
3.	MIAS	mini-Mammographic Image Analysis Society	MIAS dataset consists of 322 mammogram images from 161 patients.
Heart disease prediction			
1.	PTB Diagnostic ECG Database	Physikalisch-Technische Bundesanstalt (PTB) Diagnostic ECG Database	The dataset consists of 549 instances ECG signals from 290 patients with normal and abnormal behavior in the heart under different age groups.
2.	PhysioNet Public Database	BIDMC Congestive Heart Failure Database	The dataset consists of ECG recordings of severe congestive heart failure from 15 patients.
COVID-19 prediction			
1.	COVID-CT-Dataset	Chest CT scans	The dataset consists of 749 images of patients with COVID and non-COVID cases.

and segmentation of brain tumor, breast cancer, lung nodules, pulmonary artery, diabetic retinopathy, etc. Figure 15.3 shows the collection of papers that are published in different anatomical-wise medical image classification using DL, and it is evident that the evolution of DL in medical image

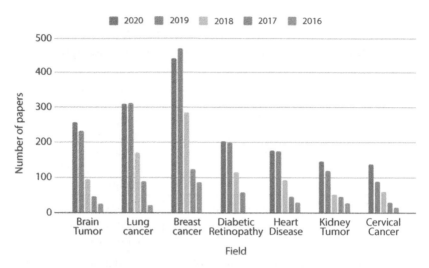

Figure 15.3 Anatomy-wise breakdown of papers in each year (2016–2020).

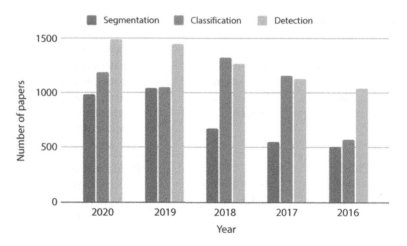

Figure 15.4 Year-wise breakdown of papers (2016–2020) based on the task.

has rapidly increased from 2016 to 2020. Figure 15.4 compares the number of publications on different analysis from the digital medical images.

15.5.1 Brain Tumor

The brain tumor is the erratic widening of cells in the brain, which can be infectious or benign. The cells that are homogeneous in composition and are not active are called benign tumor cells and the ones that are heterogeneous in composition with the presence of active cells that grow uncontrollably in the brain are categories as malignant. MRI scans can detect such tumor conditions in the brain and many more abnormal mass growths like cysts and aneurysms and swelling.

Authors in [76] proposed multi-level Gabor wavelet filters for abstracting the relevant features from the MR images and then SVM is trained on the extracted features. Conditional random fields are applied on the output of the SVM to segment the tumor. Authors in [33] proposed a skull stripping technique, fuzzy hopfield neural network for segmenting and detection of tumor in the brain images. These works use traditional

Table 15.2 Summary of papers in brain tumor classification using DL.

S. no.	Author	Data	Model	Description
1.	[76]	BRATS 2015	CRF, SVM	Multi-level Gabor wavelet filters for segmenting the important features from the MR images and then SVM is trained on the extracted features.
2.	[33]	BRATS 2015	Fuzzy Hopfield neural network	Fuzzy hopfield neural network for segmenting the tumors.
3.	[14]	BRATS 2015	U-Net	U-Net–based CNN for segmenting the tumor cells from brain images.
4.	[49]	BRATS 2015	Watershed Algorithm for Segmentation	The MRI image is transformed into the grayscale digital image (GDI) and the segmentation technique like watershed algorithm is applied on the GDI image to extract the portion of the image containing the tumor.

(Continued)

Table 15.2 Summary of papers in brain tumor classification using DL. (*Continued*)

S. no.	Author	Data	Model	Description
5.	[1]	BRATS 2015	Phase-1: CNN and SVM Phase-2: VGG, AlexNet	The phase-1 classification which includes feature extraction and classification of brain images as ordinary and abnormal is carried out using CNN and SVM algorithm. The phase-2 segmentation involves localization of the tumor in the abnormal brain images using three CNN-transfer learning techniques.
6.	[6]	BRATS 2015	RF	Classification of brain images as tumorous or not using voting average-based random forest classifier.
7.	[57]	MRI	Probabilistic Neural Network	Gray-Level Co-occurrence Matrix (GLCM) is used to abstract the features from the MRI images which increases the accuracy and reduces the time for prediction. The PNN classifier is used to find whether the image contains glioblastoma or not.

(*Continued*)

Table 15.2 Summary of papers in brain tumor classification using DL. (*Continued*)

S. no.	Author	Data	Model	Description
8.	[27]	BRATS 2015	GMM, Fuzzy Means Clustering	Wavelet transform removes noises in the BMRI images and then active contours and GMM are applied on the image to perform skull stripping on the brain images.
9.	[71]	SAR	PNN-RBF	The brain images are classified using PNN-RBF classifier and the tumor is segmented and clustered using K-means clustering.
10.	[53]	T1-W CEMRI	Hybrid Kernel–based Fuzzy C-Means clustering - Convolutional Neural Network	• This paper classifies the brain image into three types of tumor: meningioma, glioma, and pituitary tumor. • The features in the image are extracted using SIFT feature extraction technique and then CNN is applied on the extracted features to segregate the detected tumor to three classes.

(*Continued*)

Table 15.2 Summary of papers in brain tumor classification using DL. (*Continued*)

S. no.	Author	Data	Model	Description
11.	[69]	BRATS 2015	SVM, fuzzy clustering and probabilistic local ternary patterns	• Three-phase approach with phase-1 involving extracting features and classification of images as normal and abnormal using SVM algorithm. • Phase-2 uses fuzzy means clustering algorithm to find the region of the tumor in the abnormal brain images and the phase-3 consists of using probabilistic local ternary patterns to extract the tumor images using the density histogram.
12.	[51]	BRATS 2015	CNN, WT	The brain image features are extracted using wavelet transform and then CNN is applied on the extracted features to classify the brain as tumorous or not.
13.	[27]	T1CE, FLAIR	DL model	Detection of meningiomas using multiparametric deep learning model (DLM).

feature extraction methods like wavelet filters, watershed algorithms [2], thresholding, and active contour model. To accurately segment the features, recent works focus on DL networks like CNN or transfer learning models [1] for feature extraction from the images.

Table 15.2 presents the state of the art of various DL methods that are used in the classification of Brain tumors using MRI scans.

15.5.2   Lung Nodule Cancer Detection

Lung nodules are small masses in lung tissues which can either be cancerous or not. CT scans are an effective way of detecting the lung nodules at early stages. The CAD-based technique can be categorized as the detecting

Table 15.3 Paper summary—cancer detection in lung nodule by DL.

S. no.	Author	Data	Model	Description
1.	[62]	LIDC/IDRI	CNN	CNN-based cancer malignancy classification.
2.	[67]	LIDC/IDRI	CNN, DNN, and SAE	• Classification of the CT images as cancerous or not using DL models. • It is evident that CNN achieves better performance than the other two neural networks in classifying the CT scans.
3.	[39]	LIDC/IDRI	ResNet	Transfer learning-based classification model to classify the CT scans to predict if lung image contains cancer or not.
4.	[74]	18F-FDG PET/CT	CNN and ML models	• The classification of lung nodules is trained using different ML models like random forests, SVM, adaptive boosting, and artificial neural networks and a CNN model. • It is obvious from the evaluation that the ML models perform better than the CNN model in classifying the nodules as cancerous or normal.

(Continued)

Table 15.3 Paper summary—cancer detection in lung nodule by DL. (*Continued*)

S. no.	Author	Data	Model	Description
5.	[21]	LIDC/IDRI	CNN	The images obtained by the median intensity projection are concatenated and data augmentation is fitted on the images to increase the sample size, and the features from the images are extracted using CNN model and then Gaussian process model is applied on the extracted features to predict the malignancy score.
6.	[66]	LIDC/IDRI	U-Net	U-Net architecture for classifying the nodule is cancerous or not.
7.	[22]	CT, MRI	GAN	Semi-supervised model, GAN is proposed to extract the nodule information from CT and MRI scans of the patients to detect if the nodule in the lung is benign or malignant.
8.	[80]	LIDC/IDRI	AgileNet	Hybrid of LeNet and AlexNet is proposed to classify the nodules.

(*Continued*)

Table 15.3 Paper summary—cancer detection in lung nodule by DL. (*Continued*)

S. no.	Author	Data	Model	Description
9.	[26]	LIDC/IDRI	Optimal Deep Neural Network (ODNN) and Linear Discriminant Analysis (LDA)	The computation time and cost during classification can be reduced using LDA as the feature selection technique, the CT lung images are classified as normal, benign, and malignant based on the features that are extracted from the ODNN approach an optimized using Modified Gravitational Search Algorithm (MGSA) for detect the lung cancer classification.
10.	[28]	LUNA16, DSB2017	3D-Deep Neural Network	Model consists of two modules. The former is a 3D region proposal network for nodule detection. The latter selects the most relevant five nodules based on the detection confidence. Cancer probabilities are evaluated and combine them with a leaky noisy or gate.

(*Continued*)

Table 15.3 Paper summary—cancer detection in lung nodule by DL.
(*Continued*)

S. no.	Author	Data	Model	Description
11.	[20]	Lung Nodule Analysis 2016, Alibaba Tianchi Lung Cancer Detection	U-Net	The presence of nodules in the lung images does not conclude that the lung is cancerous, so a 3D DL model, U-Net, is proposed to detect the nodules in the lung CT image and then predicting if the scan is abnormal by classifying the nodules into the five class probability spaces.
12.	[79]	LIDC/IDRI	Multi-view knowledge-based collaborative	Multi-view knowledge-based collaborative model is proposed using ResNet-50 to separate the malignant nodules from benign
13.	[61]	LIDC/IDRI	Deep hierarchical semantic convolutional neural network	Deep hierarchical semantic CNN-based model to forecast the less important features and relevant features to detect if the nodule is malignant.

(*Continued*)

Table 15.3 Paper summary—cancer detection in lung nodule by DL. (*Continued*)

S. no.	Author	Data	Model	Description
14.	[8]	Chest X-Ray, LIDC-IDRI	Modified AlexNet (MAN)	• This Model examines lung pneumonia and cancer in chest X-ray • The first method is Modified AlexNet (MAN) classifies into pneumonia and normal from chest X-ray • The second method implements fusion of knowledge-based features and extracted features in the MAN to improve classification accuracy during lung cancer detection.
15.	[67]	LIDC/IDRI	CNN, DNN and SAE	• Classification of the CT images as cancerous or not using models like CNN, DNN and stacked autoencoders. • It is found that CNN performs better than the other two neural networks in classifying the CT scans

system, which segments the nodules from the tissue, and the diagnostic system which classifies the segmented nodule as benign or malignant. Identifying such nodules through CT scans manually requires experience in the field, and it may also lead to negligence and can cause severe problems.

DL is the effective way which increases the precision and accuracy of classification and detection of the infectious nodules from the CT scans of the patients. It is perceptible that many DL methods like CNN [62],

CNN-based transfer learning [39], and unsupervised DL GANs [22] extract the features from the CT images more accurately than any other means.

Table 15.3 presents the state of the art of various DL methods that are used in the detection of Lung nodule cancer using CT/MRI scans.

15.5.3   Breast Cancer Segmentation and Detection

The second major reason of death among women is breast cancer and nearly 8% of the women population gets afflicted with it. Early detection and treatment of breast cancer can elevate the process of treatment and

Table 15.4 Paper summary—classification of breast cancer by DL.

S. no.	Author	Data	Model	Description
1.	[40]	DDSM	Maximum difference feature selection (feature extraction technique)	The proposed maximum difference feature selection involves extracting the relevant tissue information from the mammograms for early detection of breast cancer.
2.	[41]	DDSM	Neural network	CAD-based approach to classify the breast mammogram images as cancer and normal by extracting the tissue features and applying neural network on the extracted features.
3.	[42]	DDSM	ANN	Intensity-based feature extraction technique to segment the features from the digital mammograms and classifying the images as normal and abnormal using ANN.

(Continued)

Table 15.4 Paper summary—classification of breast cancer by DL. (*Continued*)

S. no.	Author	Data	Model	Description
4.	[2]	WBCD	Deep-belief network	Construction of backpropagation neural network and deep belief network path to initialize the weights in the network
5.	[44]	MIAS	ANN, LDA, Naive Bayes	Various features like Wavelet Packet Transform (WPT), Local Binary Pattern (LBP), Entropy, Gray Level Co-Occurrence Matrix (GLCM), Discrete Wavelet Transform (DWT), Gray Level Run Length Matrix (GLRLM), Gabor transform, Gray Level Difference Matrix (GLDM), and trace transform are extracted from histogram and the important features are selected using ANOVA and are fed to the classifiers for classifying the breast density as two-class or three-class.
6.	[43]	MIAS	Graph-cut segmentation technique	Involves segmenting the breast regions from the image and finding the percentage of fat and dense tissue in the breast density.

(*Continued*)

Table 15.4 Paper summary—classification of breast cancer by DL. (*Continued*)

S. no.	Author	Data	Model	Description
7.	[56]	MIAS	RNN, SVM	Involves RNN for selecting the features and SVM to classify the image as normal or abnormal.
8.	[25]	MIAS	GoogleNet, Visual Geometry Group Network (VGGNet) and Residual Networks (ResNet)	Pre-trained CNN architecture for classification of mammogram images into normal or abnormal.
9.	[60]	CBIS-DDSM	Resnet50 and VGG16	Pre-trained CNN architecture for classification of mammogram images into normal or abnormal.

save the life of many patients. DL models are proven to be one the effective method for detecting the abnormal tissues in the mammograms images.

Table 15.4 presents the state of the art of various DL methods that are used in the classification of breast cancer using mammography.

15.5.4 Heart Disease Prediction

Heart disease in a nutshell is a condition that affects the heart, which includes diseases like blood vessel diseases, such as coronary artery disease, arrhythmias (heart rhythm problems), and congenital heart defects (heart defects by birth). According to the World Health Organization (WHO) heart diseases are the leading causes of deaths among the population, taking the lives of 17.9 million people world-wide each year. Therefore, an early prediction of potential heart disease is the most vital research in the medical analysis which can eventually help doctors get insight into heart failures and change their treatment accordingly. However, it is difficult to

Table 15.5 Paper summary on heart disease prediction using DL.

S. no.	Author	Data	Model	Description
1	[15]	Health system's EHR	RNN	The relation between the time-stamped events with the observation window of 12 to 18 months were detected using RNN models with Gated Recurrent Units (GRUs).
2	[52]	Physikalisch-Technische Bundesanstalt diagnostic ECG database	CNN	• The normal and MI ECG beats are detected automatically using 11-layer deep CNN. • The feature selection and extraction process are not mandatory processes as the detection can be done even in the presence of noise. • The robustness of the system is increased using 10-fold cross-validation.

(*Continued*)

Table 15.5 Paper summary on heart disease prediction using DL. (*Continued*)

S. no.	Author	Data	Model	Description
3	[77]	PhysioNet public database	MS-CNN	• The proposed method screens out the AF recordings from ECG recordings using a multiscaled fusion of deep convolutional neural networks (MS-CNN) is proposed to screen out AF recordings from single lead short electrocardiogram (ECG) recordings. • Architecture of two-stream CNN to extract features of different scales using MS-CNN.
4	[24, 34]	Cleveland heart disease dataset	DNN multilayer perceptron	Deep neural model is proposed for classification of the heart disease.
5	[47]	PhysioNet public database	CNN	A 16-layered CNN model is adapted to classify cardiac arrhythmia cases from the long-duration ECG signals.

(*Continued*)

Table 15.5 Paper summary on heart disease prediction using DL. (*Continued*)

S. no.	Author	Data	Model	Description
6	[48]	PhysioNet public database	CAE-LSTM	• A 16 layer deep CAE where the encoder comprises ECG signals in CNN. • This model reduces the signal size of arrhythmic beats. • The arrhythmias are recognized using long-short term memory (LSTM) classifiers using ECG features.
7	[29, 30]	Cleveland heart disease dataset	ANN, DNN	• $\chi 2$ statistical model and DNN for feature selection and classification, respectively. • The performance are evaluated using six different metrics, namely, accuracy, sensitivity, specificity, MCC, AUC, and ROC chart.

(*Continued*)

Table 15.5 Paper summary on heart disease prediction using DL. (*Continued*)

S. no.	Author	Data	Model	Description
8	[18]	EHR (electronic health records)	LSTM	LSTM-based model for early treatment of heart failure is a superior and novel approach compared to other methods in HF diagnosis.
9	[45]	TB diagnostic ECG and Fantasia Databases, Petersburg Institute of Cardiological Technics 12-lead Arrhythmia Database, PTB Diagnostic ECG Database and BIDMC Congestive Heart Failure Database	CNN, LSTM	ECG signals are classified into CAD, MI, and CHF conditions using CNN, followed by combined CNN and 16-layered LSTM models.
10	[9]	Health Insurance Review and Assessment Service (HIRA) - National Patients Sample (NPS)	RNN-based RetainEX	RetainVis is an analytical tool built for interpretable and interactive RNN-based models called RetainEX and visualizations for users' exploration of EMR data in the context of prediction tasks.

(*Continued*)

Table 15.5 Paper summary on heart disease prediction using DL. (*Continued*)

S. no.	Author	Data	Model	Description
11	[11, 64]	CPC of Shanxi Academy of Medical Sciences	CNN-RNN	The features of the ECG signals are extracted using the CNN and the feature sets are formed by combining the clinical features which are fed to an RNN for classification.
12	[10]	External echocardiogram videos set from Cedars-Sinai Medical Center, internal set from Stanford university	EchoNet-Dynamic	The model surpasses the performance of human experts in the critical tasks of segmenting the left ventricle, estimating ejection fraction and assessing cardiomyopathy.

manually find the risk factors of heart disease. Modern day DL techniques [16] have proven results in determining the knowledge about the factors leading to disease and medical data exploration in predicting the disease as early as possible to avoid any critical health condition.

Table 15.5 presents the state of the art of various DL methods that are used in the prediction of heart disease using ECG/EEG signals.

15.5.5   COVID-19 Prediction

COVID-19 (coronavirus disease) which originated as a mere endemic in the capital city of Wuhan, Hubei Province, China, has spread across the globe over the course of a year affecting millions of people, majority of whom have succumbed to it. The current diagnosis methods for the detection of COVID-19 patients include laboratory examinations, nasopharyngeal, and oropharyngeal swab tests. Swab tests are done by inserting a long swab into the person's nostril to collect sample secretions and cells from the nasal passage that connects it to the hind of the throat. The secretions are later tested for traces of COVID-19 genetic strains using a PCR (polymerase chain reaction) assay.

Despite the development of standard quantitative RT-PCR tests, they have been regarded as unreliable for COVID-19 diagnosis as they showed an accuracy of only 56%. CT scans have shown higher detection accuracy (around 88%) as the imaging findings of COVID-19 resembles that of MERS-CoV and SARS-CoV. The CT scans of the thoracic cavity can be used to detect the severity of infection among patients. The material-enhanced CT scans show alveolar damages which are characteristic of the coronavirus family. Hence, for early diagnosis, chest CT scans have been considered as the best method.

Table 15.6 presents the state of the art of various ML and DL methods [72] that are used in the prediction of COVID-19 patients from their chest x-ray and outlines the critical role of deep neural networks in processing the chest X-ray images.

Table 15.6 COVID-19 prediction paper summary.

S. no.	Author	Dataset	Model
1.	[78]	CT Scan	ResNet
2.	[70]	X-ray	Random Forest, REP Tree, Logistic, Random Tree, Simple Logistic, MLP, BayesNet, Naive Bayes
3.	[23]	X-ray	DenseNet
4.	[59]	X-ray	COV-ELM(ML)
5.	[5]	X-ray	VGG16
6.	[37]	X-ray	SVM, KNN, RandomForest, Naïve Bayes, Decision Tree
7.	[50]	X-ray	Inception V3, Xception, ResNet
8.	[63]	X-ray	ResNet-18, ResNet-50, SqueezeNet, DenseNet-121
9.	[7]	X-ray	ResNet-50
10.	[73]	X-ray	Inception V3
11.	[54]	X-ray	ResNet
12.	[55]	X-ray	ML Models
13.	[35]	X-ray	VGG16, VGG19, MobileNet, ResNet, DenseNet-121, InceptionV3, Xception, Inception ResNet V2
14.	[36]	X-ray	ResNet-50
15.	[58]	X-ray	CNN
16.	[32]	X-ray	AlexNet, VGGNet-19, ResNet, GoogleNet, SqueezeNet
17.	[46]	Xray	CNN

15.6 Conclusion

This study reviews nearly 80 papers on the topic of using DL in MIP, and it is obvious from this survey that DL has penetrated in all the aspects of the MIP. One of the biggest drawbacks in MIP is the data imbalance problem, where the training dataset is skewed over the abnormal class samples and could lead to the decrease in the performance of the model which, in turn, can lead to severe consequences if predicted falsely. Data augmentation and transfer learning mechanisms can be used as the techniques to terminate data imbalance problems. Another loophole in MIP is that not all data are publicly available. Finally, anatomy-wise models play an important part, as the algorithms need to construct the patient-specific models with minimum sized dataset and minimum user-interaction.

Although there are some challenges in MIP, from this survey, it is proved that DL models outperform medical practitioners in classification and segmentation of medical images. We envision that DL techniques can be used on various practical applications like image captioning, image reconstruction, content-based image retrievals and surgical robots using reinforcement learning providing an assistance to the medical practitioners and also helps in remote monitoring of patients.

Deep neural networks like CNN require a large and feature engineered dataset to train on and hypertuned parameters to outperform in the evaluation. There is no universal model that performs best for the whole pool of datasets available for analysis. The prediction and the performance of the model depend on the nature and quality of the dataset on which the model is trained.

References

1. Abd-Ellah, M., Awad, A., Khalaf, A., Hamed, H., Two-phase multi-model automatic brain tumour diagnosis system from magnetic resonance images using convolutional neural networks. *Eurasip J. Image Video Process.*, *2018*, 1, 2018, 10.1186/s13640-018-0332-4.
2. Abdel-Zaher, A. and Eldeib, A., Breast cancer classification using deep belief networks. *Expert Syst. Appl.*, *46*, 139–144, 2016, 10.1016/j.eswa.2015.10.015.
3. Abinaya, P., Ravichandran, K.S., Santhi, B., Watershed segmentation for vehicle classification and counting. *Int. J. Eng. Technol.*, *5*, 2, 770–775, 2013.
4. Mortazi, A. and Bagci, U., Automatically Designing CNN Architectures for Medical Image Segmentation. *International Workshop on Machine*

Learning in Medical Imaging, 11046, pp. 98–106, 2018, https://doi.org/10.1007/978-3-030-00919-9_12.

5. Chen, A., Jaegerman, J., Matic, D., Inayatali, H., Charoenkitkarn, N., Chan, J., Detecting Covid-19 in Chest X-Rays using Transfer Learning with VGG16. *CSBIO 20 Computational Systems - Biology and Bioinfromatics*, pp. 93–96, 2020, https://doi.org/10.1145/3429210.3429213.

6. Anitha, R. and Siva Sundhara Raja, D., Development of computer-aided approach for brain tumor detection using random forest classifier. *Int. J. Imaging Syst. Technol.*, 28, 1, 48–53, 2018, 10.1002/ima.22255.

7. Makris, A., Kontopoulos, I., Tserpes, K., *COVID-19 detection from chest X-Ray images using Deep Learning and Convolutional Neural Networks*, medRxiv 2020.05.22.20110817, 2020, https://doi.org/10.1101/2020.05.22.20110817.

8. Bhandary, A., Prabhu, G., Rajinikanth, V., Deep-learning framework to detect lung abnormality – A study with chest X-Ray and lung CT scan images. *Pattern Recognit. Lett.*, 129, 271–278, 2020, 10.1016/j.patrec.2019.11.013.

9. Kwon, B.C., Choi, M.-J., Kim, J.T., Choi, E., Kim, Y.B., Kwon, S., Sun, J., Choo, J., RetainVis: Visual Analytics with Interpretable and Interactive Recurrent Neural Networks on Electronic Medical Records. *IEEE Trans. Visual. Comput. Graphics*, 25, 1, 299–309, 2018, 10.1109/TVCG.2018.2865027.

10. Ouyang, D., He, B., Ghorbani, A., Yuan, N., Ebinger, J., Langlotz, C.P., Heidenreich, P.A., Harrington, R.A., Liang, D.H., Ashley, E.A., Zou, J.Y., Video-based AI for beat-to-beat assessment of cardiac function. *Nature, 580*, 7802, 252–256, 2020, https://doi.org/10.1038/s41586-020-2145-8.

11. Li, D., Li, X., Zhao, J., Bai, X., Automatic staging model of heart failure based on deep learning. *Biomed. Signal Process. Control*, 52, 77–83, 2019, https://doi.org/10.1016/j.bspc.2019.03.009Get.

12. Deserno, T.M., Fundamentals of Biomedical Image Processing, in: *Biomedical Image Processing. Biomedical Engineering*, 2011, 10.1007/978-3-642-15816-2 1.

13. Mhaske, D., Rajeswari, K., Tekade, R., Deep Learning Algorithm for Classification and Prediction of Lung Cancer using CT Scan Images. *ICCUBEA, 2020*, 10.1109/ICCUBEA47591.2019.9128479.

14. Dong, H., Yang, G., Liu, F., Mo, Y., Guo, Y., Automatic brain tumor detection and segmentation using U-net based fully convolutional networks. *Commun. Comput. Inf. Sci.*, 723, 506–517, 2017, 10.1007/978-3-319-60964-5_44.

15. Choi, E., Schuetz, A., Stewart, W.F., Sun, J., Using recurrent neural network models for early detection of heart failure onset. *J. Am. Med. Inf. Assoc.*, 24, 2, 361–370, 2016, https://doi.org/10.1093/jamia/ocw112.

16. Ali, F., El-Sappagh, S., Riazul Islam, S.M., Kwak, D., Ali, A., Imran, M., Kwak, K.-S., A smart healthcare monitoring system for heart disease prediction based on ensemble deep learning and feature fusion. *Inform. Fusion, 63*, 208–222, 2020, https://doi.org/10.1016/j.inffus.2020.06.008.

17. Mohan, G. and Monica Subashini, M., MRI based medical image analysis: Survey on brain tumor grade classification. *Biomed. Signal Process. Control*, 39, 139–161, 2018, https://doi.org/10.1016/j.bspc.2017.07.007.

18. Maragatham, G. and Devi, S., LSTM Model for Prediction of Heart Failure in Big Data. *J. Med. Syst.*, 43, 5, 111, 2019, https://doi.org/10.1007/s10916-019-1243-3.

19. He, K., Zhang, X., Ren, S., Sun, J., Deep Residual Learning for Image Recognition. *Proceedings of the IEEE Computer Society Conference on Computer Vision and Pattern Recognition*, 2016.

20. Huang, W. and Hu, L., Using a Noisy U-Net for Detecting Lung Nodule Candidates. *IEEE Access*, 7, 67905–67915, 2019, 10.1109/ACCESS.2019.2918224.

21. Hussein, S., Gillies, R., Cao, K., Song, Q., Bagci, U., TumorNet: Lung nodule characterization using multi-view Convolutional Neural Network with Gaussian Process. *Proceedings - International Symposium on Biomedical Imaging*, pp. 1007–1010, 2017, 10.1109/ISBI.2017.7950686.

22. Jiang, J., Hu, Y., Tyagi, N., Zhang, P., Rimner, A., Mageras, G.S., Deasy, J.O., Veeraraghavan, H., Tumor-aware, adversarial domain adaptation from CT to MRI for lung cancer segmentation. *Lect. Notes Comput. Sci. (including subseries Lecture Notes in Artifical Intelligence and Lecture Notes in Bioinformatics)*, 11071, 777–785, 2018, 10.1007/978-3-030-00934-2_86.

23. Paul Cohen, J., Dao, L., Morrison, P., Roth, K., Bengio, Y., Shen, B., Abbasi, A., Hoshmand-Kochi, M., Ghassemi, M., Li, H., Duong, T.Q., Predicting COVID-19 Pneumonia Severity on Chest X-ray with Deep Learning. *Cureus*, 12, 7, 2020, 10.7759/cureus.9448.

24. Miao, K.H. and Miao, J.H., Coronary Heart Disease Diagnosis using Deep Neural Networks. *Int. J. Adv. Comput. Sci. Appl.*, 9, 10, 1–8, 2018.

25. Khan, S., Islam, N., Jan, Z., Ud Din, I., Rodrigues, J., A novel deep learning based framework for the detection and classification of breast cancer using transfer learning. *Pattern Recognit. Lett.*, 125, 1–6, 2019, 10.1016/j.patrec.2019.03.022.

26. Lakshmanaprabu, S., Mohanty, S., Shankar, K., Arunkumar, N., Ramirez, G., Optimal deep learning model for classification of lung cancer on CT images. *Future Gener. Comput. Syst.*, 92, 374–382, 2019, 10.1016/j.future.2018.10.009.

27. Laukamp, K., Thiele, F., Shakirin, G., Fully automated detection and segmentation of meningiomas using deep learning on routine multiparametric MRI. *Eur. Radiol.*, 29, 1, 124–132, 2019.

28. Liao, F., Liang, M., Li, Z., Hu, X., Song, S., Evaluate the Malignancy of Pulmonary Nodules Using the 3-D Deep Leaky Noisy-OR Network. *IEEE Trans. Neural Netw. Learn. Syst.*, 30, 11, 3484–3495, 2019, 10.1109/TNNLS.2019.2892409.

29. Ali, L., Rahman, A., Khan, A., Zhou, M., Javeed, A., Khan., J.A., *An Automated Diagnostic System for Heart Disease Prediction Based on $\chi 2$

Statistical Model and Optimally Configured Deep Neural Network. *IEEE Access, 7*, 34938–34945, 2019, 10.1109/ACCESS.2019.2904800.

30. Ali, L., Niamat, A., Khan, J.A., Golilarz, N.A., Xingzhong, X., Noor, A., Nour, R., Ahmad C. Bukhari, S., An Optimized Stacked Support Vector Machines Based Expert System for the Effective Prediction of Heart Failure. *7*, 54007–54014, 2019.

31. Frid-Adar, M., Diamant, I., Klang, E., Amitai, M., Goldberger, J., Greenspan, H., GAN-based synthetic medical image augmentation for increased CNN performance in liver lesion classification. *Neurocomputing, 321*, 321–331, 2018, https://doi.org/10.1016/j.neucom.2018.09.013.

32. Nakrani, M.G., Sable, G.S., Shinde, U.B., Classification of COVID-19 from Chest Radiography Images Using Deep Convolutional Neural Network. *J. Xidian Univ., 14*, 565–569, 2020, https://doi.org/10.37896/jxu14.8/061.

33. Megersa, Y. and Alemu, G., Brain tumor detection and segmentation using hybrid intelligent algorithms. *IEEE AFRICON Conference, 2015*, 2015, 10.1109/AFRCON.2015.7331938.

34. Khan, M.A., An IoT Framework for Heart Disease Prediction Based on MDCNN Classifier. *IEEE Access, 8*, 34717–34727, 2020, 10.1109/ACCESS.2020.2974687.

35. Qjidaa, M., Mechbal, Y., Ben-fares, A., Amakdouf, H., Maaroufi, M., Alami, B., Qjidaa, H., Early detection of COVID19 by deep learning transfer Model for populations in isolated rural areas. *ISCV*, vol. 1, pp. 1–5, 2020, 10.1109/ISCV49265.2020.9204099.

36. Farooq, M. and Hafeez, A., COVID-ResNet: A deep learning framework for screening of COVID19 from radiographs. ArXiv, abs/2003.14395. https://arxiv.org/abs/2003.14395, 2020.

37. Imad, M., Khan, N., Ullah, F., Hassan, M.A., Hussain, A., Faiza, COVID-19 Classification based on Chest X-Ray Images Using Machine Learning Techniques. *J. Comput. Sci. Technol. Stud., 2*, 1–11, 2020, https://al-kindipublisher.com/index.php/jcsts/article/view/531.

38. Razzak, M.I., Naz, S., Zaib, A., Deep Learning for Medical Image Processing: Overview, Challenges and the Future, in: *Classification in BioApps. Lecture Notes in Computational Vision and Biomechanics*, vol. 26, 2017, https://doi.org/10.1007/978-3-319-65981-7_12.

39. Nibali, A., He, Z., Wollersheim, D., Pulmonary nodule classification with deep residual networks. *Int. J. Comput. Assist. Radiol. Surg., 12*, 10, 1799–1808, 2017, 10.1007/s11548-017-1605-6.

40. Nithya, R. and Santhi, B., Mammogram classification using maximum difference feature selection method. *J. Theor. Appl. Inf. Technol., 33*, 2, 197–204, 2011.

41. Nithya, R. and Santhi, B., Breast cancer diagnosis in digital mammogram using statistical features and neural network. *Res. J. Appl. Sci. Eng. Tech., 4*, 24, 5480–5483, 2012.

42. Nithya, R. and Santhi, B., Mammogram analysis based on pixel intensity mean features. *J. Comput. Sci.*, 8, 3, 329–332, 2012.
43. Nithya, R. and Santhi, B., Application of texture analysis method for mammogram density classification. *J. Instrum.*, 12, 7, 2017.
44. Nithya, R. and Santhi, B., Computer-aided diagnosis system for mammogram density measure and classification. *Biomed. Res.*, 28, 6, 2427–2431, 2017.
45. Lih, O.S., Jahmunah, V., San, T.R., Ciaccio, E.J., Yamakawa, T., Tanabe, M., Kobayashi, M., Faust, O., Rajendra Acharya, U., Comprehensive electrocardiographic diagnosis based on deep learning. *Artif. Intell. Med.*, 103, 2020, https://doi.org/10.1016/j.artmed.2019.101789.
46. Oyelade, O.N. and Ezugwu, A.E., *Deep Learning Model for Improving the Characterization of Coronavirus on Chest X-ray Images Using CNN*, medRXiv, 2020, https://doi.org/10.1101/2020.10.30.20222786.
47. Yildirim, O., Plawiak, P., Tan, R.-S., Rajendra Acharya, U., Arrhythmia detection using deep convolutional neural network with long duration ECG signals. *Comput. Biol. Med.*, 102, 1, 411–420, 2018, https://doi.org/10.1016/j.compbiomed.2018.09.009.
48. Yildirim, O., Baloglu, U.B., Tan, R.-S., Ciaccio, E.J., Acharya, U.R., A new approach for arrhythmia classification using deep coded features and LSTM networks. *Comput. Methods Programs Biomed.*, 176, 121–133, 2019, https://doi.org/10.1016/j.cmpb.2019.05.004.
49. Prakash, V. and Manjunathachari, K., Detection of brain tumour using segmentation. *Int. J. Eng. Technol.*, 7, 688, 2018, 10.14419/ijet.v7i2.8.10559.
50. Jain, R., Gupta, M., Taneja, S., Jude Hemanth, D., Deep learning based detection and analysis of COVID-19 on chest X-ray images. *Appl. Intell.*, 51, 1690–1700, 2020, 10.1007/s10489-020-01902-1.
51. Rajasekar, B., Brain tumour segmentation using CNN and WT. *Res. J. Pharm. Technol.*, 12, 10, 4613–4617, 2019, 10.5958/0974-360X.2019.00793.5.
52. Acharya, R., Fujita, H., Oh, S.L., Hagiwara, Y., Tan, J.H., Adam, M., Application of deep convolutional neural network for automated detection of myocardial infarction using ECG signals. *Inf. Sci.*, 415–416, 190–198, 2017, https://doi.org/10.1016/j.ins.2017.06.027.
53. Rao, S. and Lingappa, B., Image analysis for MRI based brain tumour detection using hybrid segmentation and deep learning classification technique. *Int. J. Intell. Eng. Syst.*, 12, 5, 53–62, 2019.
54. Misra, S., Jeon, S., Lee, S., Managuli, R., Jang, I.-S., Kim, C., Multi-channel transfer learning of chest x-ray images for screening of covid-19. *Electronics*, 9, 9, 1388, 2020, https://doi.org/10.3390/electronics9091388.
55. Pathari, S. and Rahul, U., *Automatic detection of COVID-19 and pneumonia from Chest X-ray using transfer learning*, MedRXiv, 2020, https://doi.org/10.1101/2020.05.27.20100297.

56. Mambou, S.J., Maresova, P., Krejcar, O., Selamat, A., Kuca, K., Breast Cancer Detection Using Infrared Thermal Imaging and a Deep Learning Model. *Sensors(Basel)*, *18*, 9, 2799, 2018, 10.3390/s18092799.

57. Selvy, P.T., Dharani, V.P., Indhuja, A., Brain Tumour Detection Using Deep Learning Techniques. *Int. J. Sci. Res. Comput. Sci. Eng. Inf. Technol.*, *169*, 175, 2019, 10.32628/cseit195233.

58. SIddiqui, S.Y., Abbas, S., Khan, M.A., Naseer, I., Masood, T., Khan, K.M., Al Ghamdi, M.A., Almotiri, S.H., Intelligent decision support system for COVID-19 empowered with deep learning. *Comput. Mater. Continua*, *66*, 1719–1732, 2021.

59. Rajpal, S., Kumar, N., Rajpal, A., COV-ELM classifier: An Extreme Learning Machine based identification of COVID-19 using Chest X-Ray Images. *Image Video Process.*, 2020.

60. Shen, L., Margolies, L., Rothstein, J., Fluder, E., McBride, R., Sieh, W., Deep Learning to Improve Breast Cancer Detection on Screening Mammography. *Sci. Rep.*, *9*, 1, 2019, 10.1038/s41598-019-48995-4.

61. Shen, S., Han, S., Aberle, D., Bui, A., Hsu, W., An interpretable deep hierarchical semantic convolutional neural network for lung nodule malignancy classification. *Expert Syst. Appl.*, *128*, 84–95, 2019, 10.1016/j.eswa.2019.01.048.

62. Shen, W., Zhou, M., Yang, F., Learning from experts: Developing transferable deep features for patient-level lung cancer prediction. *Lect. Notes Comput. Sci. (including subseries Lecture Notes in Artifical Intelligence and Lecture Notes in Bioinformatics)*, *9901*, 124–131, 2016, 10.1007/978-3-319-46723-8_15.

63. Minaee, S., Kafieh, R., Sonka, M., Yazdani, S., Soufi, G.J., Deep-COVID: Predicting COVID-19 from chest X-ray images using deep transfer learning. *Med. Image Anal.*, *65*, 2020, https://doi.org/10.1016/j.media.2020.101794.

64. Tuli, S., Basumatary, N., Gill, S.S., Kahani, M., Arya, R.C., Wander, G.S., Buyya, R., HealthFog: An ensemble deep learning based Smart Healthcare System for Automatic Diagnosis of Heart Diseases in integrated IoT and fog computing environments. *Future Gener. Comput. Syst.*, *104*, 187–200, 2020, https://doi.org/10.1016/j.future.2019.10.043.

65. Chen, S., Ma, K., Zheng, Y., Med3D: Transfer Learning for 3D Medical Image Analysis. *Comput. Vis. Pattern Recognit.*, 2019.

66. Skourt, A.B., Hassani, E.A., Majda, A., Lung CT image segmentation using deep neural networks. *Proc. Comput. Sci.*, *127*, 109–113, 2018, 10.1016/j. procs.2018.01.104.

67. Song, Q., Zhao, L., Luo, X., Using Deep Learning for Classification of Lung Nodules on Computed Tomography Images. *J. Healthcare Eng.*, *2017*, 7, 2017, 10.1155/2017/8314740.

68. Kim, S., An, S., Chikontwe, P., Park, S.H., Bidirectional RNN-based Few Shot Learning for 3D Medical Image Segmentation. *Comput. Vis. Pattern Recognit.*, 2020.

69. Sriramakrishnan, P., Kalaiselvi, T., Rajeshwaran, R., Modified local ternary patterns technique for brain tumour segmentation and volume estimation

from MRI multi-sequence scans with GPU CUDA machine. *Biocybern. Biomed. Eng.*, *39*, 2, 470–487, 2019, 10.1016/j.bbe.2019.02.002.

70. Thepade, S.D., Bang, S.V., Chaudhari, P.R., Dindorkar, M.R., Covid19 Identification from Chest X-ray Images using Machine Learning Classifiers with GLCM Features. *ELCVIA: Electron. Lett. Comput. Vis. Image Anal.*, *19*, 85–97, 2020, https://www.raco.cat/index.php/ELCVIA/article/view/375822.

71. Suhartono, Nguyen, P., Shankar, K., Hashim, W., Maseleno, A., Brain tumor segmentation and classification using KNN algorithm. *Int. J. Eng. Adv. Technol.*, *8*, 6, 706–711, 2019, 10.35940/ijeat.F1137.0886S19.

72. Bhattacharya. S., Reddy Maddikunta, P.K., Pham, Q.V., Gadekallu, T.R., Krishnan S.S.R., Chowdhary, C.L., Alazab, M., Jalil Piran, M., Deep learning and medical image processing for coronavirus (COVID-19) pandemic: A survey. *Sustain. Cities Soc.*, 2021.

73. Tan, T., Das, B., Soni, R., Fejes, M., Ranjan, S., Szabo, D.A., Melapudi, V., Shriram, K.S., Agrawal, U., Rusko, L., Herczeg, Z., Darazs, B., Tegzes, P., Ferenczi, L., Mullick, R., Avinash, G., *Pristine annotations-based multi-modal trained artificial intelligence solution totriage chest x-ray for COVID19*, arXiv, 2020, https://arxiv.org/abs/2011.05186.

74. Wang, H., Zhou, Z., Li, Y. *et al.*, Comparison of machine learning methods for classifying mediastinal lymph node metastasis of non-small cell lung cancer from 18F-FDG PET/CT images. *EJNMMI Res.*, *7*, 11, 2017. https://doi.org/10.1186/s13550-017-0260-9

75. Weiss, K., Khoshgoftaar, T.M., Wang, D., A survey of transfer learning. *J. Big Data*, *3*, 9, 2016, 10.1186/s40537-016-0043-6.

76. Wu, W., Chen, A., Zhao, L., Corso, J., Brain tumor detection and segmentation in a CRF (conditional random fields) framework with pixel-pairwise affinity and superpixel-level features. *Int. J. Comput. Assist. Radiol. Surg.*, *9*, 2, 241–253, 2014, 10.1007/s11548-013-0922-7.

77. Fan, X., Yao, Q., Cai, Y., Miao, F., Sun, F., Li, Y., Multiscaled Fusion of Deep Convolutional Neural Networks for Screening Atrial Fibrillation From Single Lead Short ECG Recordings. *IEEE J. Biomed. Health Inform.*, *22*, 1744–1753, 2018.

78. Xu, X., Jiang, X., Ma, C., Du, P., Li, X., Lv, S., Yu, L., Ni, Q., Chen, Y., Su, J., Lang, G., Li, Y., Zhao, H., Liu, J., Xu, K., Ruan, L., Sheng, J., Qiu, Y., Wu, W., Li, L., A Deep Learning System to Screen Novel Coronavirus Disease 2019 Pneumonia. *Engineering*, *6*, 10, 1122–1129, 2020, https://doi.org/10.1016/j.eng.2020.04.010.

79. Xie, Y., Xia, Y., Zhang, J., Song, Y., Feng, D., Fulham, M., Cai, W., Knowledge-based Collaborative Deep Learning for Benign-Malignant Lung Nodule Classification on Chest CT. *IEEE Trans. Med. Imaging*, *38*, 4, 991–1004,, 2019, 10.1109/TMI.2018.2876510.

80. Zhao, X., Liu, L., Qi, S., Teng, Y., Li, J., Qian, W., Agile convolutional neural network for pulmonary nodule classification using CT images. *Int. J. Comput. Assist. Radiol. Surg.*, *13*, 4, 585–595, 2018, 10.1007/s11548-017-1696-0.

16

Simulation of Self-Driving Cars Using Deep Learning

Rahul M. K.*, Praveen L. Uppunda, Vinayaka Raju S., Sumukh B. and C. Gururaj

Department of Telecommunication Engineering, B.M.S College of Engineering, Bengaluru, India

Abstract

Self-driving cars have been a popular area of research for a few decades now. However, the prevalent methods have proven inflexible and hard to scale in more complex environments. For example, in developing countries, the roads are more chaotic and unstructured as compared to developed countries. Hence, the rule-based self-driving methodologies currently being used in developed countries cannot be applied to the roads in developing countries. Therefore, in this paper, a methodology of implementing self-driving is discussed which we propose that it will be better suited to more unstructured and chaotic environments.

As discussed, there are many approaches to solving self-driving, each with its advantages and disadvantages. In this paper, the concept of end-to-end learning with behavioral cloning applied for self-driving is discussed. We have experimented with two different neural network models, Convolutional Neural Network (CNN) and Multilayer Perceptron (MLP). Also, we have two different pre-processing pipelines, that is, with and without lane feature extraction. In the final result, the goal is to find the optimal combination of these methodologies to get the highest accuracy. It was found that the end-to-end learning CNN model without lane feature extraction gave the highest accuracy compared to the other combinations.

Keywords: Self-driving, behavioral cloning, end-to-end learning, CNN, MLP

---

*Corresponding author: rahulmk8055@gmail.com

Pradeep Singh (ed.) Fundamentals and Methods of Machine and Deep Learning: Algorithms, Tools and Applications, (379–396) © 2022 Scrivener Publishing LLC

16.1   Introduction

Most self-driving cars that are currently in the market are developed for structured roads, relying heavily on lane marking, handwritten rules for specific situations and road signs, etc. [2, 3]. This method has a profound disadvantage when it encounters the roads of developing countries, as they are not as structured and often do not have clear lane markings on the roads. Thus, using handwritten rules will fail in this scenario. To solve this problem, we propose the method of end-to-end learning with behavioral cloning. This is because the need of defining handwritten rules or policies in this methodology is eliminated. Although end-to-end learning has its disadvantages [11], we propose that it will perform better than the other methods in certain environments as described above.

Also, in this paper, six combinations of three different attributes are implemented to arrive at an optimal combination. The three different attributes are type of model (CNN/MLP), type of image processing pipeline (with/without lane feature extraction), and type of output (classification/ regression).

16.2   Methodology

16.2.1   Behavioral Cloning

Behavioral cloning is a method that is used to capture human sub-cognitive skills. As a human subject performs the skill, his or her actions can be recorded along with the situation that gave rise to that action. This method can be used to construct automatic control systems for complex tasks for which classical control theory is inadequate. It can also be used for training [4, 10].

16.2.2   End-to-End Learning

End-to-end learning refers to training a complex learning system represented by a single model (usually a deep neural network) that represents the complete target system, bypassing the intermediate layers usually present in traditional pipeline designs [1].

In this end-to-end system, there are two main components, i.e., training component and the inference component [15]. The training component consists of recording all the actions of the human subject while he or she performs the task of driving, and then training the model using the collected data. In the inference component, the trained model drives the car, autonomously utilizing the knowledge of previously collected data.

16.3   Hardware Platform

In the current implementation, a physical prototype of the car is used to experiment different scenarios of processing, so that more practical insights of the model's performance can be inferred, rather than using a software simulator. The prototype car is a custom-designed 3D printed 1:16 scale car with Ackerman steering which is shown in Figure 16.1. The actuators used are DC motors, and a servo motor is used to control the Ackerman steering. The processing unit used is a Raspberry Pi 3 Model B. A smartphone is used as a camera to capture images and feed it to the model. Also, a stand-alone PC is used to run certain models that require higher computing power. In this case, the images captured are transmitted from the car to the PC and the inference predictions are sent back from the PC wirelessly to the car over WIFI using the Robotic Operating System (ROS) framework.

ROS is the software stack used which acts as the communication middleware between different components in the system.

Figure 16.1 Prototype 1:16 scale car.

16.4 Related Work

One of the first implementations of behavioral cloning in self-driving was by ALVINN [5], which predicted driving parameters from road images and laser data. Nvidia has demonstrated end-to-end behavioral cloning in self-driving using deep CNNs, and surprisingly, this performed remarkably well and reintroduced the potential of end-to-end learning in self-driving [1]. The Nvidia model has gone through further iterations to result in a model that is nearly four times smaller, which enables it to be used in embedded systems [21]. Authors in [22] highlight which region of the image influences the resulting steering angle produced by end-to-end learning models. It was shown that end-to-end models accurately determined that lane markings had the most influence in the final steering angle produced by the model.

16.5 Pre-Processing

This section describes the pre-processing steps applied on the image before feeding it to the model. Figure 16.2 indicates the Image Processing Pipeline used.

16.5.1 Lane Feature Extraction

We assume that lane markings as the primary indicator needed for inferring driving parameters by the model. Therefore, in this step, only the lane features are extracted from the image and fed to the model. Lane features are extracted using classical computer vision algorithms such as Canny edge detector [6] and Hough transform [7, 13].

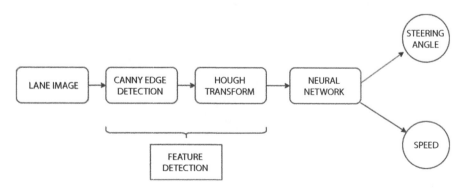

Figure 16.2 Image processing pipeline.

Figure 16.3 Original Image.

16.5.1.1   Canny Edge Detector

Canny edge detection is a technique to extract important structural information from different vision objects such as lane edges as shown in Figure 16.3. The canny output contains unwanted edge features also. Therefore, using a suitable mask, the unwanted regions are masked out. The resulting image Figure 16.4 ideally consists only of lane markings.

16.5.1.2   Hough Transform

Hough transform is the algorithm used to detect straight lines, circles, or other structures if their parametric equation is known. Here, it is used to

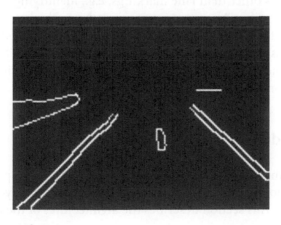

Figure 16.4 Canny edge output.

Figure 16.5 Hough lines overlaid on original image.

highlight only the lane lines as shown in Figure 16.5. This method can give robust detection even under noise and partial occlusion [20].

16.5.1.3   Raw Image Without Pre-Processing

In this method, we do not perform any pre-processing steps as described in the previous section. Instead, the raw images are fed directly to the model. The argument for this is based on the assumption that the model can make better internal learned representations of important features from the image not necessarily restricted to only lane features [8]. As stated earlier, in a situation where the roads do not contain any clear lane markings, the previous method fails, but in this method, the model can learn representations of features other than lane markings, e.g., identifying the contour of the road as a feature. Also, an argument can be made that the model can learn to extract lane features better than the previous method as the previous method uses classical methods which are very susceptible to lighting conditions, whereas a deep learning model can be more resilient to different lighting conditions [8, 9].

16.6   Model

In this implementation, we have experimented with two types of models, i.e., Convolutional Neural Network (CNN) [14] and Multilayer Perceptron (MLP) model. This section describes the architectures of the models.

16.6.1 CNN Architecture

The architecture that has been implemented is based on the model used by [1] which has been tweaked to obtain the optimal values for the model. The input size of the image is fixed to be 120 × 160. The CNN consists of five convolutional layers followed by two fully connected layers as depicted in Figure 16.6. Since the CNN requires a higher computing resource, it is not possible to run this on the Raspberry Pi 3 model B. Therefore, the images from the car are wirelessly transmitted to a stand-alone PC that is running the CNN. Then the stand-alone PC will infer from the image and transmit the driving parameters back to the car.

16.6.2 Multilayer Perceptron Model

Given its simplicity, the MLP model [19] was also considered since it has performed remarkably well in ALVINN [5]. Also, the added advantage of using MLP models is reduction in the requirement of computing resources, which makes it suitable for running it locally on the Raspberry Pi if needed. The disadvantage of MLP models is that, they are not very robust and cannot scale to different environments very easily and tend to overfit.

Similar to the previous model, the input image size is fixed to 120 × 160 pixels. It has four hidden layers with 50 neurons each and there a dropout of 0.1 in each layer as depicted by Table 16.1.

16.6.3 Regression vs. Classification

As stated before, we also experimented with type of output of the model, i.e., regression and classification. The aim is to find which among the two is better suited.

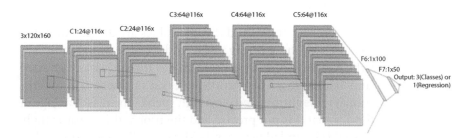

Figure 16.6 CNN model architecture.

Table 16.1 CNN architecture.

Input image 120 × 160	
Convolutional Layer 1	24@116 × 156
Convolutional Layer 2	32@112 × 152
Convolutional Layer 3	64@108 × 148
Convolutional Layer 4	64@104 × 146
Convolutional Layer 5	64 × 104 × 144
Fully connected Layer 6	1 × 00
Fully Connected Layer 7	1 × 50
Output Layer	6 (Classification)
	2 (Regression)

16.6.3.1 Regression

In regression, the output variable is continuous. The regression model used is defined by having two outputs, one for each driving parameter being steering angle and throttle. The range of steering angles is between [−M, M] degrees, where M is the maximum physical steering angle of the car and the throttle values are scaled in the range [0, 1]. The disadvantage or this is that the output is unbounded, and also regression models generally take longer to converge. The advantage of this is that the model is more precise in predicting the driving parameters.

16.6.3.2 Classification

In this method, the steering angles and throttle values are divided into discrete classes, by splitting the steering angle and throttle value intervals. For simplicity, the steering interval is divided into three classes, i.e., hard left, straight, and hard right. The throttle interval is divided into three classes, i.e., stationary, medium speed, and high speed. The disadvantage of using this method is that it is not precise and the probability error is high. However, the output is bounded between [−M, M] unlike regression. Also, classification models converge more easily.

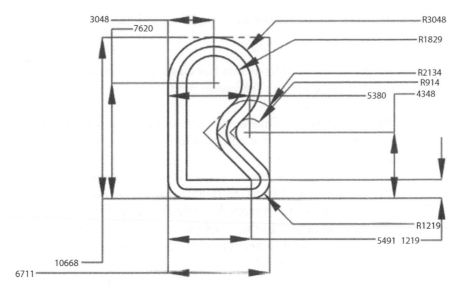

Figure 16.7 Experimental track used for training and testing.

16.7 Experiments

As stated in Section 16.2, a 1:16 scale car has been built to test the models practically. To evaluate the models, a circuit/track was built to simulate a road like environment as shown in Figure 16.7. The car is driven by a human around the track keeping within the lanes to collect the training data initially. Using this, data eight different models were trained and the performance of these models on the track was tested.

16.8 Results

Here, the model is differentiated based on three attributes:

    i) CNN model/MLP model
   ii) Regression/classification
  iii) Feature extraction pre-processing/end-to-end learning

By the combination of these three attributes, eight different models are obtained that have been named Model 1 through Model 8. Each model is independently evaluated and, in the end, the aim is to obtain the model with the best overall accuracy.

The metrics chosen to evaluate each model are as follows:

i) Accuracy
ii) Categorical cross-entropy loss (for classification models)
iii) Mean square error (for regression models)

Table 16.2 shows the definition of each model numbering from 1 through 8 each having a particular combination of the three attributes that we have chosen for comparison.

For classification models, the loss function used is the categorical cross-entropy loss. This loss function is obtained by the combination of SoftMax activation and cross-entropy loss which enables for it to be used for multi-class classification. In this implementation, there are three different classes, as mentioned in Section 16.6.3.2. This loss function treats each class with equal weightage, hence the training data needed to be normalized by having close to equal number of training samples for each class in order to avoid bias in the final model. In this case, there will be more training samples for driving straight than driving right or left, and hence it needed to be normalized.

For regression models, the loss function used is the mean squared error. This loss function is suitable for applications that have a continuous value as its output value. The mean error between the expected value and output value is squared so that it always remains positive.

Descriptions of results of some of the models which provided important insights and Table 16.3 contains the final results of each model.

From Figure 16.8, it can be seen that, as the number of epochs increases, the accuracy gradually increases.

By looking at the validation accuracy curve, it is clear that the validation accuracy also rises along with training accuracy; this is very desirable

Table 16.2 Model definition.

	MLP		CNN	
	Classif.	*Regres.*	*Classif.*	*Regres.*
End-to-End	Model 1	Model 2	Model 5	Model 6
FEP	Model 3	Model 4	Model 7	Model 8

Classif., Classification; Regres., Regression; FEP, Feature Extraction Pre-processing.

Table 16.3 Model results.

	Accuracy		Loss		MSE	
	Train	Test	Train	Test	Train	Test
Model 1	89%	86%	0.30	0.37	____	
Model 2	____				300	280
Model 3	84%	80%	0.38	0.54	____	
Model 4	____				290	380
Model 5	98%	88%	0.01	0.65	____	
Model 6	____				100	300
Model 7	98%	75%	0.01	2.2	____	
Model 8	____				85	450

MSE, mean squared error.

because it indicates that the network is not overfitting but is, in fact, learning only useful features of training data.

From Figure 16.9, it can be observed that it is decreasing as the number of epochs increase. This is a typical behavior of a model that has generalized. Specifically observing the validation loss, it can be seen that it also decreases along with the training loss, but it has an oscillating behavior which may indicate that the network is finding it a bit more difficult to

"Model 1" Evaluation (MLP/Classification/End-to-End).

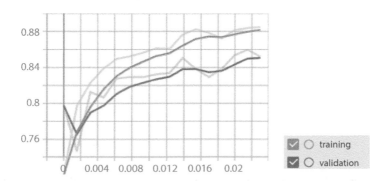

Figure 16.8 Accuracy vs. training time (hours) plot of Model 1 that uses classification method with MLP model without pre-processing.

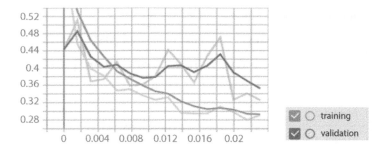

Figure 16.9 Loss vs. training time (hours) plot of Model 1 that uses classification method with MLP model without pre-processing.

classify images it has not seen before. In our testing, the car was also able to traverse successfully on an entirely different track from which it was trained on, indicating that the model has satisfactorily generalized.

In regression models, the primary evaluation measure is the mean squared error. By observing Figure 16.10, it can be seen that both the training and validation MSE decreases with increase in the number of epochs. Observing the final MSE value and curve of the validation MSE, it can be seen that it has a lower value than the training MSE value. From this, it can be inferred that the MLP has not overfitted. This is very indicative that the MLP network has very successfully generalized and is able to predict the steering angles for images it has not seen before. However, the final error value is not desirable and there is room for improvement. In this case, the validation MSE is 280, meaning that there is an average error of 16.73° in the steering angle. However, an average error of 16.73° in the steering angle

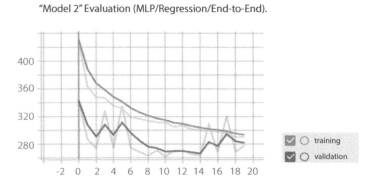

Figure 16.10 MSE vs. steps plot of Model 2 that uses classification method with MLP model without pre-processing.

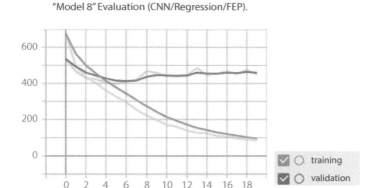

Figure 16.11 MSE vs. steps plot of Model 8 that uses classification method with MLP model with pre-processing (feature extraction).

did not have a huge impact when the car was practically tested on the track; in fact, it was able to traverse the track successfully.

Looking at the MSE plot in Figure 16.11, it can be observed that training MSE decreases in a steady pace for every epoch; however, the validation error plateaus around a value of 450.

This is indicating that the model has not generalized suitably and has in fact completely overfitted on the training data. In our testing, the car was able to navigate around the track that it was trained on; however, the car failed to navigate around a new track other than the one it was trained on.

In observing the accuracy and loss scores shown in Figure 16.12, it can be seen that this model is a well-performing model. This model has the highest training and validation accuracies compared to the rest of the models.

Observing the loss values in Figure 16.13, it can be seen that the training loss has a very low value of 0.01 and validation loss is 0.65. However, by observing the loss plot, it can be seen that the training loss decreases along with an increase in the number of epochs whereas the validation loss increases. The inference that can be drawn from this is that the model is clearly overfitting. The fact of CNNs being very robust has worked to our disadvantage in this case, because by looking at some of the feature maps the CNN has derived, it can be seen that the CNN has overfitted on the background objects rather than extracting lane features. In practical testing of this car on the track, this model has performed the best compared to the rest of the models. The car was also able to traverse successfully in a different track from which it was trained on.

Model 5 Evaluation (CNN/Classification/End-to-End).

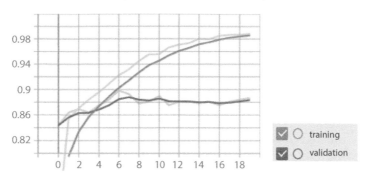

Figure 16.12 Accuracy vs. steps plot of Model 5 that uses classification method with CNN model without pre-processing.

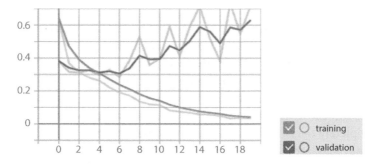

Figure 16.13 Loss vs. steps plot of Model 5 that uses classification method with model without pre-processing.

Considering all of the compiled results above, the best performing model is Model 5, which has the configuration:

    i) Convolutional Neural Network
   ii) End-to-End Learning
  iii) Classification Model

In all cases, this model performed consistently better compared to others. This result is not surprising since CNNs perform better when it comes to image classification [16].

Also, end-to-end learning has outperformed feature extraction pre-processing [17]. This means that the CNN has made better internal

Figure 16.14 Input image given to CNN.

Figure 16.15 Feature map at second convolutional layer.

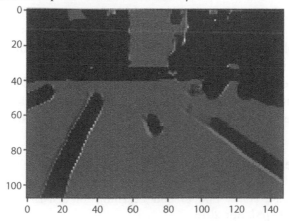

Figure 16.16 Feature map at the fifth convolutional layer.

representations of lane features better than classical image processing algorithms [18]. This result is consistent with existing literature.

Feature maps give an insight as to what the CNN actually sees and infers from for a given input image. Feature maps are obtained by convolving the filters derived by CNN with the input image Figure 16.14. These feature maps were derived using the model five configuration of CNN/classification/end-to-end. Also, techniques can be applied to get insights as to which part of the image the CNN gives more priority and weightage to calculate the final output [12].

In Figure 16.15, which is the output of the second convolutional layer, and it can be observed that at the second layer the CNN has extracted important edges from the image. It can be said that the second convolutional layer is performing an operation similar and analogous to the Canny edge detector.

In Figure 16.16, which is the output of the fifth convolutional layer, it can be observed that the final layer of the CNN has extracted only the lane features from the image and removed most of the background objects. It can be said that the fifth convolutional layer performs an operation similar and analogous to the Hough transform operation.

There are, however, limitations in using end-to-end learning for self-driving. The major limitation is the amount of training data required for the model to converge and reliably function in varied environments. The other limitation is that end-to-end systems are monoliths and do not have separate components to handle separate tasks, which makes it more difficult to train and debug specific functions within the model.

16.9   Conclusion

In this paper, the concept of behavioral cloning is explored for the task of self-driving. We have derived insights about the various methodologies used for implementing behavioral cloning, by comparing different models. These results indicate that end-to-end learning CNN model without any preprocessing steps such as lane extraction is the most optimal in terms of performance. This means that end-to-end learning has great potential to be used in environments where lane markings are absent or not clearly indicated.

References

1. Bojarski, M. *et al.*, End to End Learning for Self-Driving Cars, *arXiv: 1604.07316 [cs]*, Apr. 2016.

2. Birdsall, M., Google and ITE: The road ahead for self-driving cars. *Inst. Transp. Eng. ITE J.*, 84, 5, 36–39, 2014.
3. Shalev-Shwartz, S., Shammah, S., Shashua, A., On a Formal Model of Safe and Scalable Self-driving Cars. ArXiv, abs/1708.06374, 2017.
4. Ghasemipour, S.K.S., Zemel, R., Gu, S., A Divergence Minimization Perspective on Imitation Learning Methods. *Proceedings of the Conference on Robot Learning, in PMLR*, vol. 100, pp. 1259–1277, 2020.
5. Pomerleau, D.A., Alvinn: An autonomous land vehicle in a neural network, in: *Advances in neural information processing systems*, pp. 305–313, 1989.
6. Daigavane, P.M. and Bajaj, P.R., Road lane detection with improved canny edges using ant colony optimization, in: *2010 3rd International Conference on Emerging Trends in Engineering and Technology*, 2010, November, IEEE, pp. 76–80.
7. Saudi, A., Teo, J., Hijazi, M.H.A., Sulaiman, J., Fast lane detection with randomized hough transform, in: *2008 international symposium on information technology*, 2008, August, vol. 4, IEEE, pp. 1–5.
8. Chen, Z. and Huang, X., End-to-end learning for lane keeping of self-driving cars. *2017 IEEE Intelligent Vehicles Symposium (IV)*, Los Angeles, CA, pp. 1856–1860, 2017.
9. Kim, J., Kim, J., Jang, G.J., Lee, M., Fast learning method for convolutional neural networks using extreme learning machine and its application to lane detection. *Neural Networks*, 87, 109–12, 2017.
10. Sammut, C. and Webb, G.I., (Eds.), *Encyclopedia of machine learning*, Springer, New York ; London, 2010.
11. Glasmachers, T., Limits of end-to-end learning, in: *Proceedings of the Ninth Asian Conference on Machine Learning*, vol. 77, pp. 17–32, Proceedings of Machine Learning Research, November 2017.
12. Selvaraju, R.R., Cogswell, M., Das, A., Vedantam, R., Parikh, D., Batra, D., Grad-CAM: Visual Explanations from Deep Networks via Gradient-Based Localization, in: *2017 IEEE International Conference on Computer Vision (ICCV)*, Oct. 2017, pp. 618–626.
13. Low, C.Y., Zamzuri, H., Mazlan, S.A., Simple robust road lane detection algorithm, in: *2014 5th International Conference on Intelligent and Advanced Systems (ICIAS)*, Jun. 2014, pp. 1–4.
14. Guo, T., Dong, J., Li, H., Gao, Y., Simple convolutional neural network on image classification. *2017 IEEE 2nd International Conference on Big Data Analysis (ICBDA)*, Beijing, pp. 721–724, 2017.
15. Bojarski, M. *et al.*, Explaining How a Deep Neural Network Trained with End-to-End Learning Steers a Car, *arXiv:1704.07911 [cs]*, Apr. 2017, Accessed: Dec. 05, 2020.
16. Driss, S.B., Soua, M., Kachouri, R., Akil, M., A comparison study between MLP and convolutional neural network models for character recognition, in: *Real-Time Image and Video Processing 2017*, May 2017, vol. 10223, p. 1022306.

17. Jiang, Y. *et al.*, Expert feature-engineering vs. Deep neural networks: Which is better for sensor-free affect detection?, in: *Artificial Intelligence in Education: 19th International Conference, AIED 2018, London, UK, June 27–30, 2018, Proceedings, Part I*, Jan. 2018, pp. 198–211.

18. O'Mahony, N. et al., Deep learning vs. traditional computer vision, in: *Advances in Computer Vision Proceedings of the 2019 Computer Vision Conference (CVC)*. pp. 128–144, Springer Nature Switzerland AG, Cham, 2020.

19. Ramchoun, H., Ghanou, Y., Ettaouil, M., Idrissi, M.A.J., 'Multilayer Perceptron: Architecture Optimization and Training'. *Int. J. Interact. Multimedia Artif. Intell.*, 4, Special Issue on Artificial Intelligence Underpinning, 26–30, 2016.

20. Assidiq, A.A., Khalifa, O.O., Islam, M.R., Khan, S., Real time lane detection for autonomous vehicles. *2008 International Conference on Computer and Communication Engineering*, Kuala Lumpur, pp. 82–88, 2008.

21. Kocić, J., Jovičić, N., Drndarević, V., An end-to-end deep neural network for autonomous driving designed for embedded automotive platforms. *Sensors, Basel, Switzerland*, 9, 9, 2064, Jan. 2019.

22. Kim, J. and Canny, J., Interpretable Learning for Self-Driving Cars by Visualizing Causal Attention, in: *2017 IEEE International Conference on Computer Vision (ICCV)*, Oct. 2017, pp. 2961–2969.

17

Assistive Technologies for Visual, Hearing, and Speech Impairments: Machine Learning and Deep Learning Solutions

Shahira K. C.*, Sruthi C. J. and Lijiya A.

Department of Computer Science and Engineering, National Institute of Technology Calicut, Kozhikode, India

Abstract

Recent advancements in technology have helped researchers in computer vision (CV) to provide useful and reliable services to improve the quality of life in various aspects. These include some of the significant applications like factory automation, self-driving cars, surveillance, healthcare, assistive technology (AT), human-computer interaction, remote sensing, and agriculture. Tremendous improvement in processing power led the way toward the successful machine learning and deep learning techniques, which, in turn, made otherwise impossible CV applications to come true. AT takes a special place due to its social commitment. AT is any service, software, or product that assists a person with a disability or elderly to improve the quality of their life. Diverse AT techniques available these days makes it out of scope for a single chapter, and hence, this chapter summarizes AT fabricated for people with vision, hearing, and verbal impairment.

Keywords: Assistive technology, visual impairment, hearing and speech impairment, machine learning, deep learning

17.1 Introduction

Among all the disabilities, blindness or visual impairment is the most limiting one. Age-related muscular degeneration or diabetics is one of the primary causes of vision loss. Hence, the necessity for assisting the increasing

---

Corresponding author: shahira_p170096cs@nitc.ac.in

Pradeep Singh (ed.) Fundamentals and Methods of Machine and Deep Learning: Algorithms, Tools and Applications, (397–424) © 2022 Scrivener Publishing LLC

number of visually impaired people is indispensable. Haptic and aural modalities have a significant role in perception by the visually impaired and congenitally blind people. In earlier days, they depended mostly on braille. Later, screen readers like VoiceOver and JAWS help along to access the digital media. These adaptive technologies are attributed to the break-through in computer vision (CV) and deep learning (DL). With the promising results in image and video processing by these DL models, research in AT is beneficiary, which is not limited to: wearable technology (wearables), object detection, navigation, scene description, visual question answering, education, and also improving daily and social life. The recent trends in AT focus on making the printed media accessible and social life more manageable. We categorize the various approaches in AT for the VIP as the traditional based and the CV based and discuss the essential techniques used in each of these approaches. Effective use of the algorithms mimicking human visual system in AT and with proper training on these assistive devices, we can make their life better and easier.

Different from vision impairment, people with verbal and hearing impairment face difficulty in communication, owning to this, they feel isolated and dependent always. Assistive devices for speech and hearing is broadly categorized into assistive listening devices (ALDs), augmentative and alternative communication (AAC) devices, and alerting devices. Advancements in CV, DL, and machine learning (ML) approach had benefited improvements in AAC and alerting device developments in a significant way. People with verbal impairment communicate through sign language, which is a blend of hand gestures, facial countenance, and body stance. Recognizing this mode of communication is hard for the verbal community. An automated two-way translator that translates the verbal language to sign language and sign language to verbal language can help to reduce this communication barrier to a certain extent. Many research in this direction has tried to solve these issues. The whole chapter describes various ML, and DL-based CV techniques that are attributed to the assistive technologies (ATs) for vision, hearing, and verbal impairment.

17.2   Visual Impairment

Among all the disabilities, the most excruciating one is blindness or visual impairment. In 2020, two billion people around the globe suffer from severe or moderate vision impairments, according to WHO. Diabetics, age-related muscular degeneration, cataract, and glaucoma are the main reasons causing vision impairment in adults, while its congenital in children. Through touch and voice input and output devices, blind people learn about the world. There are haptic devices and voice recognition systems, which make use of these senses. With proper training on the new assistive devices, they can live independently like any other sighted person. There are many supporting devices developed to help the blind or low vision people. A survey on the current list of supporting devices and softwares is given in [46]. For the blind, we can explore the AT by categorizing it into conventional approaches and CV-based approaches with a more focus on DL.

17.2.1   Conventional Assistive Technology for the VIP

Many research works are available in the assistive aids for the VIP. ATs[1] can be "high tech" and "low tech" from canes and lever door knobs to voice recognition software and augmentative communication devices (speech generating devices). The AT which were in use without making use of the CV-based approaches are categorized as conventional approaches. In conventional approaches, these ATs supporting the VIP can be classified as wayfinding and reading. These conventional methods are enhanced in the future with DL to solve the challenges in navigation and reading.

17.2.1.1   Way Finding

In way finding, the movement of the blind people, both indoor and outdoor are discussed. The primary aim of navigational aids is to detect obstacles in the path. These obstacles can be a gutter in the road, pit holes, a hanging branch or any suspended obstacles. Indoor, it can be any wall or furniture or stairs. The daily movement of the visually impaired people, both indoor and outdoor, should ensure their safety. Any navigation aid should be able to detect the following:

- Obstacles in the field of vision as similar to the human eye.
- Find the obstacles not only in the ground upto certain height, but also find any objects along his/her height.
- To find the distance from the blind user to the obstacle and this result should be imparted to the user in fraction of time to avoid collisions.
- Perception and avoidance of obstacles in the immediate proximity at a faster rate than at a longer distance.
- Precise depth estimation to these objects.

---

[1]https://guides.library.illinois.edu/c.php?g=613892ssssssss p=4265891

In earlier days, the blind navigation was supported by canes and dogs or a volunteer. The traditional canes give the result on physical contact with the obstacles, but the obstacles above the feet are missed out. The challenges faced by these give rise to white canes supported by sensors, to get informed about the obstacles at a distance and at the height of the user. A widely used AT by the visually impaired people is white canes because of the ease of use and low cost. Later, improvements were added to these traditional walking sticks by adding sensors to it. The type of sensors includes ultrasonic sensors, infrared, RGBD, or LiDAR. A comparison between a few sensors used in an Electronic Travel Aid (ETA) is given in Table 17.1 [16]. An ETA is a device that gathers information from the environment and transmits it to the visually impaired user to allow independent movement. It takes in input from a sensor and an imaging device. It combines the result from these environmental inputs, and it imparts the output information as vibration or voice output. Few challenges faced by these travel aids are the following:

- Most of the ETA's are prototypes.
- Heavy and bulky.
- Unidentified or missed the hanging obstacles.
- The sensors need to be fixed without changing direction and height to ensure good obstacle avoidance accuracy [9].

Table 17.1 Comparison of sensors for obstacle detection in ETA inspired from [16].

	Ultrasound	LiDAR	RADAR	Vision sensors
Range	Short	Short-Medium	Medium-Long	Short-Medium
Accuracy	Good	Good	Good	High
Number of obstacles detected	Low	High	Medium	Medium
Effect of sunlight	No effect	Strong	No effect	Strong
Effect of rain	Yes	Yes	Yes	Yes
Night Operation	Yes	Yes	Yes	No
Cost	Low	High	Medium	Medium

But this is not possible in case of the devices, where the user change direction randomly.

- Some of the prototypes were tested on blind folded candidates. Testing should be on blind users as the cognitive ability of these two categories varies.
- To perceive the surrounding as a blind user wishes, obstacle avoidance alone is not sufficient. He might be interested in the various objects or signboards or text in a scene.

Figure 17.1 illustrates an object detection and avoidance architecture that can be integrated into several wearable devices. The information from the sensors are incorporated into white canes and "n" number of variants of the white canes are available in the market today. Ultra canes based on ultrasound, laser canes based on a laser beam, and sonar based on ultrasound are few of them. However, many of them do not meet the precise specification needed by an ETA for a VIP [20]. The navigation can be made better and reliable by incorporating sensors along with the DL models as discussed in Section 17.2.2. The DL included new versions of the walking assistants with object detection modules evolved as smart canes.

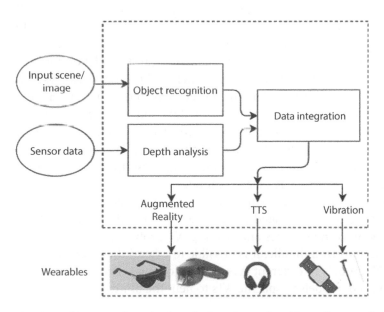

Figure 17.1 An architecture of simple obstacle detection and avoidance framework that can be integrated with different wearables.

17.2.1.2   Reading Assistance

The AT here includes those software and hardware which help the VIP to read, write, or understand the contents in a printed media or the digital media. The braille made a way to access the knowledge by the people who cannot see. These are raised dots which are read by touch. Braille is a tactile system for the blind found in 1820. Slate and stylus is a method of writing braille by hand, so the blind get the feeling of how each letter looks like. The blind people perceive the document information through audio or by touch or a volunteer reading out or by recorded voices. Adaptive technology like screen readers, Siri, and other voice-recognition software emerge with time. A screen reader is a software that uses a text-to-speech (TTS) engine to translate the textual contents of the computer screen to either speech output or a refreshable braille display. The speech synthesis technology was not initially aimed at blind users, but further advancements in this area contributed to screen reader technology. Using this, they can read documents, send an email, and use social media sites. However, unfortunately, they cannot identify the graphical contents of the page. Later, these image contents are provided as descriptions in the form of alternate text (alt-text), which can be read out by a screen reader. People prefer braille display in cases they are left with confusions in the speech so that they can feel and understand the text. All these advancements are attributed to a breakthrough in CV and DL. The recent trends in AT focus on making the printed media accessible and social life more comfortable. The refreshable braille displays also utilize the tactile perception. This has a raised set of pins that get adjusted as the user adjusts the cursor on the screen. The American Foundation for Blind gives a set of refreshable braille. In cases when a blind user is confused with the output from a screen reader, this is used. Screen reading software like JAWS and Voiceover are used to read the digital contents. The information about the figures on a web page is communicated by using the image descriptions which are produced in the real time using DL models as discussed in Sections 17.2.2.2 and 17.2.2.3. These image descriptions are represented as alt-text for the screen reader to readout.

This section focuses primarily on the categorization of AT as wayfinding related and AT related to reading. The traditional methods like cane evolved into smart canes and reading AT evolved into screen readers and mobile apps from braille. It is possible to extend the promising findings of the DL models to different ATs. The following section addresses applying various DL models to specific ATs to help the blind people.

17.2.2   The Significance of Computer Vision and Deep Learning in AT of VIP

Computer or robotic vision focuses on how camera and sensor vision can be accomplished. If a camera can be made to see and recognize objects, then the same can be applied for enhancing the visual ability of a visually challenged. Haptic and aural modalities have a major role in perception by the Visually impaired and congenitally blind people. In earlier days, they depended mostly on braille; later, screen readers help to access the digital media and improve their social life. Navigation requires scene understanding and estimation of obstacle distance in the real time. Object detection gives the best accuracy using DL methods like YOLO [38], SSD [17], and FasterRCNN [39]. The CV methods that are well accepted in the AT research for improving the reading assitance, mobility and travel includes object recognition and obstacle avoidance, scene understanding, document image understanding, visual question answering, and more. All these CV methods in AT are reciprocally related to each other.

17.2.2.1   Navigational Aids

The traveling is easy for a VIP today with the advancements in technology. The wayfinding in Section 17.2.1.1 discusses the asssitive techonologics in navigational aids and the ETA in use. Most of the ETA in support of them are costly and some apps working real time require network connectivity. ETAs have sensor inputs which can be any one or a combination of the sensors discussed in Section 17.2.1.1. Choose the sensor based on various attributes like cost, range, or other factors. Use the sensors to calculate the depth to the obstacles. There are sensors providing depth information, but are expensive. The RGB-D cameras are less costly compered to them, and they provide the per pixel depth information along with the color information. Microsoft Kinect[2] widely attained popularity because of its cost and the depth resolution and its invariant to illumination changes. Kinect have a RGB camera along with an infrared sensor to find the depth. The computational cost of the RGB-D images is high. The future of navigation research for AT is trying to incorporate the proximity sensors in the mobile phone. Integrate with the transfer learning of a DL model for object detection in a smartphone. The information about the objects in the scene can be readout. The text in natural scenes can also be given as audio output. This can be handy, unlike the earlier prototypes and also affordable.

---

[2]http://alumni.cs.ucr.edu/ klitomis/files/RGBD-intro.pdf

When a visually impaired person is traveling, he should be informed with the obstacles in the near vicinity at a faster rate to prevent the collision. The object detection deals with finding any obstacles in the path and the obstacle avoidance deals with giving an alert or feedback to the user.

One of the most challenging problems in CV is obstacle detection, and it has gained popularity because of its wide application in scene analysis, activity recognition, content-based image retrieval and pedestrian detection, lane tracking, and more. Object detection determines where objects are present in a given image, i.e., object localization together with which category each object belongs to (object classification). The object detection models consist of region selection, feature extraction and classification. The conventional methods used handcrafted features for classification. The traditional methods required separate modules for feature extraction, while the DL models have the advantage of end to end learning. The traditional methods failed to give better detection results when the image is affected by occlusion, shadows, or illumination changes. Identifying different categories of objects in the same image was difficult. Promising results toward this came with DL which could even classify multiple overlapping objects in different backgrounds. Convolutional Neural Networks (CNN) is a breakthrough in this, which works like human vision [18]. ImageNet Large-Scale Visual Recognition Challenge (ILSVRC)[3] conducted annually to find the top-performing models. Few of the CNNs are LeNet-5 [28], AlexNet [24], ResNet [50], and Inception [49]. There are different models which use Deep CNNs like R-CNN, Fast R-CNN, Faster R-CNN, and Yolo. These models can follow the following approaches:

- Region proposal–based approach
- Single-shot–based approach.

Region proposal–based methods: Region proposal–based methods are concerned with generating and extracting bounding boxes around the object of interest. It is followed by a feature extractor which is usually a CNN that can extract the features from each proposed regions. A classifier at the end classifies these features into known classes. RCNN, Fast R-CNN, and Faster R-CNN are examples which uses this approach.

In case of RCNN, region proposal is based on selective search, the feature extraction is based on AlexNet, and the final classification is using a linear SVM. In Fast RCNN [17], input is a set of region proposals from which feature is extracted by a pretrained VGG16 model. A region of

---

[3]http://www.image-net.org/challenges/LSVRC/

interest (ROI) pooling layer extracts features specific to a candidate region. Output of this CNN is given to a softmax for class prediction and also to a linear SVM for producing output for the bounding box. But this was slow process as a set of candidate region proposal needed to be proposed with each input image. Faster RCNN [39] reached the pinnacle of models in detecting the objects, by adding a CNN for proposing region and the type of object to consider along with the already existing Fast RCNN.

Single-shot–based methods: It is a single neural network which is trained end to end and predicts bounding boxes and class labels for each bounding box directly. This could process 45–155 frames per second, varying based on their versions. Yolo [38], YoloV2 [60], Fast Yolo [37], and SSD [31] are examples which uses this approach.

These DL models using CNN can be applied to problems in AT in different ways. Either we can build own model which includes training a neural network with custom dataset or do fine-tuning of the network in which we can change the hyperparameters of the model till we get a minimum error, or do transfer learning.

Transfer learning is an approach in which a model developed for one task is reused as the starting point for a model on a second task. The models trained on a different dataset and the weights are saved for future use. These weights can be used for object detection or scene description. For instance, Yolov2 [60] is developed for chinese traffic sign detection. Here, the weight vector obtained after training Yolov2 is used to classify the objects in a different dataset. Choose the models which give better accuracy in real time. An architecture of simple obstacle detection and avoidance framework that can be integrated with different wearables inspired from [41]. This gives an instance where, the result can be given as augmented reality or zoomed version of the input image or video, in case of low vision users. The voice output can be given through any wearables like headset or handsfree or smartphone. The vibration alerts can be given through watch or cane. Thus, by integrating the input from the depth sensors and camera, the object recognition improves the navigation. The smartphones are widely used for navigation and is discussed in Section 17.2.2.4.

17.2.2.2   Scene Understanding

The goal of scene understanding is to make the machines able to see like humans. Scene understanding is perceiving and analysing an environment in real time. This involves object detection and recognition integrated with the help of sensors. A scene can be a man made scene or natural scene. A scene may have different objects in various environments and different contexts. Understanding the context of the scene, identifying the objects in it and providing accurate visual information is its purpose. Visual attention contributes to scene understanding. Attention networks [56] allow to focus on some areas of the network and the visual attention is very important in locating some objects of the scene. Road scene segmentation is crucial for driving assistance. In 2020, authors in [12] introduced a fast and accurate segmentation using DL models for high and low resolution images. Apart from all these, DL has paved the way for mobile applications which can detect the objects in real time. "Tap tap see" is one among them which identifies the objects present in the input picture. The user has to click a picture; the processing happens in the cloud and gives him the voice output. Color ID Free is another app which is used to find the objects of matching color.

The scene understanding systems can analyze the images to understand the variations in the environment and identify the objects in it and interpret in human understandable form [27]. It is influenced by cognitive vision. It have applications in autonomous driving and robotic vision. The same algorithms can be customized for assisting the vision of blind people.

17.2.2.3   Reading Assistance

Visually impaired students learn to read and write with braille, with the help of a trained teacher. They can access web content or a computer with refreshable braille connected to the computer. Screen reading software allows them to read the contents on the web by converting it into speech by a TTS or through refreshable braille. They perceive the images through tactile graphics of maps, graphs and pictures. Text extraction by applications using OCR makes both the digital documents and print media easily accessible. Text localization and extraction from images helps them in different walks of life, including few listed below.

- Locate the text in natural scenes in scene understanding.
- They can access the audiobooks.
- Smartphone-based cabs that can scan the document and read out the text.
- Identify the traffic signboard, text in a catalogue, assist shopping, or read a restaurant menu card.

Smartphones provide quick and easy access to information. There are many android and iOS applications for reading assistance. SeeingAI[4] is an app by Microsoft which helps them to read the bar code of products, identify currency and also describe a scene in front of him/her. The wearable

---

[4]https://www.microsoft.com/en-us/ai/seeing-ai

Table 17.2 A comparison between few wearables.

Wearables	Sensors	Assistance	Features	Demerits	Wear On
MyEyes2.0[6], 2020	12 MP camera	Robotic vision	Text, bank notes, face detection	Costly	Finger like camera mounted to glasses
Sunu[7] [6], 2020	Sonar	Obstacle avoidance	Haptic guide light weight	Costly	Wrist band
Maptic [54], 2018	Vision sensor in chest	Obstacles in the field of vision	App process and give feedback to phone	Use GPS, Network connection required	Neck or wrist
Horus[8], 2016	Camera	Virtual assistant	Read text, face recognition, object detection	Still in prototype stage	Headset
FingerReader [48], 2015	Opticon, mini camera	Reading assistance	Printed text to voice	Camera do not auto focus, hard to adjust for different finger lengths	Finger

finger reader [45] (in Table 17.2) helps to read the document with the help of a minicamera in it. When compared to mobile applications, this finger-based approach helps a blind user to to understand the spatial layout of a document better and provide control over speed and rereading.

17.2.2.4   Wearables

The wearables for the blind can be used in different parts of the body. The mode of perception by the VIP is aural or haptics. An overview of wearable devices used by the blind people is given in [57]. They can be placed at the fingertips, wrist, tongue, ears, hands, chest, and abdomen. Figure 17.2 gives an example of a wearable glasses with sensors to understand the scene. The input information is processed using a bulky device in the backpack and the output provided as refreshable braille is felt with the fingertips. Today, the output can provided as image descriptions with the help of a TTS converters via ear pluggins. The wearable can play a very important role in education also. This is an era of intelligent assistants and intersection of them with the AT is proving

Several prototypes and wearables use sensors and give vibrational feedback or audio output. But most of them are bulky in nature and heavy. Some are in the form of head eyeglasses, heavy head sets, chest mounted devices, etc. Dakopoulos *et al.* [14] give a detailed description of these prototypes with their pros and cons. These device prototypes pass the testing, but usability by a person is very low. The cognitive ability of the user should be considered at the design stage. The user should be involved right from the design to

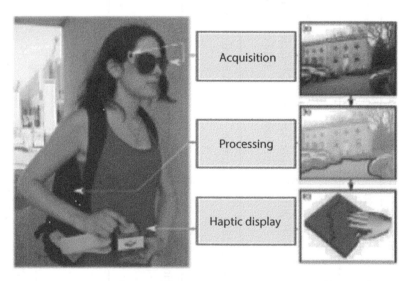

Figure 17.2 A prototype of a wearable system with image to tactile rendering from [57].

its implementation. The work [61, 62] enlists the underlying parameters that need to be considered when developing tools or devices for any activity especially for the mobility of the visually impaired. The wearables uses a camera or sensors to acquire the real world information. The processing can be done in cloud or the device and provides output as vibration or audio.

The bulky prototypes and the depth sensors that are costly increases the demand for a handy, less expensive device. Also, the increasing number of visually impaired people every year amplifies the need for a cost-effective device. The heart of the future navigational aids for the VIP lies in a smartphone. The smartphone can be used to integrate the traditional methods with CV to produce better solutions. The smartphone can act as an input and output device. The necessary steps are acquisition, processing, and output.

Acquisition: The inbuilt camera for sensing the environment. The input can be an image or a video.

Processing: The input can be processed locally in the device or on a remote server with the higher computing power. The remote device takes care of the input test data from the device. It needs to be pre-processed. The processing devices have the DL or the object detection models trained with good accuracy. Now, the input image or video is tested for the presence of objects or text or any obstacles. Processing can be done locally on the acquisition device also. DL models trained with large training set save their weights. This pre-trained weights which are trained on some other data said can be used for other task; this is transfer learning. Transfer learning of these models saves time for the time fine-tuning. The lightweight DL networks require the computational power of a smartphone.

Output: The output after processing can be the descriptions of the object or the distance provided as audio by TTS synthesis.

These wearables like a smart watch, smart glasses, or smart rings are light weight. The intelligent voice assistants like Siri by Apple, Google Assistant, or Amazon Echo are making lives easier. These virtual assistants provide easy web access by not typing in keyboard. They enable easy interaction with the wearable devices. Table 17.2 includes few wearables that helps to identify the text, currency, and face recognition. They are designed to meet specific needs of the VIP. Olli[5], designed by local motors with IBM Watson is an autonomous vehicle to meet the transportation of people with different needs. Audio cues and haptic sensors help the blind users to find seats. They can book a ride using Olli app. This uses augmented reality to use sign languages to support the deaf users. The following sections discuss the various AT supporting the deaf people.

---

[5]https://www.ibm.com/blogs/internet-of-things/olli-ai/

17.3　Verbal and Hearing Impairment

Verbal and hearing problems are another form of impairment faced by humans for decades. Partial or full verbal or hearing loss creates difficulty in communication with the verbal society. Numerous techniques have evolved to reduce the communication barrier, but the fact is that nothing was entirely successful. People suffering from verbal, hearing and language disorder faces different levels of communication problems. Some people have complete hearing loss, whereas some have partial hearing loss. Similarly, some people can hear properly, but they may be vocally disabled to communicate with society. AT is an equipment or a collection of devices that help a person with a disability to overcome their difficulty and live more comfortably. In the case of verbal, hearing, and language disorder, AT is anything which helps a person to communicate with society. A variety of assistive devices are being used to overcome the communication barrier and are mainly categorized into: ALDs, alerting devices, and AAC devices.

17.3.1　Assistive Listening Devices

Hearing loss can be partial or complete. This happens when the human hearing instrument is not sufficient to fulfil the auditory requirements of the person. ALD is amplification equipment for improving the hearing ability. The sound that we perceive is affected by numerous unwanted sound sources called noise, and this creates a problem for hard of hearing person to correctly understand the speech. ALD aims to separate noise from speech and increase speech-to-noise ratio. Significant factors that decrease the intelligibility of a speech signal are [22]:

- Distance: As the distance of the person from the sound source increases speech-to-noise ratio decreases, and the speech becomes less intelligible.
- Noise: Affect of different background noises over the speech signal diminishes its intelligibility.
- Reverberation: This is a phenomenon where a sound signal undergoes multiple reflections and persist for a long time even after its source have stopped emitting it. This diminishes the clarity of speech and thus decreases intelligibility.

ALD differs from simple hearing aids or cochlear implant, but it can be an additional module attached to these devices for better hearing in outdoor or in a specific environment. ALD ranges from a simple electronic microscope amplifier unit to more sophisticated broadcasting systems and hence are used in public places like church, theaters, and auditoriums, also for personal uses to listen to telephone and television, and for small group activities. Some of the ALDs available these days are induction loop system, FM systems, telecoils, infrared systems, personalized amplification equipment and many more [33]. Each of these mentioned ALDs are designed for specific environments and purposes but all work with the same objective to discard the adverse effects of distance, background noises, and reverberation and to provide a clear and uninterrupted speech signal to the listener. Working and contexts of each of these systems are complex and out of scope for this chapter.

17.3.2   Alerting Devices

Alerting devices, as the name suggests, alert the concerned person to audio stimuli. Hard of hearing person finds it difficult to hear or sometimes even miss out certain necessary audio signals like a doorbell, fire alarm, phone rings, alarms, barking, news alerts, and baby crying. In such cases, alternative attention seeking methods like vibrations, flashing lights or strobes, and loud horns may help. Visual or tactile means are the most effective techniques in case of hard of hearing people. Erin discusses the needs and effectiveness of strobes and tactile in different scenarios [7]. The effectiveness of strobes decreases if the person is sleeping or if he is away from it or based on the lighting in the background. Tactile, on the other hand, depends on what kind of vibrating instruments are being used. Some of the tactile instruments include bed shakers that are connected to alarms to notify the person in sleep, vibration alerts in phones, many vibrating wearable with displays showing the cause of vibration and even number of alerts are possible on smartphone applications. Some of the most commonly used alerting devices or systems are smoke alarm signalers, telephone signalers, doorbell signalers, wake up alarms, and baby signalers.

17.3.3   Augmentative and Alternative Communication Devices

Speech and audio communication can be replaced with other alternative modes of communication like speech to text, picture board, touchscreen, and many more. This becomes extremely helpful for people with complete hearing loss or for people who cannot talk. Some of the popularly used AAC are as follows [58]:

Telecommunications Device for the Deaf (TDD): The communication through telecommunication devices for a speech-impaired person is made possible by a TTS and speech to text conversion with the help of a third party. A person with the impairment communicate the message through text, the intermediate third party, or translator reads the message at the other end. The person at the other end conveys the message vocally which is converted to text by the third party and sent back to the user.

Real-Time Text (RTT): This mode of communication is very similar to TDD but is more transparent; it does not involve any third party in between. All the communications are entirely done through text messages. This differs from the conventional text messaging with a fact that it allows each user to see what the other is typing in real time like the face-to-face conversation in terms of reaction time.

Videophones: The videophone is a telecommunication device produced explicitly for people with hearing or verbal impairments. The device has a large screen in order to use it in hands-free mode while performing sign language. A videophone is necessary at both ends if both of the end-users are using sign language for communication. In the other case, an interpreter or translator translates the sign language to speech and speech to sign language during the conversation.

17.3.3.1   Sign Language Recognition

Hearing- and speech-impaired people use sign language for communication. Majority of the population cannot interpret sign language, and this hinders the social interactions of these people. They find it challenging to communicate with verbally speaking world, making it difficult for them to attain education, job, and many other basic requirements. In order to communicate with society, they need a translator. A manual translator can convert any complicated gesture sequence to speech with all the emotional modulations required for it, but it reduces the privacy of the speakers involved in the conversation. A non-manual or machine translator guarantees the privacy factor, but research is still going on to develop a complete sign language recognition system which can perform with the same accuracy as that of a human translator. The significant challenges involved in the sign language recognition system are follows:

- Sign language is very diverse; it differs from geography to geography and even differs within a region.
- Sign language involves single hand gestures, double hand gestures, facial expression, and body posture, which makes it complicated to incorporate on to a machine.
- Sign language conversation contains static and dynamic gestures performed in a sequence and hence finding the starting and ending of each gesture in the sequence become complicated.
- Interclass similarity and intraclass differences of gestures are common among sign language gestures.

- Gesturing differ from person to person based on body nature, posture, contexts, etc., making it a more challenging problem.
- Occlusion: While performing the gesture, one hand can occlude the other making it hard for the system to recognize.

Despite all these challenges, researchers are all over the world are working hard for developing an optimal sign language recognition system. Several solutions have been suggested till date but search for better one is still going on. There are many methods suggested by experts for this purpose in literature; these methods can be classified broadly into sensor-based methods and vision-based methods.

Sensor-Based Methods: These methods make use of sensors and sensor-enabled gloves to collect gesture related data. The sensors include accelerometers (ACCs), flexion (or bend) sensors, proximity sensors, and abduction sensors. The sensors are used to measure the abduction in between the fingers, finger bend angle, wrist and palm orientation, and hand movement. Values measured by the sensors provide accurate results with fewer computations. Hardware components of the sensor-based method are divided into input unit, processing unit, and output unit. The input unit deals with acquiring the data or the sensors readings and pass it to the processing unit. Some of the commonly used sensors and their uses include:

- Flex sensor: Measures finger curvature based on the resistive carbon element correlated to the bend radius.
- Light-dependent resistor (LDR): LDR changes its resistance according to the light falling on it. Amount of light received by LDR changes as the finger takes the possible bends giving different voltage values at different positions.
- Tactile sensor: It is a force-sensitive sensor that calculates the amount of force on the finger, by which it shows whether the finger is curved or straight.
- Hall effect magnetic sensor (HEMS): Sensors are placed on the fingertips, and a magnet is placed on the palm area with the south pole facing the top. When the magnet and sensors come closer, it generates electric output depending on the degree of closeness.
- Accelerometers: These sensors have a dual purpose as it can determine finger shapes, and it can capture the movement and orientation of the wrist.
- Gyroscope: This sensor measures the angular velocity and the speed with which an object spin along the axis.

- Inertial measurement unit (IMU): This unit is a combination of magnetometer, accelerometer, and a gyroscope, which can collect information with a greater degree of freedom regarding the motion and orientation of the hands.

The processing unit performs the required gesture processing to recognize the sign and to transfer the result to the output port. It collects and processes the data from the input unit using a microcontroller. Microcontrollers are of many types and differ in performance based on architecture, memory, and read-write capabilities. Some of the commonly used microcontrollers in glove-based methods are ATmega microcontroller, MSP430G2553 microcontroller, Arduino Uno board, and Odroid XU4 minicomputer [4]. Output unit as the name suggests displays the classified gestures name on computer monitor, liquid-crystal display (LCD), smartphone, or through the speaker. It also serves as a user interface and hence is an essential factor for achieving the best performance among the sign language recognition devices. Apart from the hardware components in the sensor-based methods, softwares also play a vital role in improving the system outputs. Softwares mainly come into play for the classification to recognize gestures. One of the most typical methods is to use statistical template matching, which finds the closest match of acquired sensor reading values with pre-determined training samples. ML methods like artificial neural network (ANN), support vector machines (SVM), and hidden Markov models (HMMs) are also used in literature for better classification of the obtained sensor readings in the area of gesture recognition [4]. Figure 17.3 shows the image of a DG5-V hand glove developed for Arabic sign language recognition using flex sensors and accelerometers [40]. Researchers all over the world had contributed different sensor-based methods with different combinations of sensor technologies, but the fact is that none of them covers an extensive vocabulary and the cost of many of these devices is also high based on the microcontrollers and sensors used in them. The person using it also has the burden of carrying the device whereever they travel. Table 17.3 shows some of the sensor-based methods from literature.

Vision-Based Methods: Vision-based methods use visual sensors like a camera to capture the input data. Cameras nowadays are ubiquitous device and are even present in mobile phones. This reduces the dependency of the user over different sensor devices while performing the gestures. Mostly all sign language recognition systems consist of four main modules: (1) data acquisition, (2) pre-processing, (3) feature extraction, and (4) classification. Data acquisition deals with acquiring the videos or images required for running the system. This module specifies the camera specification, the required distance between the camera and the signer, background, or outfit

Figure 17.3 DG5-V hand glove developed for Arabic sign language recognition [40].

Table 17.3 Sensor based methods from literature.

Sensors	Sign language	Gestures	Ref.
Accelerometer and IMU sensors	American	Gestures for A- Z and 0–9	[1]
5-Flex sensors	American	4 Common gestures	[36]
Flex and Accelerometer sensors	Indian	8 Common gestures	[32]
Flex, Accelerometer, and Tactile sensors	American	Gestures for A-H	[42]
Contact and multiple flex sensors	Australian	120 Common static gestures	[5]
Flex sensors and 3-D accelerometer	Arabic	40 Sentences from 80 Words	[53]
Flex sensors and gyroscope	American	3 Common gestures	[15]
Accelerometer, Bend and hall effect sensors with	–	Gestures for 0–9	[13]
Flex and Accelerometer sensors	American	Gestures for A-Z	[11]

Table 17.4 Vision based approaches.

Techniques used	Language	Gestures recognized	Ref.
3-Dimentional position trajectory with adaptive matching	Indian	20 Common actions	[26]
3-Dimensional motionlets with adaptive kernal matching	Indian	500 Common gestures	[23]
DWT(Discrete wavelet transforn) with HMM	Indian	10 Sentences	[52]
Skin-color segmentation, fingertip detection, zernike moment, and SVM	American	4 Dynamic gestures and 24 static alphabets	[25]
Fingertip and palm position, PCA, optical flow, CRF	American	9 Alphabets	[19]
SIFT (Scale Invariant Feature Transform) with key point extraction	Indian	26 Alphabets	[35]
Skin color segmentation, Fourier descriptor, distance transform, neural network	Indian	26 Alphabets and 0–9 Digits	[3]
Direct pixel value, hierarchical centroid, neural network	Indian	Digits 0–9	[44]
SMO (Sequential Minimal Optimization) with Zernike moments,	Indian	5 Alphabets	[43]
Zernike moment, SVM	American	24 Alphabets	[34]
Histogram of edge frequency, SVM	Indian	26 Alphabets	[29]
Eigen value weighted Euclidean distance	Indian	24 Static alphabets	[47]
Skin color segmentation, Zernike moment, SVM	Indian	24 Static Alphabets and 10 dynamic words	[8]
B-spline approximation and SVM	Indian	29 signs (A-Z and 0–5)	[55]
LSTM	Chinese	100 Isolated common words	[30]
Skin color segmentation and CNN	Indian	24 Static Alphabets	[48]

requirement, if any. The pre-processing module deals with the removal of unnecessary distortions, finding and segmenting the region of interest and preparing the preprocessed data for feature extraction phase, so that feature extraction is done in an unbiased manner. Some of the popularly used noise removal techniques include low-pass box filter for smoothing, median filter for salt and pepper noise, and the bilateral filter, which is a non-linear, noise-reducing, edge-preserving, and smoothing filter. Face and the two palm regions are the region of interest for any sign language recognition system. Viola-Jones face detection method [59] is the widely used solution for detecting face in an image or frame. Pre-trained TensorFlow human detection model [51] is used to find the human in the frame. Skin color segmentation [8] is the widely used hand segmentation method in the literature. Feature extraction module plays a vital role in the entire SLR system as the accuracy of the recognition process depend completely over the extracted features. Feature vectors are those vectors which can efficiently represent an image or a frame. Palm position, orientation, shape, fingertips, edges, depth, and movements are some among the crucial features considered in SLR. These features are extracted using various methods like histogram of oriented gradients (HOG) [21], Zernike moments [8], histogram of edge frequency [29], scale invariant feature transform (SIFT) [35], Fourier descriptor [2], 3-D motionlets [23], and other techniques. The last or final stage of an SLR system is the classification or recognition. ML and DL methods come into the picture in this stage. The classification has two phases: training and testing. In the training phase, features extracted are used to train the model using ML or DL algorithms, and in the testing phase, new images or videos are classified using the trained model. SVMs [8, 25, 29, 34, 55], neural network [3], and HMM [52] are the most commonly used ML models and Convolution Neural Network (CNN) [10, 48], Long short-term memory (LSTM) [30], and Recurrent Neural Network (RNN) [10]. Despite research all over the world, a complete solution covering the vocabulary of a particular sign language with acceptable accuracy is not ready. Methods proposed by researchers till date are limited to a minimal vocabulary, and hence, the scope of research in this area is high. Table 17.4 shows some of the vision-based methods from literature.

17.3.4   Significance of Machine Learning and Deep Learning in Assistive Communication Technology

ML and DL models can identify patterns from a large amount of data. The real-world problem is always very complex and multidimensional, and ML and DL models have always proved their excellence in solving these problems in various domains. Assistive communication technologies make use of self-learning and continuous improvement properties of these models, which ensures the best results compared with the traditional methods. Different from ML models, DL models even do not require feature engineering, as these models find the best features based on the provided training data. The significance of ML and DL models is evident from the extensive use of SVM, HMM, neural network, CNN, LSTM, and other models in almost all the vison-based methods. These models are even used in AAC devices, alerting devices, and sensor-based devices for automation.

17.4   Conclusion and Future Scope

The most commonly encountered sensory impairments are vision and hearing problem. We discuss the various ATs in support of these categories of people. For the visual impairment, we classify the available AT as conventional and the DL-based ones. The earlier AT available was only in navigation and reading assistance. The challenges faced by the traditional methods is resolved with the DL-based approaches. With the promising results in CV by DL models, object detection and navigation, scene description, and textual and graphical readers and wearables are beneficial. In the case of hearing and verbal impairment, we classify the available AT as ALDs, alerting devices, and AAC devices. We discuss some of the popularly used AT devices in these categories and also the significance of ML and DL models in assistive communication technology.

New developments in technologies had improved the quality of AT to a greater extend. Improvements in various sensors, cameras, and algorithms to process the data collected from these devices in lesser time can even improve the situations. Dealing with 3D data efficiently in real time can be an excellent solution for many ATs. The solutions presented throughout the chapter are still under research for further improvements hoping that even a small change can improve a person's life to the extent that we can even imagine.

References

1. Abhishek, K.S., Qubeley, L.C.F., Ho, D., Glove-based hand gesture recognition sign language translator using capacitive touch sensor, in: *2016 IEEE International Conference on Electron Devices and Solid-State Circuits (EDSSC)*, IEEE, pp. 334–337, 2016.

2. Adithya, V., Vinod, P.R., Gopalakrishnan, U., Artificial neural network based method for Indian sign language recognition, in: *Information & Communication Technologies (ICT), 2013 IEEE Conference on*, IEEE, pp. 1080–1085, 2013.

3. Adithya, V., Vinod, P.R., Gopalakrishnan, U., Artificial neural network based method for Indian sign language recognition, in: *2013 IEEE Conference on Information & Communication Technologies*, IEEE, pp. 1080–1085, 2013.

4. Ahmed, M.A. *et al.*, A review on systems-based sensory gloves for sign language recognition state of the art between 2007 and 2017. *Sensors*, 18, 7, 2208, 2018.

5. Ahmed, S.F., Ali, S.M.B., Saqib Munawwar Qureshi, Sh, Electronic speaking glove for speechless patients, a tongue to a dumb, in: *2010 IEEE Conference on Sustainable Utilization and Development in Engineering and Technology*, IEEE, pp. 56–60, 2010.

6. Alabi, A.O. and Mutula, S.M., Digital inclusion for visually impaired students through assistive technologies in academic libraries, in: *Library Hi Tech News*, University of Maryland, College Park, 2020.

7. Ashley, E.M., *Waking effectiveness of emergency alerting devices for the hearing able, hard of hearing, and deaf populations.* PhD thesis, 2007.

8. Athira, P.K., Sruthi, C.J., Lijiya, A., A signer independent sign language recognition with co-articulation elimination from live videos: an indian scenario. *J. King Saud Univ.-Comput. Inf. Sci.*, 2019. https://www.semanticscholar.org/paper/A-Sign-er-Independent-Sign-Language-Recognition-with-Athira-Sruthi/f907191849 8da2ce65984f3a32935e3d4683611e

9. Bai, J. *et al.*, Smart guiding glasses for visually impaired people in indoor environment. *IEEE Trans. Consum. Electron.*, 63, 3, 258–266, 2017.

10. Bantupalli, K. and Xie, Y., American sign language recognition using deep learning and computer vision, in: *2018 IEEE International Conference on Big Data (Big Data)*, IEEE, pp. 4896–4899, 2018.

11. Cabrera, M.E. *et al.*, Glove-based gesture recognition system, in: *Adaptive Mobile Robotics*, 5 Toh Tuck Link, Singapore pp. 747–753, World Scientific, 2012.

12. Chen, P.-R. *et al.*, DSNet: An efficient CNN for road scene segmentation. *APSIPA Trans. Signal Inf. Process.*, 9, 424–432 2020.

13. Chouhan, T. *et al.*, Smart glove with gesture recognition ability for the hearing and speech impaired, in: *2014 IEEE Global Humanitarian Technology Conference-South Asia Satellite (GHTC-SAS)*, IEEE, pp. 105–110, 2014.

14. Dakopoulos, D. and Bourbakis, N.G., Wearable obstacle avoidance electronic travel aids for blind: A survey. *IEEE Trans. Syst. Man Cybern. Part C (Appl. Rev.)*, 40, 25–35, IEEE. 2009.

15. Das, A. *et al.*, Smart glove for sign language communications, in: *2016 International Conference on Accessibility to Digital World (ICADW)*, IEEE, pp. 27–31, 2016.

16. Di Mattia, V. *et al.*, Electromagnetic technology for a new class of electronic travel aids supporting the autonomous mobility of visually impaired people,

in: *Visually Impaired: Assistive Technologies, Challenges and Coping Strategies*, Nova Science Publisher, Inc., Basel, Switzerland, 2016.

17. Girshick, R., Fast r-cnn, in: *Proceedings of the IEEE international conference on computer vision*, pp. 1440–1448, 2015.

18. Heaton, J., Goodfellow, I., Bengio, Y., Courville, A., Deep learning. Genet Program Evolvable Machines, The MIT press, 305–307, 2013. https://doi.org/10.1007/s10710-017-9314-z .

19. Hussain, I., Talukdar, A.K., Sarma, K.K., Hand gesture recognition system with real-time palm tracking, in: *2014 Annual IEEE India Conference (INDICON)*, IEEE, pp. 1–6, 2014.

20. Jeong, G.-Y. and Yu, K.-H., Multi-section sensing and vibrotactile perception for walking guide of visually impaired person. *Sensors*, 16, 7, 1070, 2016.

21. Joshi, G., Singh, S., Vig, R., Taguchi-TOPSIS based HOG parameter selection for complex background sign language recognition. *J. Visual Commun. Image Represent.*, 71, 102834, 2020.

22. Kim, J.S. and Kim, C.H., A review of assistive listening device and digital wireless technology for hearing instruments. *Korean J. Audiol.*, 18, 3, 105, 2014.

23. Kishore, P.V.V. *et al.*, Motionlets matching with adaptive kernels for 3-D Indian sign language recognition. *IEEE Sens. J.*, 18, 8, 3327–3337, 2018.

24. Krizhevsky, A., Sutskever, I., Hinton, G.E., ImageNet Classification with Deep Convolutional Neural Networks, in: *Advances in Neural Information Processing Systems 25*, F. Pereira, *et al.*, Lake Tahoe, Nevada, United States (Eds.), pp. 1097–1105, Curran Associates, Inc., 2012, http://papers.nips.cc/paper/4824-imagenet-classification-with-deep-convolutional-neural-networks.pdf.

25. Kumar, A., Thankachan, K., Dominic, M.M., Sign language recognition, in: *2016 3rd International Conference on Recent Advances in Information Technology (RAIT)*, IEEE, pp. 422–428, 2016.

26. Anil Kumar, D. *et al.*, Indian sign language recognition using graph matching on 3D motion captured signs. *Multimed. Tools Appl.*, 77, 24, 32063–32091, 2018.

27. Li, L., Socher, R., Fei-Fei, L., Towards total scene understanding: Classification, annotation and segmentation in an automatic framework, in: *2009 IEEE Conference on Computer Vision and Pattern Recognition*, pp. 2036–2043, 2009, doi: 10.1109/CVPR.2009.5206718.

28. LeCun, Y. *et al.*, LeNet-5, convolutional neural networks. In: URL: http://yann. lecun. com/exdb/lenet. 20, 5, 14, 2015. http://yann.lecun.com/exdb/lenet/ accessed on 2020/12/09

29. Lilha, H. and Shivmurthy, D., Evaluation of features for automated transcription of dual-handed sign language alphabets, in: *2011 International Conference on Image Information Processing*, IEEE, pp. 1–5, 2011.

30. Liu, T., Zhou, W., Li, H., Sign language recognition with long short-term memory, in: *2016 IEEE international conference on image processing (ICIP)*, IEEE, pp. 2871–2875, 2016.

31. Liu, W. *et al.*, Ssd: Single shot multibox detector, in: *European conference on computer vision*, Springer, pp. 21–37, 2016.

32. Lokhande, P., Prajapati, R., Pansare, S., Data gloves for sign language recognition system. *Int. J. Comput. Appl.*, 975, 8887, 2015.

33. NIH(NIDCD), *Assistive Devices for People with Hearing, Voice, Speech, or Language Disorders*, https://www.nidcd.nih.gov/health/assistive-devices-people-hearing-voice-speech-or-language-disorders. Accessed: 2020-12-09.

34. Otiniano-Rodrıguez, K.C., Cámara-Chávez, G., Menotti, D., Hu and Zernike moments for sign language recognition, in: *Proceedings of international conference on image processing, computer vision, and pattern recognition*, pp. 1–5, 2012.

35. Patil, S.B. and Sinha, G.R., Distinctive feature extraction for Indian Sign Language (ISL) gesture using scale invariant feature Transform (SIFT). *J. Inst. Eng. (India): Ser. B*, 98, 1, 19–26, 2017.

36. Praveen, N., Karanth, N., Megha, M.S., Sign language interpreter using a smart glove, in: *2014 International Conference on Advances in Electronics Computers and Communications*, IEEE, pp. 1–5, 2014.

37. Redmon, J. and Farhadi, A., YOLOv3: An Incremental Improvement. In: *arXiv, 1804.02767, 2018*.

38. Redmon, J. *et al.*, You Only Look Once: Unified, Real-Time Object Detection, in: *The IEEE Conference on Computer Vision and Pattern Recognition (CVPR)*, June 2016.

39. Ren, S. *et al.*, Faster R-CNN: Towards Real-Time Object Detection with Region Proposal Networks. *IEEE Trans. Pattern Anal. Mach. Intell.*, 39, 6, 1137–1149, June 2017.

40. Sadek, M.I., Mikhael, M.N., Mansour, H.A., A new approach for designing a smart glove for Arabic Sign Language Recognition system based on the statistical analysis of the Sign Language, in: *2017 34th National Radio Science Conference (NRSC)*, IEEE, pp. 380–388, 2017.

41. Shahira, K.C., Tripathy, S., Lijiya, A., Obstacle Detection, Depth Estimation And Warning System For Visually Impaired People, in: *TENCON 2019-2019 IEEE Region 10 Conference (TENCON)*, IEEE, pp. 863–868, 2019.

42. Sharma, D., Verma, D., Khetarpal, P., LabVIEW based Sign Language Trainer cum portable display unit for the speech impaired, in: *2015 Annual IEEE India Conference (INDICON)*, IEEE, pp. 1–6, 2015.

43. Sharma, K., Joshi, G., Dutta, M., Analysis of shape and orientation recognition capability of complex Zernike moments for signed gestures, in: *2015 2nd International Conference on Signal Processing and Integrated Networks (SPIN)*, IEEE, pp. 730–735, 2015.

44. Sharma, M., Pal, R., Sahoo, A.K., Indian Sign Language Recognition Using Neural Networks and KNN Classifiers. *ARPN J. Eng. Appl. Sci.*, 9, 8, 1255–1259, 2014.

45. Shilkrot, R. *et al.*, FingerReader: a wearable device to explore printed text on the go, in: *Proceedings of the 33rd Annual ACM Conference on Human Factors in Computing Systems*, pp. 2363–2372, 2015.

46. Singh, B. and Kapoor, M., A Survey of Current Aids for Visually Impaired Persons, in: *2018 3rd International Conference On Internet of Things: Smart Innovation and Usages (IoT-SIU)*, IEEE, pp. 1–5, 2018.

47. Singha, J. and Das, K., Indian sign language recognition using eigen value weighted euclidean distance based classification technique. In: *arXiv preprint arXiv:1303.0634*, 2013.

48. Sruthi, C.J. and Lijiya, A., Signet: A deep learning based indian sign language recognition system, in: *2019 International Conference on Communication and Signal Processing (ICCSP)*, IEEE, pp. 0596–0600, 2019.

49. Szegedy, C. *et al.*, Rethinking the inception architecture for computer vision, in: *Proceedings of the IEEE conference on computer vision and pattern recognition*, pp. 2818–2826, 2016.

50. Targ, S., Almeida, D., Lyman, K., Resnet in resnet: Generalizing residual architectures. In: *arXiv preprint arXiv:1603.08029*, 2016.

51. Tensorow Detection Model Zoo. https://medium.com/@madhawavidanapa-thirana/real-time-human-detection-in-computer-vision-part-2-c7eda27115c6. Accessed: 2020-12-09.

52. Tripathi, K., Baranwal, N., Nandi, G.C., Continuous dynamic Indian Sign Language gesture recognition with invariant backgrounds, in: *2015 International Conference on Advances in Computing, Communications and Informatics (ICACCI)*, IEEE, pp. 2211–2216, 2015.

53. Tubaiz, N., Shanableh, T., Assaleh, K., Glove-based continuous Arabic sign language recognition in user-dependent mode. *IEEE Trans. Hum.-Mach. Syst.*, 45, 4, 526–533, 2015.

54. Tucker, E., *Maptic is a wearable navigation system for the visually impaired*, Dezeen, London, Retrieved October 10 (2017), 65–84, 2019, 2018.

55. Geetha, U.C. and Manjusha, M., A Vision Based Recognition of Indian Sign Language Alphabets and Numerals Using B-Spline Approximation. *Int. J. Comput. Sci. Eng. (IJCSE)*, 4, 3, 406, 2012.

56. Vaswani, A. *et al.*, Attention is all you need, in: *Advances in neural information processing systems*, vol. 30, pp. 5998–6008, 2017.

57. Velázquez, R., Wearable assistive devices for the blind, in: *Wearable and autonomous biomedical devices and systems for smart environment*, pp. 331–349, Springer, Berlin, Heidelberg, 2010.

58. verizon, *Assistive Technologies for the Deaf and Hard of Hearing*, https://www.verizon.com/info/technology/assistive-listening-devices/. Accessed: 2020-12-09.

59. Yun, L. and Peng, Z., An Automatic Hand Gesture Recognition System Based on Viola-Jones Method and SVMs, in: *Second International Workshop on Computer Science and Engineering*, pp. 72–77, 2009.

60. Zhang, J. *et al.*, A real-time chinese traffic sign detection algorithm based on modified YOLOv2. *Algorithms*, 10, 4, 127, 2017.

61. Isaksson, J., Jansson, T., Nilsson, J., Desire of use: A hierarchical decomposition of activities and its application on mobility of by blind and low-vision individual. *IEEE Trans. Neual Syst. Rehab. Eng.,* 25, 5, 1146–1156, 2020.
62. Law, Effie L.-C., Roto, V., Hassenzahl, M., Vermeeren, A.POS, Kort, J., Understanding, scoping and defining user experience: a survey approach, in: *Proceedings of the SIGCHI conference on human factors in computing systems,* pp. 719–728, Boston, MA, USA, 2009.

18

Case Studies: Deep Learning in Remote Sensing

Emily Jenifer A. and Sudha N.*

SASTRA Deemed University, Thanjavur, India

Abstract

Interpreting the data captured by earth observation satellites in the context of remote sensing is a recent and interesting application of deep learning. The satellite data may be one or more of the following: (i) a synthetic aperture radar image, (ii) a panchromatic image with high spatial resolution, (iii) a multispectral image with good spectral resolution, and (iv) hyperspectral data with high spatial and spectral resolution. Traditional approaches involving standard image processing techniques have limitations in processing huge volume of remote sensing data with high resolution images. Machine learning has become a powerful alternative for processing such data. With the advent of GPU, the computation power has increased several folds which, in turn, support training deep neural networks with several layers. This chapter presents the different deep learning networks applied to remote sensed image processing. While individual deep networks have shown promise for remote sensing, there are scenarios where combining two networks would be valuable. Of late, hybrid deep neural network architecture for processing multi-sensor data has been given interest to improve performance. This chapter will detail a few hybrid architectures as well.

Keywords: Deep learning, remote sensing, neural network, satellite image, fusion

*Corresponding author: sudha@cse.sastra.edu; sudhanatraj@yahoo.com

Pradeep Singh (ed.) Fundamentals and Methods of Machine and Deep Learning: Algorithms, Tools and Applications, (425–438) © 2022 Scrivener Publishing LLC

18.1 Introduction

Remote sensing involves the acquisition of earth observation data using a satellite or an unmanned aerial vehicle (UAV). Interpreting remotely sensed images provides essential information in a variety of applications such as land cover classification, damage assessment during disasters, monitoring crop growth, and urban planning.

Traditional approaches for interpreting remote sensed data apply standard image processing techniques such as texture analysis and transformations. The huge volume of remote sensing data sets limitations to these approaches. A powerful alternative for dealing with huge data volume is through deep learning. Deep learning has shown great potential in improving the segmentation and classification performance in remote sensing [1]. Deep learning is achieved using deep neural networks. With the advent of graphics processing units (GPUs), computational power has increased several times allowing the training of deep neural networks in a short period of time.

A variety of deep neural networks have found applications in remote sensing. One of them is convolutional neural network (CNN). CNN performs convolutions on a remote sensed image with learnt filter kernels to compute the feature maps. CNNs are used for land cover classification, crop classification, super-resolution, pan-sharpening, and denoising hyper spectral images. Another category of deep networks, namely, recurrent neural networks (RNN), has feedback recurrent connections and they are largely used for analysing time-series data. In remote sensing, they are useful for change detection in multi-temporal images. Studying crop growth dynamics and damage assessment during disasters are typical applications of these networks. Deep learning by autoencoders (AE) performs excellent feature abstraction. This is used for remote sensing image classification to achieve high accuracy and also in pan-sharpening. Deep networks such as generative adversarial networks (GANs) are used to generate super-resolution images, pan-sharpened images, and cloud-free images.

Although individual networks have shown promise for remote sensing, there are certain scenarios where combining two different networks would be valuable. In assessing the crop damage caused by a cyclone, CNN can be used to identify the agricultural land while RNN can be used to detect the change due to damage. Further, fusing images from different sensors aids in obtaining better accuracy as one modality can complement the other. Recent research focuses on fusing evidences from different deep neural network architectures as well as data from multiple sensors to improve performance.

Section 18.2 provides the motivation behind the application of deep learning in remote sensing. Section 18.3 presents various deep neural networks used for interpreting remote sensing data. Section 18.4 describes the hybrid architectures for processing data from multiple sensors. Section 18.5 concludes the chapter.

18.2   Need for Deep Learning in Remote Sensing

In recent years, deep learning has been proved to be a very successful technique. Deep networks sometimes surpass even humans in solving intensive computational tasks. Due to these successes and thanks to the availability of high-performance computational resources, deep learning has become the model of choice in many application areas. In the field of remote sensing, satellite data poses some new challenges for deep learning. The data is multimodal, geo-tagged, time-stamped, and voluminous. Remote sensing scientists have exploited the power of deep learning to address these challenges.

Satellite images are captured with a variety of sensors. Each data modality possesses its own merits and demerits. The performance is highly enhanced when data from multiple sensors are fused together in such a way to meet the needs of a particular application. Traditionally, fusion is achieved by extracting the features from images. Feature extraction is, however, a complex procedure. Image fusion algorithms based on machine learning have been developed in recent years to overcome the complexity, and they have given promising results. Among the various methods available for fusion, deep learning is a recent and highly effective way of achieving it. The various architectures developed so far for deep fusion in remote sensing will be reviewed in this chapter.

Deep learning has played a key role in data processing in many remote sensing applications. The applications involve agriculture, geology, disaster assessment, urban planning, and remote-sensed image processing in general. The different deep learning architectures and their roles in remote-sensed data processing are discussed next.

18.3   Deep Neural Networks for Interpreting Earth Observation Data

18.3.1   Convolutional Neural Network

The CNN is the most successful deep learning network for image classification and segmentation. The CNN has emerged as a powerful tool by

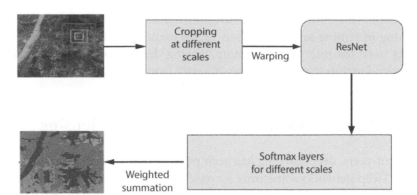

Figure 18.1 Land cover classification using CNN.

providing outstanding performance in these computer vision tasks. With the increase in the remote sensing satellites installed with a variety of sensors, CNN-based approaches may benefit from this large data availability. The CNN has been effectively applied to remote sensing for object detection and image segmentation. Building [2] and aircraft [3] detection has been achieved using CNN. The final fully connected layer generally performs the classification task. CNN has, therefore, been largely used for land use and land cover classification [4–7]. One such multi-scale classification using ResNet [8] is shown in Figure 18.1. The ground objects such as buildings, farmlands, water areas, and forests show various characteristics in varied resolution; thus, single-scale observation cannot exploit the features effectively. The ResNet-50 was adopted by the authors due to its low computational complexity compared to other pre-trained models. It has 16 residual blocks with three convolutional layers and the default input size of ResNet-50 is 224 × 224 × 3. The multi-scale patches are assigned with land cover category labels for classification through pre-trained ResNet-50, and they are combined with the boundary segmentation for efficient final projection of the land cover. Pan-sharpening is also an another important application of CNN [9].

18.3.2 Autoencoder

Autoencoder (AE) is an unsupervised deep learning model that performs non-linear transformation. The non-linear function learns the hidden surface from the unlabeled data. AE consists of an encoder network that reduces the dimension of the given input and a decoder network that reconstructs the input. Typical applications of AE in remote sensing are

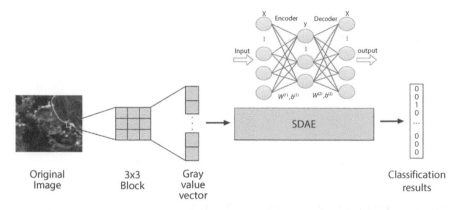

Figure 18.2 Remote sensing image classifier using stacked denoising autoencoder.

dimensionality reduction [10] and feature variation [11]. AE also performs classification efficiently with unlabeled data [12]. In specific, it is applied to snow cover mapping [13]. An image classifier using stacked denoising autoencoder (SDAE) [14] is shown in Figure 18.2. SDAE is based on the concept of adding noise to each encoder input layer and forcing to learn all the important features. It creates a stable network that is robust to noise. SDAE has bi-level learning process. Initially, the unlabeled inputs are sent to the SDAE. The features are learnt with greedy layer-wise approach for unsupervised training. It is followed by a labeled supervised training of a back propagation layer for classification.

18.3.3   Restricted Boltzmann Machine and Deep Belief Network

A restricted Boltzmann machine (RBM) is a generative stochastic model that can learn probability distribution over its input set. It has two types of nodes, hidden and visible, and the connections between nodes form a bipartite graph. Deep belief network (DBN) is formed by stacking RBMs. In remote sensing images, RBM is applied to classification [15, 16] and feature learning [17]. Figure 18.3 shows an application of RBM in hyperspectral image classification [15]. In conventional RBM, all the visible layer nodes are connected with all hidden layer nodes but nodes of visible layer or hidden layer are not connected among each other. However in [15], authors have replaced binary visible layers with Gaussian ones for effective land cover classification. The Gaussian RBM extracts the features in an unsupervised way, and these extracted land cover features are given to logistic regression unit for classification.

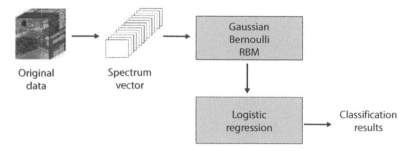

Figure 18.3 Gaussian-Bernoulli RBM for hyperspectral image classification.

18.3.4   Generative Adversarial Network

GAN is a generative model that automatically discovers and learns the patterns in the input data in such a way that the learnt model can generate new examples similar to the input data during learning. GAN is realized using two CNNs: a generator and a discriminator. In remote sensing, GAN is largely used in image synthesis for data augmentation [18, 19]. GAN is also used in generating super resolution images [20]. In [21], semi-supervised detection of airplanes from unlabeled airport images is performed using GAN. GAN has been effectively employed in pan-sharpening [22] as shown in Figure 18.4. Pan-sharpening is a process of merging high-resolution panchromatic and lower resolution multispectral images to create a single high-resolution color image. The authors in [22] aimed to solve the pan-sharpening problem by image generation with a GAN. The generator was trained in a way to learn the adaptive loss function to produce a high quality pan sharpened images.

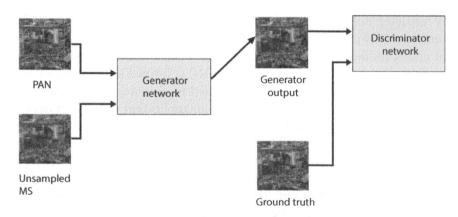

Figure 18.4 GAN for pan-sharpening with multispectral and panchromatic images.

18.3.5   Recurrent Neural Network

A RNN takes a time-series input and captures the temporal pattern present in it. RNN usually suffers from short-term memory which is addressed by long short-term memory (LSTM) and gated recurrent unit (GRU). LSTM and GRU are capable of processing long sequential inputs. In the field of remote sensing, RNN and its variants have been used for image classification [23], satellite image correction [24], and other processing with temporal data [25]. The change detection performed on multi-temporal images [26] is illustrated in Figure 18.5. During the learning process, RNN captures the relationship between the successive inputs in the temporal data and remembers the sequence. Learning the dependencies among the time-series inputs facilitates performing change detection effectively. The RNN network learns the change rule of the time sequence images efficiently through the transferability of the memory. RNN not only learns the bi-temporal changes but also the multi-temporal changes in land cover.

Change detection in crops and after-effects of the natural disasters is efficiently performed using RNN [27]. While a single deep neural network has been largely applied to various remote sensing applications, a few recent works focus on combining more than one type of network and process multi-sensor data to improve results. The next section reviews these hybrid architectures in remote sensing.

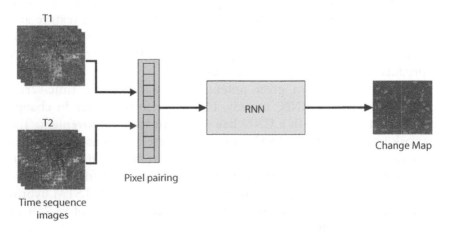

Figure 18.5 Change detection on multi-temporal images using RNN.

18.4   Hybrid Architectures for Multi-Sensor Data Processing

Independent deep architectures applied to remote sensing give only moderate performance. Recent developments in combining different deep architectures yield better results as each deep learning architecture shows some advantage for a particular application. Hybrid architectures can be very useful in change detection and classification. Hybrid deep neural networks also achieve image fusion. In remote sensing, applications such as classification and change detection deal with massive data which, in turn, increases the processing time. To address this challenge efficiently, different deep learning models are considered leveraging their capacities. The hybrid approach improves speed and accuracy by parallel processing with multiple networks. Table 18.1 displays a few existing hybrid deep architectures that process multi-sensor data.

The combination CNN-GAN has been applied to change detection [28]. The relationship between the multi-temporal images and their change maps can be learnt through generative learning process for change detection. The learning process is as follows. The CNN initially extracts the features to remove redundancy and noise from the multispectral images. The GAN is then applied to learn the mapping function.

Another application of this hybrid architecture is cloud removal. Critical information is lost in the image in the presence of cloud. The missed information needs to be reconstructed. An efficient CNN-GAN combination, proposed by [29], removes the clouds in an optical image using the corresponding SAR image in a two-step procedure. In the first step, the SAR image is converted to a simulated optical image with coarse texture and less spectral information. In the second step, the fusion of simulated optical image along with SAR and cloudy optical image is performed by a GAN to produce an optical image free from clouds.

The RNN has shown great potential in analysing the time-series images. A variant of RNN, namely, LSTM, performs better in change detection. Its fusion with a CNN has shown further improvement. The network training of CNN-LSTM for change detection is as follows. The CNN extracts the spatial and spectral features from the patches of input image while the classification using these features is performed by the LSTM network. The city expansion study done with CNN-LSTM hybrid network [30] has given a satisfactory overall accuracy rate of 98.75% as displayed in the table.

Table 18.1 Hybrid deep architectures for remote sensing.

Publication	Hybrid architecture		Inputs	Application	Results
[28]	CNN	GAN	MS images	Change detection	Overall error = 5.76%
[29]	CNN	GAN	SAR and MS	Cloud removal	SAM = 3.1621
[30]	CNN	LSTM	MS images	Change detection	Overall accuracy = 98.75%
[31]	CNN	SAE	PAN and MS	Pan sharpening	Overall accuracy = 94.82%
[32]	CNN	GAN	Near-infrared (NIR) and short-wave infrared (SWIR)	Image Fusion	ERGAS = 0.69 SAM = 0.72
[33]	CNN	RNN	MS and PAN	To find oil spill in the ocean	mIoU = 82.1%

SAM - Spectral Angle Mapper; ERGAS - Relative Dimensionless Global Error in Synthesis; mIoU - mean Intersection over Union.

Pan-sharpening has been achieved using a combination of CNN and stacked autoencoder (SAE) in order to generate a fused image of panchromatic and multispectral data. The hybrid architecture proposed by [31] deals with the spatial and spectral contents separately. The spectral features of the multispectral image are extracted by the successive layers of SAE. The spatial information present in large amount in the panchromatic images is extracted by CNN. Both the spatial and spectral features are fused and the resulting pan-sharpened image is given to a fully connected layer for classification of water and urban areas. The overall accuracy of the pan-sharpened image classification by the hybrid architecture is 94.82% which is much higher than the classification accuracies provided by individual architectures.

With the combination of CNN and RNN, a hybrid architecture has been developed and applied to ocean oil spill detection [33]. A single deep CNN can extract the features for oil spill segmentation, but it missed most of the finer details. By incorporating conditional random fields in RNN, the hybrid architecture efficiently captures the missed out finer details of the oil spill in SAR images. The evaluation index of segmentation, namely, mean intersection over union (mIoU), is computed to be 82.1%. It is much better than a CNN-only architecture. Moreover, the run time of CNN-RNN network is only 0.8 s, which is much less when compared to the fully convolutional network architecture that takes 1.4 s.

The above discussions reveal that a hybrid architecture gives much better performance than a single architecture.

18.5   Conclusion

In recent years, deep learning has played a major role in enhancing the performance and accuracy in remote sensing given the challenges posed in terms of limited availability of ground truths and cumbersome pre-processing. A review of various deep learning–based remote-sensed image processing has been presented in this chapter. Deep architectures such as CNN, RNN, AEs, and GAN applied to remote sensing have been discussed. Combination of two different architectures for fusing data from multiple sensors has also been discussed. The role of fusion in applications such as cloud removal, change detection, pan sharpening, land use land cover classification, and oil spill detection has been highlighted.

Although remote sensing is a growing application area that employs deep learning, supervised classification has so far been widely used. The enormous volume of data available from satellites and dependence on large labeled dataset pose challenges in the generation of ground truth. The design of deep unsupervised and semi-supervised neural networks is an important future direction to explore. The models can self-learn the spatial patterns from the unlabeled data and classify them without any prior information.

References

1. Zhu, X.X., Tuia, D., Mou, L., Xia, G.S., Zhang, L., Xu, F., Fraundorfer, F., Deep learning in remote sensing: A comprehensive review and list of resources. *IEEE Geosci. Remote Sens. Mag.*, 5, 4, 8–36, 2017.
2. Konstantinidis, D., Argyriou, V., Stathaki, T., Grammalidis, N., A modular CNN-based building detector for remote sensing images. *Comput. Networks*, *168*, 107034, 2020.

3. Liu, Q., Xiang, X., Wang, Y., Luo, Z., Fang, F., Aircraft detection in remote sensing image based on corner clustering and deep learning. *Eng. Appl. Artif. Intell.*, *87*, 103333, 2020.

4. Jin, B., Ye, P., Zhang, X., Song, W., Li, S., Object-oriented method combined with deep convolutional neural networks for land-use-type classification of remote sensing images. *J. Indian Soc. Remote Sens.*, *47*, 6, 951–965, 2019.

5. Rajesh, S., Nisia, T.G., Arivazhagan, S., Abisekaraj, R., Land Cover/Land Use Mapping of LISS IV Imagery Using Object-Based Convolutional Neural Network with Deep Features. *J. Indian Soc. Remote Sens.*, *48*, 1, 145–154, 2020.

6. Sharma, A., Liu, X., Yang, X., Land cover classification from multi-temporal, multi-spectral remotely sensed imagery using patch-based recurrent neural networks. *Neural Networks*, *105*, 346–355, 2018.

7. Sharma, A., Liu, X., Yang, X., Shi, D., A patch-based convolutional neural network for remote sensing image classification. *Neural Networks*, *95*, 19–28, 2017.

8. Tong, X.Y., Xia, G.S., Lu, Q., Shen, H., Li, S., You, S., Zhang, L., Land-cover classification with high-resolution remote sensing images using transferable deep models. *Remote Sens. Environ.*, *237*, 111322, 2020.

9. Masi, G., Cozzolino, D., Verdoliva, L., Scarpa, G., Pansharpening by convolutional neural networks. *Remote Sens.*, *8*, 7, 594, 2016.

10. Zabalza, J., Ren, J., Zheng, J., Zhao, H., Qing, C., Yang, Z., Marshall, S., Novel segmented stacked autoencoder for effective dimensionality reduction and feature extraction in hyperspectral imaging. *Neurocomputing*, *185*, 1–10, 2016.

11. Abdi, G., Samadzadegan, F., Reinartz, P., Spectral–spatial feature learning for hyperspectral imagery classification using deep stacked sparse autoencoder. *J. Appl. Remote Sens.*, *11*, 4, 042604, 2017.

12. Mughees, A. and Tao, L., Efficient deep auto-encoder learning for the classification of hyperspectral images, in: *2016 International Conference on Virtual Reality and Visualization (ICVRV)*, 2016, September, IEEE, pp. 44–51.

13. Mughees, A. and Tao, L., Efficient deep auto-encoder learning for the classification of hyperspectral images, in: *2016 International Conference on Virtual Reality and Visualization (ICVRV)*, 2016, September, IEEE, pp. 44–51.

14. Liang, P., Shi, W., Zhang, X., Remote sensing image classification based on stacked denoising autoencoder. *Remote Sens.*, *10*, 1, 16, 2018.

15. Tan, K., Wu, F., Du, Q., Du, P., Chen, Y., A parallel gaussian–bernoulli restricted boltzmann machine for mining area classification with hyperspectral imagery. *IEEE J. Sel. Top. Appl. Earth Obs. Remote Sens.*, *12*, 2, 627–636, 2019.

16. Qin, F., Guo, J., Sun, W., Object-oriented ensemble classification for polarimetric SAR imagery using restricted Boltzmann machines. *Remote Sens. Lett.*, *8*, 3, 204–213, 2017.

17. Taherkhani, A., Cosma, G., McGinnity, T.M., Deep-FS: A feature selection algorithm for Deep Boltzmann Machines. *Neurocomputing*, *322*, 22–37, 2018.

18. Lin, D.Y., Wang, Y., Xu, G.L., Fu, K., Synthesizing remote sensing images by conditional adversarial networks, in: *2017 IEEE International Geoscience and Remote Sensing Symposium (IGARSS)*, 2017, July, IEEE, pp. 48–50.

19. Wang, G., Dong, G., Li, H., Han, L., Tao, X., Ren, P., Remote sensing image synthesis via graphical generative adversarial networks, in: *IGARSS 2019 IEEE International Geoscience and Remote Sensing Symposium*, 2019, July, IEEE, pp. 10027–10030.

20. Ma, W., Pan, Z., Guo, J., Lei, B., Super-resolution of remote sensing images based on transferred generative adversarial network, in: *IGARSS 2018-2018 IEEE International Geoscience and Remote Sensing Symposium*, 2018, July, IEEE, pp. 1148–1151.

21. Chen, G., Liu, L., Hu, W., Pan, Z., Semi-Supervised Object Detection in Remote Sensing Images Using Generative Adversarial Networks, in: *IGARSS 2018 - 2018 IEEE International Geoscience and Remote Sensing Symposium*, 2018, July, IEEE, pp. 2503–2506.

22. Liu, X., Wang, Y., Liu, Q., PSGAN: A generative adversarial network for remote sensing image pan-sharpening, in: *2018 25th IEEE International Conference on Image Processing (ICIP)*, 2018, October, IEEE, pp. 873–877.

23. Mou, L., Ghamisi, P., Zhu, X.X., Deep recurrent neural networks for hyperspectral image classification. *IEEE Trans. Geosci. Remote Sens.*, 55, 7, 3639–3655, 2017.

24. Maggiori, E., Charpiat, G., Tarabalka, Y., Alliez, P., Recurrent neural networks to correct satellite image classification maps. *IEEE Trans. Geosci. Remote Sens.*, 55, 9, 4962–4971, 2017.

25. Pelletier, C., Webb, G.I., Petitjean, F., Temporal convolutional neural network for the classification of satellite image time series. *Remote Sens.*, 11, 5, 523, 2019.

26. Lyu, H., Lu, H., Mou, L., Learning a transferable change rule from a recurrent neural network for land cover change detection. *Remote Sens.*, 8, 6, 506, 2016.

27. Vignesh, T., Thyagharajan, K.K., Ramya, K., Change detection using deep learning and machine learning techniques for multispectral satellite images. *Int. J. Innov. Tech. Exploring Eng.*, 9, 1S, 90–93, 2019.

28. Gong, M., Niu, X., Zhang, P., Li, Z., Generative adversarial networks for change detection in multispectral imagery. *IEEE Geosci. Remote Sens. Lett.*, 14, 12, 2310–2314, 2017.

29. Gao, J., Yuan, Q., Li, J., Zhang, H., Su, X., Cloud Removal with Fusion of High Resolution Optical and SAR Images Using Generative Adversarial Networks. *Remote Sens.*, 12, 191, 1–17, 2020.

30. Mou, L. and Zhu, X.X., A recurrent convolutional neural network for land cover change detection in multispectral images, in: *IGARSS 2018-2018 IEEE International Geoscience and Remote Sensing Symposium*, 2018, July, IEEE, pp. 4363–4366.

31. Liu, X., Jiao, L., Zhao, J., Zhao, J., Zhang, D., Liu, F., Tang, X., Deep multiple instance learning-based spatial–spectral classification for PAN and MS imagery. *IEEE Trans. Geosci. Remote Sens.*, 56, 1, 461–473, 2017.

32. Palsson, F., Sveinsson, J.R., Ulfarsson, M.O., Single sensor image fusion using a deep convolutional generative adversarial network, in: *2018 9th Workshop on Hyperspectral Image and Signal Processing: Evolution in Remote Sensing (WHISPERS)*, 2018, September, IEEE, pp. 1–5.

33. Chen, Y., Li, Y., Wang, J., An end-to-end oil-spill monitoring method for multisensory satellite images based on deep semantic segmentation. *Sensors*, 20, 3, 1–14, 2020.

Index

Printed and bound by CPI Group (UK) Ltd, Croydon, CR0 4YY

27/10/2024

14580178-0003